100 YEARS OF TWICKENHAM

AND THE FIVE/SIX NATIONS CHAMPIONSHIP 1910-2010

100 YEARS OF TWICKENHAM
AND THE FIVE/SIX NATIONS CHAMPIONSHIP 1910-2010

Mick Cleary and Chris Rhys

This book has been produced for Twickenham Stadium
by Lennard Books
a division of Lennard Associates Ltd
Windmill Cottage
Mackerye End
Harpenden
Herts AL5 5DR

© Mick Cleary and Chris Rhys 2009

This edition first published in the UK in 2009
by Twickenham Stadium in association with Lennard Publishing

Distributed through Green Umbrella Publishing
The Old Bakehouse, 21 The Street, Lydiard Millicent, Swindon SN5 3LU

ISBN 978 1 85291 150 8

CONSULTANT EDITOR: Ian Robertson
PRODUCTION EDITOR: Chris Marshall
ASSOCIATE EDITORS: Kirsty Ennever and John Griffiths
DESIGNER: Paul Cooper
JACKET DESIGN: Paul Cooper

Printed and bound in the UK by Butler Tanner & Dennis

contents

Professional rugby players may be encouraged to believe that they are only as good as their next game, but the rest of us feel absolutely no guilt in looking back.

Quite the opposite if the experience of the Twickenham Centenary Ambassadors committee is anything to go by. The five of us – Grand Slam winners Dickie Jeeps (1957), Bill Beaumont (1980), Rob Andrew (1991, 1992 and 1995) and Lawrence Dallaglio (2003) were the others – were overwhelmed for choice as we tried to agree on the greatest try scored at Twickenham since that first match between England and Wales in 1910.

The memories flowed thick and fast as each video clip triggered another tale. The venue for our meeting – high in the magnificent new stand just a stone's throw from an immaculate playing area – brought home just how much the stadium itself, never mind the sport of rugby union, has evolved.

Each of us could remember with pinpoint accuracy our debut in the old Five Nations Championship and each of us, without reservation, experienced the Joy of Six at Italy's inclusion at the start of this decade.

Amid all the nostalgia, one thing we were all looking forward to was the publication of this book. *Daily Telegraph* rugby correspondent Mick Cleary has been a witty and insightful chronicler of the dramatic changes in rugby over the last quarter of a century as well as a balanced and thoughtful historian of the game. This promises to be the must-have accessory for any trip down memory lane.

Alastair Hignell

Alastair Hignell CBE
Twickenham Centenary Ambassador

foreword

66

'Billy Williams' Cabbage Patch'
has not only yielded some
stirring sporting sights down the
years, it has also given much
fun to spectators in whatever
guise they may choose to find it.

99

Introduction

History's roll-call at Twickenham is an impressive one: Adrian Stoop, Prince Alexander Obolensky, Richard Sharp, Andy Hancock, Erica Roe. (Erica Roe!?) 'Billy Williams' Cabbage Patch', a 10¼-acre market garden purchased for £5572 12s 6d in 1907, has not only yielded some stirring sporting sights down the years, it has also given much fun to spectators in whatever guise they may choose to find it. Thunderous tackles (think John Kendall-Carpenter in the 1949 Varsity Match); stupendous runs (Hancock's 80-metre effort in 1965 to deny the Scots their first victory at HQ since 1938); Grand Slams (England's winner-takes-all victory over France in 1991, perhaps); World Cup drama of the highest order (France's against-all-odds back-from-the-dead victory over the All Blacks in 1999, for instance).

And then, of course, there was Erica's streak. 'Titters at Twickers' was the jolly headline in one tabloid. Meanwhile, the esteemed journalist and former Wales and Lions full back Vivian Jenkins, editor of *Rothmans Rugby Yearbook* at the time, described the moment of her unscheduled appearance at half-time in the 1982 England v Australia match thus: '… when a lady named Erica erupted onto the field of play like a galleon in full sail, but minus her spinnakers'.

Are we in danger of undermining tales of great sporting feats by highlighting something so trivial? No, not really, for if the Twickenham experience was not essentially a fun one, then it would never exert the hold that it does. Of course, the rugby is paramount. Of course, there is drama and excellence to behold, warrior spirit to admire, courage, imagination, resilience and many other qualities to applaud, but all of these things can now be seen and replayed endlessly on television. The live occasion has to offer something different, and Twickenham has managed to do that quite splendidly down the decades.

The West Car Park is still a meeting place for old chums where tall tales are told and where, rumour has it, the occasional drop is taken. The modernisation of Twickenham, the gradual change from homespun old stadium into state-of-the-art facility, has not ignored this need to provide a sense of community alongside its obligation to provide a stage for top-class rugby. There's many a press conference taken place at Twickenham against a backdrop of still-celebrating crowds in car parks and bars.

Twickenham is now a stadium to rank alongside any in the world. Tickets are at a premium no matter what the game. Where once there were but a handful of international matches to consider, the ground now plays host to all manner of games. It is a far cry from its origins. English rugby had led a peripatetic existence prior to the first international staged at Twickenham in 1910: 14 matches were staged at Blackheath's Rectory Field, ten at the Athletic Ground in Richmond, seven at London's Kennington Oval and the same number at Manchester's Whalley Range. Welford Road (four matches) and Crystal Palace (two) also featured, as did Richardson's Field in Blackheath, Cardigan Fields in Leeds, Crown Flatt in Dewsbury, Headingley in Leeds, Upper Park in Birkenhead, Meanwood Road in Leeds, Fallowfield in Manchester, Kingsholm in Gloucester and, finally, Ashton Gate in Bristol.

Indeed it was the fact that the two matches at Crystal Palace (against New Zealand and South Africa in 1905 and 1906 respectively) were both sell-outs that prompted the RFU to look around for a suitable venue of their own. Come on down Billy Williams, a venerable RFU

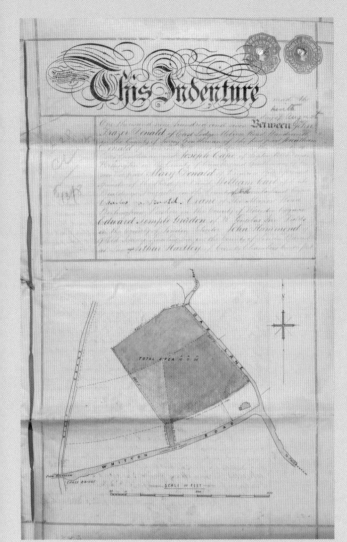

THE BIRTH OF TWICKENHAM.
ABOVE *Documents relating to the purchase of the land, and (right) initial plans for the development of the stadium.* **BELOW** *A passage from the minutes of the RFU, and (above right) details from the accounts presented by William Cail for the 1908-09 season.*

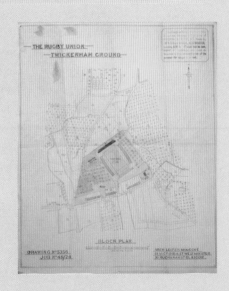

committee man, a local Twickenham resident, a former full back for Harlequins, a top-flight referee and a decent cricketer to boot who turned out for Middlesex and the MCC. That's not a bad CV. Billy swung into action in 1907, identifying the plot, now so well known, which was owned back then by the Mann family. It was essentially a market garden where cabbages had been grown, hence the nickname, and Williams set about purchasing it for the RFU. The well-respected committee man knew a good thing when he saw it. The deal was struck and construction of Twickenham Stadium was under way within a few months. Not everyone backed the scheme: some argued that the site was too far from central London; others regretted the fact that England games would now be confined to the capital. There was the matter of cost to consider, too, and in treasurer William Cail, Williams had a formidable ally. Cail recognised the potential for growth and for enlarged income.

The first stands, East and West, were constructed in 1908, the viewing areas at the south and north ends of the ground consisting of mounds of earth placed behind the goalposts. The first match was played on 2 October 1909, Harlequins taking on Richmond. A few months later, on 15 January 1910, Twickenham staged its first international game, England against Wales, before a capacity crowd of 20,000.

These days a raft of costly PR people would be commissioned to explore strategies for raising and enhancing the profile of the new venture. A poster campaign, perhaps, glitzy celebrities to cut the string, a glossy brochure to lay out the wares and a top-billing act to

THIS PAGE After England had travelled to Edinburgh for their first rugby international in the 1870-71 season, the Kennington Oval was the venue for the return match the following year and continued to host the fixture on and off until 1878. ABOVE RIGHT The Scottish team that travelled to London in 1876. BELOW RIGHT The strong Irish team that beat England at Richmond in 1898 to record their third successive win in the fixture.

launch the show. Well, no such thoughts back then, although Wales were certainly considered quality opposition, having dominated the championship between the Home Unions since the early 1900s, sweeping the board in 1900, 1902, 1905, 1908 and 1909. England had not beaten them since 1898 and so might have been entitled to a few concerns as they took their bow at their new home.

There was no need for stage management. Adrian Stoop did the business himself. Wales kicked off deep into the English 25 where Stoop, the home side's captain, decided that this was no time for cautious, safety-first rugby and set off upfield. Ten seconds later his bold initiative had resulted in a try in the corner, scored by Freddie Chapman. Now that's what you call beginning with a bang.

Inspired by Stoop, unfancied England rallied to the cause. As half-time approached, Dai Gent, who (unsurprisingly with his name) had once had a Wales trial before throwing in his lot with England, made a telling break from a loose scrum to send Bert Solomon over for the second try of the afternoon. Stout defence kept Wales in check thereafter, enabling England to win 11-6. It was the perfect way to celebrate the dawning of a new era, and England went on to claim their first outright championship title since 1892 (the 1897 and 1898 tournaments were not completed). Billy Williams' investment on behalf of the RFU was already paying dividends.

Twickenham expanded to meet demand over the coming years. The fact that it was used for grazing sheep and cattle during World War I is a reminder of how rural the ground's original environs were. A stand was built above the North Terrace in 1921, while the East Stand was extended into a two-tier unit six years later. The South Terrace was extended to a capacity of 20,000 at the same time.

Twickenham became the focal point for so much dramatic sport. The gentleman's game did not always live up to its reputation, however. The 1925 match against New Zealand produced one of the most sensational events of that time, with All Black forward Cyril Brownlie being sent off by referee Mr Freethy. The Welshman had been obliged to lecture both packs sternly three times in the opening six minutes. After ten minutes a line out degenerated into another fracas. A shrill

ABOVE The Welsh team to play England in 1907. This side won 22-0, maintaining an unbeaten run against England which went back to 1898 and eventually ended at Twickenham in 1910. BELOW The England team that avenged three successive defeats at the hands of the Irish with a 13-3 win at Richmond in 1908.

TWICKENHAM'S WARTIME ROLE.
ABOVE LEFT The West Stand was used as a swarf store, the West Car Park (above) as a coal dump, and the committee room (left) became a tea room for the ARP ladies.

blast of Freethy's whistle was followed by the sight of Brownlie trudging towards the sideline. Reports say that there was not a sound from the crowd as the shocked All Black left the field. Never before had a player been given his marching orders in an international match. The Prince of Wales, the future Edward VIII, was a spectator at the match and reportedly pleaded in vain at half-time for the New Zealander to be allowed back. The All Blacks were not to be downed, though. Even with 14 men, New Zealand were too strong for England and ran out 17-11 winners, trumping England's two tries with four of their own, one of them scored by Brownlie's brother Maurice.

It was to be 11 years before England were able to claim the New Zealand scalp in 1936. And they needed the significant help of a Russian prince to do it. Alexander Obolensky scored two of the most sensational tries ever witnessed at Twickenham to put paid to any hopes the All Blacks had of victory. Obolensky turned his marker inside out and outstripped the defence with a straight run of 40 metres for his first try after 20 minutes. Then on the stroke of half-time his turn of pace took him on an unorthodox cross-field run. He weaved this way and that, losing his own support in the process, but he did not hesitate. On and on went Obolensky, louder and louder rose the cheers, until he touched down. New Zealand never recovered, eventually losing 13-0.

After the hiatus of World War II, during which Twickenham played its part as a storage facility and Civil Defence headquarters, Five Nations rugby returned to the 'Cabbage Patch' in March 1947. In 1957 England recorded their first clean sweep for 29 years, completing the feat with a 16-3 win over Scotland at Twickenham. The occasion prompted the first noted use of the term 'Grand Slam', referring to an invincible championship season. It was to be a long wait until England's next one in 1980.

THE EVOLUTION OF THE MODERN STADIUM.
ABOVE LEFT *The annotated aerial view that was used for some years on the front of Twickenham programmes. The South Stand was the first significant change in 1981.*
ABOVE *A bit of fun for the workforce after the topping-out ceremony, with the new stand in the background.* TOP *The view from the South Stand – the other three stands await their turn for modernisation.* LEFT *The same view 25 years later.*

15

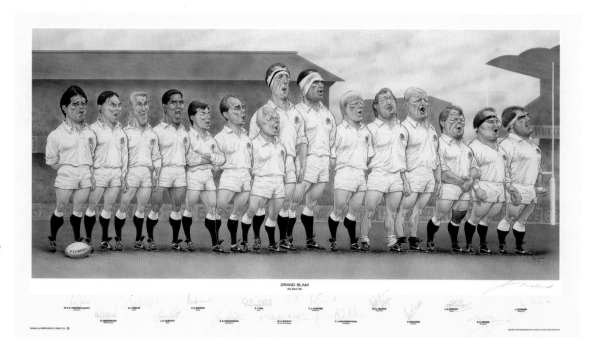

The 1960s saw some tremendous players, such as Richard Sharp and Ireland's Mike Gibson, show off their sumptuous skills at Headquarters. But the decade will be remembered best, perhaps, for Andy Hancock's try against Scotland in March 1965, the wing's 80-metre dash along the west touch line in the dying moments enabling England to secure a 3-3 draw.

From the addition of a new West Stand, with RFU offices, in 1932, Twickenham kept its familiar shape and colour for almost 50 years, through to 1981 when the South Terrace was rebuilt as the South Stand. Once that modern, open-faced edifice went up it would be only a matter of time before demand grew to improve the whole stadium. And so it proved, with the early 1990s seeing massive regeneration work done to the East and West Stands to complement the renovations carried out on the North Stand in the late 1980s. Fittingly, the team itself began to repay the considerable investment in bricks and mortar with several years of achievement.

In 1991 Will Carling's England nailed a Grand Slam in splendid fashion, beating France 21-19 at Twickenham in what was only the fourth ever winner-takes-all Grand Slam match. The result aside, it was a contest notable for the invigorating play of France and for the try scored by Philippe Saint-André, a classic piece of Gallic flair and daring. Simon Hodgkinson, who had nudged England ahead with an early penalty, missed with a further attempt. The England players made the mistake of turning their backs to get ready for the restart. Whoops! France were off and away, the extraordinary counterattack being launched by the incomparable Serge Blanco from behind his own posts and finished off several seconds later at the other end of the field by Saint-André. Carling's England, though, were made of stern stuff and came through to claim their first Grand Slam of that era. Two more followed in quick succession in what was a rich period for English rugby, in which the side also reached the 1991 World Cup final (won by Australia 12-6) and achieved, in 1993, another victory over the All Blacks (15-9), both of these matches taking place at Twickenham.

England, inevitably, featured in many classic games at the famous old stadium, but perhaps the tag of the greatest game ever played there must go to New Zealand against France in the 1999 World Cup. Indeed, that semi-final encounter ranks as one of the finest matches ever played anywhere. The All Blacks were overwhelming favourites to go through to meet Australia in the final of the tournament at Cardiff. France, meanwhile, had struggled to get to the semi-final stage and earlier that year had been beaten 54-7 by New Zealand in Wellington. No one gave them a chance, even less so when the All Blacks led 24-10 five minutes into the second half. They were cruising. Then it all went horribly wrong.

Christophe Lamaison launched the fightback with a couple of neat dropped goals. Still no alarm bells rang. Two penalties followed. The palms of New Zealand supporters began to moisten as the game headed towards the last quarter. Christophe Dominici, the smallest man on the field, who will haunt Kiwi dreams for many years to come, then touched down, Richard Dourthe following suit shortly afterwards. Both tries were converted, and France had gone from 24-10 down to 36-24 up in the space of 13 minutes. Philippe Bernat-Salles then scored another, also converted by Lamaison, who finished with 28 points. The final scoreboard read 43-31 to France. Never before had the All Blacks conceded 33 points without reply – although they did finally respond with a converted try in the last minute – and never before had they given away 43 points in a Test match.

Billy Williams would have been proud to witness that. As Twickenham expands and with the Rugby World Cup to be hosted by England in 2015, the future for the old 'Cabbage Patch' looks to be a rich one.

BELOW LEFT The roof goes on the new South Stand in 2008, and the stadium is complete.
FACING PAGE TOP Will Carling's Grand Slam team of 1991 as depicted by caricaturist John Ireland.
BELOW LEFT AND BOTTOM LEFT More memories rekindled in the Walk of Legends, introduced around the ground in 2008.

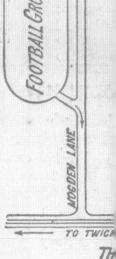

> "How often have we thanked the Lord for France being part of the brotherhood: for their style, for their flair and for a sense of the other?"

1910s

Bienvenue. **Welcome.** How often have we thanked the Lord for France being part of the brotherhood: for their style, for their flair and for a sense of the other? Without them, the championship would be that bit greyer, that bit more monochrome. Intense still, perhaps, but without that whiff of danger, that spicy sense of exoticism, that hint of the unpredictable. Yes, OK, the occasional bit of biff and brutality, all surpassed by wondrous helpings of elegance and grace and abandon.

Their arrival into the ranks in 1910 triggered the start of something special, helping to create a European carnival of rugby that has stood the test of time and has caused millions of brain cells to be destroyed in the annual quest to forge new friendships round the great capital cities.

France in those early days also served to boost a team's statistical benefits. They were the whipping boys of the championship, securing only one win in five seasons (1910–14), against Scotland (16-15) at Stade Colombes in 1911. France conceded 95 tries over the five seasons up to the outbreak of World War I, and shipped 415 points. But no one questioned their right to be there. No one wanted to turn back the clock. *Les Français étaient arrivés.*

The Great War looms over any account of this decade. How could it not? Several men who made their names on the rugby field were to show an even greater sense of valour and camaraderie in an altogether more hostile and unforgiving arena. How they would have yearned for those gentle times of mere sporting combat.

Adrian Stoop, a fine tactician, was to become a great figure in the land for his military and civil achievements as well as his sporting prowess. Of Dutch descent, Stoop won Blues at Oxford while a member of the Harlequins club, for whom he played from 1902 to 1919. A barrister, he was president of the club from 1920 to 1950, and was president of the Rugby Football Union in 1932–33. Stoop, who was a captain in the Queen's (Royal West Surrey)

BELOW Adrian Stoop (right) talking to one of his Harlequins team-mates in November 1911. Stoop made his debut for Quins against Oxford University in 1902 and although he played his last game for the club in 1939, he retired from regular play in 1919.

1911: FRANCE VISIT TWICKENHAM FOR THE FIRST TIME.
ABOVE *The French team for the encounter with England.* BELOW AND
BELOW LEFT *The match programme.* LEFT *Captaining the team was Marcel
Communeau, who had led France to their first win in the championship
earlier that season, 16-15 against Scotland.*

LEFT *Edgar Mobbs, depicted in a panel from the memorial in his honour at the Garden of Remembrance near All Saints' Church, Northampton.*
ABOVE *Ronnie Poulton captaining Oxford University against Richmond in 1911. Poulton, who later changed his name to Poulton-Palmer as a condition of his Huntley and Palmer inheritance, was killed by a sniper's bullet in Belgium while serving with The Royal Berkshire Regiment.* BELOW LEFT *A collection of caps owned by Adrian Stoop and now on display at Twickenham in the World of Rugby Museum.*

Regiment, was wounded in Mesopotamia and was awarded the Military Cross (MC) in 1919. The Harlequins ground in London – the Twickenham Stoop Stadium, formerly the Stoop Memorial Ground, or simply 'the Stoop' – bears his name.

Stoop was one of many heroic figures who came to prominence in the decade beginning in 1910. Edgar Mobbs made only the faintest of statistical marks on the Five Nations Championship in that the 1910 game in Paris was his last for his country. But his name lives on, in rugby's own world as well as in the annals of military folklore, with the annual match between the Barbarians and the East Midlands still there as a tribute to a man of great substance. Mobbs won only seven caps for England but scored four tries. Although initially refused a commission on the outbreak of war on grounds of age, being 32 at the time, he was not to be deterred. He enlisted as a private and recruited some 400 volunteers, many of them rugby players, 264 of which became D Company of 7th (Service) Battalion, The Northamptonshire Regiment. Mobbs eventually rose to command the 7th Battalion as a lieutenant-colonel and was awarded the Distinguished Service Order (DSO). He lost his life in 1917 near Passchendaele, and his name is inscribed with thousands of others on the Menin Gate at Ypres. Fittingly, perhaps, the first Mobbs Memorial Match, played on 10 February 1921, was refereed by Stoop.

There was a considerable roll-call of the fallen: Ronnie Poulton-Palmer – captain of England in their Grand Slam year of 1914 and chairman of the Huntley and Palmer biscuit empire – was one of 27 England international rugby players to lose their lives. Altogether 125 rugby internationals from the eight major rugby-playing countries perished in the conflict.

On the playing side Wales had come into the decade on the back of two successive Home Nations Grand Slams and it was no surprise that they should take advantage of the callowness of the French team to record two championship landmarks in the 1910 season – 88 points and 21 tries. The points total stood until 1976; the try total remained unsurpassed until England's 29-score haul in 2001.

There were hat-tricks for three players in 1910: Reggie Gibbs (for Wales against France), Johnny Williams (for Wales against Ireland) and Jim Tennent (for Scotland against France). Tennent also gained another claim to fame. The Scotland fly half twice had to leave the field against Wales with elbow and leg injuries, cuts which may have been caused by poor studs. New safety regulations regarding footwear were introduced for the next season.

If there were points aplenty in games featuring France, there was the rarity of a 0-0 draw between Ireland and England at Twickenham. How different the mood of the crowd that February day from the one that had attended England's opening game of the championship at the stadium a month earlier. Freddie Chapman had scored from the kick-off in what was the first international held at Twickenham, the land on which the ground was built having been acquired by the Rugby Football Union (RFU) three years earlier, in 1907, for just less than £5573.

Ireland didn't set the pulses racing in any regard in that first Five Nations year. They scored only three tries and 11 points in all in four games. Quite apart from the sterile 0-0 tie against England, they also drew a blank against Scotland, losing 14-0 at the Royal Ulster Agricultural Ground in Belfast.

England took that inaugural Five Nations Championship, although there was nothing as gaudy as a trophy in sight. Such brash things did not appear on the scene until the 1990s. The Calcutta Cup was the only bauble on offer and it went to England following their 14-5 victory at Inverleith.

The key games in the 1910 championship both involved Wales. They set a cracking pace with their 49-14 victory over France at St Helen's in Swansea, a result that still contains Wales's highest score and most tries in a championship match. It also represented Wales's biggest winning margin in the championship until 2008 when they beat Italy 47-8. Jack Bancroft's eight conversions in that 1910 game remained a championship record until Jonny Wilkinson slotted nine against Italy in 2001, while his 19 points overall stood as a landmark until equalled by Keith Jarrett in 1967.

The pivotal game, though, was Wales's next match against England at Twickenham, alluded to above. Chapman, the Westoe wing, scored one of the quickest tries ever seen in the championship, declaring England's intent from the first whistle. England fielded eight new caps – five forwards and three backs – and beat Wales for the first time since 1898. This was Wales's first defeat in the championship in nine games.

ABOVE A woodcut which paid tribute to the sacrifice made by the many rugby players who lost their lives in the Great War. BELOW LEFT A recruitment poster which encouraged others to follow the 'glorious example' set by rugby players.

England + Wales. January 1910.

ENGLAND AGAINST WALES IN 1910, THE FIRST INTERNATIONAL MATCH TO BE PLAYED AT TWICKENHAM. TOP *The Prince of Wales, soon to be King George V, provides a royal presence at the game.* ABOVE *Action conveyed by an illustrator for a magazine of the day.* RIGHT *The team line-ups from the match programme.*

ENGLAND v WALES,
SATURDAY, JAN. **15**th, 1910. Kick-off 2.45 p.m.

ENGLAND (white)

Back.
W. R. JOHNSTON (Bristol)

Three-Quarters,

RIGHT			LEFT
F. E. CHAPMAN	J. G. G. BIRKETT	B. SOLOMON	R. W. POULTON
(Westoe)	(Harlequins)	(Redruth)	(Oxford)

Half-Backs,
A. D. STOOP (Harlequins)   D. R. GENT (Gloucester)

Forwards

E. L. CHAMBERS	L. HAIGH	W. JOHNS	H. J. S. MORTON
(Bedford)	(Manchester)	(Gloucester)	(Blackheath)
H. BERRY	L. E. BARRINGTON WARD	D. F. SMITH	C. H. PILLMAN
(Gloucester)	(Edin. Univ.)	(Richmond)	(Blackheath)

Touch Judge. T. C. PRING, President, Rugby Union.

REFEREE ⬭ J. D. DALLAS, Scottish Union.

Touch Judge, E. & LYNE, President, Welsh Union.

Forwards.

J. WEBB	IVOR MORGAN	D. J. THOMAS	C. M. PRITCHARD
(Abertillery)	(Swansea)	(Swansea)	(Newport)
H. JARMAN	J. PUGSLEY	T. EVANS	B. GRONOW
(Newport)	(Cardiff)	(Llanelly)	(Bridgend)

Half-Backs
R. M. OWEN (Swansea)   R. JONES (Swansea)

Three-Quarters

LEFT			RIGHT
P. HOPKINS	J. P. JONES	W. J. TREW, Capt.	R. A. GIBBS
(Swansea)	(Newport)	(Swansea)	(Cardiff)

Back
J. BANCROFT (Swansea)

WALES

The Public are **particularly** requested not to go on the field of play at half time, as at this time of the year it is **essential** that the game **should not be delayed.**

Wales were not in the doldrums for long. They became the first Five Nations Grand Slam winners the following year – and in some style. It was a fine championship, with 247 points scored, a mark that was overtaken only in 1972, by which time the try had been upgraded to four points.

France, captained by the impressive Marcel Communeau, had their flickering moment of glory in beating Scotland 16-15, two of their four tries being scored by new cap Pierre Failliot, a strapping wing from Racing Club who picked up a silver medal in the 4 x 400m relay at the Stockholm Olympics of 1912. Tarbes scrum half Guillaume Laterrade and his half-back partner from Périgueux, Georges Peyroutou, touched down for the other tries. One player, though, missed the historic win. Stade Français' Christian Vareilles, selected in the centre, popped off the train at Melun to buy a sandwich, only for the train to chug off into the distance without him. He arrived after the game had begun to discover that his place had gone to André Francquenelle, another future Olympian, who went on to represent France in the pole vault at Antwerp in 1920. Vareilles never played for France again. Now that's what you call a costly sandwich.

Wales clinched the Triple Crown and Grand Slam at Cardiff Arms Park in March 1911. With Ireland also tilting for a Triple Crown, fans flocked to the ground for the clash. There were more than 40,000 inside and thousands locked out. Several spectators were injured after falling from the top of a stand. Reggie Gibbs went out with a flourish, scoring his thirteenth championship career try (and his seventeenth international try for Wales overall) in his final game. He scored five tries in that championship, including a hat-trick against Scotland, who finished with the Wooden Spoon, their defeat at Twickenham ending a run of nine wins in ten games at various English grounds. Gibbs's wing partner, Johnny Williams, also retired after claiming that historic Grand Slam, with a championship career total of 15 tries (17 for Wales overall) to his name.

It was a distinctive championship, defined by some notable characters. George Hamlet, the outstanding Irish forward of the era, also chose to end his international career in 1911. Hamlet played 30 times for Ireland, a world record for a forward at the time, and was president of the Irish Rugby Football Union (IRFU) in 1926-27. Meanwhile, the 22-point haul of Douglas Lambert against the benighted French remained an English record until Simon Hodgkinson improved on it by one against Argentina in November 1990. Lambert, who had scored five tries on

BELOW The team that represented Scotland on their first visit to Twickenham in 1911. The side was captained by goal-kicking forward John MacCallum.

Result Saturday March 18th 1911
England 2 gls 1 try - 13 pts
Scotland 1 gl 1 try - 8 pts

ENGLAND.

Back
S. H. WILLIAMS (Newport)

Three-Quarters

A. D. ROBERTS (Northern)	J. G G. BIRKETT (Harlequins)	R. W. POULTON (Oxford)	P. W. LAWRIE (Leicester)

Half-Backs

A. L. H. GOTLEY (Capt.) (Blackheath)   A. D. STOOP (Harlequins)

Forwards

A. L. KEWNEY (Rosslyn)	J. A. KING (Headingley)	Lieut. N. A. WODEHOUSE (R.N.)	L. HAIGH (Manchester)
L. G. BROWN (Oxford)	R. DIBBLE (Bridgwater)	R. O. LAGDEN (Oxford)	C. H. PILLMAN (Blackheath)

REFEREE ⬭ Mr. T. D. SCHOFIELD

Forwards

J. C. McCALLUM (Capt.) (Watsonians)	R. FRASER (Cambridge)	G. M. FREW (Glasgow High School)	A. F. HUTCHISON (Glasgow High School)
C. D. STUART (West of Scotland)	F. H. TURNER (Oxford)	D. M. BAIN (Oxford)	J. D. DOBSON (Glasgow Academicals)

Half-Backs

E. MILROY (Watsonians)   J. Y. HENDERSON (Watsonians)

Three-Quarters

S. STEYN (London Scottish)	R. F. SIMSON (London Scottish)	G. CUNNINGHAM (London Scottish)	W. R. SUTHERLAND (Hawick)

Back
C. OGILVY (Hawick)

SCOTLAND.

The Public are **particularly** requested not to go on the field of play at half time. The Committee also **specially** request gentlemen not to cross the field after the match.

RUGBY FOOTBALL UNION.

ENGLAND v SCOTLAND
At TWICKENHAM
Saturday, March 18th, 1911,
KICK OFF AT 3.30 P.M.

Price **6/=**
If purchased before the day.
Should the match be postponed and eventually played, no money will be returned, but this ticket will be available on the later date.

Block X   Admit to '**B' COVERED STAND**
Row 11
Seat No 248   C. J. B. Marriott

ENTRANCE, OAK LANE   RETAIN THIS PORTION   Secretary.
The Entrance to the Stand is at the back of the Stand
N.B.—OFFICIAL PROGRAMMES can be purchased inside the ground ONLY

ABOVE AND LEFT Souvenirs of Scotland's first game at Twickenham. The programme annotation shows the result to have been 13-8 to the hosts; that is, two converted tries and a try to one converted try and a try.

his England debut against France four years previously, in 1907, also bowed out of international rugby in 1911. He was another later killed in the Great War – at Loos in 1915.

The 1912 championship was shared by England and Ireland, although some would grant the title to England on points difference. Competition rules were sketchy on that point. Whereas Ireland's only defeat of the campaign came at Twickenham, 15-0, Scotland had the pleasure of inflicting a triple whammy of misery on England (not that you'd find a Scotsman ever making mention of the fact), their 8-3 victory at Inverleith depriving the Auld Enemy of

the Grand Slam, Triple Crown and Calcutta Cup in one fell swoop.

Indeed, Scotland were in rampaging scoring form in that championship, ending with more points, 53, than anyone else and equalling England's mark of 12 tries but still finishing only third. That year the championship bid adieu to that fine Brighton and Harlequins centre John Birkett and also to a trio of Welshmen, Dicky Owen, Jim Webb and Ivor Morgan.

The two remaining championships of that war-ravaged decade belonged to England, who claimed Grand Slams in successive seasons. They scored 13 tries in the 1913 campaign and didn't see their try line crossed once. The only points scored against them came from an Irish dropped goal. The final game of the season was held on Easter Monday – in the morning, as Easter had been declared 'too hot' for rugby.

England's decisive victory came against Wales. Their 12-0 win was their first in the Principality since 1895. They fielded seven players new to the Five Nations, including Cyril Lowe, soon to become one of the finest wings of his or any other generation.

The 1914 championship was marred by the fact that Scotland refused to play France after the crowd trouble in Paris the previous year. England took little notice of such diplomatic shenanigans en route to their second successive Grand Slam, led by the formidable presence of Ronnie Poulton-Palmer.

Like Stoop, Poulton-Palmer was regarded by his peers as a master tactician on the field. The Harlequins centre was pretty potent with ball in hand, too, scoring four tries in the final game against France. Cyril Lowe scored a landmark eight tries in the championship, while there was a last sighting of Jack Bancroft, younger brother of Billy and an acclaimed cricketer with Glamorgan to boot.

The dark clouds of war were already beginning to gather, and like other branches of civilian and sporting life, rugby was to play its part in the coming conflict. The toll was heavy on so many fronts.

FACING PAGE BOTTOM The last season before World War I resulted in a Grand Slam for England. Their first game was at home against Wales and ended in a 10-9 victory.
ABOVE LEFT The published teams for the match against Ireland at Twickenham on Valentine's Day 1914 – a 17-12 win. BELOW Ronnie Poulton-Palmer (front row, centre) with his England team in Edinburgh where they managed to defeat Scotland 16-15. ABOVE A French magazine cover welcomes England to Paris for what was to be the last championship match of the decade – a 39-13 triumph for England.

Five Nations Results 1910-14

1909-10

01.01.1910 ST HELEN'S, SWANSEA
Wales 49 *T*: RA Gibbs 3, I Morgan 2, HT Maddocks 2, WJ Trew, JP Jones, B Gronow *C*: J Bancroft 8
PG: J Bancroft
France 14 *T*: R Laffitte, P Mauriat *C*: A Menrath
PG: A Menrath 2
Referee: W Williams (England)

15.01.1910 TWICKENHAM
England 11 *T*: FE Chapman, B Solomon
C: FE Chapman *PG*: FE Chapman
Wales 6 *T*: RA Gibbs, J Webb
Referee: JD Dallas (Scotland)

22.01.1910 INVERLEITH, EDINBURGH
Scotland 27 *T*: JM Tennent 3, IPM Robertson 2, AW Angus, GC Gowlland *C*: JC MacCallum 3
France 0
Referee: GA Harris (Ireland)

05.02.1910 CARDIFF ARMS PARK
Wales 14 *T*: J Pugsley, W Spiller, AM Baker, I Morgan
C: J Bancroft
Scotland 0
Referee: GHB Kennedy (Ireland)

12.02.1910 TWICKENHAM
England 0
Ireland 0
Referee: TD Schofield (Wales)

26.02.1910 ROYAL ULSTER AGRICULTURAL GROUND, BELFAST
Ireland 0
Scotland 14 *T*: MW Walter 2, JD Dobson, CD Stuart
C: JC MacCallum
Referee: VH Cartwright (England)

03.03.1910 PARC DES PRINCES, PARIS
France 3 *T*: M Communeau
England 11 *T*: A Hudson 2, H Berry *C*: FE Chapman
Referee: G Bowden (Scotland)

12.03.1910 LANSDOWNE ROAD, DUBLIN
Ireland 3 *T*: G McIldowie
Wales 19 *T*: JL Williams 3, RA Gibbs, LM Dyke
DG: PF Bush
Referee: JD Dallas (Scotland)

19.03.1910 INVERLEITH, EDINBURGH
Scotland 5 *T*: DG Macpherson *C*: JC MacCallum
England 14 *T*: JGG Birkett 2, H Berry, JAS Ritson
C: FE Chapman
Referee: GHB Kennedy (Ireland)

28.03.1910 PARC DES PRINCES, PARIS
France 3 *T*: P Guillemin
Ireland 8 *T*: C Thompson, T Smyth *C*: AN McClinton
Referee: VH Cartwright (England)

	P	W	D	L	FOR	AGAINST	PTS
England	4	3	1	0	36	14	7
Wales	4	3	0	1	88	28	6
Scotland	4	2	0	2	46	28	4
Ireland	4	1	1	2	11	36	3
France	4	0	0	4	20	95	0

1910-11

02.01.1911 STADE COLOMBES, PARIS
France 16 *T*: P Failliot 2, G Laterrade, G Peyroutou
C: P Decamps 2
Scotland 15 *T*: JC MacCallum, P Munro, CH Abercrombie *C*: FH Turner *DG*: J Pearson
Referee: AO Jones (England)

21.01.1911 ST HELEN'S, SWANSEA
Wales 15 *T*: RA Gibbs, I Morgan, W Spiller, J Pugsley
PG: FW Birt
England 11 *T*: AD Roberts, AL Kewney, JA Scholfield
C: D Lambert
Referee: JI Gillespie (Scotland)

28.01.1911 TWICKENHAM
England 27 *T*: D Lambert 2, CH Pillman 2, WE Mann, AD Stoop, NA Wodehouse *C*: D Lambert 5
PG: D Lambert 2
France 0
Referee: EA Johns (Wales)

04.02.1911 INVERLEITH, EDINBURGH
Scotland 10 *T*: FH Turner, JMB Scott *DG*: P Munro
Wales 32 *T*: RA Gibbs 3, W Spiller 2, JL Williams 2, R Thomas *C*: LM Dyke 2 *DG*: W Spiller
Referee: IG Davidson (Ireland)

11.02.1911 LANSDOWNE ROAD, DUBLIN
Ireland 3 *T*: T Smyth
England 0
Referee: JD Dallas (Scotland)

25.02.1911 INVERLEITH, EDINBURGH
Scotland 10 *T*: JT Simson, AW Angus *DG*: P Munro
Ireland 16 *T*: CT O'Callaghan, AR Foster, C Adams, JP Quinn *C*: WP Hinton, RA Lloyd
Referee: VH Cartwright (England)

28.02.1911 PARC DES PRINCES, PARIS
France 0
Wales 15 *T*: I Morgan, JL Williams, RM Owen
C: J Bancroft 3
Referee: W Williams (England)

11.03.1911 CARDIFF ARMS PARK
Wales 16 *T*: T Evans, J Webb, RA Gibbs *C*: J Bancroft 2
PG: J Bancroft
Ireland 0
Referee: FC Potter-Irwin (England)

18.03.1911 TWICKENHAM
England 13 *T*: JGG Birkett, PW Lawrie, NA Wodehouse *C*: RO Lagden 2
Scotland 8 *T*: RF Simson, WR Sutherland
C: G Cunningham
Referee: TD Schofield (Wales)

25.03.1911 MARDYKE, CORK
Ireland 25 *T*: ARV Jackson 2, JP Quinn, CT O'Callaghan, MR Heffernan *C*: RA Lloyd 3
DG: RA Lloyd
France 5 *T*: P Failliot *C*: F Dutour
Referee: JC Findlay (Scotland)

	P	W	D	L	FOR	AGAINST	PTS
Wales	4	4	0	0	78	21	8
Ireland	4	3	0	1	44	31	6
England	4	2	0	2	61	26	4
France	4	1	0	3	21	92	2
Scotland	4	0	0	4	43	77	0

1911-12

01.01.1912 PARC DES PRINCES, PARIS
France 6 *T*: R Paoli, J Dufau
Ireland 11 *T*: AS Taylor, AR Foster, RA Lloyd
C: RA Lloyd
Referee: AO Jones (England)

20.01.1912 INVERLEITH, EDINBURGH
Scotland 31 *T*: WR Sutherland 2, AW Gunn, J Pearson, JG Will, FH Turner *C*: FH Turner 5 *PG*: J Pearson
France 3 *T*: M Communeau
Referee: JJ Coffey (Ireland)

20.01.1912 TWICKENHAM
England 8 *T*: H Brougham, JA Pym *C*: FE Chapman
Wales 0
Referee: JT Tulloch (Scotland)

03.02.1912 ST HELEN'S, SWANSEA
Wales 21 *T*: GL Hirst, I Morgan, RCS Plummer
C: J Bancroft 2 *DG*: WJ Trew, FW Birt
Scotland 6 *T*: JG Will, E Milroy
Referee: FC Potter-Irwin (England)

10.02.1912 TWICKENHAM
England 15 *T*: AD Roberts 2, JGG Birkett, H Brougham, RW Poulton*
Ireland 0
Referee: TD Schofield (Wales)
* RW Poulton changed his name to RW Poulton-Palmer in 1913 but will be referred to as RW Poulton throughout this section.

24.02.1912 LANSDOWNE ROAD, DUBLIN
Ireland 10 *T*: AR Foster, RA Lloyd *DG*: RA Lloyd
Scotland 8 *T*: FH Turner, JG Will *C*: JC MacCallum
Referee: FC Potter-Irwin (England)

09.03.1912 BALMORAL SHOWGROUNDS, BELFAST
Ireland 12 *T*: CV McIvor, GS Brown *C*: RA Lloyd
DG: RA Lloyd
Wales 5 *T*: W Davies *C*: J Bancroft
Referee: JD Dallas (Scotland)

16.03.1912 INVERLEITH, EDINBURGH
Scotland 8 *T*: WR Sutherland, CM Usher
C: JC MacCallum
England 3 *T*: D Holland
Referee: F Gardiner (Ireland)

25.03.1912, RODNEY PARADE, NEWPORT
Wales 14 *T*: DEG Davies 2, RCS Plummer, JP Jones
C: H Thomas
France 8 *T*: E Lesieur, L Larribau *C*: M Boyau
Referee: AO Jones (England)

08.04.1912 PARC DES PRINCES, PARIS
France 8 *T*: J Dufau, P Failliot *C*: M Boyau
England 18 *T*: JGG Birkett, H Brougham, JH Eddison, AD Roberts, CH Pillman *DG*: H Coverdale
Referee: TD Schofield (Wales)

	P	W	D	L	FOR	AGAINST	PTS
England	4	3	0	1	44	16	6
Ireland	4	3	0	1	33	34	6
Scotland	4	2	0	2	53	37	4
Wales	4	2	0	2	40	34	4
France	4	0	0	4	25	74	0

1912-13

01.01.1913 PARC DES PRINCES, PARIS
France 3 *T*: J Sebedio
Scotland 21 *T*: WA Stewart 3, RE Gordon 2
C: FH Turner 3
Referee: JW Baxter (England)

18.01.1913 CARDIFF ARMS PARK
Wales 0
England 12 *T*: VHM Coates, CH Pillman
C: JE Greenwood *DG*: RW Poulton
Referee: SH Crawford (Ireland)

25.01.1913 TWICKENHAM
England 20 *T*: VHM Coates 3, CH Pillman 2, RW Poulton *C*: JE Greenwood
France 0
Referee: J Games (Wales)

01.02.1913 INVERLEITH, EDINBURGH
Scotland 0
Wales 8 *T:* JMC Lewis, T Jones *C:* JMC Lewis
Referee: SH Crawford (Ireland)

08.02.1913 LANSDOWNE ROAD, DUBLIN
Ireland 4 *DG:* RA Lloyd
England 15 *T:* VHM Coates 2, CH Pillman, JAS Ritson
PG: JE Greenwood
Referee: JRC Greenlees (Scotland)

22.02.1913 INVERLEITH, EDINBURGH
Scotland 29 *T:* WA Stewart 4, CM Usher, TC Bowie,
WDCL Purves *C:* FH Turner 4
Ireland 14 *T:* FG Schute, P Stokes *C:* RA Lloyd 2
DG: RA Lloyd
Referee: JW Baxter (England)

27.02.1913 PARC DES PRINCES, PARIS
France 8 *T:* P Failliot, G Andre *C:* P Struxiano
Wales: 11 *T:* JMC Lewis, Rev JA Davies, T Williams
C: JMC Lewis
Referee: JH Miles (England)

08.03.1913 ST HELEN'S, SWANSEA
Wales 16 *T:* B Lewis 2, JP Jones *C:* J Bancroft 2
PG: J Bancroft
Ireland 13 *T:* JP Quinn, AL Stewart *C:* RA Lloyd 2
PG: RA Lloyd
Referee: JG Cunningham (Scotland)

15.03.1913 TWICKENHAM
England 3 *T:* LG Brown
Scotland 0
Referee: TD Schofield (Wales)

24.03.1913 MARDYKE, CORK
Ireland 24 *T:* JP Quinn 3, W Tyrrell 2, Rd'A Patterson
C: RA Lloyd 3
France 0
Referee: JH Miles (England)

	P	W	D	L	FOR	AGAINST	PTS
England	4	4	0	0	50	4	8
Wales	4	3	0	1	35	33	6
Scotland	4	2	0	2	50	28	4
Ireland	4	1	0	3	55	60	2
France	4	0	0	4	11	76	0

1913-14

01.01.1914 PARC DES PRINCES, PARIS
France 6 *T:* J Lacoste, G Andre
Ireland 8 *T:* JP Quinn, GH Wood *C:* RA Lloyd
Referee: EW Calver (England)

17.01.1914 TWICKENHAM
England 10 *T:* LG Brown, CH Pillman
C: FE Chapman 2
Wales 9 *T:* W Watts *C:* J Bancroft *DG:* GL Hirst
Referee: JRC Greenlees (Scotland)

07.02.1914 CARDIFF ARMS PARK
Wales 24 *T:* IT Davies, J Wetter, GL Hirst
C: J Bancroft 2 *PG:* J Bancroft *DG:* GL Hirst, JMC Lewis
Scotland 5 *T:* WA Stewart *C:* AD Laing
Referee: V Drennon (Ireland)

14.02.1914 TWICKENHAM
England 17 *T:* CN Lowe 2, WJA Davies, CH Pillman,
AD Roberts *C:* FE Chapman
Ireland 15 *T:* ARV Jackson, JP Quinn *C:* RA Lloyd
DG: RA Lloyd
Referee: TD Schofield (Wales)

28.02.1914 LANSDOWNE ROAD, DUBLIN
Ireland 6 *T:* JP Quinn, V McNamara
Scotland 0
Referee: JW Baxter (England)

02.03.1914 ST HELEN'S, SWANSEA
Wales 31 *T:* J Wetter 2, H Uzzell 2, GL Hirst,
Rev JA Davies, WH Evans *C:* J Bancroft 5
France 0
Referee: JH Miles (England)

14.03.1914 BALMORAL SHOWGROUNDS, BELFAST
Ireland 3 *T:* AR Foster
Wales 11 *T:* JB Jones, IT Davies, J Wetter
C: JMC Lewis
Referee: JT Tulloch (Scotland)

21.03.1914 INVERLEITH, EDINBURGH
Scotland 15 *T:* JG Will 2, JL Huggan *C:* FH Turner
DG: TC Bowie
England 16 *T:* CN Lowe 3, RW Poulton
C: HC Harrison 2
Referee: TD Schofield (Wales)

13.04.1914 STADE COLOMBES, PARIS
France 13 *T:* G Andre, JL Capmau, M-F Lubin-Lebrere
C: L Besset 2
England 39 *T:* RW Poulton 4, CN Lowe 3, WJA Davies,
JHD Watson *C:* JE Greenwood 6
Referee: J Games (Wales)

	P	W	D	L	FOR	AGAINST	PTS
England	4	4	0	0	82	49	8
Wales	4	3	0	1	75	18	6
Ireland	4	2	0	2	29	34	4
Scotland	3	0	0	3	20	46	0
France	3	0	0	3	19	78	0

Scotland and France did not meet

"

England won four Grand Slams, a magnificent haul, only to see Scotland looking to eclipse them in the closing years of the decade.

"

1920s

The economic turmoil in the world at large was reflected in the topsy-turvy nature of the championship during the 1920s. There were switchback fortunes for nearly every side. England won four Grand Slams, a magnificent haul, only to see Scotland looking to eclipse them in the closing years of the decade, during which they claimed four titles in five years, albeit two of them were shared with Ireland. Inexplicably, in 1928, in the middle of this streak, Scotland went from heroes to zeros, picking up just two points, only for England to lift their fourth Grand Slam of the era. Make sense of that!

Ireland, meanwhile, went from relative no-hopers to contenders, four successive lowly placings being followed swiftly by two runners-up spots and two shared titles. Wales constantly wandered up and down the table during the course of the 1920s. Only France were consistent, consistently vulnerable that is, winning only seven matches in the entire decade. It was an improvement of sorts, but they brought up the rear for much of the time. 'Flair, but no discipline,' was the assessment of one commentator. Now, where have we heard that before? *Plus ça change*.

Scotland were Grand Slam winners in 1925. Their fans ought to have embraced the moment, for although their side did them proud in the following years, it was to be a long, long wait until they were next to savour the Grand Slam feeling – 59 years to be precise, Jim Aitken's men finally scooping the pot in 1984. Seize the day, for it may be some time before it comes round again. There's many who'll raise a glass to that sentiment.

Murrayfield, with its wide-open terraces, came into our midst during the 1920s, and was a suitably raucous, appreciative backdrop for the success of 1925, the first year of the stadium's use. It was becoming increasingly obvious that there was an appetite for watching rugby. Crowds were growing. The Wales v Scotland game in Swansea in 1921 was almost called off after the crowd of more than 50,000 continually spilled onto the pitch. The captains were called together and the visitors wanted the game abandoned but saw sense as they were about to claim their first win in Wales in 29 years.

England even experimented with taking the Five Nations to the shires, Welford Road hosting the 1923 game between England and Ireland. That initiative, commendable in so many ways, was not deemed a success in that fewer than 20,000 turned out to watch. The small acorn theory didn't hold good for the RFU grandees, Five Nations matches returned to 'Billy Williams' Cabbage Patch', and Twickenham remained the centre of the English rugby universe.

The decade witnessed other curios. That same year, 1923, it became illegal to use more than three players in the front row, while in 1922, in the game between Wales and England at Cardiff, both sides wore numbers on the backs of their jerseys for the first time in an international. Wales lorded it that day, effectively sealing the 1922 championship in the opening match of the tournament. Wales scored tries through eight different players in their 28-6 victory but could manage only two conversions. All five Swansea players got on the scoresheet as Wales revelled in the muddy conditions.

But if there was one overriding feature of the 1920s it lay in the quality of the performers. There are names from that decade that resonate still. For France, fly half Yves du Manoir made his debut in 1925 and captained his country against Scotland in 1927 aged 22, only to have his life tragically cut short just a year later. On 2 January 1928, with France and Scotland about to meet at Stade Colombes, du Manoir, not selected for the game, was killed when his aircraft came down during a military flying examination; the Yves du Manoir stadiums at Colombes and Montpellier are both named in his memory.

Great Scots of the period included Phil Macpherson, Ian Smith and A.C. 'Johnny' Wallace, as well as Eric Liddell, who won the first of his seven Scottish caps in 1922. 'Flying Scotsman' Liddell was educated at Eltham College in London, going on to play rugby for Edinburgh University and Scotland. But his time in rugby was brief and he played in his last international, against England, in March 1923. His sporting calling was athletics. At the 1924 Olympic Games in Paris, Liddell won the gold medal in the 400m (in a world record time of 47.60 seconds) after declining to run in his favourite 100m because of the heats having been scheduled on a Sunday – events immortalised in the Oscar-winning film *Chariots of Fire*. Liddell had been born in China, the son of missionaries, and his beliefs shaped his life. He returned to China in 1925 and entered the ministry, dying in a Japanese internment camp in 1945 from a brain tumour.

Among the leading English rugby players of the 1920s was one Wavell Wakefield. 'Wakers' played for England from 1920 to 1927 as a back-five forward, was on the winning side in 20 of his 30 championship games and won three Grand Slams – in 1921, in 1923 and as captain in 1924. Overall he represented England 31 times (a record until surpassed by Budge Rogers in 1969), leading the side on 13 occasions. Wakefield was a man with presence, a man with a mind as well as character – easy virtues to denote; far more difficult to locate in any one individual – and he takes his place alongside such players as Martin Johnson, Will Carling and Bill Beaumont in the pantheon of notable English captains. Furthermore, Wakefield was an all-round talent: he was also the RAF 440 yards champion and played cricket for the MCC. After retiring from rugby, he was MP for Swindon from 1935 to 1945 and for St Marylebone from 1945 to 1963, when he was elevated to the peerage as Baron Wakefield of Kendal, having already been knighted in 1944. Wakefield was president of Harlequins from 1950 to 1980 and of the RFU in 1950-51.

Yet if Wakefield was an all-rounder, how about Stanley Harris for a Renaissance man? Harris was a *Boy's Own* hero. As well as winning rugby caps for England against Ireland and Scotland in 1920, he played polo for England, played Davis Cup tennis for South Africa and won the South African light-heavyweight boxing title. Harris even turned down a place in the Great Britain Olympic modern pentathlon team in 1920 to play rugby, and legend has it he may once have been a runner-up in the world ballroom dancing championships. In 1924, having returned to South Africa, he was called up by the touring Lions and played two Tests. Apart from all that, Stan Harris led a quiet, sedentary life.

There were numerous farewells to be made during the 1920s: to Cyril Lowe, that try scorer extraordinaire, the man whose radar was tuned to the white line. Some wings today would do well to take note. Lowe's record of 18 international tries stood as an English record until overtaken by Rory Underwood in 1990 (although Underwood himself scored no more than 18 career tries in the Five Nations). Lowe won his 25 caps in succession but did not open his try-scoring account until his seventh Test, against Ireland at Twickenham in 1914. Once he got the

ABOVE Ian Smith and Phil Macpherson, two Scotland greats of the 1920s.

RULES AS TO
PROFESSIONALISM

The Rugby Union Committee deem it advisable, as the game spreads in all parts of the country, to draw the attention of all players to these rules.

THE PRINCIPAL RULES AS AFFECT THE INDIVIDUAL ARE AS FOLLOWS:—

1. Professionalism is illegal.

2. Acts of Professionalism are :—

Asking, receiving, or relying on a promise, direct or implied, to receive any money consideration whatever, actual or prospective, any employment or advancement, any establishment in business, or any compensation whatever for :—

   (a) Playing football or rendering any service to a football organisation (provided however, that the Secretary and Treasurer of a Club who has definitely ceased playing football may be excepted under special conditions).

   (b) Training, or loss of time connected therewith.

   (c) Time lost in playing football or in travelling in connection with football.

   (d) Expenses in excess of the amount actually disbursed on account of reasonable hotel or travelling expenses.

Playing for a Club while receiving, or after having received from such Club, any consideration whatever for acting as an official, or for doing or having done any work about the Club's ground or in connection with the Club's affairs, unless such work was done before the receiver became a football player.

Remaining on tour at his Club's expense longer than is reasonable.

Giving or receiving any money testimonial. Or, giving or receiving any other testimonial, except under the authority of this Union.

Playing on any ground where gate money is taken :—

   (a) During the close season (that is between 21st April and 1st September, except when the Tuesday in Easter Week falls later than 21st April, when the close season shall commence from the Wednesday in the Easter Week), except where special permission for the game has been granted by this Committee.

   (b) In any match or contest where it is previously agreed that less than 15 players on each side shall take part (except where, in exceptional cases, this Committee may have granted special permission for less than 15 players aside to take part).

Knowingly playing with or against any expelled or suspended player or Club, or with or against any professional player or Club.

Refusing to give evidence or otherwise assist in carrying out these rules when requested by this Union to do so.

Being registered as, or declared a professional, or suspended by any National Rugby Union or by the Football Association.

Playing within 8 days of any accident for which he has claimed or received insurance compensation, if insured under these rules.

Playing in any benefit match connected with football (except where this Committee has given permission for a *bona fide* charity match).

Knowingly playing or acting as referee or touch judge on the ground of an expelled or suspended club.

Receiving money or other valuable consideration from any person or persons as an inducement towards playing football.

Signing any form of the Northern Union (Rugby League).

Advocating or taking steps to promote Northern Union (Rugby League) or other professional football.

The penalty for breach of these Rules is suspension or expulsion. (Expulsion carries with it the formal declaration of professionalism).

This Union shall have power to deal with all acts which it may consider as acts of professionalism and which are not specifically provided for.

October, 1924.   *BY ORDER OF THE COMMITTEE.*

IGNORANCE OF THE RULES IS NO DEFENCE.

LEFT *'Rules as to Professionalism'*
announced by the Rugby Union Committee
in 1924.

the 1920s

taste for it, though, he was nigh on impossible to stop, and he went on to score a championship record eight tries in that campaign, including hat-tricks against Scotland and France. 'Get the ball to Cyril' was about as much of a team talk as was necessary.

It's not as if Lowe were the Jonah Lomu of his day. He weighed in at no more than 8½ stone and stood only 5ft 6ins. Yet Lowe's impact on the side is easy to gauge: he was on the winning England side on 21 occasions. The son of a parson from Holbeach in Lincolnshire and educated at Dulwich College and Cambridge, Lowe served as a fighter pilot in the Great War and was awarded the MC and Distinguished Flying Cross (DFC).

ABOVE *Cyril Lowe, W.J.A. Davies and Cecil Kershaw, who all left international rugby after England's Grand Slam in 1923.* BELOW *A letter from Windsor Castle congratulating Davies on his team's performance and his own personal achievements.*

Two other long-serving England players retired along with Lowe after the 1923 Grand Slam – Welsh-born fly half W.J.A. Davies and fellow United Services man scrum half Cecil Kershaw. They formed a splendid double act, appearing in international partnership at half back a then-record 14 times. William John Abbott Davies, known by his initials or as 'Dave', captained England to that 1923 Grand Slam and on 11 occasions in total. In an international career that began in 1913, he had an overall record as a player of 20 wins, one draw and just one defeat. Davies rounded off matters in 1923 in some style, dropping a goal in Paris to help clinch the Slam. And on his honeymoon, too. Bet his bride was appreciative – nothing else to do in Paris, after all.

The committee men kept an eagle eye on events during the 1920s. Funny how there has always been the occasional point of friction between players and men in blazers. Neil Macpherson, a forward who won seven caps for Scotland as well as four for the Lions, was originally banned *sine die* in 1924 by the Scottish Rugby Union (SRU) for accepting a gift from Newport RFC of a watch in recognition of the unbeaten 1922-23 season. The International Rugby Football Board (IRFB), as it was called at the time, had stated that no gift of greater value than £2 could be accepted; the watch was valued at £21. The SRU also banned its players from having any playing contact with those from Newport. Macpherson was eventually reinstated but never played for Scotland again.

Wales's Ossie Male also found himself in hot water in 1924. His supposed misdemeanour was to play for his

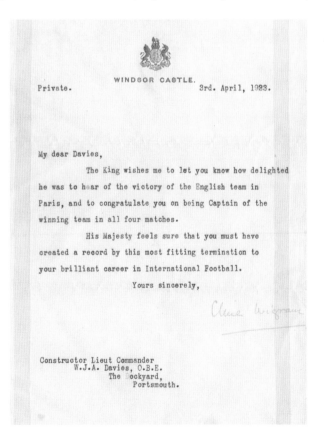

Private.   WINDSOR CASTLE.   3rd. April, 1923.

My dear Davies,

The King wishes me to let you know how delighted he was to hear of the victory of the English team in Paris, and to congratulate you on being Captain of the winning team in all four matches.

His Majesty feels sure that you must have created a record by this most fitting termination to your brilliant career in International Football.

Yours sincerely,

Constructor Lieut Commander
W.J.A. Davies, O.B.E.
The Dockyard,
Portsmouth.

RIGHT Ossie Male, restored to the Welsh team after his three-year absence, attempts a conversion against England at Twickenham in 1927.

club, Cardiff, within a week of an international, which was contrary to Welsh Rugby Union (WRU) regulations. As the Wales team travelled up to London on their way to Paris for the France game, the WRU decided to suspend Male; he was sent home when the party reached Paddington. It was to be three years before Male played for Wales again, although he did go on to captain his country in 1927 against Scotland and in 1928 against Scotland and France.

The 1920 championship was a three-way tie, although had the points-difference system been in place at the time, the game between Wales and England at Swansea on 17 January would have proved decisive: Wales's 19-5 margin of victory would have settled the issue in favour of the home side at the final reckoning. Jerry Shea, the Newport centre, scored 16 points on championship debut, while Leicester and Army wing Harold Day scored England's points.

Day played because, as the record would have it, 'he was better suited to a wet day', even though it had been W.M. Lowry of Birkenhead Park who had been photographed in the team line-up.

There was a dutiful sense of remembrance about this first championship since hostilities ceased. The war had taken a heavy toll. If that was the predominant emotion, there was also a sense of hope and renewal in the air. Certainly that was reflected in the team sheets, with all the sides fielding a host of new caps – inevitably so. Some countries fared better than others in this enforced transition. Ireland lost all four matches for the first time, conceding a record 76 points and 19 tries.

France's 15-7 victory in Ireland was their first away win since their entry into the championship in 1910. Racing Club wing Adolphe Jauréguy touched down twice, as did beret-wearing Perpignan wing Raoul Got. Jauréguy was to become a star of his time. This was the year that French rugby began, admittedly slowly, to get its act together, the Fédération Française de Rugby (FFR) coming into being to take over the running of French rugby from the Union des Sociétés Françaises de Sports Athlétiques.

The RFU's jubilee year in 1921 had a suitable point of celebration – England's third Grand Slam. England were in a league of their own, as can be deduced from their 'points against' column. They conceded only nine points in total in their four games. Miserly, mean and very well organised, England fully deserved their Grand Slam. They weren't too scruffy, either, when it came to crossing the opposition try line, scoring 13 tries in all, eight more than the next best sides. France slipped into the reckoning, albeit fleetingly, finishing as runners-up alongside Wales after victories over Scotland and Ireland.

Not surprisingly, England came into the championship the following year with confidence. Their critics would say that they always have such assumptions. There was no doubting the merits of the claim this time around, though. Even so, they were to come up short in a championship noted for narrow margins in many instances – there were three drawn games – but for an overwhelming margin in the game that really mattered, that between Wales

BELOW The teams as listed in the programme for the match against France in January 1920, England's first game at Twickenham after the war. RIGHT The England team photo taken before the game in Dublin later that season.

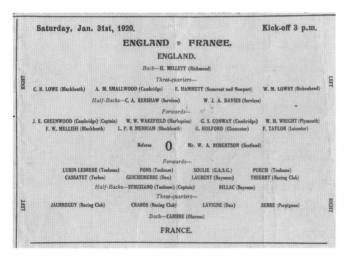

and England at Cardiff Arms Park. English embarrassment knew no bounds as Wales scored eight tries. In partial mitigation, England were without their orchestrator and chosen captain, W.J.A. Davies.

For the first time in an international match, both sides wore numbers. The only numbers, though, that really mattered were there on the scoreboard – Wales 28 England 6. Len 'Bruno' Brown's international career for England ended that day after 18 caps. Brown, who had won the MC in the Great War, returned to Brisbane and was instrumental in the founding of the Australian Rugby Union (ARU) in 1949.

France could count themselves terribly unlucky to come away with only a draw from their visit to Twickenham. They outscored England by three tries to one in a game that ended 11-11, England preserving their unbeaten championship record at Twickenham thanks to a late try from Gloucester forward Tommy Voyce, great uncle of present-day Gloucester back Tom Voyce. Aimé Cassayet, Raoul Got and René Lasserre scored France's tries.

England reigned supreme for the next couple of years, winning back-to-back Grand Slams in 1923 and 1924, the second time that they had achieved such a feat. That they managed the second Slam without the formidable services of Davies, Kershaw and Lowe, all of whose boots had been well and truly hung up, seemed to emphasise England's strength in depth.

England didn't have things all their own way, though, sneaking home 8-6 in Scotland in 1923 by dint of a conversion from Devonport Services forward William Luddington. England's crucial score was an interception try from Tommy Voyce. The Grand Slam was clinched in Paris with a 12-3 win, tries coming from Geoffrey Conway and Wavell Wakefield.

While England enjoyed exalted status, Wales were obliged to dwell on their fortunes after a poor season in 1924. They won only one championship match, against France at Stade Colombes – their worst return in many a year. After much agonising and soul-searching, the 'Big Five' selection panel was born, the panacea for all ills in the Welsh game. Or so the thinking went.

Saturday, Feb. 25th, 1922. *Kick-off 3 p.m.*

ENGLAND v FRANCE.

ENGLAND

Back—R. C. W. PICKLES
(Bristol)

Threequarters—

C. N. LOWE (1) E. MYERS (2) M. S. BRADBY (3) H. L. V. DAY (4)
(Blackheath) (Bradford) (Navy) (Leicester and Army)

Half-Backs—W. J. A. DAVIES (5) (Captain) C. A. KERSHAW (6)
(Navy) (Navy)

Forwards—

G. S. CONWAY (10) R. COVE-SMITH (14) R. F. H. DUNCAN (7) R. EDWARDS (9)
(Cambridge) (Cambridge) (Guy's Hospital) (Newport)

E. R. GARDNER (11) J. E. MAXWELL-HYSLOP (13) A. T. VOYCE (8) W. W. WAKEFIELD (12)
(Navy) (Oxford) (Gloucester) (Cambridge and R.A.F.)

0

Forwards—

C. BIRABIN (2) J. BOUBÉE (8) A. CASSAYET (5) C. GONNET (1)
(Dax) (Biarritz) (Stade Gaudinois) (Albi)

R. LASSERRE (7) (Capt.) G. LUBIN LEBRÈRE (4) J. SEBEDIO (6) E. SOULIE (3)
(Cognac) (Toulouse) (Carcassonne) (Société Générale, Paris)

Half Backs—R. PITEU (9) G. PASCOT (10)
(Pau) (Perpignan)

Threequarters—

A. LAFFONT (11) R. CRABOS (14) F. BORDES (13) R. RAMIS (12)
(Bayonne) (St. Sevres) (Toulouse) (Perpignan)

Back—J. CLEMENT (15)
(Valence)

FRANCE

Referee—Mr. J. M. TENNANT (Scotland)

AFTER CONSIDERABLE THOUGHT YESTERDAY THE RUGBY SELECTION COMMITTEE CHOSE ENGLAND'S XV TO PLAY WALES.

THEY ENTICED SUB-LT. K.A.SELLAR FROM THE NAVY TO PLAY FULL BACK.

HAMILTON WICKES
GIBBS
MORTON
LAIRD
WAKEFIELD

THEY HAVE CHOSEN NO FEWER THAN FIVE HARLEQUINS. — A THIRD OF THE TEAM!

2 FROM BRISTOL. L. J. CORBETT ENGLAND'S NEW CAPTAIN.

AND J. S. TUCKER THE HOOKER.

H. M. LOCKE ONE FROM BIRKENHEAD PARK.

T. COULSON FROM COVENTRY

TWO FORWARDS FROM PLYMOUTH ALBION. E. STANBURY and J. HANLEY.

H.G. PERITON FROM WATERLOO (KING'S + AND LIVERPOOL STREET ARE JEALOUS OF THIS)

K. J. STARK, OLD ALLEYNIANS AND

— THE LAST PLACE GOES TO R. COVE-SMITH O.M.Ts.

RIGHT How the cartoonist saw the forthcoming match between England and Wales at Twickenham in 1927. As it turned out Wavell Wakefield was replaced by Geoffrey Conway (facing page top).

There was another different venue on the official records this year, with France obliged to play their game against Scotland at the Stade Pershing after the Seine burst its banks and flooded Stade Colombes. England also played their first international in Ulster, winning 14-3 at Ravenhill.

Towards the end of the 1925 championship, Inverleith gave way to Murrayfield as Scotland's home ground, a move vindicated in the very first game at the new venue, 80,000 cramming in to see Scotland's 14-11 victory over England. Money well spent, as they might say in those parts. Indeed, the anticipation and subsequent opening of Murrayfield seemed to have a galvanising effect, Scotland winning all their four matches that season to claim their first title of the Five Nations era. Centre Phil Macpherson, part of an all-Oxford-educated Scottish threequarter line, led the side with vigour. (A clock was later installed in Macpherson's memory at Murrayfield, donated by his widow.) Yet there was no doubt as to the star of the emerging Scotland team, the prodigiously talented wing Ian Smith. He scored four tries in each of successive games against France and Wales. His wing partner, A.C. 'Johnny' Wallace, was no slouch, either. Wallace scored at least once in every game in 1925.

Ireland took second place that year with England, whose 'Golden Era' appeared to be on the wane. In the 11 championships since the start of the Five Nations, England had won the title eight times and been runners-up twice, including shared placings in both cases. They had won 35 of 44 championship matches played, their record including a 13-match sequence without defeat – no mean achievement.

France, without the influential René Crabos, lost all four games. Crabos had been forced to retire after breaking his leg against Ireland the previous year. Crabos had been the midfield linchpin of a threatening back line, the stand-out French player in his 17 internationals, and had played a part in each of France's four post-war wins to date. He captained the French Army side, and then the national side on 12 occasions. Crabos went on to be a manager of the French team in later years and also president of the FFR in 1952.

The 1926 championship was a humdrum affair, Scotland and Ireland sharing the title. The former experienced defeat at Murrayfield against the latter who, in turn, lost to Wales to ruin their hopes of a Grand Slam. The Scotland v Ireland clash in Edinburgh was close, Ireland winning 3-0 courtesy of a last-ditch try in the corner from Jack Gage.

In 1927 Scotland recorded their first ever hat-trick of titles, even though they once again shared the championship spoils with Ireland. Wales and France finished as also-rans, the latter's 3-0 win over England in Paris in their final game being more than welcome. There was trouble on the political front in French rugby, grievances and difficulties that were soon to come to a head.

Meanwhile, the game itself had become sterile, a situation that many commentators put down to the 3-2-3 scrum. The back row were the defensive hit men, the scourge of any attacking player. The weather during the 1927 championship did not help matters. Cats and dogs. That sort of thing.

LEFT The England team to play Scotland at Twickenham in 1928. Back row (left to right): H.G. Periton, C.D. Aarvold, K.J. Stark, J. Hanley, F.D. Prentice, G.V. Palmer, T.H. Vile (referee). Middle row: W.J. Taylor, J.V. Richardson, E. Stanbury, R. Cove-Smith (capt), J.S. Tucker, T.W. Brown, R.H.W. Sparks. Front row: H.C.C. Laird, A.T. Young.
FOLLOWING PAGES Action from the 1928 England v Scotland game: H.G. 'Joe' Periton breaks through a Scottish tackle.

Ireland's 6-0 win over Scotland was played out in arctic conditions. Several players were said afterwards to be suffering from hypothermia. Nonetheless, Ireland did manage two tries, from prop Ted (later Sir Theodore) Pike and wing James Ganly. For the second successive season, Ireland deprived Scotland of a Grand Slam and Triple Crown.

Aimé Cassayet, one of the finest forwards of his generation, played his final game for France against Wales at Swansea that year. He passed away just months after that match following a painful illness. A robust player, athletic too, Cassayet won 31 caps. He played initially for Tarbes, helping them to the championship in 1920, before moving to Narbonne, who have a stadium named in his memory.

The two sides who dominated the era, England and Scotland, were to close the decade with a title each. In 1928 England achieved their sixth Grand Slam, a mighty return – although they would have to wait until 1957 before they next accomplished the feat. Indeed, in 1928, England had to scrap for the mythical bauble, overcoming Wales and Ireland only by narrow margins. But if there was little of the swagger and superiority of previous Grand Slams, there was still plenty to admire in England's fortitude as they came through 10-8 in Swansea and by an even narrower margin, 7-6, in Dublin.

At St Helen's England pounced on a defensive error to score in the first half, wing William Taylor getting that touchdown and Colin Laird scoring the visitors' second try. John Bartlett and Dai John were the Welsh try scorers, and Wales were seemingly denied a winning score when an offside decision thwarted Neath forward Tom Hollingdale on his debut.

England prevailed at Lansdowne Road, too, even though outscored two tries to one. Lansdowne wing Jack 'Joxer' Arigho and Wanderers scrum half Mark Sugden scored Ireland's tries, while Birkenhead Park centre James Richardson crossed for England. Yet it was Richardson's dropped goal, worth four points, that made the difference. It was England's fifth win in six games at Lansdowne Road and Ireland's only defeat of the 1928 championship. Indeed, Ireland were making a mark, outscoring the champions elect during that campaign, finishing with 12 tries to the nine of all-conquering England. Scotland's curious slump saw them record just a solitary victory, 15-6 in Paris against fellow stragglers France, who did, however, gain their first ever win against Wales, a welcome respite after 13 defeats in a row.

The decade closed with Scotland once again in the ascendant. They won their fourth title in five seasons, in marked contrast to France, who ended up without a point for the third time in five seasons.

FACING PAGE FAR LEFT Jack 'Joxer' Arigho and Mark Sugden, both try scorers for Ireland in their close defeat to England in 1928.
BOTTOM The match-programme line-ups for England's Grand Slam game against Scotland the same year.

BELOW Twickenham in 1929.

45

Five Nations Results 1920-29

1919-20

01.01.1920 PARC DES PRINCES, PARIS
France 0
Scotland 5 *T:* GB Crole *C:* F Kennedy
Referee: FC Potter-Irwin (England)

17.01.1920 ST HELEN'S, SWANSEA
Wales 19 *T:* WJ Powell, J Shea *C:* J Shea *PG:* J Shea
DG: J Shea
England 5 *T:* HLV Day *C:* HLV Day
Referee: JT Tulloch (Scotland)

31.01.1920 TWICKENHAM
England 8 *T:* WJA Davies *C:* JE Greenwood
PG: JE Greenwood
France 3 *T:* R Crabos
Referee: WA Robertson (Scotland)

07.02.1920 INVERLEITH, EDINBURGH
Scotland 9 *T:* AT Sloan *PG:* F Kennedy 2
Wales 5 *T:* A Jenkins *C:* A Jenkins
Referee: SH Crawford (Ireland)

14.02.1920 LANSDOWNE ROAD, DUBLIN
Ireland 11 *T:* JAN Dickson, RA Lloyd *C:* RA Lloyd
PG: RA Lloyd
England 14 *T:* CN Lowe, FW Mellish, E Myers,
WW Wakefield *C:* JE Greenwood
Referee: WA Robertson (Scotland)

17.02.1920 STADE COLOMBES, PARIS
France 5 *T:* A Jaureguy *C:* P Struxiano
Wales 6 *T:* B Williams, WJ Powell
Referee: Col WSD Craven (England)

28.02.1920 INVERLEITH, EDINBURGH
Scotland 19 *T:* GB Crole 2, AW Angus, A Browning
C: F Kennedy 2 *PG:* F Kennedy
Ireland 0
Referee: JW Baxter (England)

13.03.1920 CARDIFF ARMS PARK
Wales 28 *T:* B Williams 3, A Jenkins, J Whitfield,
T Parker *C:* A Jenkins 2, J Wetter *DG:* A Jenkins
Ireland 4 *DG:* BAT McFarland
Referee: FC Potter-Irwin (England)

20.03.1920 TWICKENHAM
England 13 *T:* SW Harris, CA Kershaw, CN Lowe
C: JE Greenwood 2
Scotland 4 *DG:* JH Bruce-Lockhart
Referee: TD Schofield (Wales)

03.04.1920 LANSDOWNE ROAD, DUBLIN
Ireland 7 *T:* AH Price *DG:* RA Lloyd
France 15 *T:* R Got 2, A Jaureguy 2, W Gayraud
Referee: JM Tennent (Scotland)

	P	W	D	L	FOR	AGAINST	PTS
Wales	4	3	0	1	58	23	6
Scotland	4	3	0	1	37	18	6
England	4	3	0	1	40	37	6
France	4	1	0	3	23	26	2
Ireland	4	0	0	4	22	76	0

1920-21

15.01.1921 TWICKENHAM
England 18 *T:* AM Smallwood 2, CA Kershaw,
CN Lowe *C:* EDG Hammett *DG:* WJA Davies
Wales 3 *T:* J Ring
Referee: JC Sturrock (Scotland)

22.01.1921 INVERLEITH, EDINBURGH
Scotland 0
France 3 *T:* E Billac
Referee: WP Hinton (Ireland)

05.02.1921 ST HELEN'S, SWANSEA
Wales 8 *DG:* A Jenkins 2
Scotland 14 *T:* AE Thomson, JCR Buchanan, AT Sloan
C: GHHP Maxwell *PG:* GHHP Maxwell
Referee: JW Baxter (England)

12.02.1921 TWICKENHAM
England 15 *T:* AF Blakiston, LG Brown, CN Lowe
C: BS Cumberlege *DG:* CN Lowe
Ireland 0
Referee: TD Schofield (Wales)

26.02.1921 CARDIFF ARMS PARK
Wales 12 *T:* J Williams, W Hodder *PG:* A Jenkins 2
France 4 *DG:* R Lasserre
Referee: PMR Royds (England)

26.02.1921 LANSDOWNE ROAD, DUBLIN
Ireland 9 *T:* DJ Cussen, GV Stephenson,
WA Cunningham
Scotland 8 *T:* J Hume, AT Sloan *C:* GHHP Maxwell
Referee: JW Baxter (England)

**12.03.1921 BALMORAL SHOWGROUNDS,
BELFAST**
Ireland 0
Wales 6 *T:* MG Thomas *PG:* T Johnson
Referee: JM Tennent (Scotland)

19.03.1921 INVERLEITH, EDINBURGH
Scotland 0
England 18 *T:* LG Brown, ER Gardner, QEMA King,
T Woods *C:* EDG Hammett 3
Referee: JC Crawford (Ireland)

28.03.1921 STADE COLOMBES, PARIS
France 6 *PG:* R Crabos 2
England 10 *T:* AF Blakiston, CN Lowe
C: EDG Hammett 2
Referee: JC Sturrock (Scotland)

09.04.1921 STADE COLOMBES, PARIS
France 20 *T:* R Piteu 2, A Cassayet, J Boubee
C: R Crabos 4
Ireland 10 *T:* P Stokes 2 *C:* TG Wallis 2
Referee: JG Cunningham (Scotland)

	P	W	D	L	FOR	AGAINST	PTS
England	4	4	0	0	61	9	8
France	4	2	0	2	33	32	4
Wales	4	2	0	2	29	36	4
Scotland	4	1	0	3	22	38	2
Ireland	4	1	0	3	19	49	2

1921-22

02.01.1922 STADE COLOMBES, PARIS
France 3 *T:* A Jaureguy
Scotland 3 *T:* A Browning
Referee: HC Harrison (England)

21.01.1922 CARDIFF ARMS PARK
Wales 28 *T:* W Bowen, WJ Delahay, I Evans,
D Hiddlestone, T Parker, F Palmer, C Richards,
J Whitfield *C:* J Rees 2
England 6 *T:* HLV Day, CN Lowe
Referee: JM Tennent (Scotland)

04.02.1922 INVERLEITH, EDINBURGH
Scotland 9 *T:* A Browning 2 *PG:* A Browning
Wales 9 *T:* W Bowen *C:* F Samuel *DG:* I Evans
Referee: RA Lloyd (Ireland)

11.02.1922 LANSDOWNE ROAD, DUBLIN
Ireland 3 *T:* TG Wallis
England 12 *T:* CN Lowe, ER Gardner, JE Maxwell-
Hyslop, AM Smallwood
Referee: JM Tennent (Scotland)

25.02.1922 INVERLEITH, EDINBURGH
Scotland 6 *T:* WE Bryce, EH Liddell
Ireland 3 *T:* JAB Clarke
Referee: TD Schofield (Wales)

25.02.1922 TWICKENHAM
England 11 *T:* AT Voyce *C:* HLV Day *PG:* HLV Day 2
France 11 *T:* A Cassayet, R Got, R Lasserre *C:* R Crabos
Referee: JM Tennent (Scotland)

11.03.1922 ST HELEN'S, SWANSEA
Wales 11 *T:* J Whitfield 2, I Evans *C:* F Samuel
Ireland 5 *T:* P Stokes *C:* TG Wallis
Referee: JC Sturrock (Scotland)

18.03.1922 TWICKENHAM
England 11 *T:* CN Lowe 2, WJA Davies *C:* GS Conway
Scotland 5 *T:* JC Dykes *C:* DM Bertram
Referee: RA Lloyd (Ireland)

23.03.1922 STADE COLOMBES, PARIS
France 3 *T:* A Jaureguy
Wales 11 *T:* J Whitfield, W Cummins, I Evans
C: A Jenkins
Referee: RW Harland (Ireland)

08.04.1922 LANSDOWNE ROAD, DUBLIN
Ireland 8 *T:* GV Stephenson *C:* TG Wallis
PG: TG Wallis
France 3 *T:* J Pascot
Referee: JM Tennent (Scotland)

	P	W	D	L	FOR	AGAINST	PTS
Wales	4	3	1	0	59	23	7
England	4	2	1	1	40	47	5
Scotland	4	1	2	1	23	26	4
France	4	0	2	2	20	33	2
Ireland	4	1	0	3	19	32	2

1922-23

20.01.1923 INVERLEITH, EDINBURGH
Scotland 16 *T:* E McLaren 2, WE Bryce, EH Liddell
C: D Drysdale 2
France 3 *GM*:* L Beguet
Referee: TH Vile (Wales)
* goal from mark

20.01.1923 TWICKENHAM
England 7 *T:* HL Price *DG:* AM Smallwood
Wales 3 *T:* G Michael
Referee: JMB Scott (Scotland)

03.02.1923 CARDIFF ARMS PARK
Wales 8 *T:* JMC Lewis *C:* A Jenkins *PG:* A Jenkins
Scotland 11 *T:* EH Liddell, LM Stuart, AL Gracie
C: D Drysdale
Referee: JW Baxter (England)

10.02.1923 WELFORD ROAD, LEICESTER
England 23 *T:* CN Lowe, LJ Corbett, HL Price,
AT Voyce, AM Smallwood *C:* GS Conway 2
DG: WJA Davies
Ireland 5 *T:* TA McClelland *C:* WE Crawford
Referee: TH Vile (Wales)

24.02.1923 LANSDOWNE ROAD, DUBLIN
Ireland 3 *T:* DJ Cussen
Scotland 13 *T:* EH Liddell, SB McQueen, A Browning
C: A Browning 2
Referee: TH Vile (Wales)

24.02.1923 ST HELEN'S, SWANSEA
Wales 16 *T:* WR Harding, MG Thomas, A Baker
C: A Jenkins 2 *PG:* J Rees
France 8 *T:* M Lalande, R Lasserre *C:* L Beguet
Referee: JB McGowan (Ireland)

10.03.1923 LANSDOWNE ROAD, DUBLIN
Ireland 5 *T:* DJ Cussen *C:* WE Crawford
Wales 4 *DG:* J Powell
Referee: JM Tennent (Scotland)

17.03.1923 INVERLEITH, EDINBURGH
Scotland 6 *T:* AL Gracie, E McLaren
England 8 *T:* AM Smallwood, AT Voyce
C: WGE Luddington
Referee: TH Vile (Wales)

02.04.1923 STADE COLOMBES, PARIS
France 3 *PG:* L Beguet
England 12 *T:* GS Conway, WW Wakefield
C: WGE Luddington *DG:* WJA Davies
Referee: AE Freethy (Wales)

14.04.1923 STADE COLOMBES, PARIS
France 14 *T:* A Jaureguy 2, L Beguet, P Moureu
C: L Beguet
Ireland 8 *T:* AC Douglas, TA McClelland
C: WE Crawford
Referee: PMR Royds (England)

	P	W	D	L	FOR	AGAINST	PTS
England	4	4	0	0	50	17	8
Scotland	4	3	0	1	46	22	6
Wales	4	1	0	3	31	31	2
France	4	1	0	3	28	52	2
Ireland	4	1	0	3	21	54	2

1923-24

01.01.1924 STADE PERSHING, PARIS
France 12 *T:* A Jaureguy, E Piquiral, H Galau, P Moureu
Scotland 10 *T:* AC Wallace *PG:* DS Davies
DG: H Waddell
Referee: E Roberts (Wales)

19.01.1924 ST HELEN'S, SWANSEA
Wales 9 *T:* T Johnson, T Jones, A Owen
England 17 *T:* HC Catcheside 2, HP Jacob, HM Locke, E Myers *C:* GS Conway
Referee: AW Angus (Scotland)

26.01.1924 LANSDOWNE ROAD, DUBLIN
Ireland 6 *T:* GV Stephenson, AP Atkins
France 0
Referee: AA Lawrie (Scotland)

02.02.1924 INVERLEITH, EDINBURGH
Scotland 35 *T:* IS Smith 3, WE Bryce, DM Bertram, AC Wallace, H Waddell, GPS Macpherson
C: D Drysdale 4 *PG:* D Drysdale
Wales 10 *T:* VM Griffiths, I Jones *C:* BO Male 2
Referee: JB McGowan (Ireland)

09.02.1924 RAVENHILL, BELFAST
Ireland 3 *T:* AC Douglas
England 14 *T:* HC Catcheside 2, LJ Corbett, RH Hamilton-Wickes *C:* GS Conway
Referee: TH Vile (Wales)

23.02.1924 TWICKENHAM
England 19 *T:* HP Jacob 3, HC Catcheside, AT Young
C: GS Conway 2
France 7 *T:* J Ballarin *DG:* A Behoteguy
Referee: AE Freethy (Wales)

23.02.1924 INVERLEITH, EDINBURGH
Scotland 13 *T:* H Waddell 2, DM Bertram
C: D Drysdale 2
Ireland 8 *T:* GV Stephenson 2 *C:* GV Stephenson
Referee: TH Vile (Wales)

08.03.1924 CARDIFF ARMS PARK
Wales 10 *T:* C Richards, C Pugh *DG:* E Watkins
Ireland 13 *T:* TR Hewitt, FS Hewitt, HWV Stephenson
C: WE Crawford 2
Referee: JT Tulloch (Scotland)

15.03.1924 TWICKENHAM
England 19 *T:* HC Catcheside, E Myers, WW Wakefield *C:* GS Conway 3 *DG:* E Myers
Scotland 0
Referee: TH Vile (Wales)

27.03.1924 STADE COLOMBES, PARIS
France 6 *T:* A Behoteguy, M-F Lubin-Lebrere
Wales 10 *T:* E Finch, AR Rickards *DG:* VM Griffiths
Referee: RA Roberts (England)

	P	W	D	L	FOR	AGAINST	PTS
England	4	4	0	0	69	19	8
Scotland	4	2	0	2	58	49	4
Ireland	4	2	0	2	30	37	4
Wales	4	1	0	3	39	71	2
France	4	1	0	3	25	45	2

1924-25

01.01.1925 STADE COLOMBES, PARIS
France 3 *T:* E Ribere
Ireland 9 *T:* M Sugden, GV Stephenson
PG: WE Crawford
Referee: J McGill (Scotland)

17.01.1925 TWICKENHAM
England 12 *T:* RH Hamilton-Wickes, HJ Kittermaster, AT Voyce *PG:* R Armstrong
Wales 6 *T:* C Thomas, WP James
Referee: AA Lawrie (Scotland)

24.01.1925 INVERLEITH, EDINBURGH
Scotland 25 *T:* IS Smith 4, AC Wallace 2, AC Gillies
C: AC Gillies, D Drysdale
France 4 *DG:* Y du Manoir
Referee: Dr E DeCourcy Wheeler (Ireland)

07.02.1925 ST HELEN'S, SWANSEA
Wales 14 *T:* WJ Hopkins, WI Jones, RA Cornish
C: D Parker *PG:* D Parker
Scotland 24 *T:* IS Smith 4, AC Wallace 2 *C:* D Drysdale
DG: D Drysdale
Referee: JW Baxter (England)

14.02.1925 TWICKENHAM
England 6 *T:* AM Smallwood 2
Ireland 6 *T:* TR Hewitt, HWV Stephenson
Referee: TH Vile (Wales)

28.02.1925 LANSDOWNE ROAD, DUBLIN
Ireland 8 *T:* HWV Stephenson *C:* WE Crawford
PG: WE Crawford
Scotland 14 *T:* AC Wallace, DJ MacMyn
C: D Drysdale, JC Dykes *DG:* H Waddell
Referee: AE Freethy (Wales)

28.02.1925 CARDIFF ARMS PARK
Wales 11 *T:* E Finch 2, WJ Delahay *C:* D Parker
France 5 *T:* M de Labordiere *C:* J Ducousso
Referee: RW Harland (Ireland)

14.03.1925 RAVENHILL, BELFAST
Ireland 19 *T:* TJ Millin, GV Stephenson, WF Browne, HWV Stephenson *C:* GV Stephenson 2
PG: GV Stephenson
Wales 3 *T:* BR Turnbull
Referee: JW Baxter (England)

21.03.1925 MURRAYFIELD
Scotland 14 *T:* JB Nelson, AC Wallace *C:* D Drysdale, AC Gillies *DG:* H Waddell
England 11 *T:* RH Hamilton-Wickes, WW Wakefield
C: WGE Luddington *PG:* WGE Luddington
Referee: AE Freethy (Wales)

13.04.1925 STADE COLOMBES, PARIS
France 11 *T:* E Barthe, M Besson, L Cluchague
C: J Ducousso
England 13 *T:* RH Hamilton-Wickes, WW Wakefield
C: WGE Luddington 2 *GM*:* WGE Luddington
Referee: AE Freethy (Wales)
* goal from mark

	P	W	D	L	FOR	AGAINST	PTS
Scotland	4	4	0	0	77	37	8
Ireland	4	2	1	1	42	26	5
England	4	2	1	1	42	37	5
Wales	4	1	0	3	34	60	2
France	4	0	0	4	23	58	0

1925-26

02.01.1926 STADE COLOMBES, PARIS
France 6 *T:* E Piquiral *PG:* C-A Gonnet
Scotland 20 *T:* AC Wallace 3, DJ MacMyn, JM Bannerman *C:* D Drysdale *PG:* AC Gillies
Referee: W Llewellyn (Wales)

16.01.1926 CARDIFF ARMS PARK
Wales 3 *T:* GE Andrews
England 3 *T:* WW Wakefield
Referee: WH Acton (Ireland)

23.01.1926 RAVENHILL, BELFAST
Ireland 11 *T:* GV Stephenson 2 *C:* TR Hewitt
PG: GV Stephenson
France 0
Referee: AA Lawrie (Scotland)

06.02.1926 MURRAYFIELD
Scotland 8 *T:* H Waddell *C:* D Drysdale *PG:* AC Gillies
Wales 5 *T:* RC Herrera *C:* WA Everson
Referee: D Hellewell (England)

13.02.1926 LANSDOWNE ROAD, DUBLIN
Ireland 19 *T:* DJ Cussen 2, FS Hewitt, GV Stephenson
C: GV Stephenson 2 *PG:* GV Stephenson
England 15 *T:* LW Haslett, HG Periton, AT Young
C: TES Francis 3
Referee: W Llewellyn (Wales)

27.02.1926 MURRAYFIELD
Scotland 0
Ireland 3 *T:* JH Gage
Referee: BS Cumberlege (England)

27.02.1926 TWICKENHAM
England 11 *T:* AR Aslett 2, HJ Kittermaster
C: TES Francis
France 0
Referee: AE Freethy (Wales)

13.03.1926 ST HELEN'S, SWANSEA
Wales 11 *T:* WR Harding, T Hopkins, RC Herrera
C: TE Rees
Ireland 8 *T:* CJ Hanrahan *C:* GV Stephenson
PG: GV Stephenson
Referee: BS Cumberlege (England)

20.03.1926 TWICKENHAM
England 9 *T:* JS Tucker, AT Voyce, JWG Webb
Scotland 17 *T:* IS Smith 2, H Waddell *C:* H Waddell 2
DG: JC Dykes
Referee: WH Acton (Ireland)

Five Nations Results 1920-29

05.04.1926 STADE COLOMBES, PARIS
France 5 *T:* G Gerintes *C:* C-A Gonnet
Wales 7 *T:* E Watkins *DG:* RA Cornish
Referee: RW Harland (Ireland)

	P	W	D	L	FOR	AGAINST	PTS
Scotland	4	3	0	1	45	23	6
Ireland	4	3	0	1	41	26	6
Wales	4	2	1	1	26	24	5
England	4	1	1	2	38	39	3
France	4	0	0	4	11	49	0

1926-27

01.01.1927 STADE COLOMBES, PARIS
France 3 *T:* E Ribere
Ireland 8 *T:* EO'D Davy *C:* GV Stephenson
PG: GV Stephenson
Referee: RL Scott (Scotland)

15.01.1927 TWICKENHAM
England 11 *T:* LJ Corbett *C:* E Stanbury
PG: E Stanbury *GM*:* LJ Corbett
Wales 9 *T:* GE Andrews, WR Harding *PG:* BO Male
Referee: RL Scott (Scotland)
* goal from mark

22.01.1927 MURRAYFIELD
Scotland 23 *T:* H Waddell 2, IS Smith 2
C: AC Gillies 3, D Drysdale *PG:* AC Gillies
France 6 *T:* E Piquiral, R Hutin
Referee: BS Cumberlege (England)

05.02.1927 CARDIFF ARMS PARK
Wales 0
Scotland 5 *T:* DS Kerr *C:* AC Gillies
Referee: WH Jackson (England)

12.02.1927 TWICKENHAM
England 8 *T:* JC Gibbs, HCC Laird *C:* E Stanbury
Ireland 6 *T:* H McVicker *PG:* GV Stephenson
Referee: TH Vile (Wales)

26.02.1927 LANSDOWNE ROAD, DUBLIN
Ireland 6 *T:* TO Pike, JB Ganly
Scotland 0
Referee: BS Cumberlege (England)

26.02.1927 ST HELEN'S, SWANSEA
Wales 25 *T:* J Roberts 2, WR Harding 2, W Thomas,
GE Andrews, WG Morgan *C:* BO Male 2
France 7 *T:* A Prevost *DG:* A Verger
Referee: WH Jackson (England)

12.03.1927 LANSDOWNE ROAD, DUBLIN
Ireland 19 *T:* GV Stephenson 2, JB Ganly 2
C: GV Stephenson 2 *PG:* GV Stephenson
Wales 9 *T:* WG Morgan *C:* WC Powell *DG:* WH Lewis
Referee: BS Cumberlege (England)

19.03.1927 MURRAYFIELD
Scotland 21 *T:* IS Smith 2, JC Dykes, GPS Macpherson,
JW Scott *C:* AC Gillies *DG:* H Waddell
England 13 *T:* JC Gibbs, HCC Laird *C:* E Stanbury,
KJ Stark *PG:* KJ Stark
Referee: NM Purcell (Ireland)

02.04.1927 STADE COLOMBES, PARIS
France 3 *T:* E Vellat
England 0
Referee: AE Freethy (Wales)

	P	W	D	L	FOR	AGAINST	PTS
Scotland	4	3	0	1	49	25	6
Ireland	4	3	0	1	39	20	6
England	4	2	0	2	32	39	4
Wales	4	1	0	3	43	42	2
France	4	1	0	3	19	56	2

1927-28

02.01.1928 STADE COLOMBES, PARIS
France 6 *T:* H Haget, A Camel
Scotland 15 *T:* WM Simmers, JR Paterson, JC Dykes,
PS Douty, JW Scott
Referee: RM Magrath (Ireland)

21.01.1928 ST HELEN'S, SWANSEA
Wales 8 *T:* JD Bartlett, DE John *C:* Ivor Jones
England 10 *T:* WJ Taylor, HCC Laird
C: JV Richardson 2
Referee: RW Harland (Ireland)

28.01.1928 RAVENHILL, BELFAST
Ireland 12 *T:* JB Ganly 2, JE Arigho 2
France 8 *T:* E Ribere, H Behoteguy *C:* A Behoteguy
Referee: C Anderson (Scotland)

04.02.1928 MURRAYFIELD
Scotland 0
Wales 13 *T:* A Jenkins, DE John, J Roberts
C: BO Male 2
Referee: RW Harland (Ireland)

11.02.1928 LANSDOWNE ROAD, DUBLIN
Ireland 6 *T:* JE Arigho, M Sugden
England 7 *T:* JV Richardson *DG:* JV Richardson
Referee: AE Freethy (Wales)

25.02.1928 TWICKENHAM
England 18 *T:* HG Periton 2, GV Palmer 2
C: JV Richardson 3
France 8 *T:* J Galia, A Jaureguy *C:* A Verger
Referee: AE Freethy (Wales)

25.02.1928 MURRAYFIELD
Scotland 5 *T:* DS Kerr *C:* D Drysdale
Ireland 13 *T:* JB Ganly, EO'D Davy, GV Stephenson
C: GV Stephenson 2
Referee: BS Cumberlege (England)

10.03.1928 CARDIFF ARMS PARK
Wales 10 *T:* DE John, A Jenkins *C:* Ivor Jones 2
Ireland 13 *T:* JE Arigho 2, JB Ganly
C: GV Stephenson 2
Referee: THH Warren (Scotland)

17.03.1928 TWICKENHAM
England 6 *T:* J Hanley, HCC Laird
Scotland 0
Referee: TH Vile (Wales)

09.04.1928 STADE COLOMBES, PARIS
France 8 *T:* R Houdet 2 *C:* A Behoteguy
Wales 3 *T:* WC Powell
Referee: RW Harland (Ireland)

	P	W	D	L	FOR	AGAINST	PTS
England	4	4	0	0	41	22	8
Ireland	4	3	0	1	44	30	6
Wales	4	1	0	3	34	31	2
France	4	1	0	3	30	48	2
Scotland	4	1	0	3	20	38	2

1928-29

**31.12.1928 STADE YVES DU MANOIR
(COLOMBES), PARIS**
France 0
Ireland 6 *T:* EO'D Davy, GV Stephenson
Referee: BS Cumberlege (England)

19.01.1929 TWICKENHAM
England 8 *T:* H Wilkinson 2 *C:* GS Wilson
Wales 3 *T:* JC Morley
Referee: RW Harland (Ireland)

19.01.1929 MURRAYFIELD
Scotland 6 *T:* JR Paterson *PG:* AH Brown
France 3 *T:* A Behoteguy
Referee: BS Cumberlege (England)

02.02.1929 ST HELEN'S, SWANSEA
Wales 14 *T:* J Roberts 2, WG Morgan, H Peacock
C: Ivor Jones
Scotland 7 *PG:* AH Brown *DG:* AH Brown
Referee: D Hellewell (England)

09.02.1929 TWICKENHAM
England 5 *T:* RW Smeddle *C:* GS Wilson
Ireland 6 *T:* EO'D Davy, M Sugden
Referee: AE Freethy (Wales)

23.02.1929 LANSDOWNE ROAD, DUBLIN
Ireland 7 *T:* JE Arigho *DG:* EO'D Davy
Scotland 16 *T:* GPS Macpherson, JM Bannerman,
IS Smith, WM Simmers *C:* JC Dykes, JW Allan
Referee: BS Cumberlege (England)

23.02.1929 CARDIFF ARMS PARK
Wales 8 *T:* T Arthur, R Barrell *C:* D Parker
France 3 *T:* M Camel
Referee: HEB Wilkins (England)

09.03.1929 RAVENHILL, BELFAST
Ireland 5 *T:* EO'D Davy *C:* HC Browne
Wales 5 *T:* FL Williams *C:* D Parker
Referee: J McGill (Scotland)

16.03.1929 MURRAYFIELD
Scotland 12 *T:* IS Smith 2, CHC Brown, JB Nelson
England 6 *T:* SSC Meikle, AL Novis
Referee: Dr JR Wheeler (Ireland)

**01.04.1929 STADE YVES DU MANOIR
(COLOMBES), PARIS**
France 6 *T:* R Houdet, E Ribere
England 16 *T:* CD Aarvold 2, CHA Gummer,
HG Periton *C:* E Stanbury 2
Referee: AE Freethy (Wales)

	P	W	D	L	FOR	AGAINST	PTS
Scotland	4	3	0	1	41	30	6
Wales	4	2	1	1	30	23	5
Ireland	4	2	1	1	24	26	5
England	4	2	0	2	35	27	4
France	4	0	0	4	12	36	0

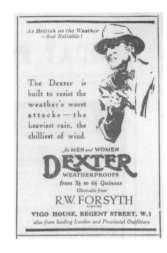

"
After repeated warnings over payments to players in club rugby, the Home Unions finally lost patience with France in February 1931. A large boot was applied to the French derrière.
"

1930s

ENGLAND v FRANCE IN 1930.
ABOVE *Aerial view of the ground and the West Car Park.* BELOW
French scrum half Lucien Serin scores the visitors' only try.
BELOW RIGHT *Details from the programme. The next visit to*
Twickenham for the French was to be 17 years later.

Rugby Football Union

OFFICIAL PROGRAMME

2 d.

ENGLAND v. FRANCE

Saturday, 22nd February, 1930.   Kick-off **3** p.m.

England		REFEREE Mr. A. E. FREETHY (Wales)	France	
No.			No.	
15	J. G. ASKEW (Cambridge University)	FULL BACK	15	M. PIQUEMAL (Tarbes)
		THREEQUARTERS		
14	J. S. R. REEVE (Harlequins)	R. WING L. WING	11	R. SAMATAN (Agen)
13	M. ROBSON (Oxford University)	R. CENTRE L. CENTRE	12	M. BAILLETTE (Quillan)
12	A. L. NOVIS (The Army and Blackheath)	L. CENTRE R. CENTRE	13	G. GERALD (Racing Club de France)
11	H. P. JACOB (Blackheath)	L. WING R. WING	14	P. HOUDET (Stade Français, Paris)
9	R. S. SPONG (Old Millhillians)	STAND-OFF HALF	10	C. MAGNANOU (Bayonne)
10	W. H. SOBEY (Old Millhillians)	SCRUM HALF	9	L. SERIN (Béziers)
8	H. G. PERITON (Waterloo)		8	A. BIOUSSA (Toulouse)
7	P. D. HOWARD (Oxford Univ. and Old Millhillians)		7	A. AMBERT (Toulouse)
6	H. WILKINSON (Halifax)		6	E. RIBERE (Captain) (Quillan)
5	B. H. BLACK (Oxford University)		5	M. CAMEL (Toulouse)
4	J. W. FORREST (R.N. & United Services, Portsmouth)	FORWARDS	4	R. MAJERUS (Stade Français, Paris)
3	A. H. BATESON (Otley)		3	G. GALIA (Quillan)
2	J. S. TUCKER (Captain) (Bristol)		2	J. CHOYS (Narbonne)
1	H. REW (The Army and Exeter)		1	G. BIGOT (Quillan)

For List of Matches at Twickenham *see inside*

Tickets may be obtained from ALFRED HAYS, Ltd. (Sole Official Agents),
26 Old Bond Street, W.1 (Regent 3400); 74 Cornhill, E.C.3 (Avenue 3300);
or 62 Strand, W.C.2 (Chancery 7532), for the Matches marked *

WALKER & CO. (PRINTERS) LTD., TWICKENHAM.

The dastardly French! Paying players! The nerve of it! Didn't they realise that it was a chaps' game? No need for filthy lucre. Well, not for another 60 years or so.

After repeated warnings over payments to players in club rugby and amid concerns over a breakaway movement within the French club game, the Home Unions finally lost patience with France in February 1931. The French did well to last the course in the championship of that year, for the FFR seemed powerless to control the club scene. A large boot was applied to the French derrière. They were not to feature in the championship for another 16 years, although they were actually readmitted in July 1939. By then, though, minds were elsewhere as gloom once again descended over Europe.

There were some in France who missed the championship. But there was little doubt that the championship missed the French. As has been the case ever since, they brought a sense of difference to proceedings. It's part verbal language but mainly body language. The French even look different on a rugby field. They align differently, run and pass differently, and celebrate differently. It's taken a while for kissing to catch on. Stiff upper lips and the occasional prim handshake have been the order of the day elsewhere.

The expulsion left no sense of shame hanging over the game in France. In fact, you might argue that it benefited world rugby greatly. Without an international outlet into the championship, France were forced to reconsider their position within Europe. They didn't sulk particularly or turn inwards. Quite the opposite. They broadened their horizons. France were the first to adopt a pan-European outlook. They arranged fixtures with the likes of Germany, Italy and Romania. The Fédération Internationale de Rugby Amateur (FIRA) was formed in Paris in 1934 as a parallel body to the IRFB, and their office was located within the FFR for many years.

That alliance of nations did European rugby a heap of good. Upon their readmission to the championship after the war, France maintained contact with their FIRA confrères through their 'A' team, and the countries persevered and grew in number, forming their own European league of up to three divisions.

France's involvement laid the foundations from which significant things grew. Italian rugby benefited from the contact, as did rugby in Romania, who became a force from 1950 to 1990. To a lesser degree, the game in Spain, Portugal and Georgia also flourished as a result of France's presence. The long-term beneficiary was Rugby World Cup (RWC). Would they all have got there without France? Perhaps. But FIRA became an important influence and remains so. For that, the sport should be thankful.

Even so, the pariahs did have a couple of years at the start of the 1930s to show their worth. And they finished in some style, beating England 14-13 in April 1931 in their final match before expulsion to consign their cross-Channel neighbours to the Wooden Spoon. Even though England outscored the hosts by three tries to two that Easter Monday in Paris, France came through with dropped goals (still worth four points) from Marcel Baillette and Racing Club centre Géo Gérald, whose strike decided the match.

There were many Frenchmen to salute as they went off into exile, notably Adolphe Jauréguy, who was forced to retire even before the Home Unions delivered their banishment edict, injury having brought an end to his fine career in 1930. He was the younger brother of Pierre, who won four caps in 1913 and introduced him to the game. Adolphe Jauréguy played at Tarbes, where he met that midfield maestro René Crabos, then fought in the Great War. Jauréguy later played alongside Crabos at Racing Club after winning the 1919 Coupe de l'Espérance (the wartime French championship) with Tarbes. He moved on to Toulouse, winning championships there in 1922 and 1923, before returning to Paris with Stade Français. He was 12 times captain of France and scored 14 tries in 31 Tests.

Eugène Ribère was to be the last captain of France before their expulsion. Ribère, a back-row forward of distinction, played orginally for Perpignan, with whom he won the 1925 championship, before moving to the provincial club US Quillan, about 50 miles inland from Perpignan, and helping them to three consecutive finals, 1928–30. Ribère had an excellent try-scoring record for a back-row forward, touching down on four occasions against Ireland during his career. He was France's most capped player with 34 caps until overtaken by Jean Prat, who gained his thirty-fifth against Italy in 1952.

Never mind the French paying their players – or more precisely their being paid in the club game (there was never any suggestion that they received money for their championship feats) – there were a few occasions during the 1930s when the spectators might have merited payment. Tough and uncompromising as the rugby was, it was not always exceptional. That said, there were high spots, such as the 1938 season, which was a feast of points and tries.

RIGHT AND FACING PAGE
RFU hospitality for the Irish team after the game in 1931, which Ireland won 6-5. Lavish fare and much speech-making.
FACING PAGE FAR RIGHT
Eugène Ribère (top) and George Stephenson, influential players for France and Ireland respectively whose championship careers were coming to a close at the start of the 1930s. Ribère played his final Five Nations match against England in 1931; Stephenson retired from international rugby in 1930.

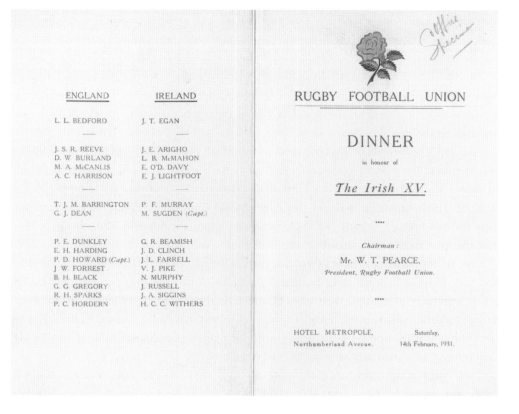

ENGLAND	IRELAND
L. L. BEDFORD	J. T. EGAN
J. S. R. REEVE	J. E. ARIGHO
D. W. BURLAND	L. B. McMAHON
M. A. McCANLIS	E. O'D. DAVY
A. C. HARRISON	E. J. LIGHTFOOT
T. J. M. BARRINGTON	P. F. MURRAY
G. J. DEAN	M. SUGDEN (Capt.)
P. E. DUNKLEY	G. R. BEAMISH
E. H. HARDING	J. D. CLINCH
P. D. HOWARD (Capt.)	J. L. FARRELL
J. W. FORREST	V. J. PIKE
B. H. BLACK	N. MURPHY
G. G. GREGORY	J. RUSSELL
R. H. SPARKS	J. A. SIGGINS
P. C. HORDERN	H. C. C. WITHERS

RUGBY FOOTBALL UNION

DINNER

in honour of

The Irish XV.

••••

Chairman :

Mr. W. T. PEARCE,
President, Rugby Football Union.

••••

HOTEL METROPOLE,   Saturday,
Northumberland Avenue.   14th February, 1931.

After the dominance of England and Scotland through the 1920s, there was no one country that came to the fore in the 1930s and stayed there. True, England and Scotland did manage two Triple Crowns apiece, but Wales and Ireland also made their mark at different times on the championship honours board.

The more competitive nature of the championship had its own appeal. Certainly the first tournament of the decade was to prove one of the closest ever, and the most fiercely contested since the Five Nations came into being. England took the title with five points while Scotland were Wooden Spoonists with three.

CHURCHMAN'S CIGARETTES

E. RIBERE

Yet if there was little vintage rugby to celebrate, there were, once again, some notable characters in the championship's midst. Ireland's George Stephenson made his debut against France in 1920, played through his country's doldrum years, and was one of the key figures in their turnaround from also-rans to championship contenders and winners. When he called it a day after the 1930 tournament, Stephenson was Ireland's most capped player with 42 caps and leading try scorer with 15 tries; a breakdown of his career shows 20 wins and 20 losses with two draws. As Ireland improved, so did Stephenson become more prominent. A formidable centre and occasional wing, he was first-choice kicker for much of his career, finishing just six shy of a century of points for his country. A psychiatrist by profession, Stephenson settled in Hertfordshire, England. Other Irishmen to bow out during the 1930s included scrum half Mark Sugden and forwards Jamie Clinch and Jimmy Farrell – fine players and good men to boot.

PLAYER'S CIGARETTES.

G. V. STEPHENSON

TOAST LIST.

H.M. THE KING.

THE SILENT TOAST.

THE IRISH XV.

Proposed by Mr. R. F. OAKES,
Vice-President Rugby Football Union.

Reply by Mr. M. SUGDEN, Captain, Irish XV.

THE ENGLISH XV.

Proposed by Mr. J. G. MUSGRAVE,
President, Irish Rugby Football Union.

Reply by Mr. P. D. HOWARD, Captain, English XV.

THE REFEREE.

Proposed by Mr. A. D. STOOP,
Vice-President Rugby Football Union.

Reply by Mr. A. E. FREETHY.

THE GUESTS.

Proposed by THE PRESIDENT.
Reply by Mr. JAMES BAXTER and Mr. F. D. PRENTICE.

MENU.

Cocktails.
* *
VINS.

Gonzalez Royal Pale Sherry

Dry Pouilly Reserve

Lanson 1921

* *

Courvoisier V.O.

Graham's Fine Old Vintage

* *

Corona Chicas

Turkish and Virginia Cigarettes

Hors d'Oeuvre Vatel
Saumon Fumé

Consommé Double Alexandra
Crème Lison

Filets de Sole Cardinal

Poularde Diva
Cépes à la Crème

Carré d'Agneau Persillé
Pommes Chateau
Salade Française

Soufflé Glacé Fedora
Friandises

Canapé Rabelais

Café

W. WOOLLER

V. G. J. JENKINS

The 1930s saw the arrival on the scene of two of the most admired and acknowledged Welshmen of this or any other era – Wilf Wooller and Vivian Jenkins, both of whom made their international debuts against England in 1933. These were men of real stature in the game, both within Wales and at large. Wooller, from north Wales, was that bit more versatile than Jenkins as a sportsman. In fact, Wooller was that bit more versatile than almost any other sportsman in the land. Born near Colwyn Bay and making his first appearance for Wales from Rydal School, he went on to win 18 caps, playing his club rugby for Cardiff – and his club football, too. As if that weren't enough, Wooller also captained Glamorgan CCC for 14 years from 1947, having had to retire from rugby as a result of the effects of life as a POW in Singapore during World War II. In a first-class cricket career for Cambridge University and Glamorgan that ran overall from 1935 to 1962, Wooller scored 13,593 runs and took 958 wickets; he also led Glamorgan to their first County Championship title in 1948 and was a Test selector from 1955 to 1961, although he never played international cricket.

Jenkins, meanwhile, was no mean all-round sportsman himself, also playing first-class cricket (for Oxford University and Glamorgan, 1931–37) besides representing Wales at rugby. Against Ireland in 1934, he became the first Welshman to score a try from full back. A rock under the high ball, Jenkins played 14 times for Wales but in just one Test for the Lions, against South Africa in 1938. His tour was plagued by hamstring problems, but he did have the distinction of landing a penalty from 65 metres in the first Test at Johannesburg in that one international outing. If Jenkins was an authority on the field, he was to become an even more distinguished presence off it as rugby correspondent of *The Sunday Times* and editor of *Rothmans Rugby Yearbook*. Jenkins died in 2004 aged 92.

The Scots also had their men of note. The 1933 season was to be the final campaign for Ian Smith, flying wing and that year's captain of Scotland as they won the championship and Triple Crown. Born in Melbourne, Australia, but educated at Winchester College and Oxford University, Smith racked up 24 international tries in his career (a world record until overtaken by Wallaby David Campese in 1987), including eight in 1925 to equal the season record for the Five Nations held by England's Cyril Lowe. After 11 tries in his first five games for

ABOVE Wilf Wooller (left, in Cambridge colours) and Vivian Jenkins, who were to become stalwarts of the Welsh side during the 1930s. BELOW 1932 and it is the turn of Phil Macpherson and his Scottish team to enjoy a meal at the Hotel Metropole, the regular post-match venue in the West End. They had earlier lost 16-3 at Twickenham.

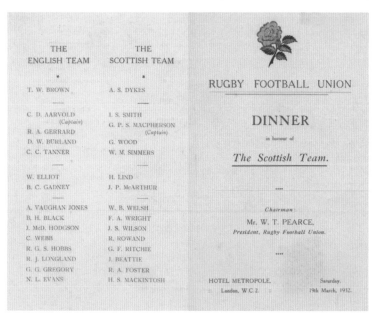

THE ENGLISH TEAM	THE SCOTTISH TEAM
T. W. BROWN	A. S. DYKES
C. D. AARVOLD (Captain)	I. S. SMITH
R. A. GERRARD	G. P. S. MACPHERSON (Captain)
D. W. BURLAND	G. WOOD
C. C. TANNER	W. M. SIMMERS
W. ELLIOT	H. LIND
B. C. GADNEY	J. P. McARTHUR
A. VAUGHAN JONES	W. B. WELSH
B. H. BLACK	F. A. WRIGHT
J. McD. HODGSON	J. S. WILSON
C. WEBB	R. ROWAND
R. G. S. HOBBS	G. F. RITCHIE
R. J. LONGLAND	J. BEATTIE
G. G. GREGORY	R. A. FOSTER
N. L. EVANS	H. S. MACKINTOSH

RUGBY FOOTBALL UNION

DINNER

in honour of

The Scottish Team.

Chairman:

Mr. W. T. PEARCE,
President, Rugby Football Union.

HOTEL METROPOLE,   Saturday,
London, W.C.2   19th March, 1932.

ABOVE *Prince Alexander Obolensky (11) is pursued by Ken Fyfe of Scotland at Twickenham in 1936.*

Scotland, he managed only four in the last 14 of a total of 32 internationals for his country, but his later maturity brought him the Scottish captaincy. Smith still holds the Scottish record for international tries, although the mark was equalled by Tony Stanger in 1998 and Chris Paterson had scored 22 at the time of writing.

It is no disrespect to the achievements of the players described above to suggest that one name from the 1930s retains a significance that is beyond even them, that of Prince Alexander Obolensky. Celebrity has always had its allure, even in those austere times, and while others achieved more, some, Obolensky among them, managed to strike a chord that resonates still. A Russian in the white of England, Obolensky abided by the old showbiz maxim of 'leave 'em wanting more', playing a single season of international rugby in 1936 while at Oxford University. Obolensky was born in St Petersburg, the son of a prince who fled to London's Muswell Hill during the 1917 revolution in Russia (not many in those parts had Muswell Hill located on their radar at the time). Becoming a British citizen only in 1936, the year of his debut, young 'Obo' scored twice against New Zealand on an astonishing first international appearance as England beat the All Blacks 13-0 at Twickenham. One try was a curved run from right to left over half the pitch, in which Obolensky left defenders trailing. Style and potency, not a bad mix. Small wonder he is still spoken of.

ABOVE John Snagge (left) and Teddy Wakelam in the Twickenham commentary box in the 1930s. Wakelam had given the first ever live sports commentary on the BBC with coverage of England v Wales at Twickenham in 1927. LEFT The Radio Times announces its live radio commentary on England v Wales in January 1933.

That New Zealand game has achieved mythical status, for thereafter in the championship the dashing prince barely received a pass. The glum air of the championship, with its attritional play and dearth of tries, found fitting expression in the opening game between England and Wales at St Helen's. Expectations deserved to be high, for both sides had recently beaten the All Blacks. Yet the scoreline, 0-0, tells you all you need to know.

Obolensky didn't see the ball; nor did the crowd for that matter. He was only to play two more games for his adopted country, his final match being England's sole win of that championship, a 9-8 victory over Scotland at Twickenham. Obolensky, who played club rugby for Leicester and Rosslyn Park, won his second Blue at Oxford in 1937. He lost his life in a flying accident in Norfolk in 1940, aged 24, having joined the RAF, and is buried at Ipswich.

The first championship of the decade went to England, their 0-0 draw with Scotland in their last match enough for them to take the title. The 1930 tournament was notable, though, for France's vivid early burst of form. Victories came over Scotland and Ireland, the first time France had won two championship matches since 1921, but this promising run was followed by defeat to England. Even so, France might have sneaked the championship at the death, but in their final match against Wales they lost composure, a complaint that has a familiar ring to it. The overall number of tries scored in 1930, 25, and the points total, 128, were both the lowest since the Five Nations Championship came into being.

Wales ruled the roost in 1931, winning the championship for the first time since 1922, scoring 15 tries and only dropping a point to England in an 11-11 draw at Twickenham. Wales had suffered eight consecutive defeats at Twickenham, and they might even have fully nailed that bogey but for the reinstatement of Don Burland's conversion of his own try, originally deemed to have missed. Nonetheless, Wales had a measure of justifiable reprieve in that Wick Powell scored a rare goal from a mark when England forgot that they were entitled to charge down the kick. The draw with Wales apart, England were utterly in the doldrums, and finished with the Wooden Spoon for the first time since 1907, before the Five Nations began. They conceded 59 points, a sign of their lack of confidence, their line being easily breached – not a

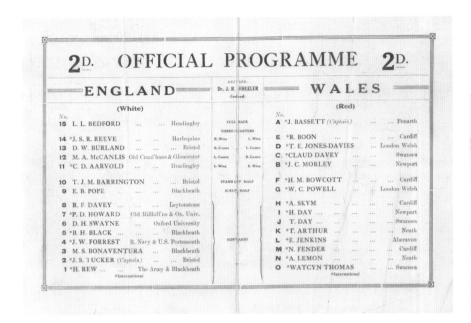

2d. OFFICIAL Programme 2d.

Rugby Football Union

TWICKENHAM.

England *v.* **Wales**

SATURDAY, 17th JANUARY, 1931.

Kick-off - 2.45 p.m.

failing that is usually ascribed to an England side; they were lean times, indeed, that year. Two classy scrum halves retired in 1931, Scotland's James Nelson and Mark Sugden of Ireland. Sugden, with 28 caps, was Ireland's most capped scrum half until overtaken by Michael Bradley in 1993.

The 1932 championship reverted to four teams with the expulsion of France. It was not a high-quality tournament, the result a three-way tie between Ireland, Wales and England, with Ireland having scored most points, most tries and having similar points difference to Wales. Irish fans cared little for the overall quality as they saluted their side's first championship since 1927. The key game, perhaps, was Ireland's 12-10 victory over Wales at Cardiff Arms Park. In a season in which Bennie Osler's all-conquering Springboks had set the tone of negative play, it was heartening to see six tries scored, four of them by Ireland. The Irish, captained well by George Beamish (later Air Marshal Sir George Beamish), finished the championship with most points scored, 40, and most tries, nine.

Scotland were in yo-yo mode: having lost all three games in 1932, they soared back to win all three matches in 1933 and take the title. In their first game against Wales at Swansea they fielded eight new caps and gave the captaincy to Ian Smith, a shrewd strategic move. Scotland won the title on the final day of the championship by beating Ireland 8-6, scoring two dropped goals to Ireland's two tries.

That year, Wales recorded their first ever win at Twickenham in ten visits with a 7-3 victory. Ronnie Boon, the Cardiff wing, was the Welsh hero with a dropped goal and a try, but the pack, led by the outstanding Watcyn Thomas, made an important contribution. This was to be the last international appearance of Carl Aarvold, captain of England and a Test skipper on the 1930 Lions tour of New Zealand and Australia. He was called to the Bar in 1932, became Judge Aarvold and presided at the 1965 trial of the Kray twins. Aarvold, knighted in 1968, was also

ABOVE England took the Wooden Spoon in 1931. Although they started well with a draw against a strong Welsh side, they proceeded to lose their remaining three games.

59

WALES'S FIRST WIN AT TWICKENHAM: A TENTH-GAME VICTORY.

A LINE-OUT DURING THE RUGBY INTERNATIONAL BETWEEN ENGLAND AND WALES, WHICH WALES WON BY SEVEN POINTS TO THREE: ENGLISH FORWARDS (IN WHITE) JUMPING FOR THE BALL—SHOWING SOME OF THE CROWD OF 40,000 WHO WATCHED THE MATCH.

ABOVE A memorable day for Welsh fans in 1933 as their team ended their long wait for a first win at Twickenham. RIGHT Throw-in practice for England captain Carl Aarvold at a training session before the 1933 game with Wales.

president of the Lawn Tennis Association from 1963 to 1981. Sir Carl Aarvold died in 1991, aged 83.

England conceded only six points in claiming the title and Triple Crown in 1934. Although Cardiff Arms Park had a new North Stand, which raised the capacity to over 50,000, the enhanced crowd had little to cheer when England visited in January of that year, seeing England score three tries to defeat their side 9-0. Wales, to much criticism, fielded 13 new caps. Nonetheless, this was to be Wales's only defeat in the championship.

In 1935 Ireland didn't begin well, losing 14-3 at Twickenham, but rallied to win the title, an achievement that owed something to the failings of others – the dropped point in the draw between England and Wales proved crucial to their cause. England also slipped up at Murrayfield, as has often been the case, losing for the sixth time in succession north of the border. Ireland had to wait for that Calcutta Cup result after finishing their campaign with a 9-3 win over Wales at Ravenhill, the sole try coming from Bective Rangers wing Jack Doyle in his one and only international. Ireland had to play much of the game with 14 men after Doyle's wing partner, Joseph O'Connor, broke his collarbone. Jack Siggins led a young and inexperienced Ireland team to that 1935 championship. The Belfast Collegian captained

BELOW FAR RIGHT A poor start to a good season. Ireland centre Ernest Ridgeway misses a conversion at Twickenham in 1935 and his side lose 14-3, but there were better things to come for the Irish that year. BELOW Jack Siggins (left), captain of the championship-winning Irish side of 1935, and wing Joseph O'Connor, who broke his collarbone in the crucial clash with Wales.

CHURCHMAN'S CIGARETTES

J. A. SIGGINS

CHURCHMAN'S CIGARETTES

J. J. O'CONNOR

ENGLAND v WALES IN 1937.
ABOVE *Welsh training session at Richmond: Albert Freethy and Wilf Wooller (left and second left) discuss plans with Idwal Rees, Bill Clement (about to make his Wales debut) and Haydn Tanner.*
RIGHT *Haydn Tanner sets up the Welsh backs.*
LEFT AND BELOW *The programme for the game, which England won 4-3.*

OFFICIAL PROGRAMME

ENGLAND (White)				WALES (Red)	
			REFEREE : Mr. R. A. BEATTIE (Scotland)		
15	H. G. OWEN SMITH	St. Mary's Hospital	Full Backs	A	V. G. J. JENKINS	London Welsh
			Threequarters			
11	H. S. SEVER	Sale	L. Wing R. Wing	B	IDWAL REES	Swansea
12	P. CRANMER	Richmond	L. Centre R. Centre	C	CLAUD DAVEY (Captain)	London Welsh
13	P. L. CANDLER	St. Bartholomew's Hospital	R. Centre L. Centre	D	W. WOOLLER	Cardiff
14	*A. G. BUTLER	Harlequins	R. Wing L. Wing	E	*W. H. CLEMENT	Llanelly
			Half Backs :			
10	*T. A. KEMP	Cambridge University	Standoff	G	W. T. H. DAVIES	Swansea
9	J. L. GILES	Coventry	Scrum	F	H. TANNER	Swansea
1	*D. A. CAMPBELL	Cambridge University		H	BRYN EVANS	Llanelly
2	*D. L. K. MILMAN	Bedford		I	T. J. REES	Newport
3	W. H. WESTON	Northampton		J	*EMRYS EVANS	Llanelly
4	*T. F. HUSKISSON	Old Merchant Taylors		K	HAROLD THOMAS	Neath
5	*A. WHEATLEY	Coventry	Forwards	L	*D. L. THOMAS	Neath
6	*R. E. PRESCOTT	Harlequins		M	J. LANG	Swansea
7	H. B. TOFT	Waterloo		N	A. M. REES	London Welsh
8	R. J. LONGLAND	Northampton		O	E. LONG	Swansea
	* NEW INTERNATIONAL				* NEW INTERNATIONAL	
Touch Judge: Mr. H. A. HAIGH SMITH (Rugby Football Union Committee)				Touch Judge : Major IDRIS EVANS		

[Programme cover:] Rugby Football Union Twickenham. 2D. OFFICIAL PROGRAMME 2D. ENGLAND v. WALES. SATURDAY, 16th JANUARY, 1937. Kick-off 2.30 p.m. PRICE TWOPENCE. Copyright. Photo by Aerofilms Ltd.

61

Ireland ten times in all and went on to be president of the IRFU in 1962-63; he was also manager of the 1955 Lions to South Africa.

The clamp came on in 1936, with no team totalling more than 16 points from their three games. The negative tone was set from the off, with England and Wales sharing a 0-0 draw in Swansea. The crowds, though, were not to be deterred, with some 70,000 cramming into the Arms Park in March to see Vivian Jenkins' boot deliver a 3-0 victory over Ireland, and the title, to the home side.

In the following campaign, the ruling order was once again turned on its head, with England winning all three games, while champions Wales lost the lot. Runners-up Ireland (24) and third-placed Scotland (20) both managed to score more points than the championship winners, who acquired only 19. England did at least manage to lay their Murrayfield bogey, winning 6-3 in Edinburgh with tries from Rosslyn Park debutant Jimmy Unwin and Sale's Hal Sever. Sever had a good season, also landing a dropped goal to help beat Wales and a try in the defeat of Ireland.

Out of the gloom came shafts of sunlight. Where there had been caution and restrictiveness, suddenly there was adventure and abandon. The 1938 season was one of points and tries. Even Ireland, who lost all their games and finished with the Wooden Spoon, scored more points, 33, than any of the five previous champions. Scotland were champions, but third-placed England scored 60 points in an aggregate total for the championship of 176. This figure and the 35 tries scored were records for a six-match tournament, eclipsing the mark of 142 points in 1908 and the 32-try championship of 1904.

Ireland and England contributed to a breathless spectacle. Whereas in 1936 there had been only 59 points and 12 tries scored in the entire championship, the 1938 Ireland v England contest at Lansdowne Road ended in a 36-14 win for the visitors and produced 11 tries from 11 different players. The margin might have been closer, but Gloucester full back Grahame Parker, also a first-class cricketer for Cambridge University and Gloucestershire, collected 15 points by converting six of the seven English tries and kicking a penalty goal – and all on his debut.

It was to be Scotland's title, though, and deservedly so. The 21-16 scoreline in their favour at Twickenham might suggest the match was a close affair, but the Scots outscored their opponents by five tries to one. The win confirmed Scotland as Triple Crown winners and champions. Wilson Shaw, restored at fly half that season after spending 1937 in the threequarters, led the side well. His swerving run that day at Twickenham produced the decisive score three minutes from the end. Shaw went on to be president of the SRU in 1970-71.

There were other notable characters of the day. Wales fly half Cliff Jones helped shape the template of Welsh No. 10s, those jinking, imaginative, courageous souls who dared to

BELOW Three leading figures in the 1938 championship: (left to right) Wilson Shaw (Scotland), Peter Cranmer (England) and Cliff Jones (Wales).

CHURCHMAN'S CIGARETTES

R. W. SHAW

CHURCHMAN'S CIGARETTES

P. CRANMER

CHURCHMAN'S CIGARETTES

CLIFF W. JONES

ENGLAND v IRELAND IN 1939, THE LAST CHAMPIONSHIP GAME TO BE PLAYED AT TWICKENHAM BEFORE WAR WAS DECLARED IN SEPTEMBER THAT YEAR.
ABOVE *The England team that day. Back row (left to right): J.C.H. Ireland (referee), R.S.L. Carr, R.M. Marshall, J.K. Watkins, J.T.W. Berry, H.D. Freakes, G.E. Hancock, R.H. Guest, D.E. Teden. Middle row: H.F. Wheatley, J. Heaton, H.B. Toft (capt), T.F. Huskisson, R.E. Prescott. Front row: G.A. Walker, P. Cooke. Gus Walker was to lose an arm in the war but later became an international referee and president of the RFU. He was knighted in 1962 and became Deputy C-in-C Allied Forces Central Europe in 1967 as an air chief marshal.* ABOVE LEFT *A sign of things to come – security measures at the ground.* LEFT AND BELOW *Souvenirs of the occasion.*

challenge the opposition no matter what the circumstances. Along with Vivian Jenkins and Arthur Rees, Jones made up a trio of Welsh internationals of the time who hailed from Llandovery College.

Another fine man to call it a day in 1938 was England centre Peter Cranmer, who was said to have brought the best out of Prince Obolensky in that famous game against the All Blacks in 1936. Cranmer, who also played county cricket for Warwickshire for some 20 years, came within a whisker of being a dual international. In his final season of international rugby, he captained England twice, showing his customary perception and strength of character. Later, he was to become a distinguished journalist with the BBC.

Just when fans had got used to the thrills and spills of attacking championship rugby, 1939 delivered a tepid tournament, in keeping with the mood at large. Wales, Ireland and England shared the laurels with two wins apiece. Once again, however, thoughts turned to graver matters.

Five Nations Results 1930-39

1929-30

01.01.1930 STADE YVES DU MANOIR (COLOMBES), PARIS
France 7 *T:* A Biossa *DG:* C Magnanou
Scotland 3 *T:* WM Simmers
Referee: D Hellewell (England)

18.01.1930 CARDIFF ARMS PARK
Wales 3 *T:* TE Jones-Davies
England 11 *T:* JSR Reeve 2 *C:* BH Black *PG:* BH Black
Referee: RW Jeffares (Ireland)

25.01.1930 RAVENHILL, BELFAST
Ireland 0
France 5 *T:* R Samatan *C:* A Ambert
Referee: BS Cumberlege (England)

01.02.1930 MURRAYFIELD
Scotland 12 *T:* WM Simmers 2 *C:* FH Waters
DG: H Waddell
Wales 9 *T:* G Jones *C:* Ivor Jones *DG:* G Jones
Referee: Dr JR Wheeler (Ireland)

08.02.1930 LANSDOWNE ROAD, DUBLIN
Ireland 4 *DG:* PF Murray
England 3 *T:* AL Novis
Referee: AE Freethy (Wales)

22.02.1930 TWICKENHAM
England 11 *T:* HG Periton, JSR Reeve, M Robson
C: BH Black
France 5 *T:* L Serin *C:* A Ambert
Referee: AE Freethy (Wales)

22.02.1930 MURRAYFIELD
Scotland 11 *T:* DStC Ford, GPS Macphersn,
FH Waters *C:* FH Waters
Ireland 14 *T:* EO'D Davy 3, MP Crowe *C:* PF Murray
Referee: BS Cumberlege (England)

08.03.1930 ST HELEN'S, SWANSEA
Wales 12 *T:* A Skym, T Arthur, H Jones* *PG:* J Bassett
Ireland 7 *PG:* PF Murray *DG:* EO'D Davy
Referee: D Hellewell (England)
* also claimed by H Peacock

15.03.1930 TWICKENHAM
England 0
Scotland 0
Referee: RW Jeffares (Ireland)

21.04.1930 STADE YVES DU MANOIR (COLOMBES), PARIS
France 0
Wales 11 *T:* A Skym *DG:* WG Morgan, WC Powell
Referee: D Hellewell (England)

	P	W	D	L	FOR	AGAINST	PTS
England	4	2	1	1	25	12	5
Wales	4	2	0	2	35	30	4
Ireland	4	2	0	2	25	31	4
France	4	2	0	2	17	25	4
Scotland	4	1	1	2	26	30	3

1930-31

01.01.1931 STADE YVES DU MANOIR (COLOMBES), PARIS
France 3 *T:* E Ribere
Ireland 0
Referee: TH Vile (Wales)

17.01.1931 TWICKENHAM
England 11 *T:* DW Burland *C:* DW Burland
PG: BH Black 2
Wales 11 *T:* TE Jones-Davies, JC Morley *C:* J Bassett
GM:* WC Powell
Referee: Dr JR Wheeler (Ireland)
* goal from mark

24.01.1931 MURRAYFIELD
Scotland 6 *PG:* JW Allan 2
France 4 *DG:* L Servole
Referee: RW Jeffares (Ireland)

07.02.1931 CARDIFF ARMS PARK
Wales 13 *T:* JC Morley, W Thomas, RW Boon
C: J Bassett 2
Scotland 8 *T:* D Crichton-Miller 2 *C:* JW Allan
Referee: JG Bott (England)

14.02.1931 TWICKENHAM
England 5 *T:* BH Black *C:* BH Black
Ireland 6 *T:* LB McMahon *PG:* PF Murray
Referee: AE Freethy (Wales)

28.02.1931 LANSDOWNE ROAD, DUBLIN
Ireland 8 *T:* M Sugden, VJ Pike *C:* PF Murray
Scotland 5 *T:* HS Mackintosh *C:* JW Allan
Referee: BS Cumberlege (England)

28.02.1931 ST HELEN'S, SWANSEA
Wales 35 *T:* AR Ralph 2, EC Davey, N Fender, J Lang,
FL Williams, T Arthur *C:* J Bassett 5 *DG:* WC Powell
France 3 *T:* C Petit
Referee: RW Harland (Ireland)

14.03.1931 RAVENHILL, BELFAST
Ireland 3 *T:* JAE Siggins
Wales 15 *T:* JC Morley 2, EC Davey *C:* J Bassett
DG: AR Ralph
Referee: MA Allan (Scotland)

21.03.1931 MURRAYFIELD
Scotland 28 *T:* HS Mackintosh 2, IS Smith 2,
DStC Ford, WR Logan *C:* JW Allan 5
England 19 *T:* JA Tallent 2, JSR Reeve 2 *C:* BH Black 2
PG: BH Black
Referee: Dr JR Wheeler (Ireland)

06.04.1931 STADE YVES DU MANOIR (COLOMBES), PARIS
France 14 *T:* A Clady, J Galia *DG:* M Baillette, G Gerald
England 13 *T:* DW Burland, RW Smeddle, JA Tallent
C: BH Black, JW Forrest
Referee: AE Freethy (Wales)

	P	W	D	L	FOR	AGAINST	PTS
Wales	4	3	1	0	74	25	7
Scotland	4	2	0	2	47	44	4
France	4	2	0	2	24	44	4
Ireland	4	2	0	2	17	28	4
England	4	0	1	3	38	59	1

1931-32

16.01.1932 ST HELEN'S, SWANSEA
Wales 12 *T:* RW Boon *C:* J Bassett *PG:* J Bassett
DG: RW Boon
England 5 *T:* E Coley *C:* RJ Barr
Referee: FJC Moffat (Scotland)

06.02.1932 MURRAYFIELD
Scotland 0
Wales 6 *T:* RW Boon *PG:* J Bassett
Referee: T Bell (Ireland)

13.02.1932 LANSDOWNE ROAD, DUBLIN
Ireland 8 *T:* SL Waide *C:* PF Murray *PG:* PF Murray
England 11 *T:* DW Burland *C:* DW Burland
PG: DW Burland 2
Referee: W Burnet (Scotland)

27.02.1932 MURRAYFIELD
Scotland 8 *T:* G Wood, WM Simmers *C:* JW Allan
Ireland 20 *T:* EJ Lightfoot, EWF de Vere Hunt,
SL Waide *C:* PF Murray 4
Referee: BS Cumberlege (England)

12.03.1932 CARDIFF ARMS PARK
Wales 10 *T:* EC Davey, AR Ralph *DG:* AR Ralph
Ireland 12 *T:* WMcC Ross 2, EJ Lightfoot, SL Waide
Referee: E Holmes (England)

19.03.1932 TWICKENHAM
England 16 *T:* CD Aarvold 2, BH Black, CC Tanner
C: DW Burland 2
Scotland 3 *T:* IS Smith
Referee: Dr JR Wheeler (Ireland)

	P	W	D	L	FOR	AGAINST	PTS
Ireland	3	2	0	1	40	29	4
Wales	3	2	0	1	28	17	4
England	3	2	0	1	32	23	4
Scotland	3	0	0	3	11	42	0

France did not take part in the championship from 1932 until 1947

1932-33

21.01.1933 TWICKENHAM
England 3 *T:* W Elliot
Wales 7 *T:* RW Boon *DG:* RW Boon
Referee: T Bell (Ireland)

04.02.1933 ST HELEN'S, SWANSEA
Wales 3 *T:* T Arthur
Scotland 11 *T:* IS Smith, KLT Jackson *C:* KC Fyfe
PG: KC Fyfe
Referee: JG Bott (England)

11.02.1933 TWICKENHAM
England 17 *T:* AL Novis 2, LA Booth, BC Gadney,
EH Sadler *C:* DA Kendrew
Ireland 6 *T:* EWF de Vere Hunt *PG:* PF Murray
Referee: MA Allan (Scotland)

11.03.1933 RAVENHILL, BELFAST
Ireland 10 *T:* RJ Barnes *PG:* JAE Siggins
DG: EO'D Davy
Wales 5 *T:* HM Bowcott *C:* VGJ Jenkins
Referee: MA Allan (Scotland)

18.03.1933 MURRAYFIELD
Scotland 3 *T:* KC Fyfe
England 0
Referee: Dr JR Wheeler (Ireland)

01.04.1933 LANSDOWNE ROAD, DUBLIN
Ireland 6 *T:* MP Crowe, PF Murray
Scotland 8 *DG:* KLT Jackson, H Lind
Referee: BS Cumberlege (England)

	P	W	D	L	FOR	AGAINST	PTS
Scotland	3	3	0	0	22	9	6
Ireland	3	1	0	2	22	30	2
England	3	1	0	2	20	16	2
Wales	3	1	0	2	15	24	2

1933-34

20.01.1934 CARDIFF ARMS PARK
Wales 0
England 9 *T:* GWC Meikle 2, AL Warr
Referee: FW Haslett (Ireland)

03.02.1934 MURRAYFIELD
Scotland 6 *T:* WR Logan *PG:* JM Ritchie
Wales 13 *T:* BTV Cowey 2, JI Rees *C:* VGJ Jenkins 2
Referee: HLV Day (England)

10.02.1934 LANSDOWNE ROAD, DUBLIN
Ireland 3 *T:* GJ Morgan
England 13 *T:* HA Fry 2, GWC Meikle
C: GG Gregory 2
Referee: MA Allan (Scotland)

24.02.1934 MURRAYFIELD
Scotland 16 *T:* RCS Dick 2, JA Crawford *C:* RW Shaw 2
PG: JW Allan
Ireland 9 *T:* J Russell 2, JJ O'Connor
Referee: BS Cumberlege (England)

10.03.1934 ST HELEN'S, SWANSEA
Wales 13 *T:* A Fear, BTV Cowey, VGJ Jenkins
C: VGJ Jenkins 2
Scotland 0
Referee: W Burnet (Scotland)

17.03.1934 TWICKENHAM
England 6 *T:* LA Booth, GWC Meikle
Scotland 3 *T:* RW Shaw
Referee: FW Haslett (Ireland)

	P	W	D	L	FOR	AGAINST	PTS
England	3	3	0	0	28	6	6
Wales	3	2	0	1	26	15	4
Scotland	3	1	0	2	25	28	2
Ireland	3	0	0	3	12	42	0

1934-35

19.01.1935 TWICKENHAM
England 3 *PG:* HJ Boughton
Wales 3 *T:* W Wooller
Referee: FW Haslett (Ireland)

02.02.1935 CARDIFF ARMS PARK
Wales 10 *T:* CW Jones, W Wooller *DG:* VGJ Jenkins
Scotland 6 *T:* DA Thom, RW Shaw
Referee: FW Haslett (Ireland)

09.02.1935 TWICKENHAM
England 14 *T:* JL Giles *C:* HJ Boughton
PG: HJ Boughton 3
Ireland 3 *T:* JJ O'Connor
Referee: MA Allan (Scotland)

23.02.1935 LANSDOWNE ROAD, DUBLIN
Ireland 12 *T:* JJ O'Connor, PJ Lawlor, AH Bailey,
EC Ridgeway
Scotland 5 *T:* RW Shaw *C:* KC Fyfe
Referee: J Hughes (England)

09.03.1935 RAVENHILL, BELFAST
Ireland 9 *T:* JI Doyle *PG:* JAE Siggins, AH Bailey
Wales 3 *PG:* TO James
Referee: MA Allan (Scotland)

16.03.1935 MURRAYFIELD
Scotland 10 *T:* KC Fyfe, LB Lambie *C:* KC Fyfe 2
England 7 *T:* LA Booth *DG:* P Cranmer
Referee: RW Jeffares (Ireland)

	P	W	D	L	FOR	AGAINST	PTS
Ireland	3	2	0	1	24	22	4
England	3	1	1	1	24	16	3
Wales	3	1	1	1	16	18	3
Scotland	3	1	0	2	21	29	2

1935-36

18.01.1936 ST HELEN'S, SWANSEA
Wales 0
England 0
Referee: FW Haslett (Ireland)

01.02.1936 MURRAYFIELD
Scotland 3 *T:* HM Murray
Wales 13 *T:* W Wooller, EC Davey, CW Jones
C: VGJ Jenkins 2
Referee: CH Gadney (England)

08.02.1936 LANSDOWNE ROAD, DUBLIN
Ireland 6 *T:* AH Bailey, CV Boyle
England 3 *T:* HS Sever
Referee: MA Allan (Scotland)

22.02.1936 MURRAYFIELD
Scotland 4 *DG:* WCW Murdoch
Ireland 10 *T:* S Walker, LB McMahon *DG:* VA Hewitt
Referee: JW Faull (Wales)

14.03.1936 CARDIFF ARMS PARK
Wales 3 *PG:* VGJ Jenkins
Ireland 0
Referee: CH Gadney (England)

21.03.1936 TWICKENHAM
England 9 *T:* R Bolton, PL Candler, P Cranmer
Scotland 8 *T:* RW Shaw *C:* KC Fyfe *PG:* KC Fyfe
Referee: TH Phillips (Wales)

	P	W	D	L	FOR	AGAINST	PTS
Wales	3	2	1	0	16	3	5
Ireland	3	2	0	1	16	10	4
England	3	1	1	1	12	14	3
Scotland	3	0	0	3	15	32	0

1936-37

16.01.1937 TWICKENHAM
England 4 *DG:* HS Sever
Wales 3 *T:* W Wooller
Referee: RA Beattie (Scotland)

06.02.1937 ST HELEN'S, SWANSEA
Wales 6 *T:* W Wooller 2
Scotland 13 *T:* RCS Dick 2, RW Shaw *C:* GD Shaw 2
Referee: CH Gadney (England)

13.02.1937 TWICKENHAM
England 9 *T:* AG Butler, HS Sever *PG:* P Cranmer
Ireland 8 *T:* FG Moran 2 *C:* AH Bailey
Referee: JW Faull (Wales)

27.02.1937 LANSDOWNE ROAD, DUBLIN
Ireland 11 *T:* R Alexander, LB McMahon, FG Moran
C: AH Bailey
Scotland 4 *DG:* I Shaw
Referee: CH Gadney (England)

20.03.1937 MURRAYFIELD
Scotland 3 *PG:* GD Shaw
England 6 *T:* HS Sever, EJ Unwin
Referee: S Donaldson (Ireland)

03.04.1937 RAVENHILL, BELFAST
Ireland 5 *T:* AH Bailey *C:* S Walker
Wales 3 *PG:* WG Legge
Referee: MA Allan (Scotland)

	P	W	D	L	FOR	AGAINST	PTS
England	3	3	0	0	19	14	6
Ireland	3	2	0	1	24	16	4
Scotland	3	1	0	2	20	23	2
Wales	3	0	0	3	12	22	0

1937-38

15.01.1938 CARDIFF ARMS PARK
Wales 14 *T:* A McCarley, JI Rees *C:* VGJ Jenkins
PG: VGJ Jenkins 2
England 8 *T:* PL Candler, HS Sever *C:* HD Freakes
Referee: RA Beattie (Scotland)

05.02.1938 MURRAYFIELD
Scotland 8 *T:* WH Crawford *C:* WH Crawford
PG: WH Crawford
Wales 6 *T:* A McCarley 2
Referee: CH Gadney (England)

12.02.1938 LANSDOWNE ROAD, DUBLIN
Ireland 14 *T:* AH Bailey, GE Cromey, MJ Daly,
RB Mayne *C:* P Crowe
England 36 *T:* JL Giles, R Bolton, RM Marshall,
BE Nicholson, RE Prescott, FJ Reynolds, EJ Unwin
C: GW Parker 6 *PG:* GW Parker
Referee: JCH Ireland (Scotland)

26.02.1938 MURRAYFIELD
Scotland 23 *T:* JGS Forrest 2, DJ Macrae,
AH Drummond *C:* WH Crawford 2 *PG:* AH Drummond
DG: TF Dorward
Ireland 14 *T:* GE Cromey, DB O'Loughlin, FG Moran,
GJ Morgan *C:* S Walker
Referee: CH Gadney (England)

12.03.1938 ST HELEN'S, SWANSEA
Wales 11 *T:* AR Taylor, WH Clement *C:* WG Legge
PG: W Wooller
Ireland 5 *T:* FG Moran *C:* HR McKibbin
Referee: JCH Ireland (Scotland)

19.03.1938 TWICKENHAM
England 16 *T:* EJ Unwin *PG:* GW Parker 3
DG: FJ Reynolds
Scotland 21 *T:* WN Renwick 2, RW Shaw, RCS Dick
PG: WH Crawford 2
Referee: I David (Wales)

	P	W	D	L	FOR	AGAINST	PTS
Scotland	3	3	0	0	52	36	6
Wales	3	2	0	1	31	21	4
England	3	1	0	2	60	49	2
Ireland	3	0	0	3	33	70	0

1938-39

21.01.1939 TWICKENHAM
England 3 *T:* DE Teden
Wales 0
Referee: JCH Ireland (Scotland)

04.02.1939 CARDIFF ARMS PARK
Wales 11 *T:* MJ Davies, WH Travers *C:* W Wooller
PG: W Wooller
Scotland 3 *PG:* WH Crawford
Referee: AS Bean (England)

11.02.1939 TWICKENHAM
England 0
Ireland 5 *T:* JWS Irwin *C:* HR McKibbin
Referee: JCH Ireland (Scotland)

25.02.1939 LANSDOWNE ROAD, DUBLIN
Ireland 12 *T:* FG Moran, JD Torrens *PG:* HR McKibbin
GM*: HJM Sayers
Scotland 3 *T:* JRS Innes
Referee: CH Gadney (England)
* goal from mark

11.03.1939 RAVENHILL, BELFAST
Ireland 0
Wales 7 *T:* WTH Davies *DG:* WTH Davies
Referee: JCH Ireland (Scotland)

18.03.1939 MURRAYFIELD
Scotland 6 *T:* WCW Murdoch, RW Shaw
England 9 *PG:* J Heaton 3
Referee: I David (Wales)

	P	W	D	L	FOR	AGAINST	PTS
Wales	3	2	0	1	18	6	4
Ireland	3	2	0	1	17	10	4
England	3	2	0	1	12	11	4
Scotland	3	0	0	3	12	32	0

"
Good time to be an Irishman. Good time to think that the paltry times were behind their team and a golden future beckoned.
"

1940s

THE WAR YEARS.

Although the championship did not get under way again until 1947, some international matches were played during the war and immediately afterwards. ABOVE England play Scotland at Wembley in 1942. LEFT AND BELOW Twickenham hosted its first post-war international in 1946, when England played Scotland in a 'friendly' non-championship match.

Results:
England - 1 pen g* 1g 1 drop g* = 12 pts.
Scotland - 1g 1 try = 8 pts.

OFFICIAL PROGRAMME

ENGLAND (WHITE)		REFEREE: IVOR DAVID (West)	SCOTLAND (BLUE)	
15 H. J. M. UREN	Waterloo	Full Backs	15 K. I. GEDDES (Captain)	London Scottish
		Threequarters		
11 H. F. GREASLEY	Coventry	L. Wing R. Wing	14 C. W. DRUMMOND	Melrose
12 E. K. SCOTT	St. Mary's Hospital	L. Centre R. Centre	13 W. H. MUNRO	Glasgow H.S. F.P. & Army
13 J. HEATON (Captain)	Waterloo	R. Centre L. Centre	12 C. R. BRUCE	Glasgow Academicals & Army
14 R. S. L. CARR	Old Cranleighans & Manchester	R. Wing L. Wing	11 J. R. S. INNES	Aberdeen Grammar School F.P.
		Half-backs:		
10 N. M. HALL	St. Mary's Hospital	Stand-off	10 I. J. M. LUMSDEN	Watsonians
9 W. K. T. MOORE	Devonport Services	Scrum	9 K. H. S. WILSON	Watsonians & London Scottish
8 J. W. THORNTON	Gloucester		1 I. C. HENDERSON	Academicals-Wanderers
7 E. BOLE	Cambridge University		2 G. LYALL	Gala
6 D. B. VAUGHAN	R.N.E. College		3 R. AITKEN	London Scottish
5 H. R. PEEL	Headingley	Forwards	4 A. G. M. WATT	Academicals-Wanderers
4 J. MYCOCK	Sale		5 J. KIRK	Academicals-Wanderers
3 G. A. KELLY	Bedford		6 W. I. D. ELLIOT	Academicals-Wanderers
2 F. C. H. HILL	Bristol		7 D. W. DEAS	Heriot's F.P.
1 T. W. PRICE	Gloucester		8 J. H. ORR	Heriot's F.P.

Rugby Football Union
Twickenham

3D

OFFICIAL PROGRAMME

England v. Scotland

SATURDAY, 16th MARCH, 1946
Kick-off 3.0 p.m.

PRICE THREEPENCE

Good time to be an Irishman. Good time to cheer the likes of Jackie Kyle, Karl Mullen, Barney Mullan and a host of other emerald-clad warriors. Good time to think that the paltry times were behind their team and a golden future beckoned.

Well, it wasn't bad, but after 1948 they weren't to sample the sweet taste of Grand Slam success again for 61 years, until 2009. They tried and tried, came agonisingly close, were contenders, were even favourites, but little did those toasting Ireland's 1948 Slam think that they would have to wait so long before the next one. In some ways their success in 1948 was something of a surprise. True, they had a decent championship in 1947, thumping England by 22-0, a sign of gathering prowess, but their limp 16-3 defeat to Australia at Lansdowne Road just a month before the start of the 1948 championship didn't speak of great things to come. Perhaps that was just the jolt that the side needed, for there was talent there. But they needed to gel as a team, needed to believe in each other and in the cause.

The 1948 success was not a Grand Slam in an imperious, swaggering sense. Ireland did not overwhelm or leave opponents quaking at the prospect of meeting them. Ireland scored only 36 points across their four games, one of the lowest hauls ever recorded in achieving a Slam. No matter. A Grand Slam is what it was. And about time, too. Ireland did score tries, mind, ten of them, but failed to put real distance on the scoreboard between themselves and their opponents for lack of a goal-kicker.

Kyle and Mullen, both medical men, were the master strategists. Mullen, who was Ireland captain for most of that Slam season, was already a high-quality international hooker by the end of 1947. He was the man who set the tone, who shaped the tactics, who drew people together. Mullen was as good on the opposition as he was on his own men. He devised tactics to suit the strengths of his side and then factored in how the opposition might fancy taking a chunk out of Ireland. The style became known as 'Triple Crown rugby', with the forwards showing a precise mastery of the skills and the backs, aware of their limitations, being shrewd and opportunistic.

Kyle, a delightful as well as astute man, was able to implement whatever plan was laid

ABOVE Swansea also hosted a wartime international between Wales and England in 1943. BELOW Ground preparations at Twickenham before the 1947 game against France. Although it was mid-April, hard frosts were still a problem.

before him or, crucially, to adapt to whatever came up in front of him on the field of play. Like all the great players of previous or future generations, Kyle had time on the ball. Little fazed him. He had an intuitive understanding of what his pack of forwards needed at any given time; and then he had the skills to exploit any advantage. Place Kyle alongside any of the great fly halves in the history of the sport – Barry John, John Rutherford or Hugo Porta, for example – and no one would quibble.

The Irish didn't have things all their own way in this truncated decade, albeit they did win two of the three championships. A host of players came to the fore from the other countries, too: from Wales,

FRANCE VISIT TWICKENHAM FOR THE FIRST TIME SINCE 1930.
LEFT The French team. Back row (left to right): E. Pebeyre, M. Sorondo, M. Terreau, A. Alvarez, Y. Bergougnan, L. Junquas (capt), H. Dutrain. Front row: A. Moga, R. Soro, L. Caron, G. Basquet, J. Matheu, E. Buzy, J. Prat, M. Jol.
BELOW LEFT The programme from the match, which was the last international outing for England captain Jack Heaton.

Bleddyn Williams, Ken Jones, Billy Cleaver, Jack Matthews and Rees Stephens, while forwards Jean Prat and Alban Moga are revered wherever rugby is played in France's *l'Ovalie*. The year 1947 also saw Don White and Micky Steele-Bodger wear the white of England for the first time.

France, restored to the fold after their financial and political shenanigans in the 1930s, came back in some style, beating Scotland 8-3 in Paris in the first Five Nations game since World War II. To Toulouse wing Jean Lassègue, known as 'the Buffalo', went the honour of scoring the first try since resumption.

The 1947 championship, though, was shared between England and Wales with three wins apiece. For their clash with the English at the Arms Park, the Welsh picked Ken Jones on the right wing. He was to stay there in every game for the next ten seasons, finishing up in 1957 with a record 44 caps and 17 tries for Wales. Bleddyn Williams and Rees Stephens were with him much of the way. The Wales captain in the years immediately after the war was Haydn Tanner, who had made his international debut as an 18 year old in Wales's 13-12 victory over New Zealand at Cardiff in December 1935, having also been in the Swansea side that defeated the All Blacks 11-3. By the time he called it a day in 1949, with 25 Wales caps and a single Lions Test to his name, Tanner was the last Test player of the pre-war era still playing international rugby. He died in June 2009, aged 92, and the 15-year span of his international career, straddling the war, remains a Wales record.

Wales's pivotal game of the 1947 championship came against Ireland at Swansea. In a match that was postponed from the scheduled 8 March date because of a frozen pitch, Wales proved too strong in the eventual muddy conditions, snuffing out Irish hopes of a Triple Crown. Newport back-

OFFICIAL PROGRAMME
ENGLAND · FRANCE
AT TWICKENHAM
SATURDAY, 19th APRIL, 1947   Kick-off 3 p.m.

OFFICIAL		PROGRAMME	
ENGLAND (WHITE)		REFEREE: Mr Trevor Jones (Wales)	**FRANCE** (LIGHT BLUE)
15 S. C. NEWMAN	Oxford University and Blackheath	Full Backs	15 A. J. ALVAREZ ... U.S. Tyrossaise
14 D. W. SWARBRICK	Oxford University	Threequarters: L. Wing R. Wing	14 E. PEBEYRE ... C. A. Briviste
13 N. O. BENNETT	St. Mary's Hospital	L. Centre R. Centre	13 L. M. SORONDO ... U.S. Montalbanaise
12 J. HEATON (Capt.)	Waterloo	R. Centre L. Centre	12 L. JUNQUAS (Capt.) ... Aviron Bayonnais
11 R. H. GUEST	Waterloo	R. Wing L. Wing	11 H. DUTRAIN ... Stade Toulousain
10 N. M. HALL	St. Mary's Hospital	Half-backs: Stand Off	10 M. M. TERREAU ... U.S. Bressane
9 J. O. NEWTON THOMPSON Oxford University and Blackheath		Scrum	9 Y. BERGOUGNAN ... Stade Toulousain
8 V. G. ROBERTS	Penryn		8 J. M. J. MATHEU ... Castres Olympique
7 R. H. G. WEIGHILL	R.A.F. and Harlequins		7 G. J. R. E. BASQUET ... S.U. Agenais
6 M. R. STEELE BODGER Cambridge University and Harlequins			6 J. PRAT ... F. C. Lourdais
5 J. MYCOCK	Sale	Forwards	5 ALBAN MOGA ... C.A. Bèglais
4 J. GEORGE	Falmouth		4 R. V. P. SORO ... U.S. Romanaise
3 G. A. GIBBS	Bristol		3 L. CARON ... Lyon Ol. Univ.
2 A. P. HENDERSON	Cambridge University		2 E. BUZY ... F.C. Lourdais
1 H. WALKER	Coventry		1 M. JOL ... Biarritz Olympique

row forward Bob Evans scored the only try of the match, while lock Bill Tamplin of Cardiff added a penalty.

Ireland had already gone down at home to France but picked up a couple of wins in the campaign, including that assertive victory over England in Dublin alluded to earlier. Ireland scored five tries that day, two apiece for wings Bertie O'Hanlon and Barney Mullan and one for back-row forward Bill McKay. The 22-0 scoreline represented Ireland's biggest winning margin against England until the 43-13 victory at Croke Park in 2007. And it was no false portent. Mullan, with a brace of tries that day, featured on the scoresheet with regularity that year and in 1948. A representative of the Clontarf club, Mullan was a cattle salesman and also a member of the Ireland clay-pigeon-shooting team. Six tries (plus six conversions and two penalties) in eight Tests made for a significant contribution.

The year 1948, quite apart from being Ireland's annus mirabilis, was noteworthy for France's progress. They gained their first win in Wales, 11-3 in Swansea, after nine straight defeats and then beat England by 15 points to 0, their highest score and winning margin against England up to that point. France finished in joint second place with Scotland. Having been the championship's perennial whipping boys so often in the early years, France had found another identity. It wasn't difficult to know which they preferred. For England, meanwhile, times were hard, with just one point from the campaign and the Wooden Spoon.

The first game of the 1948 championship was perhaps the most significant, with Ireland triumphing 13-6 in Paris. The French pack were in

ABOVE Enthusiastic Welsh supporters arrive at Paddington Station in January 1948, but their team, containing no fewer than ten representatives of the Cardiff club, could manage only a 3-3 draw at Twickenham. BELOW Three of the Welsh heroes from that 1948 team: (left to right) Ken Jones, Bleddyn Williams and Haydn Tanner.

WRU CENTENARY 1881-1981

Ken Jones

WRU CENTENARY 1881-1981

Bleddyn Williams

WRU CENTENARY 1881-1981

Hadyn Tanner

OFFICIAL PROGRAMME

ENGLAND (WHITE)				SCOTLAND (BLUE)	
15	A. GRAY	Otley	1	K. I. GEDDES	London Scottish
14	C. B. HOLMES	Manchester	2	T. G. H. JACKSON	London Scottish
13	N. O. BENNETT	St. Mary's	3	C. W. DRUMMOND	Melrose
12	J. HEATON (Capt.)	Waterloo	4	W. H. MUNRO	Glasgow High School F.P.
11	R. H. GUEST	Waterloo	5	D. D. MACKENZIE	Edinburgh University
10	N. M. HALL	St. Mary's	6	C. R. BRUCE (Capt.)	Glasgow Academicals
9	J. O. NEWTON THOMPSON	Oxford University	7	E. ANDERSON	Stewart's F.P.
8	D. F. WHITE	Army and Northampton	8	T. P. L. McGLASHAN	R. High School F.P.
7	R. H. G. WEIGHILL	RAF and Harlequins	9	A. T. FISHER	Waterloo and Watsonians
6	M. R. STEELE BODGER	Cambridge University	10	H. H. CAMPBELL	Cambridge University and London Scottish
5	J. MYCOCK	Sale	11	F. H. COUTTS	Army and Melrose
4	J. GEORGE	Falmouth	14	I. C. HENDERSON	Edinburgh A. Wanderers
3	G. A. KELLY	Bedford	13	D. D. VALENTINE	Hawick
2	A. P. HENDERSON	Cambridge University	12	D. McLEAN	R. High School F.P.
1	H. WALKER	Coventry	15	W. I. D. ELLIOT	Edinburgh A. Wanderers

RESERVE: Mr. Ivor David (Wales)

Touch Judges: Mr. H. A. Haigh Smith (England) and Mr. M. A. Allan (Scotland)

OFFICIAL 3D PROGRAMME

ENGLAND v SCOTLAND
AT TWICKENHAM
SATURDAY, 15th MARCH, 1947. Kick-off 3 p.m.

Patron: HIS MAJESTY THE KING
President: Mr. J. Daniell

ENGLAND v SCOTLAND

Rugby Football Union Ground, Twickenham
SATURDAY, MARCH 15th, 1947. Kick-off 3 p.m.

Price 10/-
(Including Tax and Admission to Ground)

S. F. Cooper
Engineer-Commander, R.N.,
Secretary, R.F.U.

North Stand

ROW J

SEAT 173

As every reasonable precaution has been taken for the safety of spectators, the Rugby Football Union disclaims responsibility for injury or damage to the holder of this ticket, either from accident or otherwise.

Should the match be postponed and eventually played, no money will be returned, but this ticket will be available for the new date. This ticket is issued on the condition that no re-sale is effected for more than its face value.

IMPORTANT — Please occupy your seat by 2.40 p.m.

ENGLAND v SCOTLAND IN 1947.
ABOVE AND LEFT *Souvenirs from the match. In the team line-ups, note the England back row of Don White, Bob Weighill and Micky Steele-Bodger, all new to international rugby that year. Bob Weighill was later secretary of the RFU, Micky Steele-Bodger became president of the Barbarians and Don White was appointed the first England coach in 1969.* BELOW *The teams line up before the kick-off.*

OFFICIAL PROGRAMME

ENGLAND (WHITE)		REFEREE Mr. Trevor Jones (Welsh)	IRELAND (GREEN)	
15 R. UREN	Waterloo	Full Backs	15 J. MATTSON	Wanderers
*11 C. B. HOLMES	Manchester	Threequarters: L. Wing R. Wing	14 B. O'HANLON	Dolphin
*12 E. K. SCOTT (Capt.)	Redruth	L. Centre R. Centre	13 W. D. McKEE	N.I.F.C.
*13 N. O. BENNETT	United Services	R. Centre L. Centre	12 P. REID	Garryowen
*14 R. H. GUEST	Waterloo	R. Wing L. Wing	11 B. MULLAN	Clontarf
10 I. PREECE	Coventry	Half-Backs: Stand-Off	10 J. W. KYLE	Queen's University
*9 R. J. P. MADGE	Exeter	Scrum	9 H. de LACY	Garryowen and Harlequins
*8 M. R. STEELE-BODGER	Edinburgh University		1 A. A. McCONNELL	Collegians
*7 D. B. VAUGHAN	Dev. Services		2 C. MULLEN (Capt.)	Old Belvedere
*6 D. F. WHITE	Northampton		3 J. C. DALY	London Irish
*5 H. F. LUYA	Headingley		4 C. CALLAN	Lansdowne
*4 S. V. PERRY	Cambridge University	Forwards	5 J. E. NELSON	Malone
*3 G. A. GIBBS	Bristol		6 W. J. McKAY	Queen's University
*2 A. P. HENDERSON	Cambridge University		7 D. O'BRIEN	London Irish
*1 H. WALKER	Coventry		8 J. McCARTHY	Dolphin
* International				
Touch Judge: H. A. HAIGH SMITH			Touch Judge: W. R. JEFFARES, I.R.F.U.	

bristling form and scored tries from back-row forward and captain Guy Basquet and lock Robert Soro, but Ireland had more variety and claimed three tries, one each from new cap Jim McCarthy and Paddy Reid in his second game, plus one from Barney Mullan, who also added two conversions.

The great day dawned for Ireland on 13 March 1948. Prop J.C. Daly was the Irish hero for scoring the try that won the Grand Slam at Ravenhill. The home side and visitors Wales were level at half-time, with Jackie Kyle having sent Mullan in for a try before Bleddyn Williams crossed to equalise. Then, a few minutes into the second half, Daly of London Irish found himself in the right place to profit from a kick ahead. He made no mistake. The match ended 6-3 and Ireland were Grand Slam and Triple Crown champions. Daly never played for Ireland again, signing for rugby league club Huddersfield.

Suffice to say, the scenes at Ravenhill as the final whistle sounded were rather joyous. Rumour has it that a drop or two of drink was taken. And Ireland showed that their success was no fluke when they retained the championship the following year, their first ever back-to-back outright titles.

Wales were bottom that season with three defeats in four games, although an element of quirkiness to the campaign saw them score five tries, the same as champions Ireland, and concede only 19 points, fewer than anyone else. Meanwhile, England, France and Scotland had a more even tournament with two wins apiece. The 1949 championship was notable for England's Nim Hall becoming the first to score a three-point dropped goal after the change in value, England's only points in a 9-3 defeat against Wales at Cardiff. Indeed, England had been

ABOVE AND ABOVE LEFT 1948: Grand Slam year for Ireland. The programme for Ireland's 11-10 win against England, the first match as captain of Ireland for Karl Mullen, who is given as C. Mullen in the line-up. FAR LEFT Jackie Kyle goes over for an early try at Twickenham to inspire the Irish to the second win of their 1948 campaign.

ABOVE *J.C. Daly wins the ball in Ireland's decisive 1948 match against Wales at Ravenhill. He was later to score the try that secured the Grand Slam.* LEFT *Jackie Kyle (near left) and Karl Mullen, two of the most influential players in the Irish team of 1948.*
FACING PAGE *Nim Hall, scorer of the first three-point dropped goal in England's game against Wales in 1949.*

winless in the championship since beating France 6-3 at Twickenham in April 1947, only breaking that sequence in the third game of the 1949 campaign – the seventh since their last victory – in which they once again beat France, also at Twickenham, this time by 8 points to 3.

Ireland's repeat Grand Slam quest perished at the first hurdle when they lost 16-9 at home to France. This was France's third victory in succession in Ireland, having triumphed 5-0 in Belfast in 1930 before winning once again in 1947, on that occasion 12-8 in Dublin. The fair city had plenty of attraction for Frenchmen. In 1949, Jean Prat contributed ten points with the boot and was becoming an increasingly influential figure. Indeed the victory was a further sign of the growing strength of French rugby. There were other signs, too, mutterings about the sort of dealings on the club scene that had caused so many problems before.

Ireland, however, recovered from that faltering start, using the same virtues of efficiency and pragmatism that had characterised their Grand Slam campaign. And of course there was the genius that was Kyle. Ireland had also found a truly reliable place-kicker in George Norton, whose 26-point return for the 1949 season was a new Irish record for the championship. The Triple Crown and championship were clinched with a 5-0 victory over Wales at St Helen's, Ireland's first win in Swansea in 11 attempts since 1889. Grand days indeed.

Five Nations Results 1947-49

1946-47

01.01.1947 STADE COLOMBES, PARIS
France 8 *T:* J Lassegue, M Terreau *C:* J Prat
Scotland 3 *PG:* KI Geddes
Referee: CH Gadney (England)

18.01.1947 CARDIFF ARMS PARK
Wales 6 *T:* JRG Stephens, GW Evans
England 9 *T:* DF White *C:* A Gray *DG:* NM Hall
Referee: RA Beattie (Scotland)

25.01.1947 LANSDOWNE ROAD, DUBLIN
Ireland 8 *T:* JW McKay *C:* B Mullan
PG: B Mullan
France 12 *T:* J Lassegue 2, J Prat, M Sorondo
Referee: JBG Whittaker (England)

01.02.1947 MURRAYFIELD
Scotland 8 *T:* WID Elliot *C:* KI Geddes
PG: KI Geddes
Wales 22 *T:* KJ Jones 2, BL Williams, WB Cleaver,
L Williams *C:* WE Tamplin 2 *PG:* WE Tamplin
Referee: Capt MJ Dowling (Ireland)

08.02.1947 LANSDOWNE ROAD, DUBLIN
Ireland 22 *T:* B O'Hanlon 2, B Mullan 2, JW McKay
C: B Mullan 2 *PG:* B Mullan
England 0
Referee: MA Allan (Scotland)

22.02.1947 MURRAYFIELD
Scotland 0
Ireland 3 *T:* B Mullan
Referee: CH Gadney (England)

15.03.1947 TWICKENHAM
England 24 *T:* NO Bennett, RH Guest, AP Henderson,
CB Holmes *C:* J Heaton 4 *DG:* NM Hall
Scotland 5 *T:* TGH Jackson *C:* KI Geddes
Referee: I David (Wales)

22.03.1947 STADE COLOMBES, PARIS
France 0
Wales 3 *PG:* WE Tamplin
Referee: AS Bean (England)

29.03.1947 ST HELEN'S, SWANSEA
Wales 6 *T:* RT Evans *PG:* WE Tamplin
Ireland 0
Referee: JBG Whittaker (England)

19.04.1947 TWICKENHAM
England 6 *T:* RH Guest, VG Roberts
France 3 *PG:* J Prat
Referee: T Jones (Wales)

	P	W	D	L	FOR	AGAINST	PTS
Wales	4	3	0	1	37	17	6
England	4	3	0	1	39	36	6
Ireland	4	2	0	2	33	18	4
France	4	2	0	2	23	20	4
Scotland	4	0	0	4	16	57	0

1947-48

01.01.1948 STADE COLOMBES, PARIS
France 6 *T:* G Basquet, R Soro
Ireland 13 *T:* PJ Reid, JS McCarthy, B Mullan
C: B Mullan 2
Referee: TN Pearce (England)

17.01.1948 TWICKENHAM
England 3 *PG:* SC Newman
Wales 3 *T:* KJ Jones
Referee: RA Beattie (Scotland)

24.01.1948 MURRAYFIELD
Scotland 9 *T:* TGH Jackson *PG:* WCW Murdoch 2
France 8 *T:* R Lacaussade *C:* A Alvarez *PG:* J Prat
Referee: AS Bean (England)

07.02.1948 CARDIFF ARMS PARK
Wales 14 *T:* BL Williams, J Matthews, KJ Jones
C: WE Tamplin *PG:* WE Tamplin
Scotland 0
Referee: TN Pearce (England)

14.02.1948 TWICKENHAM
England 10 *T:* RH Guest 2 *C:* R Uren 2
Ireland 11 *T:* JW Kyle, JW McKay, WD McKee
C: B Mullan
Referee: T Jones (Wales)

21.02.1948 ST HELEN'S, SWANSEA
Wales 3 *PG:* O Williams
France 11 *T:* G Basquet, M Terreau, M Pomathios
C: A Alvarez
Referee: AS Bean (England)

28.02.1948 LANSDOWNE ROAD, DUBLIN
Ireland 6 *T:* B Mullan, JW Kyle
Scotland 0
Referee: CH Gadney (England)

13.03.1948 RAVENHILL, BELFAST
Ireland 6 *T:* B Mullan, JC Daly
Wales 3 *T:* BL Williams
Referee: MA Allan (Scotland)

20.03.1948 MURRAYFIELD
Scotland 6 *T:* CW Drummond, WB Young
England 3 *PG:* R Uren
Referee: NH Lambert (Ireland)

29.03.1948 STADE COLOMBES, PARIS
France 15 *T:* M Pomathios, J Prat, R Soro *C:* A Alvarez
DG: Y Bergougnan
England 0
Referee: T Jones (Wales)

	P	W	D	L	FOR	AGAINST	PTS
Ireland	4	4	0	0	36	19	8
France	4	2	0	2	40	25	4
Scotland	4	2	0	2	15	31	4
Wales	4	1	1	2	23	20	3
England	4	0	1	3	16	35	1

1948-49

15.01.1949 STADE COLOMBES, PARIS
France 0
Scotland 8 *T:* WID Elliot, PW Kininmonth
C: WD Allardice
Referee: TN Pearce (England)

15.01.1949 CARDIFF ARMS PARK
Wales 9 *T:* L Williams 2, A Meredith
England 3 *DG:* NM Hall
Referee: NH Lambert (Ireland)

29.01.1949 LANSDOWNE ROAD, DUBLIN
Ireland 9 *PG:* GW Norton 3
France 16 *T:* G Basquet, J Lassegue *C:* J Prat 2
PG: J Prat 2
Referee: TN Pearce (England)

05.02.1949 MURRAYFIELD
Scotland 6 *T:* LG Gloag, DWC Smith
Wales 5 *T:* BL Williams *C:* RF Trott
Referee: NH Lambert (Ireland)

12.02.1949 LANSDOWNE ROAD, DUBLIN
Ireland 14 *T:* B O'Hanlon, WD McKee *C:* GW Norton
PG: GW Norton 2
England 5 *T:* CB van Ryneveld *C:* WB Holmes
Referee: RA Beattie (Scotland)

26.02.1949 TWICKENHAM
England 8 *T:* LB Cannell *C:* WB Holmes *DG:* I Preece
France 3 *DG:* A Alvarez
Referee: T Jones (Wales)

26.02.1949 MURRAYFIELD
Scotland 3 *PG:* WD Allardice
Ireland 13 *T:* JS McCarthy 2 *C:* GW Norton 2
PG: GW Norton
Referee: AS Bean (England)

12.03.1949 ST HELEN'S, SWANSEA
Wales 0
Ireland 5 *T:* JS McCarthy *C:* GW Norton
Referee: TN Pearce (England)

19.03.1949 TWICKENHAM
England 19 *T:* CB van Ryneveld 2, RH Guest,
GRd'A Hosking, RD Kennedy *C:* BH Travers 2
Scotland 3 *PG:* GA Wilson
Referee: NH Lambert (Ireland)

26.03.1949 STADE COLOMBES, PARIS
France 5 *T:* J Lassegue *C:* A Alvarez
Wales 3 *T:* KJ Jones
Referee: NH Lambert (Ireland)

	P	W	D	L	FOR	AGAINST	PTS
Ireland	4	3	0	1	41	24	6
England	4	2	0	2	35	29	4
France	4	2	0	2	24	28	4
Scotland	4	2	0	2	20	37	4
Wales	4	1	0	3	17	19	2

LEFT *Regular television coverage of rugby from Twickenham was introduced in the 1950s.* BELOW *Peter West (right) and Wilf Wooller provide commentary for England v Wales in 1955.*

" France were bold, rigorous, adventurous and disciplined – a notable array of virtues, ones that they have battled incessantly to keep hold of. "

1950s

The 1950s saw France begin to flex their muscles. Now, there have been times when such activities from our friends across the Channel have not been too wholesome. *Le Crunch* on all fronts. However, in the 1950s France were bold, rigorous, adventurous and disciplined – a notable array of virtues, ones that they have battled incessantly to keep hold of – and their significant advance over the decade culminated with their first ever championship in 1959.

A sure sign of France's rise to prominence came in 1950 with their third championship victory in succession over England. There were notable Gallic names to admire, men who are still revered in French rugby; men of stature and integrity, players who, in their robustness and unquenchable drive, typified the new approach.

It was Lucien Mias, an early-day version of Martin Johnson, who led France to the title in 1959. Mias was a big man in all senses, the Mazamet lock commanding huge respect from friend and foe alike. Discipline was top of Mias' agenda, as was an emphasis on forward play. Not only were France technically proficient, they attacked with great elan and cleverness from first phase, notably from the line out, the forwards interposing with the dexterity of backs. That was not the last time we were to see that little trick. No one attacks with such verve in these situations as the French. Man, ball, space, support, pass – glory.

Mias, who made his debut against Scotland in 1951 and went on to win 29 caps, only became captain by default, taking over on the 1958 tour of South Africa when Michel Celaya was injured. Originally a schoolmaster, Mias changed career midstream, taking up medicine in his mid-twenties and becoming a doctor at the age of 29. At the end of France's championship-winning season, Mias – or 'Doctor Pack', as he was known – retired to follow his new profession.

ABOVE Guy Basquet from a team photograph taken before the game against Ireland at Stade Colombes in 1952, won 11-8 by the visitors. RIGHT Jean Prat leads his team out at Twickenham in 1953. France went down 11-0, one of England's tries being scored by Jeff Butterfield on his first international appearance.

Among the other distinguished names on the French roll of honour of the 1950s are Guy Basquet and Jean Prat. The former, a back-row forward with the Agen club, made his debut in 1945 and finally called time on his international career in 1952, as his country's most capped No. 8 with 33 caps, 24 of them as captain. Basquet was a real leader, a man of raw presence with a finely tuned radar locked on to the try line. He scored eight tries for his country, but more significant than his points contribution was that he managed to instil a sense of direction and order in the French team, qualities notably lacking from the French game in earlier times and upon which the likes of Mias were able to build. Basquet was later to become vice-president of the FFR.

Prat was, and still is, a legend in French rugby. Dubbed 'Monsieur Rugby', he played on the flank for his home-town club, Lourdes, and helped them to six French championship titles, having no need of the holy waters to work his magic. Prat also played in 51 of a possible 52 internationals, after making his debut in 1945 against the British Army, a match for which the French awarded caps. His brother Maurice, a centre, played alongside him in 18 of those Tests.

Yet France did not have it all their own way during the 1950s. Far from it. In fact, it was Wales who lorded it over the rest, with at least a share in five of the first seven championships, including a Grand Slam in the opening year of the decade, 1950. Their triumph was a surprise, Wales having been Wooden Spoonists only a year earlier. It was their first Grand Slam since 1911.

As ever, the collective was the thing, teams impressing and producing as a group rather than as individuals. But if rugby is the great team sport, it is also a sport that throws up outstanding characters. There were several vying for the spotlight across the 1950s, but two names resonate still with followers of the game – Cliff Morgan and Jackie Kyle.

It would be hard to find two more distinguished players from any era. Fly halves of note, certainly, but more than that, men of distinction. Morgan, wise, wry and devilishly difficult to pin down on the field; Kyle, too, a fly half with wit and spirit. The pair will be bracketed together whenever pub debate turns to talk of the greatest ever outside halves. Fitting then that they should bow out in the same season, 1958. Kyle, as accomplished in his medical career as he was on the rugby field, was a pivotal figure in the Irish side that enjoyed success

ABOVE The Wales team that beat France at Cardiff Arms Park to win the Grand Slam in 1950. Back row (left to right): I. Jones, J.D. Robins, D.J. Hayward, E.R. John, R.T. Evans, W.R. Cale, W.B. Cleaver. Front row: K.J. Jones, M.C. Thomas, B.L. Jones, J.A. Gwilliam (capt), J. Matthews, C. Davies, G. Williams. Front row: W.R. Willis, D.M. Davies.

immediately after World War II. Three championships in four seasons included that Grand Slam of 1948, which until 2009 was a lone point of all-conquering championship success in Irish rugby history.

Kyle, who played for North of Ireland FC (NIFC) as well as Queen's University, Belfast, won 46 caps for Ireland and six for the Lions and retired as Ireland's, indeed the world's, most capped fly half. His last Test was against Scotland, in which Ireland recorded their only win of the 1958 championship. The Scots were glad to see the back of him after 11 wins in 11 championship appearances against them.

Cliff Morgan encapsulated so many fine attributes, with his passion for the sport and his unbridled emotion. His values were those of both a competitor and a sportsman. Morgan, who came from the Rhondda, played for Cardiff as well as for Bective Rangers in Ireland. He was part of the Wales side that won or shared four titles from 1952 to 1956 and was a key figure in Wales's 13-8 victory over the All Blacks in December 1953 as well as the brains of the Lions side in South Africa in 1955. Like Kyle, he retired as his country's most capped fly half, in Morgan's case with 29 appearances. Joining the BBC in the same year as he retired, Morgan went on to have an equally distinguished post-playing career, holding a number of sports-related posts with the corporation, eventually becoming Head of Sport and Outside Broadcasts for BBC Television.

Add in several other notable players from that era – Karl Mullen, Noel Henderson, Jim McCarthy and Des O'Brien from Ireland; Norman 'Nim' Hall, Don White, Eric Evans, Peter Jackson and Jeff Butterfield from England; Peter Kininmonth and Doug Elliot, who persevered in arduous times for Scotland; Bleddyn Williams and Ken Jones for Wales – and it's not difficult to see why the decade saw Twickenham's first ever all-ticket international (England against Wales in 1954) and a greater demand for the grainy images of rugby internationals to be transmitted on television.

The popularity of the game was growing for all sorts of reasons. The sport, of course, was not without its kinks, flaws and lulls, but the trend was upwards. Wales decided to move fixtures away from the evocative St Helen's in Swansea after more than 40 years of competition, the 1954 match against Scotland being the last rugby international played at the ground. St Helen's simply could not accommodate the growing demand, all the more so during those boom years for Welsh rugby in the early 1950s.

Wales enjoyed a splendid first half of the decade, a surprising development given their laboured end to the previous one. The Welsh declared their intentions in the grandest possible manner with an 11-5 victory at Twickenham in 1950 in front of a crowd of almost 76,000, an attendance that prompted the Rugby Football Union to look towards their policy of all-ticket matches.

A new Welsh star was revealed in the form of Lewis Jones, the youngest member of the side that day at 18 years and nine months. The debutant full back produced a superb break to set up Cliff Davies for a try, as well as kicking a penalty goal and a conversion. Jones became something of a folk hero, although the adulation was short-lived. Like so many after him,

Players who were to leave their stamp on the decade: Cliff Morgan (top right), Eric Evans (left), Jeff Butterfield (above), Doug Elliot (right), Peter Jackson (far right).

83

ENGLAND v WALES IN 1950.

RIGHT Debutant Lewis Jones makes his appearance at the top of the Welsh line-up in the programme against an England side which included six players from the Oxford University team. ABOVE RIGHT Ray Cale goes over for the first Welsh try. BELOW Happy Welsh supporters carry Lewis Jones from the field at the end of the game.

FACING PAGE Lewis Jones and his captain John Gwilliam as portrayed by the cartoonist Gren in a series of cigarette cards commemorating the WRU centenary.

OFFICIAL PROGRAMME

ENGLAND (WHITE)		REFEREE: Mr. N. H. LAMBERT (Ireland)	WALES (RED)	
15 M. B. HOFMEYR	Oxford University	Full Backs	1 L. JONES	Neath and Devonport Services
14 I. J. BOTTING	Oxford University	Threequarters: L. Wing R. Wing	2 *K. JONES	Newport
13 *L. B. CANNELL	Oxford University	L. Centre R. Centre	3 *J. MATTHEWS	Cardiff
12 B. BOOBBYER	Oxford University	R. Centre L. Centre	4 *B. L. WILLIAMS (Capt.)	Cardiff
11 J. V. SMITH	Cambridge University	R. Wing L. Wing	5 *M. THOMAS	Newport and Devonport Services
10 *I. PREECE (Capt.)	Coventry	Half Backs: Stand-Off	6 *W. B. CLEAVER	Cardiff
9 *G. RIMMER	Waterloo	Scrum	7 W. R. WILLIS	Cardiff
8 *J. McG. KENDALL-CARPENTER	Oxford University	Forwards	8 D. M. DAVIES	Somerset Police
7 *E. EVANS	Sale		9 J. D. ROBINS	Birkenhead Park
6 W. A. HOLMES	Nuneaton		10 *C. DAVIES	Cardiff
5 *G. R. D'A. HOSKING	Devonport Services and Royal Navy		11 *R. STEPHENS	Neath
4 H. A. JONES	Barnstaple		12 *D. HAYWARD	Newbridge
3 H. D. SMALL	Oxford University		13 *R. CALE	Pontypool
2 *D. B. VAUGHAN	Headingley		14 *J. GWILLIAM	Newport and Edinburgh Wanderers
1 J. J. CAIN	Waterloo		15 *R. T. EVANS	Newport
			*International	
Touch Judge: Col. G. WARDEN			Touch Judge: Mr. W. H. HARRIS.	

Jones's attention was turned north by the lure of the rugby league shilling. Leeds RL fans were the beneficiaries.

That match against England was also the first as captain for the influential John Gwilliam as Wales won at Twickenham for the first time since 1933. Gwilliam gained the captaincy after just six international appearances and was to skipper Wales on 13 occasions. Like hooker Dai Davies (Somerset Police) and prop John Robins (Birkenhead Park), the back-row forward played club rugby outside Wales during his international career, for Cambridge University, Edinburgh Wanderers and later Gloucester. Gwilliam was a schoolmaster, educated at Monmouth School before going on to Cambridge, and played his early rugby for Newport and London Welsh.

Lewis Jones

If there was merited joy when Wales clinched the Triple Crown in Belfast with a hard-fought 6-3 win over Ireland, it was soon dissipated when 80 travelling fans were killed in a plane crash on their way home, the aircraft coming down at Llandow near Cardiff. Wales supporters paid their respects before the final game, a Grand Slam-winning 21-0 success over France at the Arms Park a fortnight later.

Ireland's purple patch in the championship found due reward with the title in 1951. They did it by the narrowest of margins, edging out second-placed France 9-8 in Dublin. How different things might have been for France if their principal goal-kicker, Jean Prat, had not been ruled out on the morning of the game with flu. Each side scored two tries of which the French converted one, the sides being separated by a penalty goal from Noel Henderson, who landed his first kick in international rugby.

J. A. Gwilliam

France were on the move, showing that the decision to readmit them to the fold (see the 1930s) had been the right one, although misgivings and suspicions about professionalism in the country remained. What was not in question was the growing excellence of French play. How much greyer and flatter a place would the championship have been down the years without France!

France claimed their first victory at Twickenham during this campaign, winning comfortably 11-3, with tries from two of their most influential players, Guy Basquet and Jean Prat. England were in the doldrums and finished joint bottom of the championship pile, their only note of consolation coming with a 5-3 victory over Scotland at Twickenham.

Scotland had a rum season, again struggling to make a mark – one staggering result apart. They beat defending Grand Slam champions Wales 19-0 at Murrayfield, an astonishing reversal of fortunes. They were set on their way by an extraordinary dropped goal from the touch line by No. 8 and captain Peter Kininmonth. Two tries from Bob Gordon on debut plus another from Hamish Dawson followed. In many ways, this was one of the most remarkable results in the entire history of the championship. Scotland had to wait until 1955 for their next international victory – coincidentally against Wales at Murrayfield – their run of 17 losses including 15 in the championship. Strange thing, sport.

Unexpectedly, perhaps, given the nature of selectors, the result prompted no great purge in the Welsh ranks. Indeed, only one player, fly half Glyn Davies, was never to play for Wales again. He gave way to one Clifford Isaac Morgan, who made his debut at Cardiff in the following match, against one of his heroes – Ireland's Jackie Kyle.

ENGLAND v FRANCE IN 1951.
ABOVE RIGHT The players leave the field after France's memorable first Twickenham victory in 1951. The score was 11-3, the French points provided by Guy Basquet and Jean Prat. **LEFT** The French team that made history that day. Back row (left to right): L. Mias, H. Fourès, P. Bertrand, P. Pascalin, R. Bernard, J. Prat, V.S. Llewellyn (referee). Middle row: A. Porthault, G. Brun, G. Basquet (capt), R. Arcalis, M. Pomathios, G. Belletante. Front row: A. Alvarez, G. Dufau. **PREVIOUS PAGES** The game took place on a murky, muddy day.

The following year Wales achieved another Grand Slam, and Morgan was a key component of the side. Among the other stars was Ken Jones, who scored four tries during that 1952 championship, including two against England at Twickenham. The Welsh try scorers were backed up by Malcolm Thomas and Lewis Jones, who both weighed in with important points with the boot, a talent that the latter was to take up to Leeds that October.

Indeed, the Twickenham match between Wales and a resurgent England was the decisive game of the campaign. England, giving notice that they were a force to be reckoned with, took full advantage of the temporary absence of Lewis Jones, who was receiving treatment for an injury, to score tries through Albert Agar and Ted Woodward. The faster Wales outfit, though, eventually had the better of them, overcoming the six-point deficit through Ken Jones and one Thomas conversion to take the game 8-6. For his first try, Jones split then outpaced the England defence from almost halfway; the second was a sweeping, curving run to the right corner.

England learnt their lesson, noting that they needed more bite in attack. The next season they became more positive in their approach and more threatening near the try line, to the extent that their points aggregate of 54 was the highest since the resumption of the championship after the war. England's total was bolstered by a six-try thumping of Scotland in their final game, Nim Hall converting four of the scores.

The Scots, now in their alarming slump, were proving to be the whipping boys of the championship, Ireland also giving them a pasting by the same 26-8 scoreline at Murrayfield. It was no surprise that they should finish bottom for the second time in consecutive seasons, conceding 75 points in the process.

ENGLAND v WALES IN 1952. ABOVE RIGHT *In Cliff Morgan's first international appearance at Twickenham the Welsh had a narrow 8-6 win, which set them on the way to another Grand Slam.* RIGHT *Ken Jones touches down for one of his two tries in the game.*

In fact Ireland were in decent attacking form themselves, equalling England's 54 points scored and running in 12 tries, one more than the eventual champions. Against Scotland, debutant wing Seamus Byrne scored a hat-trick, the first Irishman to do so since Eugene Davy had also made the Scots suffer in 1930. In addition the 26 points scored against Scotland in 1953 set a mark for Ireland not attained again for 31 years, when the Irish beat England 26-21 at Twickenham, and not surpassed until Ireland's 27-12 victory over Australia in Brisbane in 1979.

For the second successive season, the championship hinged on the second game, England gaining revenge for their defeat by Wales the previous year with a fine 8-3 win in Cardiff. The Welsh left out Cliff Morgan because his half-back partner, Rex Willis, had fractured his shoulder. The plan failed, Wales managing only a penalty from full back Terry Davies. England scored the only try of the game through centre Lewis Cannell.

Captain Nim Hall and Don White were crucial elements of that championship-winning England side. White was a stout member of the back row as well as a faithful servant of

ABOVE England and Ireland battle through the Twickenham snow in 1952 in a game that England won thanks to a single unconverted try by Brian Boobbyer.

Northampton, where he was involved in the family shoe business. He went on to become an England selector and was coach from 1969 to 1971. Hall, meanwhile, was a utility back who could kick points and was renowned for landing long-range dropped goals. A Yorkshireman, he was something of a versatile figure away from the field, too, with jobs in insurance, medicine and the pub trade. Hall captained England on 13 occasions, although following the 1953 triumph he was to play for England only twice more, against Wales and Ireland in 1955.

The 1954 tournament proved to be a three-way split for honours between England, France and Wales, the dominant teams of the day. The sides finished level on points with three wins apiece. Those of a Scottish persuasion should perhaps cover their eyes now lest they read that their team scored a paltry six – yes, six – points in their four matches. Scotland lost all four games for the third season in succession, an unprecedented state of affairs for any country. Doom and gloom north of the border.

Up where the sun shone brightly, at the top of the table, the decisive day was 10 April, when all three contenders were in action. Frost had forced the postponement of the Wales v Scotland game from January, and the rearrangement certainly added spice to the day's events.

England did not manage to trouble France unduly in Paris, scoring only a single try from flanker Tug Wilson in an 11-3 defeat at Stade Colombes. France came through with scores from André Boniface and Maurice Prat, with brother Jean on the mark with his kicking. Wales duly beat Scotland, running in four tries from prop Billy Williams, Ray Williams, Bryn Meredith and Cliff Morgan to win 15-3 in the final championship match to be played at St Helen's.

The championship was close again the following year, Wales and France this time sharing the title, with almost identical points for and against, in a tournament that featured a high

1953: A CHAMPIONSHIP-WINNING SEASON FOR ENGLAND.

ABOVE *S.J. 'Akker' Adkins is brought down as England try to break through the French defence during their 11-0 win at Twickenham.* **BELOW** *The Coventry lock was selected against Scotland in England's following match and scored on what was his last international appearance.* **LEFT** *Adrian Stoop's season ticket for the 1954-55 season.*

RUGBY FOOTBALL UNION, TWICKENHAM
Season 1954-55

ENGLAND *v* **FRANCE**, 26th Feb., 1955, at 3.0 p.m.
ENGLAND *v* **SCOTLAND**, 19th Mar., 1955, at 3.0 p.m.

WEST LOWER STAND

ENTRANCE	ROW	SEAT
E	6	156

NOTE.—Ticket holders are requested to occupy their seats at least 15 minutes before the kick-off, please.

Price 30/-
(including Admission to Ground)

Secretary
P.T.O.

Note:—In the event of being postponed and eventually played returned, but this Ticket will be available on the later date.

As every reasonable precaution is taken for the safety of spectators, the holder of this Ticket agrees to accept all risks of injury or damage from accident or otherwise.

This Ticket is issued on the condition that no re-sale is effected for more than its face value. **852**

RENEWAL OF TICKETS.
Application for the renewal of this Seat for International Matches Season 1955-56 MUST BE REC... BY 1st OCTOBER, 1955, and be accompanied by this...

Issued to A. D. Stoop Esq

2006/234

RUGBY FOOTBALL UNION

ENGLAND *v* **SCOTLAND**

TWICKENHAM
SATURDAY 21st MARCH
1953
OFFICIAL PROGRAMME
ONE SHILLING

	ENGLAND			SCOTLAND
1.	N. M. HALL — Richmond (CAPTAIN)	**FULL-BACKS**	1.	I. H. M. THOMSON — Army and Heriot's F.P.
		THREE-QUARTERS		
2.	R. C. BAZLEY — Waterloo	LEFT WING / RIGHT WING	2.	T. G. WEATHERSTONE — Stewart's F.P.
3.	W. P. C. DAVIES — Harlequins	LEFT CENTRE / RIGHT CENTRE	3.	A. CAMERON — Glasgow H.S. F.P. (CAPTAIN)
4.	J. BUTTERFIELD — Northampton	RIGHT CENTRE / LEFT CENTRE	4.	D. CAMERON — Glasgow H.S. F.P.
5.	J. E. WOODWARD — Wasps	RIGHT WING / LEFT WING	5.	J. S. SWAN — St. Andrews University
		HALF-BACKS		
6.	M. REGAN — Liverpool	STAND OFF	6.	L. BRUCE LOCKHART — London Scottish
7.	D. W. SHUTTLEWORTH — Army and Headingley	SCRUM	7.	A. F. DORWARD — Gala
		FORWARDS		
8.	R. V. STIRLING — R.A.F. and Leicester		8.	J. C. DAWSON — Glasgow Academicals
9.	E. EVANS — Sale		9.	J. H. F. KING — Selkirk
10.	W. A. HOLMES — Nuneaton		10.	R. L. WILSON — Gala
11.	D. T. WILKINS — R.N. and U.S. Portsmouth		11.	J. H. HENDERSON — Oxford University
12.	S. J. ADKINS — Coventry	KICK-OFF 3 P.M.	12.	J. J. HEGARTY — Hawick
13.	A. O. LEWIS — Bath		13.	W. KERR — London Scottish
14.	J. MacG. K. KENDALL-CARPENTER — Bath		14.	W. L. K. COWIE — Edinburgh Wanderers
15.	D. F. WHITE — Northampton		15.	K. H. D. McMILLAN — Sale
	Touch Judge Col. G. WARDEN, O.B.E.	Referee Capt. M. J. DOWLING (Ireland)		Touch Judge J. GRAHAM

ABOVE RIGHT *The England team before the game against France in their 1957 Grand Slam season. Back row (left to right): R.C. Williams (referee), J. Butterfield, W.P.C. Davies, P.H. Thompson, R.W.D. Marques, J.D. Currie, P.G.D. Robbins, C.R. Jacobs, R. Challis, Dr N.M. Parkes (touch judge). Middle row: P.B. Jackson, G.W.D. Hastings, E. Evans (capt), A. Ashcroft, R, Higgins. Front row: R.M. Bartlett, R.E.G. Jeeps.*

turnover of players. Scotland, with their fans in a state of distress, managed to pull off a shock and highly significant victory over Wales, not only ending a catalogue of 15 straight defeats in the championship but also Wales's Grand Slam aspirations. One of Scotland's tries in the 14-8 win was scored by Cambridge University wing Arthur Smith, a future Scotland and Lions captain who was making the first of 33 international appearances for his country.

Besides remarkable arrivals, the season also saw some notable retirements, among them that of Bleddyn Williams, the 'Prince of Centres', who finished on a high with a win over England. Williams won 27 caps for Wales and the Lions and played his part in four Five Nations title wins (three shared). He scored a record 185 career tries for Cardiff, where his centre partner was none other than Jack Matthews, a legendary tackler who had made his Wales debut against England in 1947, in the same match as Williams, and himself won 23 Wales and Lions caps up to 1951.

Hopes were high that 1956 would be a vintage championship following the enthralling Lions series in South Africa the previous summer. The rubber had been drawn 2-2 and had been characterised by some fine expansive rugby by the tourists. Yet the anticipated bonanza didn't materialise. Wales were outright champions but managed to score only 25 points in their four games, one of the lowest ever hauls by a title-winning side. It was not a championship that stirred the soul. Wales were demonstrably the best side on display but failed to land the Triple Crown, losing 11-3 to Ireland at Lansdowne Road.

England's time was coming, though, and duly arrived in 1957, when they claimed a Grand Slam in commendable manner. They made a virtue of having a settled side, making only two changes throughout the championship and conceding just eight points in four games. Many a modern-day professional defence coach would be proud of that miserly return. Teamwork brings its reward in many ways.

Four of England's six tries were scored by their wings – three by Peter Jackson – an indication that they were prepared to use the ball, too, after a slowish start to the campaign.

THE BRITISH BROADCASTING CORPORATION

HEAD OFFICE: BROADCASTING HOUSE, LONDON, W.1

TELEVISION CENTRE: WOOD LANE, LONDON, W.12

TELEGRAMS & CABLES: BROADCASTS, LONDON, TELEX   *   INTERNATIONAL TELEX 2-2182

TELEPHONE: SHEPHERDS BUSH 8030

16th May, 1957.

Dear Douglas,

I am enclosing four photographs which are
taken from the telerecording of the arrival of
the Queen and the Duke of Edinburgh at Twickenham
on the 16th March.   The quality if not staggeringly
good but it is the best one can get from the blowing
up of single frames from the film.

I hope to see you occasionally at Lord's this
year.

Best wishes,

Yours sincerely,

(Antony Craxton)

Colonel F.D. Prentice,
Rugby Football Union,
Twickenham,
Middx.
ACr/DMS

ENGLAND v. SCOTLAND

at the Rugby Football Union Ground, Twickenham

Saturday, 16th March, 1957   Kick-off 3.0 p.m.

ENTRANCE **C**   WEST LOWER STAND

ROW **4**   £1

SEAT **51**

ABOVE The Queen and Prince Philip visit Twickenham for the 1957 Calcutta Cup match. FAR LEFT The BBC's Outside Broadcasts producer Antony Craxton sent the 'grainy' photograph with this accompanying letter to the then secretary of the RFU, Doug Prentice, as a souvenir of the occasion.

Even so, England were helped on their way to a Grand Slam by a momentary aberration from Neath wing Keith Maddocks, who was caught offside under his own posts in England's opening game of the championship in Cardiff. The resultant point-blank penalty goal from full back Fenwick Allison was the only score of the match.

England saved their best for last, beating Scotland 16-3 at Twickenham, tries from Phil Davies, Reg Higgins and Peter Thompson seeing them to their seventh Grand Slam and their first since 1928. Eric Evans led England with admirable assurance throughout the tournament. The Sale hooker, a schoolmaster, made his debut against Australia in 1948 and captained England in 13 of his 30 internationals in a distinguished career that also saw him accumulate over 100 appearances for Lancashire.

Scotland's next match, against Wales at Murrayfield, brought to a close the international career of Ken Jones. An Olympic relay silver medallist at the 1948 London Games, Jones was self-evidently blessed with exceptional pace, but he was also known as a sound defender. When he called it a day in 1957, he had 44 international caps for Wales, a world record, plus three for the Lions. Wales lost several other players that year, including back-row forward Rees Stephens, who like Jones had made his debut against England in 1947.

The closing two years of the decade were formative. England took the title again in 1958, the hallmark of their triumph once again being their solid defensive work: they conceded a miserly six points in four matches. Nevertheless the most interesting feature of the championship was the gathering force that was France. In 1957 they had lost all four matches for the first time since 1929, despite showing promise, in particular against Wales. Now, in

TWICKENHAM JUBILEE MATCH

WEST LOWER STAND

ENGLAND & WALES v. SCOTLAND & IRELAND
Rugby Football Union Ground, Twickenham
SATURDAY 17th OCTOBER 1959

ENTRANCE **E** ROW **19** SEAT 161

This ticket is issued on the condition that the Rugby Football Union, its servants or agents will not be liable for any loss, injury or damage howsoever caused to the holder of this ticket.

KICK-OFF 3.15 p.m.
IMPORTANT—PLEASE OCCUPY YOUR SEAT BY 3 p.m.

PRICE **£1**
(Including Admission to Ground)

SECRETARY.

1958, they were beaten in their opening two games, but the second defeat, a sound 14-0 thumping by England in Paris, led to six changes for the next championship match and finally a combination that looked as if it might deliver.

So it proved. France proceeded to claim their first win in Cardiff, beating Wales 16-6 to begin a run that was to culminate in a series win in South Africa and an historic first ever championship title in 1959. France outplayed Wales that day in Cardiff, scoring tries through Pierre Danos and Pierre Tarricq, both of which were converted, with full back Michel Vannier adding a couple of dropped goals. Three weeks later, France beat Ireland 11-6 in Paris. *Les Bleus* were on their way.

Nevertheless France had to work mighty hard for their first ever outright title. In a season in which only two points separated the five teams, France claimed the honours with two wins and a draw, losing their final game 9-5 in Dublin. France had enough discipline and togetherness to prevail in what was a decidedly humdrum championship. England, for example, conceded just one try but scored none in reply. The overall tallies of just 12 tries and 93 points were, and always remained, record lows for a Five Nations season in which all sides competed.

No matter. It was to be a seminal moment for French rugby. The French back row of Michel Crauste, Jean Barthe and François Moncla was all-consuming, particularly in the all-important 11-3 victory over Wales. Furthermore, captain Lucien Mias was a fine leader. At long last, France had proved themselves.

TEAMS:

ENGLAND AND WALES	SCOTLAND AND IRELAND
T. E. DAVIES (W)	K. J. F. SCOTLAND (S)
P. B. JACKSON (E)	A. R. SMITH (S)
M. C. THOMAS (W)	M. K. FLYNN (I)
W. M. PATTERSON (Sale)	D. HEWITT (I)
J. R. C. YOUNG (E)	A. J. F. O'REILLY (I)
A. B. W. RISMAN (E)	G. SHARPE (Stewarts College F.P.)
R. E. G. JEEPS (Capt.) (E)	A. A. MULLIGAN (I)
R. PROSSER (W)	H. F. McLEOD (S)
B. U. MEREDITH (W)	A. R. DAWSON (Capt.) (I)
G. J. BENDON (E)	S. MILLAR (I)
R. H. WILLIAMS (W)	J. W. Y. KEMP (S)
J. D. CURRIE (E)	W. A. J. MULCAHY (I)
H. MORGAN (W)	N. A. A. MURPHY (I)
J. R. FAULL (W)	J. T. GREENWOOD (S)
A. ASHCROFT (E)	G. K. SMITH (S)

Referee:
Mon. J. F. SAMPIERI (*France*)

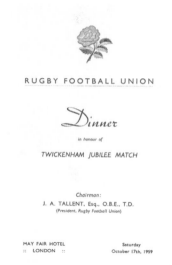

RUGBY FOOTBALL UNION

Dinner

in honour of

TWICKENHAM JUBILEE MATCH

Chairman:

J. A. TALLENT, Esq., O.B.E., T.D.
(President, Rugby Football Union)

MAY FAIR HOTEL :: LONDON ::   Saturday October 17th, 1959

Twickenham Jubilee Match

Dinner in Honour of the Teams

The President and Committee of the Rugby Football Union request the pleasure of

's Company at the

May Fair Hotel, Berkeley Street

On Saturday, 17th October, 1959, at 8.15 p.m. (for 8.30)

Dinner Jacket

R.S.V.P. to
The Secretary
Rugby Football Union
Twickenham

FACING PAGE TOP Dickie Jeeps waits to catch a greasy ball in England's 6-0 win against Ireland on their way to the championship title in 1958. BOTTOM André Boniface (11) watches as Antoine Labazuy is successful with his penalty attempt in France's 3-3 draw at Twickenham in 1959. THIS PAGE Fifty years of Twickenham was celebrated in October 1959 with a jubilee match followed by dinner at the May Fair Hotel. TOP John Currie, representing England and Wales, forces his way over the line.

Five Nations Results 1950-59

1949-50

14.01.1950 MURRAYFIELD
Scotland 8 *T:* R Macdonald, GM Budge
C: L Bruce-Lockhart
France 5 *T:* J Merquey *C:* J Prat
Referee: T Jones (Wales)

21.01.1950 TWICKENHAM
England 5 *T:* JV Smith *C:* MB Hofmeyr
Wales 11 *T:* WR Cale, C Davies *C:* BL Jones
PG: BL Jones
Referee: NH Lambert (Ireland)

28.01.1950 STADE COLOMBES, PARIS
France 3 *DG:* P Lauga
Ireland 3 *PG:* JH Burges
Referee: TN Pearce (England)

04.02.1950 ST HELEN'S, SWANSEA
Wales 12 *T:* MC Thomas, KJ Jones *PG:* BL Jones
DG: WB Cleaver
Scotland 0
Referee: Capt MJ Dowling (Ireland)

11.02.1950 TWICKENHAM
England 3 *T:* VG Roberts
Ireland 0
Referee: RA Beattie (Scotland)

25.02.1950 LANSDOWNE ROAD, DUBLIN
Ireland 21 *T:* J Blayney, AB Curtis, L Crowe
C: GW Norton 3 *PG:* GW Norton 2
Scotland 0
Referee: TN Pearce (England)

25.02.1950 STADE COLOMBES, PARIS
France 6 *T:* F Cazenave, J Pilon
England 3 *T:* JV Smith
Referee: NH Lambert (Ireland)

11.03.1950 RAVENHILL, BELFAST
Ireland 3 *PG:* GW Norton
Wales 6 *T:* KJ Jones, MC Thomas
Referee: RA Beattie (Scotland)

18.03.1950 MURRAYFIELD
Scotland 13 *T:* DA Sloan 2, JG Abercrombie
C: T Gray 2
England 11 *T:* JV Smith 2 *C:* MB Hofmeyr
PG: MB Hofmeyr
Referee: Capt MJ Dowling (Ireland)

25.03.1950 CARDIFF ARMS PARK
Wales 21 *T:* KJ Jones 2, ER John, J Matthews
C: BL Jones 3 *PG:* BL Jones
France 0
Referee: Capt MJ Dowling (Ireland)

	P	W	D	L	FOR	AGAINST	PTS
Wales	4	4	0	0	50	8	8
Scotland	4	2	0	2	21	49	4
Ireland	4	1	1	2	27	12	3
France	4	1	1	2	14	35	3
England	4	1	0	3	22	30	2

1950-51

13.01.1951 STADE COLOMBES, PARIS
France 14 *T:* L Mias, A Porthault *C:* J Prat *PG:* J Prat 2
Scotland 12 *T:* DM Rose *PG:* T Gray 2
Referee: TN Pearce (England)

20.01.1951 ST HELEN'S, SWANSEA
Wales 23 *T:* J Matthews 2, MC Thomas 2, KJ Jones
C: BL Jones 4
England 5 *T:* GC Rittson-Thomas *C:* EN Hewitt
Referee: Capt MJ Dowling (Ireland)

27.01.1951 LANSDOWNE ROAD, DUBLIN
Ireland 9 *T:* JE Nelson, T Clifford *PG:* NJ Henderson
France 8 *T:* D Olive, J Matheu *C:* P Bertrand
Referee: TN Pearce (England)

03.02.1951 MURRAYFIELD
Scotland 19 *T:* R Gordon 2, JC Dawson *C:* HM Inglis,
IHM Thomson *PG:* IHM Thomson *DG:* PW Kininmonth
Wales 0
Referee: Capt MJ Dowling (Ireland)

10.02.1951 LANSDOWNE ROAD, DUBLIN
Ireland 3 *PG:* D McKibbin
England 0
Referee: T Jones (Wales)

24.02.1951 TWICKENHAM
England 3 *T:* B Boobbyer
France 11 *T:* G Basquet, J Prat *C:* J Prat *DG:* J Prat
Referee: VS Llewellyn (Wales)

24.02.1951 MURRAYFIELD
Scotland 5 *T:* DA Sloan *C:* IHM Thomson
Ireland 6 *T:* DJ O'Brien *DG:* NJ Henderson
Referee: TN Pearce (England)

10.03.1951 CARDIFF ARMS PARK
Wales 3 *PG:* B Edwards
Ireland 3 *T:* JW Kyle
Referee: WCW Murdoch (Scotland)

17.03.1951 TWICKENHAM
England 5 *T:* DF White *C:* WG Hook
Scotland 3 *T:* A Cameron
Referee: Capt MJ Dowling (Ireland)

07.04.1951 STADE COLOMBES, PARIS
France 8 *T:* A Alvarez *C:* J Prat *PG:* A Alvarez
Wales 3 *T:* KJ Jones
Referee: Capt MJ Dowling (Ireland)

	P	W	D	L	FOR	AGAINST	PTS
Ireland	4	3	1	0	21	16	7
France	4	3	0	1	41	27	6
Wales	4	1	1	2	29	35	3
Scotland	4	1	0	3	39	25	2
England	4	1	0	3	13	40	2

1951-52

12.01.1952 MURRAYFIELD
Scotland 11 *T:* IF Cordial *C:* IHM Thomson
PG: IHM Thomson 2
France 13 *T:* J Prat, G Basquet *C:* J Prat 2 *PG:* J Prat
Referee: I David (Wales)

19.01.1952 TWICKENHAM
England 6 *T:* AE Agar, JE Woodward
Wales 8 *T:* KJ Jones 2 *C:* MC Thomas
Referee: NH Lambert (Ireland)

26.01.1952 STADE COLOMBES, PARIS
France 8 *T:* J Prat *C:* J Prat *PG:* J Prat
Ireland 11 *T:* NJ Henderson, JS McCarthy *C:* JR Notley
PG: NJ Henderson
Referee: TN Pearce (England)

02.02.1952 CARDIFF ARMS PARK
Wales 11 *T:* KJ Jones *C:* MC Thomas *PG:* MC Thomas 2
Scotland 0
Referee: Capt MJ Dowling (Ireland)

23.02.1952 LANSDOWNE ROAD, DUBLIN
Ireland 12 *T:* MF Lane, JW Kyle, NJ Henderson
PG: NJ Henderson
Scotland 8 *T:* JNG Davidson *C:* IHM Thomson
PG: IHM Thomson
Referee: I David (Wales)

08.03.1952 LANSDOWNE ROAD, DUBLIN
Ireland 3 *PG:* JGMW Murphy
Wales 14 *T:* RCC Thomas, KJ Jones, JRG Stephens
C: BL Jones *PG:* BL Jones
Referee: Dr PF Cooper (England)

15.03.1952 MURRAYFIELD
Scotland 3 *T:* J Johnston
England 19 *T:* E Evans, JMK Kendall-Carpenter,
CE Winn, JE Woodward *C:* NM Hall 2 *DG:* AE Agar
Referee: Capt MJ Dowling (Ireland)

22.03.1952 ST HELEN'S, SWANSEA
Wales 9 *PG:* BL Jones 2 *DG:* AG Thomas
France 5 *T:* M Pomathios *C:* J Prat
Referee: AWC Austin (Scotland)

29.03.1952 TWICKENHAM
England 3 *T:* B Boobbyer
Ireland 0
Referee: I David (Wales)

05.04.1952 STADE COLOMBES, PARIS
France 3 *T:* M Pomathios
England 6 *PG:* NM Hall 2
Referee: WCW Murdoch (Scotland)

	P	W	D	L	FOR	AGAINST	PTS
Wales	4	4	0	0	42	14	8
England	4	3	0	1	34	14	6
Ireland	4	2	0	2	26	33	4
France	4	1	0	3	29	37	2
Scotland	4	0	0	4	22	55	0

1952-53

10.01.1953 STADE COLOMBES, PARIS
France 11 *T:* J-R Bourdeu *C:* P Bertrand
PG: P Bertrand *DG:* J Carabignac
Scotland 5 *T:* DM Rose *C:* NW Cameron
Referee: OB Glasgow (Ireland)

17.01.1953 CARDIFF ARMS PARK
Wales 3 *PG:* TJ Davies
England 8 *T:* LB Cannell *C:* NM Hall *PG:* JE Woodward
Referee: Capt MJ Dowling (Ireland)

24.01.1953 RAVENHILL, BELFAST
Ireland 16 *T:* PJ Lawler, JS McCarthy, JW Kyle,
M Mortell *C:* RJ Gregg 2
France 3 *DG:* J Carabignac
Referee: TE Priest (England)

07.02.1953 MURRAYFIELD
Scotland 0
Wales 12 *T:* BL Williams 2, KJ Jones *PG:* TJ Davies
Referee: Dr PF Cooper (England)

14.02.1953 LANSDOWNE ROAD, DUBLIN
Ireland 9 *T:* M Mortell *PG:* NJ Henderson 2
England 9 *T:* E Evans *PG:* NM Hall 2
Referee: AWC Austin (Scotland)

28.02.1953 TWICKENHAM
England 11 *T:* J Butterfield, E Evans, JE Woodward
C: NM Hall
France 0
Referee: VJ Parfitt (Wales)

28.02.1953 MURRAYFIELD
Scotland 8 *T:* JH Henderson *C:* IHM Thomson
PG: IHM Thomson
Ireland 26 *T:* SJ Byrne 3, JS McCarthy, M Mortell,
JR Kavanagh *C:* RJ Gregg 4
Referee: I David (Wales)

14.03.1953 ST HELEN'S, SWANSEA
Wales 5 *T:* GM Griffiths *C:* TJ Davies
Ireland 3 *T:* AC Pedlow
Referee: Dr PF Cooper (England)

21.03.1953 TWICKENHAM
England 26 *T:* RC Bazley 2, SJ Adkins, J Butterfield, RV Stirling, JE Woodward *C:* NM Hall 4
Scotland 8 *T:* JH Henderson, TG Weatherstone *C:* IHM Thomson
Referee: Capt MJ Dowling (Ireland)

28.03.1953 STADE COLOMBES, PARIS
France 3 *PG:* P Bertrand
Wales 6 *T:* GM Griffiths 2
Referee: OB Glasgow (Ireland)

	P	W	D	L	FOR	AGAINST	PTS
England	4	3	1	0	54	20	7
Wales	4	3	0	1	26	14	6
Ireland	4	2	1	1	54	25	5
France	4	1	0	3	17	38	2
Scotland	4	0	0	4	21	75	0

1953-54

09.01.1954 MURRAYFIELD
Scotland 0
France 3 *T:* R Brejassou
Referee: I David (Wales)

16.01.1954 TWICKENHAM
England 9 *T:* JE Woodward 2, CE Winn
Wales 6 *T:* G Rowlands *PG:* G Rowlands
Referee: Capt MJ Dowling (Ireland)

23.01.1954 STADE COLOMBES, PARIS
France 8 *T:* M Prat 2 *C:* J Prat
Ireland 0
Referee: AI Dickie (Scotland)

13.02.1954 TWICKENHAM
England 14 *T:* J Butterfield, M Regan, DS Wilson *C:* I King *PG:* I King
Ireland 3 *PG:* J Murphy-O'Connor
Referee: AI Dickie (Scotland)

27.02.1954 RAVENHILL, BELFAST
Ireland 6 *T:* M Mortell 2
Scotland 0
Referee: VJ Parfitt (Wales)

13.03.1954 LANSDOWNE ROAD, DUBLIN
Ireland 9 *T:* JT Gaston *PG:* NJ Henderson, S Kelly
Wales 12 *PG:* V Evans 3 *DG:* D Thomas
Referee: AWC Austin (Scotland)

20.03.1954 MURRAYFIELD
Scotland 3 *T:* MK Elgie
England 13 *T:* DS Wilson 2, PD Young *C:* N Gibbs 2
Referee: OB Glasgow (Ireland)

27.03.1954 CARDIFF ARMS PARK
Wales 19 *T:* GM Griffiths, WOG Williams *C:* V Evans 2 *PG:* V Evans 3
France 13 *T:* R Martine, R Baulon *C:* J Prat 2 *PG:* J Prat
Referee: AI Dickie (Scotland)

10.04.1954 STADE COLOMBES, PARIS
France 11 *T:* A Boniface, M Prat *C:* J Prat *DG:* J Prat
England 3 *T:* DS Wilson
Referee: I David (Wales)

10.04.1954 ST HELEN'S, SWANSEA
Wales 15 *T:* WOG Williams, Ray Williams, BV Meredith, CI Morgan *PG:* V Evans
Scotland 3 *T:* JH Henderson
Referee: Dr PF Cooper (England)

	P	W	D	L	FOR	AGAINST	PTS
Wales	4	3	0	1	52	34	6
England	4	3	0	1	39	23	6
France	4	3	0	1	35	22	6
Ireland	4	1	0	3	18	34	2
Scotland	4	0	0	4	6	37	0

1954-55

08.01.1955 STADE COLOMBES, PARIS
France 15 *T:* A Boniface, J Prat, A Domenech, G Dufau *PG:* M Vannier
Scotland 0
Referee: HB Elliott (England)

22.01.1955 LANSDOWNE ROAD, DUBLIN
Ireland 3 *PG:* NJ Henderson
France 5 *T:* A Domenech *C:* M Vannier
Referee: I David (Wales)

22.01.1955 CARDIFF ARMS PARK
Wales 3 *PG:* AB Edwards
England 0
Referee: OB Glasgow (Ireland)

05.02.1955 MURRAYFIELD
Scotland 14 *T:* AR Smith, JA Nichol *C:* MK Elgie *PG:* MK Elgie *DG:* JT Docherty
Wales 8 *T:* TJ Brewer 2 *C:* JRG Stephens
Referee: Capt MJ Dowling (Ireland)

12.02.1955 LANSDOWNE ROAD, DUBLIN
Ireland 6 *T:* AJF O'Reilly *PG:* NJ Henderson
England 6 *T:* J Butterfield, GWD Hastings
Referee: AI Dickie (Scotland)

26.02.1955 TWICKENHAM
England 9 *T:* R Higgins *PG:* DStG Hazell 2
France 16 *T:* R Baulon, M Celaya *C:* M Vannier 2 *DG:* J Prat 2
Referee: R Mitchell (Ireland)

26.02.1955 MURRAYFIELD
Scotland 12 *T:* JS Swan *PG:* MK Elgie 2 *DG:* A Cameron
Ireland 3 *PG:* S Kelly
Referee: LM Boundy (England)

12.03.1955 CARDIFF ARMS PARK
Wales 21 *T:* CC Meredith, GM Griffiths, CI Morgan, HT Morris *C:* G Owen 3 *PG:* G Owen
Ireland 3 *PG:* NJ Henderson
Referee: AI Dickie (Scotland)

19.03.1955 TWICKENHAM
England 9 *T:* IDS Beer, FD Sykes *PG:* DStG Hazell
Scotland 6 *T:* A Cameron *PG:* A Cameron
Referee: DC Joynson (Wales)

26.03.1955 STADE COLOMBES, PARIS
France 11 *T:* R Baulon *C:* M Vannier *PG:* M Vannier *DG:* M Prat
Wales 16 *T:* AG Thomas, HT Morris *C:* G Owen 2 *PG:* G Owen 2
Referee: OB Glasgow (Ireland)

	P	W	D	L	FOR	AGAINST	PTS
Wales	4	3	0	1	48	28	6
France	4	3	0	1	47	28	6
Scotland	4	2	0	2	32	35	4
England	4	1	1	2	24	31	3
Ireland	4	0	1	3	15	44	1

1955-56

14.01.1956 MURRAYFIELD
Scotland 12 *T:* JWY Kemp 2 *PG:* AR Smith, A Cameron
France 0
Referee: Capt MJ Dowling (Ireland)

21.01.1956 TWICKENHAM
England 3 *PG:* DF Allison
Wales 8 *T:* CL Davies, RJ Robins *C:* G Owen
Referee: R Mitchell (Ireland)

28.01.1956 STADE COLOMBES, PARIS
France 14 *T:* A Boniface, R Baulon *C:* M Vannier *DG:* M Vannier, J Bouquet
Ireland 8 *T:* AJF O'Reilly *C:* AC Pedlow *PG:* AC Pedlow
Referee: Dr PF Cooper (England)

04.02.1956 CARDIFF ARMS PARK
Wales 9 *T:* HP Morgan, CI Morgan, CL Davies
Scotland 3 *PG:* A Cameron
Referee: LM Boundy (England)

11.02.1956 TWICKENHAM
England 20 *T:* J Butterfield, E Evans, PB Jackson *C:* JD Currie *PG:* JD Currie 2, DF Allison
Ireland 0
Referee: AI Dickie (Scotland)

25.02.1956 LANSDOWNE ROAD, DUBLIN
Ireland 14 *T:* NJ Henderson, AJF O'Reilly, JW Kyle, JA O'Meara *C:* AC Pedlow
Scotland 10 *T:* EJS Michie, AR Smith *C:* T McClung 2
Referee: HB Elliott (England)

10.03.1956 LANSDOWNE ROAD, DUBLIN
Ireland 11 *T:* MJ Cunningham *C:* AC Pedlow *PG:* AC Pedlow *DG:* JW Kyle
Wales 3 *PG:* G Owen
Referee: AI Dickie (Scotland)

17.03.1956 MURRAYFIELD
Scotland 6 *T:* GD Stevenson *PG:* AR Smith
England 11 *T:* JE Williams *C:* JD Currie *PG:* JD Currie 2
Referee: Capt MJ Dowling (Ireland)

24.03.1956 CARDIFF ARMS PARK
Wales 5 *T:* CD Williams *C:* G Owen
France 3 *T:* J Bouquet
Referee: Dr PF Cooper (England)

14.04.1956 STADE COLOMBES, PARIS
France 14 *T:* J Dupuy, G Pauthe *C:* A Labazuy *PG:* A Labazuy 2
England 9 *T:* PH Thompson *PG:* DF Allison 2
Referee: I David (Wales)

	P	W	D	L	FOR	AGAINST	PTS
Wales	4	3	0	1	25	20	6
England	4	2	0	2	43	28	4
Ireland	4	2	0	2	33	47	4
France	4	2	0	2	31	34	4
Scotland	4	1	0	3	31	34	2

1956-57

12.01.1957 STADE COLOMBES, PARIS
France 0
Scotland 6 *PG:* KJF Scotland *DG:* KJF Scotland
Referee: LM Boundy (England)

19.01.1957 CARDIFF ARMS PARK
Wales 0
England 3 *PG:* DF Allison
Referee: AI Dickie (Scotland)

26.01.1957 LANSDOWNE ROAD, DUBLIN
Ireland 11 *T:* NH Brophy, JW Kyle *C:* AC Pedlow *PG:* AC Pedlow
France 6 *PG:* M Vannier 2
Referee: LM Boundy (England)

02.02.1957 MURRAYFIELD
Scotland 9 *T:* AR Smith *PG:* KJF Scotland *DG:* AF Dorward
Wales 6 *T:* RH Davies *PG:* TJ Davies
Referee: RC Williams (Ireland)

Five Nations Results 1950-59

09.02.1957 LANSDOWNE ROAD, DUBLIN
Ireland 0
England 6 *T:* PB Jackson *PG:* R Challis
Referee: AI Dickie (Scotland)

23.02.1957 TWICKENHAM
England 9 *T:* PB Jackson 2, E Evans
France 5 *T:* C Darrouy *C:* M Vannier
Referee: RC Williams (Ireland)

23.02.1957 MURRAYFIELD
Scotland 3 *PG:* KJF Scotland
Ireland 5 *T:* PJA O'Sullivan *C:* PJ Berkery
Referee: LM Boundy (England)

09.03.1957 CARDIFF ARMS PARK
Wales 6 *PG:* TJ Davies 2
Ireland 5 *T:* JR Kavanagh *C:* AC Pedlow
Referee: JAS Taylor (Scotland)

16.03.1957 TWICKENHAM
England 16 *T:* WPC Davies, R Higgins, PH Thompson
C: R Challis 2 *PG:* R Challis
Scotland 3 *PG:* KJF Scotland
Referee: R Mitchell (Ireland)

23.03.1957 STADE COLOMBES, PARIS
France 13 *T:* J Dupuy, M Prat, A Sanac *C:* J Bouquet 2
Wales 19 *T:* R Prosser, G Howells, J Faull, BV Meredith
C: TJ Davies 2 *PG:* TJ Davies
Referee: Dr PF Cooper (England)

	P	W	D	L	FOR	AGAINST	PTS
England	4	4	0	0	34	8	8
Wales	4	2	0	2	31	30	4
Ireland	4	2	0	2	21	21	4
Scotland	4	2	0	2	21	27	4
France	4	0	0	4	24	45	0

1957-58

11.01.1958 MURRAYFIELD
Scotland 11 *T:* GD Stevenson, IR Hastie
C: RWT Chisholm *PG:* RWT Chisholm
France 9 *T:* J Dupuy *PG:* M Vannier 2
Referee: LM Boundy (England)

18.01.1958 TWICKENHAM
England 3 *T:* PH Thompson
Wales 3 *PG:* TJ Davies
Referee: RC Williams (Ireland)

01.02.1958 CARDIFF ARMS PARK
Wales 8 *T:* GT Wells, JR Collins *C:* TJ Davies
Scotland 3 *PG:* AR Smith
Referee: Dr NM Parkes (England)

08.02.1958 TWICKENHAM
England 6 *T:* A Ashcroft *PG:* JGG Hetherington
Ireland 0
Referee: G Burrell (Scotland)

01.03.1958 STADE COLOMBES, PARIS
France 0
England 14 *T:* PH Thompson 2, PB Jackson
C: GWD Hastings *PG:* GWD Hastings
Referee: WJ Evans (Wales)

01.03.1958 LANSDOWNE ROAD, DUBLIN
Ireland 12 *T:* AC Pedlow 2 *PG:* NJ Henderson,
PJ Berkery
Scotland 6 *T:* AR Smith, TG Weatherstone
Referee: WN Gillmore (England)

15.03.1958 LANSDOWNE ROAD, DUBLIN
Ireland 6 *T:* JA O'Meara *PG:* NJ Henderson
Wales 9 *T:* HJ Morgan, BV Meredith, C Roberts
Referee: Dr NM Parkes (England)

15.03.1958 MURRAYFIELD
Scotland 3 *PG:* C Elliot
England 3 *PG:* GWD Hastings
Referee: RC Williams (Ireland)

29.03.1958 CARDIFF ARMS PARK
Wales 6 *T:* JR Collins *PG:* TJ Davies
France 16 *T:* P Danos, P Tarricq *C:* A Labazuy 2
DG: M Vannier 2
Referee: AI Dickie (Scotland)

19.04.1958 STADE COLOMBES, PARIS
France 11 *T:* P Danos *C:* A Labazuy *PG:* A Labazuy
DG: M Vannier
Ireland 6 *PG:* NJ Henderson 2
Referee: Dr NM Parkes (England)

	P	W	D	L	FOR	AGAINST	PTS
England	4	2	2	0	26	6	6
Wales	4	2	1	1	26	28	5
France	4	2	0	2	36	37	4
Scotland	4	1	1	2	23	32	3
Ireland	4	1	0	3	24	32	2

1958-59

10.01.1959 STADE COLOMBES, PARIS
France 9 *T:* F Moncla *DG:* P Lacaze 2
Scotland 0
Referee: DG Walters (Wales)

17.01.1959 CARDIFF ARMS PARK
Wales 5 *T:* DIE Bebb *C:* TJ Davies
England 0
Referee: RC Williams (Ireland)

07.02.1959 MURRAYFIELD
Scotland 6 *T:* NS Bruce *PG:* KJF Scotland
Wales 6 *T:* MJ Price *C:* TJ Davies
Referee: RC Williams (Ireland)

14.02.1959 LANSDOWNE ROAD, DUBLIN
Ireland 0
England 3 *PG:* ABW Risman
Referee: DG Walters (Wales)

28.02.1959 TWICKENHAM
England 3 *PG:* JGG Hetherington
France 3 *PG:* A Labazuy
Referee: RC Williams (Ireland)

28.02.1959 MURRAYFIELD
Scotland 3 *PG:* KJF Scotland
Ireland 8 *T:* JF Dooley *C:* D Hewitt *PG:* D Hewitt
Referee: LM Boundy (England)

14.03.1959 CARDIFF ARMS PARK
Wales 8 *T:* C Ashton, MJ Price *C:* TJ Davies
Ireland 6 *T:* AJF O'Reilly *PG:* D Hewitt
Referee: G Burrell (Scotland)

21.03.1959 TWICKENHAM
England 3 *PG:* ABW Risman
Scotland 3 *PG:* KJF Scotland
Referee: DG Walters (Wales)

04.04.1959 STADE COLOMBES, PARIS
France 11 *T:* F Moncla 2 *C:* A Labazuy *PG:* A Labazuy
Wales 3 *PG:* TJ Davies
Referee: Dr NM Parkes (England)

18.04.1959 LANSDOWNE ROAD, DUBLIN
Ireland 9 *T:* NH Brophy *PG:* D Hewitt
DG: MAF English
France 5 *T:* J Dupuy *C:* P Lacaze
Referee: DG Walters (Wales)

	P	W	D	L	FOR	AGAINST	PTS
France	4	2	1	1	28	15	5
Ireland	4	2	0	2	23	19	4
Wales	4	2	0	2	21	23	4
England	4	1	2	1	9	11	4
Scotland	4	1	1	2	12	25	3

"

The Swinging Sixties?
Perhaps swinging from a
rope if you were an
England fan.

"

1960s

The Swinging Sixties? Perhaps swinging from a rope if you were an England fan. It was to be a fallow decade for those in white, with a lone outright championship title to their credit in 1963, the year in which they famously triumphed in Cardiff, 13-6. So famously, in fact, that virtually every one of that side was to find himself being interviewed for years to come about England's exploits on that bitterly cold day long ago. Little did anyone realise at the time that it would be another 28 years before England were to cross into Wales without fear in their souls and with the prospect of victory on the horizon. It was to be an astonishingly barren run.

The portents had not been too doom-laden. True, there were seven new caps introduced for the opening match of the first season of the decade. However, one of them, the redoubtable Don Rutherford, helped propel England into a 14-0 lead against Wales in the curtain-raiser at Twickenham, while the arrival on the international scene of another, fly half Richard Sharp, was to generate memories that lasted through many a dark winter.

England, in fact, went unchanged throughout that campaign, one that saw them finish level with France at the top of the table with seven points. England secured a Triple Crown on the strength of an uplifting 21-12 victory at Murrayfield in their final game, three tries contributing to their highest points total in an international in seven years. The fast, reliable service of captain Dickie Jeeps at scrum half made best use of the glut of possession secured by a pack in which, once again, those Harlequins buddies-in-arms David Marques and John 'Muscles' Currie were to the fore. Rivals in their Oxbridge days, the pair were a formidable partnership.

And yet so much England promise yielded so little in tangible terms across the ensuing years, the 1963 achievement excepted. Instead it was to be the tricolour that flew proudly. Although England did manage to trade on level terms at the start of the decade, sharing two

RIGHT A good start to the 1960s: Don Rutherford lands his second penalty to increase England's lead against Wales at Twickenham in 1960.
FACING PAGE TOP Caricaturist John Ireland captures the deceptive speed of Richard Sharp. BOTTOM The French laid on some lavish hospitality for the England team after their 3-3 draw in Paris in 1960: the illustrated cover for the menu and the programme for the evening ahead.

draws in 1960 and 1961, they could not match France's record for the period in terms of titles. The French began the 1960s by adding to their success of 1959 with three further titles in succession, including the shared spoils of 1960, no mean feat for the last of the sides to be admitted to the brotherhood and for a country that had seen such turbulent times. And there was more to come for France, including their first ever Grand Slam in 1968.

The musketeer mentality prevailed, and how could it not under the charismatic leadership of the indomitable Racing Club and Lourdes flanker Michel Crauste. An engaging captain, Crauste was blessed with an even temperament and a strong, magnetic personality and led his country 22 times between 1961 and 1966. In 1962, Crauste scored a hat-trick of tries in the 13-0 victory over England at Stade Colombes. It was the first time a forward had touched down three times in a championship match since before France entered the competition – since 1903, in fact. When he left the international scene in 1966, Crauste had set a new French appearance record, having won 63 caps.

Richard Sharp

There were other characters to savour, among them Pierre 'Monsieur Le Drop' Albaladejo, who revealed his signature play when landing three dropped goals against Ireland in the 23-6 victory at Stade Colombes in 1960, the first time the feat had been achieved in the championship. Having played two internationals in 1954, Albaladejo had been recalled for the previous match against Wales; he bowed out in 1964. Although Jonny Wilkinson may be the player most associated with dropping goals in modern times, it was Albaladejo who raised the art to a new level. His legend lives on in his home town of Dax.

Two pairs of French brothers, the Camberaberos and the Bonifaces, were also to make their mark in the 1960s. The former were a half-back combination – Lilian at scrum half and elder

ENGLAND			FRANCE
15. J. G. WILLCOX Oxford University & Lancashire	FULL BACKS	15. ¹P. DEDIEU Béziers	
	THREE-QUARTERS		
14. P. B. JACKSON Coventry & Warwickshire	RIGHT WING	LEFT WING	11. C. DARROUY Mont-de-Marsan
13. M. S. PHILLIPS Fylde & Lancashire	RIGHT CENTRE	LEFT CENTRE	12. A. BONIFACE Mont-de-Marsan
12. M. P. WESTON Durham City & Durham	LEFT CENTRE	RIGHT CENTRE	13. G. BONIFACE Mont-de-Marsan
11. J. ROBERTS Sale & Middlesex	LEFT WING	RIGHT WING	14. P. BESSON Brive
	HALF BACKS		
10. R. A. W. SHARP Wasps & Cornwall (CAPTAIN)	STAND-OFF	10. P. ALBALADEJO Dax	
9. S. J. S. CLARKE Cambridge University & Sussex	SCRUM	9. P. LACROIX Agen (CAPTAIN)	
	FORWARDS		
1. ¹K. J. WILSON Gloucester & Gloucestershire		1. F. MAS Béziers	
2. J. D. THORNE Bristol & Gloucestershire		2. J. ROLLET Bayonne	
3. N. J. DRAKE-LEE Cambridge Univ. & Leicestershire		3. F. ZAGO Montauban	
4. T. A. PARGETTER Coventry & Warwickshire		4. M. LIRA La Voulte	
5. J. E. OWEN Coventry & Warwickshire	Referee: Mr. D. C. J. McMAHON (Scotland)	5. J.-P. SAUX Pau	
7. D. P. ROGERS Bedford & East Midlands		6. J. FABRE Toulouse Stadium	
8. ¹D. G. PERRY Bedford & Surrey	KICK-OFF 2.30 p.m.	8. H. ROMERO Montauban	
6. D. C. MANLEY Exeter & Devon	¹ A New Cap	7. M. CRAUSTE Lourdes	
Touch Judge: Mr. J. W. BLAKE (Northumberland) 14		Touch Judge: Msr. M. LAURENT (F.F.R.) 15	

brother Guy at stand-off. André and Guy Boniface, on the other hand, were a centre pairing, and were to be a pivotal part of the French attack, partnering one another a then world record 18 times in internationals, although not all those matches were against member countries of the IRFB (which comprised only the 'big eight' until 1987). André was older by three years and played for France for 13 seasons from 1954, while Guy started his Test career in 1960; both left international rugby after the Wales match of 1966. The Bonifaces played for Mont-de-Marsan, and the grief to be found in that town at news of Guy's death in a car crash on New Year's Day 1968, aged just 30, spread throughout the rugby world.

Meanwhile, another Mont-de-Marsan man, Christian Darrouy, was to create ripples of admiration around Europe with his clever, elusive play on the French wing. He made his debut as a 20-year-old in 1957 against Ireland, and was to score a hat-trick against them in 1963. Darrouy, who ended his international career as captain of France on the 1967 tour of South Africa, was his country's leading try scorer with 23 at the time of his retirement.

But enough of France. It was not they alone who etched traces of glory across the decade. So, too, did Wales. They won three titles outright and shared the honours with Scotland in 1964. By the end of the decade the signs were clear, a generation rich in talent, character and skill – nay, genius – was about to be revealed in all its finery. That Wales won the title in 1969 was a portent of things to come. They closed out the deal with a thumping 30-9 victory over England in Cardiff, with local hero Maurice Richards on the wing scoring four tries to equal the Welsh individual record for a single match. The other try came from a trademark ghosting run from fly half Barry John. His partnership with Gareth Edwards was approaching double figures by that time: assured, authoritative and potent, there was probably never a finer half-back duo in the history of the game. How fans delighted in their presence. How opposition back rows plotted and fretted.

By that stage, J.P.R. Williams and Mervyn Davies, too, were coming through; they were in their first international season in 1969, both having made their

Barry John

Gareth Edwards

debuts against Scotland at Murrayfield. As these two made their grand entrance, one of sport's great figures, Keith Jarrett, was about to depart stage left. Jarrett still has iconic status in Wales. How many others have scored 19 points on debut – equalling the then record individual tally for Wales in an international – and against England? Rarely has a single game become so laden with myth-making potential, Jarrett's extraordinary feat helping bring about Wales's only victory of the 1967 campaign. His try from 40 metres was spoken of in reverential tones for many a year. Wales were in flux and had seemingly found a new hero. Those bearing cheque books from

LEFT Welsh legend Keith Jarrett, who almost single-handedly destroyed England on his debut at Cardiff in 1967, converts yet another goal-kick attempt on that memorable occasion. FACING PAGE TOP An impressive line-up for France in 1963. Yet although there was a try for Guy Boniface, converted by Pierre Albaladejo, England won by a single point thanks to two penalties from John Willcox. BOTTOM Barry John and Gareth Edwards, whose golden partnership was well established by the end of the decade.

the north obviously thought so, too, for in 1969 Jarrett was lured away to rugby league by Barrow. But the legend lived on. In that final season, Jarrett ended his time in a Wales union shirt with a national season record 31 points in the championship.

There were so many others to assume the mantle left behind by Jarrett. In that sensational 34-21 victory of 1967, two tries were registered by a certain T.G.R. Davies. Switching from centre in summer 1969, Gerald Davies was to become one of the finest wings not only of his generation but in history, with his jinking and swerving and his shirt worn collar up. He remains also one of the sport's real ambassadors, a gent in every sense. By the time he retired in 1978, Davies had scored a national record 20 tries, a mark shared with Gareth Edwards that stood until surpassed by Ieuan Evans in 1994.

The Arms Park underwent a significant rebuild after the 1967 England game. As the stadium took on a new face, so too did the side itself. Wales closed out the decade with a Triple Crown and championship under the studied tutelage of Clive Rowlands. The benefits of bringing the players together for squad sessions paid off handsomely. Squad sessions are now the norm, of course, but Rowlands helped create the template.

There was little succour for the Scots and Irish throughout the decade. The dismal pattern was set early for Ireland, who in 1960 lost all four games for the first time in 40 years, collecting the Wooden Spoon in what was Tom Kiernan's debut season. Scotland, at least, had a share of the title in 1964 to boost spirits. They won three games, more than Wales, but lost the key match in Cardiff, 11-3.

ENGLAND v WALES IN THE EARLY 1960s.
ABOVE RIGHT *Prime Minister Sir Alec Douglas-Home is introduced to Wales captain Clive Rowlands at Twickenham in 1964. Rowlands was to mastermind a revival in Welsh fortunes. However, four years earlier (right and above) it had been somewhat different, England new caps Don Rutherford and Jim Roberts combining to inflict a 14-6 defeat on the Welsh.* **BELOW** *A commiserating pat on the back for the Welsh players as they leave the field at the end of that 1960 game.*

ENGLAND

1. ¹D. RUTHERFORD — Percy Park
2. J. R. C. YOUNG — Harlequins
3. M. S. PHILLIPS — Oxford University
4. ¹M. P. WESTON — Richmond
5. ¹J. ROBERTS — Old Millhillians & Sale
6. A. B. W. RISMAN — Manchester University
7. R. E. G. JEEPS — Northampton (CAPTAIN)
8. L. H. WEBB — Bedford
9. ¹S. A. M. HODGSON — Durham City
10. ¹P. T. WRIGHT — Blackheath
11. R. W. D. MARQUES — Harlequins
12. J. D. CURRIE — Harlequins
13. P. G. D. ROBBINS — Moseley
14. ¹W. G. D. MORGAN — Medicals
15. R. E. SYRETT — Wasps

Touch Judge: MR. R. J. TODD (Hampshire)
14

FULL BACKS
THREE-QUARTERS
RIGHT WING / LEFT WING
RIGHT CENTRE / LEFT CENTRE
LEFT CENTRE / RIGHT CENTRE
LEFT WING / RIGHT WING
HALF BACKS
STAND OFF
SCRUM
FORWARDS

Referee
Mr. J. A. S. TAYLOR (Scotland)

KICK-OFF 2.30 P.M.

¹ A new cap

WALES

1. T. E. DAVIES — Llanelly
5. D. BEBB — Carmarthen T.C. & Swansea
4. ¹G. WINDSOR LEWIS — Richmond
3. M. J. PRICE — R.A.F. & Pontypool
2. J. COLLINS — Aberavon
6. C. ASHTON — Aberavon
7. ¹C. EVANS — Pontypool
8. R. PROSSER — Pontypool
9. B. V. MEREDITH — Newport
10. L. J. CUNNINGHAM — Aberavon
11. ¹G. W. PAYNE — Army & Pontypridd
12. R. H. WILLIAMS — Llanelly (CAPTAIN)
13. ¹B. CRESSWELL — Newport
14. J. FAULL — Swansea
15. H. J. MORGAN — Abertillery

Touch Judge: MR. D. M. HUGHES (Llanelly)
15

If the 1960s were intent on swinging on the cultural front, then rugby wanted a piece of the action, too. The 1960 championship boasted 31 tries and 187 points, the best tally since 1931. England played a part. After failing to score a try in the previous championship, they managed seven this time around, with wing Jim Roberts of Old Millhillians scoring three of them, two on debut against Wales in England's championship opener. Encouraged by the inventive, challenging play of Richard Sharp, England then racked up 21 points to Scotland's 12 at Murrayfield. (They were not to surpass 21 points in Edinburgh until Bill Beaumont's side scored 30 in 1980.) That emphatic win brought a fourteenth Triple Crown for England. Yet after a narrow 8-5 win over Ireland at Twickenham, England had had their eyes on a clean sweep, only to stumble against France. They had to make do with a share of the spoils in Paris (and eventually in the championship overall), Mike Weston scoring the only try of the game in a 3-3 draw. Michel Vannier kicked a penalty for France. Don Rutherford showed well at full back, as did the back row of Morgan, Robbins and Syrett. Stern defence was the order of the day.

Any hopes England harboured of taking the championship outright the following season quickly evaporated. Beaten 5-0 by South Africa at Twickenham in early January, England then subsided to defeats in their opening two rounds of the Five Nations, losing 6-3 in Cardiff and then going down 11-8 at Lansdowne Road. England could at least hold their heads high when France came to Twickenham, playing out a creditable 5-5 draw against the eventual champions. Torrential rain took a role in proceedings, with defences dominating. Cambridge University lock Vic Harding opened the scoring with a try on debut, John Willcox converting. Five minutes later, though, Crauste's try was converted by Vannier.

During this tournament, the England selectors got themselves into a bit of a pickle over the relative merits of the available fly halves. In the event, they began with Bev Risman, then compromised by reintroducing Richard Sharp and moving Risman to centre. Risman, however, was to move to rugby league by the end of the championship, with Phil Horrocks-Taylor stepping into the fly half breach for the final game against Scotland, Sharp being unavailable through injury. Horrocks-Taylor landed a penalty to complement the try scored by Jim Roberts in a 6-0 victory. Scotland had come to Twickenham looking for their first win there since 1938 and with a Triple Crown on the line, but England held firm.

For their part France didn't even have to worry about their final game, having wrapped up their third successive championship before the side headed to Lansdowne Road. They rounded off in style, however, beating Ireland 15-3. The key game for the French had been the previous one, a hard-fought 8-6 win over Wales in Paris. Wales led 6-3 with tries

BELOW The England team originally selected to play Scotland in 1961. Back row (left to right): M.P. Weston, T.P. Wright, J.G. Willcox, W.G.D. Morgan, V.S.J. Harding, R.J. French, D.P. Rogers, L.I. Rimmer. Front row: R.A.W. Sharp, J. Roberts, E. Robinson, R.E.G. Jeeps (capt), C.R. Jacobs, J.R.C. Young, A.B.W. Risman. To illustrate the problems facing the England selectors that year, three of these players were not in the side that eventually took the field a few days later. Bev Risman was replaced by Bill Patterson, Phil Horrocks-Taylor took over from Richard Sharp and Peter Jackson came in for John Young.

either side of the interval from Alun Pask, in his first international, and Dewi Bebb before Guy Boniface levelled the scores. Michel Vannier converted to nudge France towards the title. In general, this Five Nations campaign was characterised by the large number of players tried out by the various countries. Only Scotland managed to keep the same side for two matches in a row. Wales led the way with 26 players used; England and Ireland fielded 25 and 23 respectively.

French domination continued in 1962, splendid wins at Murrayfield (11-3) and against England (13-0), during which Crauste roamed free in scoring a hat-trick, setting up France as worthy champions. However, if France had earlier captured the imagination with their verve and brio in attack, then it was their defence which impressed in 1962. They conceded only six points in the championship, both from kicks. If that was miserly defence at its meanest, then the attacking productivity of Wales and Ireland was correspondingly minimalist. These countries scored only 18 points between them in eight matches, nine apiece – a pitiful return.

Yet Wales it was who dented France's Grand Slam ambitions, Kel Coslett landing the penalty goal that led to France's first reverse in the championship since 1959. Wales won that match just 3-0, and indeed in the 1962 tournament failed to score a try for the first time since 1889. The Wooden Spoon was not decided until the autumn, the original Ireland v Wales game being postponed from its original date in March after an outbreak of smallpox in the Rhondda Valley. The match was drawn 3-3, with Ireland finishing bottom of the table with just a solitary point.

At the end of the 1962 season, England bade farewell to a distinguished player, Dickie Jeeps, who brought down the curtain on a fine career but not before participating that summer in his third Lions tour. Jeeps had made his England bow in 1956, having already made four Test

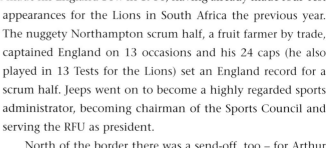

appearances for the Lions in South Africa the previous year. The nuggety Northampton scrum half, a fruit farmer by trade, captained England on 13 occasions and his 24 caps (he also played in 13 Tests for the Lions) set an England record for a scrum half. Jeeps went on to become a highly regarded sports administrator, becoming chairman of the Sports Council and serving the RFU as president.

North of the border there was a send-off, too – for Arthur Smith, who scored two tries against Ireland on his penultimate appearance for his country and helped them finish outright second that year, their best placing since 1950. Like Jeeps, Smith went with the Lions to South Africa in 1962, having also been in the 1955 party; indeed this time he was tour captain, adding three Tests as Lions skipper to his 15 as captain of Scotland out of a total of 36 internationals. Immensely gifted academically as well as in the field of sport, Arthur Smith died from cancer in 1975 at the tragically young age of 42.

The 1963 championship-winning England side were a durable lot, as their final points difference of just ten showed.

BELOW Dickie Jeeps enjoys the close attention of prop Amédée Domenech in England's 5-5 draw with France in 1961.
FACING PAGE TOP The free-running Michel Crauste, who scored the French try, sets up another attack in the same game. BOTTOM Scotland captain and right wing Arthur Smith, on his last visit to Twickenham, is brought down by Mike Weston in England's 6-0 Calcutta Cup win in 1961.

LEFT New cap John Owen, who also scored in the game, wins a line out against Wales in England's win in Cardiff in 1963. ABOVE André Boniface makes a break for France, but England edged home 6-5 at Headquarters on their way to winning the 1963 championship. BELOW M. James, the Welsh touch judge, looks delighted as Dewi Bebb scores against England at Twickenham in 1964.

LEFT The 1963 England team to face the French at Twickenham. Back row (left to right): J.D. Thorne, K.J. Wilson, D.P. Rogers, M.P. Weston, T.A. Pargetter, D.G. Perry, J.E. Owen, D.C. Manley, N.J. Drake-Lee, D.C.J. McMahon (referee). Front row: M.S. Phillips, P.B. Jackson, R.A.W. Sharp (capt), J. Roberts, J.G. Willcox, S.J.S. Clarke.

The margins of victory were generally narrow and success had to be earned. Their biggest win came in their opening game, that landmark win in Cardiff. On a bitterly cold day, England warmed the cockles of their travelling fans' hearts with a grafting 13-6 victory. England's seven new caps did them proud, none more so than debutant Coventry lock John Owen, who scored one of England's two tries; Fylde centre Malcolm Phillips touched down for the other.

The England pack was callow beyond belief. Not only were there six new caps but of the remaining two forwards Brian Wightman was making only his second appearance, while Budge Rogers was the veteran with seven caps to his name. Wales fielded six new caps themselves but did not gel as well as England did. Dai Hayward's try came too late to affect the outcome.

England's chances of a Grand Slam disappeared in the Dublin mud, a scoreless draw doing little to lift the spirits. After a narrow 6-5 win over France at Twickenham, victory chiselled out by two penalty kicks from full back John Willcox, England finished the campaign with a 10-8 Calcutta Cup victory at Twickenham. It was Sharp who turned the game England's way, the captain selling three dummies en route to the try line to round off his championship career with a memorable score. Willcox converted and England were home, just.

It was a fitting finale to the championship careers of two other England stalwarts, wings Peter Jackson and Jim Roberts. Jackson bowed out of international rugby altogether after the match, and although Sharp was to be recalled to the colours against Australia in 1967 and Roberts played against New Zealand in 1964, the 1963 Calcutta Cup match was the last time England supporters were to see this trio in action in the Five Nations. They were to be missed. England were to win only two of their next 17 internationals. And to think that there were some who doubted Sharp. He later became a schoolmaster at Sherborne and a correspondent on *The Sunday Telegraph*.

ABOVE The programme line-up for England v Ireland in 1964 shows the debutant Mike Gibson at fly half. The evergreen Gibson (below) would make his final championship appearance more than 15 years later.

Mike Gibson

England had also suffered at the hands of Ireland at Twickenham, or, more pertinently, at the hands of one Mike Gibson, who made his debut in the 18-5 victory and played a prominent role in bringing to an end a sequence of seven successive Irish defeats at the ground.

The England back line was breaking up. The respected Malcolm Phillips, an outstanding threequarter who played 25 times in all for England, was next to go, the following season, as England began to flounder. They beat France 6-3 in Paris, drew with Wales 6-6 at Twickenham but finished on a low with a 15-6 defeat at Murrayfield, Scotland regaining the Calcutta Cup for the first time since 1950.

After seven scratchy years, Wales took a share in the title, finishing equal with Scotland on six points. Rugby in Wales had been mired in introspection following the first New Zealand Test victory in Cardiff in late December 1963. There was talk of bringing in coaches to help Wales compete on level terms with the southern hemisphere. Wales's progress in the championship helped alleviate some of the gloom, although their form was patchy through the tournament, only a try late in the game from Stuart Watkins and an accurate conversion from centre Keith Bradshaw allowing them to salvage an 11-11 draw against France in their final match. Even so, Wales did inflict Scotland's only defeat (11-3), Bradshaw touching down for the first try before Neath lock Brian Thomas stormed over from a line out to put matters beyond doubt.

England continued to wobble at the start of 1965, unhinged partly by poor weather in their opening games of the championship but also by their own inability to impose themselves. First Wales (14-3) and then Ireland (5-0) needed no second bidding. Mike Weston was drafted for the first home game of the championship against France, moving infield from his customary position in the centre to direct operations from fly half. His tactical kicking proved decisive as England eked out a 9-6 victory.

If there was little to suggest a significant upturn in England's fortunes, it did not deter Her Majesty Queen Elizabeth II from attending the Calcutta Cup game. Even if rugby were not to rank at the top of her sporting preferences, she would still be able to entertain her future rugby-mad grandchildren with tales of Andy Hancock's solo try in the dying minutes. Scotland were leading 3-0 when the ball reached Weston in the England 25 and the fly half threw out a pass to Hancock. With virtually the pitch's length separating him from the Scottish try line, the Northampton wing set off, certainly more in hope than anything else. 'I just ran and ran,' he said later. And so he did, a lung-bursting sprint along the touch line ending with him diving over at the north end of the ground at the finish of what is believed to be the longest touchdown run in Test history.

It was Wales's title, outright this time, wrapped up with victories in their first three matches, in which they totalled seven tries. They lost their final game 22-13 to France, yet still managed to cross the try line three times, both they and their conquerors on the day finishing the season with ten touchdowns. Clive Rowlands made his last international appearance in that Paris match, his fourteenth Test and his fourteenth as captain. Rowlands has been a formidable presence on the rugby scene, responsible for many major developments and serving as national coach from 1968 to 1974. He was also involved in that infamous 1963 match of interminable line outs, 111 reported in the game against Scotland. According to Newport lock Brian Price, 'Clive kept kicking it in and the opposition kept throwing it back to me! All I had to do was give it back to Clive who just kicked it back into touch. I think I caught all 111 as the ball just seemed to keep coming to me wherever I was.'

While 1966 was to bring glory and acclaim in the round-ball game, England's rugby decline continued, as they went winless and collected the Wooden Spoon outright for the first time since 1950. The 'points for' column showed just 15 with only two tries to their name, an even worse return than in the Wooden Spoon year of 1948, when England had last registered just a single championship point. They used 26 players in all, their only salvation coming in the form of a 6-6 draw with Ireland at Twickenham.

In general that year's Five Nations was a humdrum affair, Wales coming through at the death with a remarkable 9-8 victory over France in the last game, having been 8-0 down. Tries from Bernard Duprat and Jean-Joseph Rupert had seemingly given France a decisive advantage, but with Keith Bradshaw kicking two penalties to haul his side back into contention, Wales were at least on the scoreboard. France were still making most of the running. Well, they were until the ball was intercepted by Newport wing Stuart Watkins, who raced in from 75 metres for the match-winning score. Even then the drama was not quite finished. Bill Morris was penalised for throwing the ball into touch, but Claude Lacaze could not land the goal. It was to be the last the championship saw of three great French players – Crauste and the Boniface brothers.

LEFT Andy Hancock on the burst in his debut match against France in 1965. But no try for him in this game: his moment was to come later in the season against Scotland. BELOW Dinner at the London Hilton for the teams that played out the 6-6 draw that gave England their solitary point in the 1966 championship. FOLLOWING PAGES Alun Pask makes a spectacular touchdown for Wales in their 11-6 win over England in the opening game of the 1966 Five Nations.

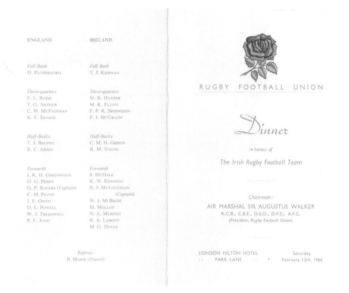

Wales could not sustain their position. The holders went from top to bottom in 1967 as France carried off the title in a championship that stood out for a glut of scoring: more than 200 points (230 in all) were scored in the tournament for the first time since 1931. Curiously, despite recording two victories, Ireland managed only 17 of them, 36 fewer than bottom-placed Wales, who rounded off with that morale-restoring, Jarrett-inspired win over England.

England had come to Cardiff that day in search of the Triple Crown after wins over Ireland (8-3) and Scotland, a burst of late scoring helping England to a 27-14 Calcutta Cup victory. Although England went down in Cardiff, they did register 21 points to top the championship scoring charts with 68. Bristol full back Roger Hosen was the mainstay, his four penalty goals at the Arms Park taking his total to 38 points for the championship, at that time a national record.

ENGLAND		Referee : D. P. d'ARCY (Ireland)		FRANCE	
15.	R. W. HOSEN Bristol & Cornwall	FULL BACKS		15.	C. LACAZE Angouleme
14	K. F. SAVAGE Northampton & East Midlands	RIGHT WING THREE-QUARTERS LEFT WING		11.	A. CAMPAES (Lourdes)
13.	R. D. HEARN Bedford & Warwickshire	RIGHT CENTRE LEFT CENTRE		12.	J. P. LUX (Saint Vincent, Tyrosse)
12.	C. R. JENNINS Waterloo & Lancashire	LEFT CENTRE RIGHT CENTRE		13.	C. DOURTHE Dax
11.	C. W. McFADYEAN Moseley & Somerset	LEFT WING RIGHT WING		14.	B. DUPRAT Bayonne
10.	J. F. FINLAN Moseley & North Midlands	HALF BACKS STAND-OFF		10.	G. CAMBERABERO La Voulte
9.	R. D. A. PICKERING Bradford & Yorkshire	SCRUM-HALF		9.	L. CAMBERABERO La Voulte
8.	J. N. PALLANT Notts & Notts, Lincs & Derbyshire	FORWARDS NO. 8		8.	A. HERRERO Toulon
7.	R. B. TAYLOR Northampton & East Midlands	OPEN-SIDE		7.	C. CARRERE Toulon
6.	D. M. ROLLITT Bristol & Gloucestershire	BLIND-SIDE		6.	M. SITJAR Agen
5.	D. E. J. WATT Bristol & Gloucestershire	LOCK		5.	B. DAUGA Mont-de-Marsan
4.	J. BARTON Coventry & Warwickshire	LOCK		4.	W. SPANGHERO Narbonne
3.	M. J. COULMAN Moseley & North Midlands	PROP		3.	J.-C. BEREJNOI Tulle
2.	S. B. RICHARDS Richmond & Middlesex	HOOKER		2.	J. M. CABANIER Montauban
1.	P. E. JUDD Coventry & Warwickshire (CAPTAIN)	PROP		1.	A. GRUARIN Toulon
Touch Judge : H. J. LUXON (Somerset) 12		KICK-OFF 3 p.m.		Touch Judge : M. ROBERT CALMET 13	

RUGBY FOOTBALL UNION

ENGLAND
v
FRANCE

TWICKENHAM
SATURDAY 25th FEBRUARY
1967
OFFICIAL PROGRAMME
ONE SHILLING AND SIXPENCE

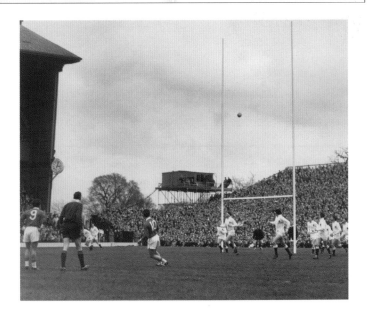

VARYING FORTUNES AGAINST FRANCE.
ABOVE RIGHT The Camberabero brothers form the half-back combination against England in 1967. RIGHT Lilian (9) watches as brother Guy (10) adds to his eventual tally of ten points as France win 16-12. TOP Budge Rogers leads his side out two years later on what was to be a happier day for England, as they put France to the sword 22-8.

Nevertheless it was France who took the honours, clinching the title with an 11-6 win in Dublin. Guy Camberabero partnered brother Lilian at half back to steer his country to the finishing line. Guy's eight points at Lansdowne Road took him to 32 points for the championship, a new French record. The game was the last championship outing for France captain Christian Darrouy, who went into international retirement after that summer's tour of South Africa.

The crowning glory for that generation of French players came the following season, 1968, when they landed their first ever Five Nations Grand Slam since joining the championship in 1910. The opening game against Scotland provided France with their biggest challenge. The eventual champions came through only 8-6 at Murrayfield, with tries from Bernard Duprat and André Campaes, the latter converted by Guy Camberabero. It had been a tense encounter, but it was as good as it got that year for Scotland, who lost all four matches for the first time since 1954.

The Camberabero brothers, from the tiny La Voulte club on the banks of the Rhone south of Lyon, kept their side on the straight and narrow. There was to be no flamboyant, showy rugby, but plenty of tough, shoulder-to-shoulder resistance. The Slam was landed on 23 March in muddy Cardiff, where France won 14-9, the tries coming from captain Christian Carrère and Lilian Camberabero, backed up with eight points from the boot of brother Guy.

ABOVE The Scotland team at Twickenham in 1969. Included in the line-up is BBC rugby correspondent Ian Robertson. He was to be on the losing side this time but the following year was in a winning team at Murrayfield before injury ruled him out of the international game. Back row (left to right): D.H. Collier (touch judge), G.C. Connell, A.B. Carmichael, W. Lauder, A.F. McHarg, P.C. Brown, R.J. Arneil, J.N.M. Frame, W.C.C. Steele, J. McLauchlan, C. Durand (referee). Front row: I. Robertson, C.F. Blaikie, W.D. Jackson, J.W. Telfer (capt), F.A.L. Laidlaw, C.M. Telfer.

This final season of the decade was notable for two significant new rulings. Replacements were allowed for players injured during the course of a game, with Scotland's Ian McCrae becoming the first official substitute when he came on for Gordon Connell in Paris. The 'Australian dispensation' rule was also adopted, under which kicking a ball directly into touch from outside a defender's 25 resulted in a line out level with the point at which the kick was made. As a device intended to produce a more open game, the latter seemed to make an immediate impact, the 1969 championship generating 234 points, the most since 247 were scored in 1911. Of the 32 tries scored, 14 were recorded by Wales, who hinted at what splendour was to come in the 1970s. France fell from the dizzy heights of the previous season, losing their first three games in 1969 and finishing with the Wooden Spoon, their sole point earned in an 8-8 draw with Wales in Paris. Ireland, meanwhile, gathered themselves and won their first three matches, before heading to Cardiff on a quest for the Grand Slam and a record sixth championship win in a row. Instead, they were well beaten 24-11 in a rough-house match during which Noel Murphy was felled by Wales skipper Brian Price. The Swinging Sixties took on a whole new meaning after that punch.

Five Nations Results 1960-69

1959-60

09.01.1960 MURRAYFIELD
Scotland 11 *T:* AR Smith 2 *C:* C Elliot *PG:* C Elliot
France 13 *T:* S Meyer, S Mericq, F Moncla
C: M Vannier 2
Referee: DG Walters (Wales)

16.01.1960 TWICKENHAM
England 14 *T:* J Roberts 2 *C:* D Rutherford
PG: D Rutherford 2
Wales 6 *PG:* TJ Davies 2
Referee: JAS Taylor (Scotland)

06.02.1960 CARDIFF ARMS PARK
Wales 8 *T:* DIE Bebb *C:* N Morgan *PG:* N Morgan
Scotland 0
Referee: KD Kelleher (Ireland)

13.02.1960 TWICKENHAM
England 8 *T:* RWD Marques *C:* D Rutherford
DG: RAW Sharp
Ireland 5 *T:* MG Culliton *C:* TJ Kiernan
Referee: DG Walters (Wales)

27.02.1960 STADE COLOMBES, PARIS
France 3 *PG:* M Vannier
England 3 *T:* MP Weston
Referee: JAS Taylor (Scotland)

27.02.1960 LANSDOWNE ROAD, DUBLIN
Ireland 5 *T:* BGM Wood *C:* D Hewitt
Scotland 6 *T:* RH Thomson *DG:* KJF Scotland
Referee: DG Walters (Wales)

12.03.1960 LANSDOWNE ROAD, DUBLIN
Ireland 9 *T:* NAA Murphy *PG:* S Kelly 2
Wales 10 *T:* B Cresswell, DO Brace *C:* N Morgan 2
Referee: DA Brown (England)

19.03.1960 MURRAYFIELD
Scotland 12 *T:* AR Smith *PG:* KJF Scotland 3
England 21 *T:* J Roberts, RE Syrett, JRC Young
C: D Rutherford 3 *PG:* D Rutherford *DG:* RAW Sharp
Referee: RC Williams (Ireland)

26.03.1960 CARDIFF ARMS PARK
Wales 8 *T:* B Cresswell *C:* N Morgan *PG:* N Morgan
France 16 *T:* M Celaya, P Lacroix, S Mericq, J Dupuy
C: M Vannier, P Albaladejo
Referee: Dr NM Parkes (England)

09.04.1960 STADE COLOMBES, PARIS
France 23 *T:* M Celaya, A Domenech, F Moncla,
H Rancoule *C:* J Bouquet *DG:* P Albaladejo 3
Ireland 6 *T:* NH Brophy 2
Referee: DG Walters (Wales)

	P	W	D	L	FOR	AGAINST	PTS
France	4	3	1	0	55	28	7
England	4	3	1	0	46	26	7
Wales	4	2	0	2	32	39	4
Scotland	4	1	0	3	29	47	2
Ireland	4	0	0	4	25	47	0

1960-61

07.01.1961 STADE COLOMBES, PARIS
France 11 *T:* G Boniface *C:* P Albaladejo
PG: P Albaladejo *DG:* P Albaladejo
Scotland 0
Referee: RC Williams (Ireland)

21.01.1961 CARDIFF ARMS PARK
Wales 6 *T:* DIE Bebb 2
England 3 *T:* JRC Young
Referee: KD Kelleher (Ireland)

11.02.1961 LANSDOWNE ROAD, DUBLIN
Ireland 11 *T:* JR Kavanagh *C:* JW Moffett
PG: JW Moffett 2
England 8 *T:* J Roberts, DP Rogers *C:* ABW Risman
Referee: GJ Treharne (Wales)

11.02.1961 MURRAYFIELD
Scotland 3 *T:* AR Smith
Wales 0
Referee: RC Williams (Ireland)

25.02.1961 TWICKENHAM
England 5 *T:* VSJ Harding *C:* JG Willcox
France 5 *T:* M Crauste *C:* M Vannier
Referee: DG Walters (Wales)

25.02.1961 MURRAYFIELD
Scotland 16 *T:* KI Ross 2, J Douglas *C:* KJF Scotland 2
PG: KJF Scotland
Ireland 8 *T:* JR Kavanagh, D Hewitt *C:* JW Moffett
Referee: MHR King (England)

11.03.1961 CARDIFF ARMS PARK
Wales 9 *T:* KHL Richards *PG:* KHL Richards 2
Ireland 0
Referee: DCJ McMahon (Scotland)

18.03.1961 TWICKENHAM
England 6 *T:* J Roberts *PG:* JP Horrocks-Taylor
Scotland 0
Referee: KD Kelleher (Ireland)

25.03.1961 STADE COLOMBES, PARIS
France 8 *T:* G Boniface, J-P Saux *C:* M Vannier
Wales 6 *T:* AEI Pask, DIE Bebb
Referee: Dr NM Parkes (England)

15.04.1961 LANSDOWNE ROAD, DUBLIN
Ireland 3 *PG:* TJ Kiernan
France 15 *T:* J Gachassin, P Albaladejo *PG:* M Vannier, P Albaladejo
DG: J Bouquet, P Albaladejo
Referee: GJ Treharne (Wales)

	P	W	D	L	FOR	AGAINST	PTS
France	4	3	1	0	39	14	7
Wales	4	2	0	2	21	14	4
Scotland	4	2	0	2	19	25	4
England	4	1	1	2	22	22	3
Ireland	4	1	0	3	22	48	2

1961-62

13.01.1962 MURRAYFIELD
Scotland 3 *PG:* AR Smith
France 11 *T:* H Rancoule *C:* P Albaladejo
PG: P Albaladejo 2
Referee: RC Williams (Ireland)

20.01.1962 TWICKENHAM
England 0
Wales 0
Referee: JAS Taylor (Scotland)

03.02.1962 CARDIFF ARMS PARK
Wales 3 *DG:* A Rees
Scotland 8 *T:* RJC Glasgow, FH ten Bos *C:* KJF Scotland
Referee: Dr NM Parkes (England)

10.02.1962 TWICKENHAM
England 16 *T:* J Roberts, RAW Sharp, MR Wade
C: RAW Sharp 2 *PG:* RAW Sharp
Ireland 0
Referee: DG Walters (Wales)

24.02.1962 STADE COLOMBES, PARIS
France 13 *T:* M Crauste 3 *C:* P Albaladejo 2
England 0
Referee: DG Walters (Wales)

24.02.1962 LANSDOWNE ROAD, DUBLIN
Ireland 6 *T:* WR Hunter *PG:* WR Hunter
Scotland 20 *T:* AR Smith 2, RC Cowan *C:* KJF Scotland
PG: KJF Scotland 2 *DG:* S Coughtrie
Referee: Dr NM Parkes (England)

17.03.1962 MURRAYFIELD
Scotland 3 *PG:* KJF Scotland
England 3 *PG:* JG Willcox
Referee: KD Kelleher (Ireland)

24.03.1962 CARDIFF ARMS PARK
Wales 3 *PG:* K Coslett
France 0
Referee: KD Kelleher (Ireland)

14.04.1962 STADE COLOMBES, PARIS
France 11 *T:* B Mommejat, C Lacaze, M Crauste
C: P Albaladejo
Ireland 0
Referee: JAS Taylor (Scotland)

Delayed match

17.11.1962 LANSDOWNE ROAD, DUBLIN
Ireland 3 *DG:* MAF English
Wales 3 *PG:* GTR Hodgson
Referee: JAS Taylor (Scotland)

	P	W	D	L	FOR	AGAINST	PTS
France	4	3	0	1	35	6	6
Scotland	4	2	1	1	34	23	5
England	4	1	2	1	19	16	4
Wales	4	1	2	1	9	11	4
Ireland	4	0	1	3	9	50	1

1962-63

12.01.1963 STADE COLOMBES, PARIS
France 6 *PG:* P Albaladejo *DG:* A Boniface
Scotland 11 *T:* RH Thomson *C:* KJF Scotland
PG: KJF Scotland *DG:* KJF Scotland
Referee: RC Williams (Ireland)

19.01.1963 CARDIFF ARMS PARK
Wales 6 *T:* DJ Hayward *PG:* GTR Hodgson
England 13 *T:* JE Owen, MS Phillips *C:* RAW Sharp 2
DG: RAW Sharp
Referee: KD Kelleher (Ireland)

26.01.1963 LANSDOWNE ROAD, DUBLIN
Ireland 5 *T:* AJF O'Reilly *C:* TJ Kiernan
France 24 *T:* C Darrouy 3, G Boniface
C: P Albaladejo 3 *DG:* P Albaladejo, A Boniface
Referee: FG Price (Wales)

02.02.1963 MURRAYFIELD
Scotland 0
Wales 6 *PG:* GTR Hodgson *DG:* DCT Rowlands
Referee: RC Williams (Ireland)

09.02.1963 LANSDOWNE ROAD, DUBLIN
Ireland 0
England 0
Referee: HB Laidlaw (Scotland)

23.02.1963 TWICKENHAM
England 6 *PG:* JG Willcox 2
France 5 *T:* G Boniface *C:* P Albaladejo
Referee: DCJ McMahon (Scotland)

23.02.1963 MURRAYFIELD
Scotland 3 *PG:* S Coughtrie
Ireland 0
Referee: GJ Treharne (Wales)

09.03.1963 CARDIFF ARMS PARK
Wales 6 *T:* G Jones *DG:* D Watkins
Ireland 14 *T:* PJ Casey *C:* TJ Kiernan *PG:* TJ Kiernan 2
DG: MAF English
Referee: AC Luff (England)

16.03.1963 TWICKENHAM
England 10 *T:* NJ Drake-Lee, RAW Sharp
C: JG Willcox 2
Scotland 8 *T:* RJC Glasgow *C:* S Coughtrie
DG: KJF Scotland
Referee: DG Walters (Wales)

23.03.1963 STADE COLOMBES, PARIS
France 5 *T:* G Boniface *C:* P Albaladejo
Wales 3 *PG:* GTR Hodgson
Referee: PG Brook (England)

	P	W	D	L	FOR	AGAINST	PTS
England	4	3	1	0	29	19	7
France	4	2	0	2	40	25	4
Scotland	4	2	0	2	22	22	4
Ireland	4	1	1	2	19	33	3
Wales	4	1	0	3	21	32	2

1963-64

04.01.1964 MURRAYFIELD
Scotland 10 *T:* IHP Laughland, RH Thomson
C: S Wilson 2
France 0
Referee: RC Williams (Ireland)

18.01.1964 TWICKENHAM
England 6 *T:* DG Perry, JM Ranson
Wales 6 *T:* DIE Bebb 2
Referee: KD Kelleher (Ireland)

01.02.1964 CARDIFF ARMS PARK
Wales 11 *T:* K Bradshaw, BE Thomas *C:* K Bradshaw
PG: K Bradshaw
Scotland 3 *T:* IHP Laughland
Referee: PG Brook (England)

08.02.1964 TWICKENHAM
England 5 *T:* DP Rogers *C:* JG Willcox
Ireland 18 *T:* MK Flynn 2, PJ Casey, NAA Murphy
C: TJ Kiernan 3
Referee: DG Walters (Wales)

22.02.1964 STADE COLOMBES, PARIS
France 3 *T:* C Darrouy
England 6 *T:* MS Phillips *PG:* RW Hosen
Referee: DG Walters (Wales)

22.02.1964 LANSDOWNE ROAD, DUBLIN
Ireland 3 *PG:* TJ Kiernan
Scotland 6 *PG:* S Wilson 2
Referee: AC Luff (England)

07.03.1964 LANSDOWNE ROAD, DUBLIN
Ireland 6 *PG:* FS Keogh 2
Wales 15 *T:* SJ Watkins, SJ Dawes, D Watkins
C: K Bradshaw 3
Referee: AC Luff (England)

21.03.1964 MURRAYFIELD
Scotland 15 *T:* RJC Glasgow, NS Bruce, JW Telfer
C: S Wilson 3
England 6 *T:* DP Rogers *PG:* RW Hosen
Referee: RC Williams (Ireland)

21.03.1964 CARDIFF ARMS PARK
Wales 11 *T:* SJ Watkins *C:* K Bradshaw *PG:* K Bradshaw 2
France 11 *T:* M Crauste *C:* P Albaladejo
PG: P Albaladejo 2
Referee: HB Laidlaw (Scotland)

11.04.1964 STADE COLOMBES, PARIS
France 27 *T:* C Darrouy 2, M Crauste, M Lira,
M Arnaudet, A Herrero *C:* P Albaladejo 3 *DG:* P Dedieu
Ireland 6 *T:* PJ Casey *DG:* CMH Gibson
Referee: DG Walters (Wales)

	P	W	D	L	FOR	AGAINST	PTS
Wales	4	2	2	0	43	26	6
Scotland	4	3	0	1	34	20	6
France	4	1	1	2	41	33	3
England	4	1	1	2	23	42	3
Ireland	4	1	0	3	33	53	2

1964-65

09.01.1965 STADE COLOMBES, PARIS
France 16 *T:* C Darrouy 2, J Gachassin, J Pique
C: P Dedieu 2
Scotland 8 *T:* BC Henderson 2 *C:* KJF Scotland
Referee: KD Kelleher (Ireland)

16.01.1965 CARDIFF ARMS PARK
Wales 14 *T:* SJ Watkins 2, HJ Morgan *C:* TG Price
DG: D Watkins
England 3 *PG:* D Rutherford
Referee: KD Kelleher (Ireland)

23.01.1965 LANSDOWNE ROAD, DUBLIN
Ireland 3 *T:* MG Doyle
France 3 *T:* C Darrouy
Referee: DG Walters (Wales)

06.02.1965 MURRAYFIELD
Scotland 12 *PG:* S Wilson 2 *DG:* BM Simmers 2
Wales 14 *T:* SJ Watkins, NR Gale *C:* TG Price
PG: TG Price 2
Referee: RW Gilliland (Ireland)

13.02.1965 LANSDOWNE ROAD, DUBLIN
Ireland 5 *T:* RA Lamont *C:* TJ Kiernan
England 0
Referee: HB Laidlaw (Scotland)

27.02.1965 TWICKENHAM
England 9 *T:* CM Payne *PG:* D Rutherford 2
France 6 *T:* C Darrouy *PG:* P Dedieu
Referee: RW Gilliland (Ireland)

27.02.1965 MURRAYFIELD
Scotland 6 *PG:* S Wilson *DG:* IHP Laughland
Ireland 16 *T:* PJ McGrath, RM Young, NAA Murphy
C: TJ Kiernan 2 *DG:* CMH Gibson
Referee: DG Walters (Wales)

13.03.1965 CARDIFF ARMS PARK
Wales 14 *T:* D Watkins, DIE Bebb *C:* TG Price
PG: TG Price *DG:* TG Price
Ireland 8 *T:* MK Flynn *C:* TJ Kiernan *PG:* TJ Kiernan
Referee: PG Brook (England)

20.03.1965 TWICKENHAM
England 3 *T:* AW Hancock
Scotland 3 *DG:* DH Chisholm
Referee: DG Walters (Wales)

27.03.1965 STADE COLOMBES, PARIS
France 22 *T:* G Boniface 2, A Herrero, J-M Cabanier
C: P Dedieu 2 *PG:* P Dedieu *DG:* J-C Lasserre
Wales 13 *T:* SJ Dawes, SJ Watkins, DIE Bebb
C: TG Price 2
Referee: RW Gilliland (Ireland), replaced by
B Marie (France)

	P	W	D	L	FOR	AGAINST	PTS
Wales	4	3	0	1	55	45	6
France	4	2	1	1	47	33	5
Ireland	4	2	1	1	32	23	5
England	4	1	1	2	15	28	3
Scotland	4	0	1	3	29	49	1

1965-66

15.01.1966 TWICKENHAM
England 6 *T:* DG Perry *PG:* D Rutherford
Wales 11 *T:* AEI Pask *C:* TG Price *PG:* TG Price 2
Referee: RW Gilliland (Ireland)

15.01.1966 MURRAYFIELD
Scotland 3 *T:* DJ Whyte
France 3 *PG:* C Lacaze
Referee: DM Hughes (Wales)

29.01.1966 STADE COLOMBES, PARIS
France 11 *T:* C Darrouy 2 *C:* C Lacaze *PG:* C Lacaze
Ireland 6 *PG:* CMH Gibson *DG:* TJ Kiernan
Referee: PG Brook (England)

05.02.1966 CARDIFF ARMS PARK
Wales 8 *T:* DK Jones 2 *C:* K Bradshaw
Scotland 3 *PG:* S Wilson
Referee: MH Titcomb (England)

12.02.1966 TWICKENHAM
England 6 *T:* JRH Greenwood *PG:* D Rutherford
Ireland 6 *T:* PJ McGrath *PG:* TJ Kiernan
Referee: B Marie (France)

26.02.1966 STADE COLOMBES, PARIS
France 13 *T:* A Boniface, J Gachassin, A Gruarin
C: C Lacaze 2
England 0
Referee: DG Walters (Wales)

26.02.1966 LANSDOWNE ROAD, DUBLIN
Ireland 3 *PG:* TJ Kiernan
Scotland 11 *T:* AJW Hinshelwood 2, D Grant
C: S Wilson
Referee: DM Hughes (Wales)

12.03.1966 LANSDOWNE ROAD, DUBLIN
Ireland 9 *T:* FPK Bresnihan *PG:* CMH Gibson
DG: CMH Gibson
Wales 6 *T:* GJ Prothero *PG:* K Bradshaw
Referee: RP Burrell (Scotland)

19.03.1966 MURRAYFIELD
Scotland 6 *T:* DJ Whyte *PG:* CF Blaikie
England 3 *DG:* CW McFadyean
Referee: KD Kelleher (Ireland)

26.03.1966 CARDIFF ARMS PARK
Wales 9 *T:* SJ Watkins *PG:* K Bradshaw 2
France 8 *T:* B Duprat, J-J Rupert *C:* C Lacaze
Referee: KD Kelleher (Ireland)

	P	W	D	L	FOR	AGAINST	PTS
Wales	4	3	0	1	34	26	6
France	4	2	1	1	35	18	5
Scotland	4	2	1	1	23	17	5
Ireland	4	1	1	2	24	34	3
England	4	0	1	3	15	36	1

1966-67

14.01.1967 STADE COLOMBES, PARIS
France 8 *T:* B Duprat, C Carrere *C:* J Gachassin
Scotland 9 *PG:* S Wilson 2 *DG:* BM Simmers
Referee: KD Kelleher (Ireland)

04.02.1967 MURRAYFIELD
Scotland 11 *T:* AJW Hinshelwood, JW Telfer
C: S Wilson *DG:* DH Chisholm
Wales 5 *T:* SJ Watkins *C:* TG Price
Referee: KD Kelleher (Ireland)

Five Nations Results 1960-69

11.02.1967 LANSDOWNE ROAD, DUBLIN
Ireland 3 *PG:* TJ Kiernan
England 8 *T:* CW McFadyean *C:* RW Hosen
PG: RW Hosen
Referee: DM Hughes (Wales)

25.02.1967 TWICKENHAM
England 12 *PG:* RW Hosen 3 *DG:* JF Finlan
France 16 *T:* C Dourthe, B Duprat *C:* G Camberabero 2
PG: G Camberabero *DG:* G Camberabero
Referee: DP d'Arcy (Ireland)

25.02.1967 MURRAYFIELD
Scotland 3 *PG:* S Wilson
Ireland 5 *T:* NAA Murphy *C:* TJ Kiernan
Referee: DM Hughes (Wales)

11.03.1967 CARDIFF ARMS PARK
Wales 0
Ireland 3 *T:* ATA Duggan
Referee: MH Titcomb (England)

18.03.1967 TWICKENHAM
England 27 *T:* CW McFadyean 2, RB Taylor, RE Webb
C: RW Hosen 3 *PG:* RW Hosen 2 *DG:* JF Finlan
Scotland 14 *T:* AJW Hinshelwood, JWC Turner
C: S Wilson *PG:* S Wilson 2
Referee: DP d'Arcy (Ireland)

01.04.1967 STADE COLOMBES, PARIS
France 20 *T:* G Camberabero, B Dauga, C Dourthe
C: G Camberabero *PG:* G Camberabero
DG: G Camberabero 2
Wales 14 *T:* DIE Bebb *C:* TG Price *PG:* TG Price 2
DG: D Watkins
Referee: DP d'Arcy (Ireland)

15.04.1967 LANSDOWNE ROAD, DUBLIN
Ireland 6 *T:* MG Molloy *PG:* TJ Kiernan
France 11 *T:* J-M Cabanier *C:* G Camberabero
DG: G Camberabero 2
Referee: RP Burrell (Scotland)

15.04.1967 CARDIFF ARMS PARK
Wales 34 *T:* TGR Davies 2, WD Morris, DIE Bebb,
KS Jarrett *C:* KS Jarrett 5 *PG:* KS Jarrett 2
DG: WH Raybould
England 21 *T:* J Barton 2, KF Savage *PG:* RW Hosen 4
Referee: DCJ McMahon (Scotland)

	P	W	D	L	FOR	AGAINST	PTS
France	4	3	0	1	55	41	6
England	4	2	0	2	68	67	4
Scotland	4	2	0	2	37	45	4
Ireland	4	2	0	2	17	22	4
Wales	4	1	0	3	53	55	2

1967-68

13.01.1968 MURRAYFIELD
Scotland 6 *T:* GJ Keith *PG:* S Wilson
France 8 *T:* B Duprat, A Campaes *C:* G Camberabero
Referee: KD Kelleher (Ireland)

20.01.1968 TWICKENHAM
England 11 *T:* CW McFadyean, BW Redwood
C: R Hiller *PG:* R Hiller
Wales 11 *T:* GO Edwards, R Wanbon *C:* KS Jarrett
DG: B John
Referee: DP d'Arcy (Ireland)

27.01.1968 STADE COLOMBES, PARIS
France 16 *T:* A Campaes, B Dauga *C:* P Villepreux 2
PG: P Villepreux *DG:* J Gachassin
Ireland 6 *PG:* WMcM McCombe 2
Referee: GC Lamb (England)

03.02.1968 CARDIFF ARMS PARK
Wales 5 *T:* WK Jones *C:* KS Jarrett
Scotland 0
Referee: GC Lamb (England)

10.02.1968 TWICKENHAM
England 9 *PG:* R Hiller 2 *DG:* JF Finlan
Ireland 9 *PG:* TJ Kiernan 3
Referee: M Joseph (Wales)

24.02.1968 STADE COLOMBES, PARIS
France 14 *T:* J Gachassin *C:* G Camberabero
PG: G Camberabero *DG:* L Camberabero, C Lacaze
England 9 *PG:* R Hiller 2 *DG:* MP Weston
Referee: HB Laidlaw (Scotland)

24.02.1968 LANSDOWNE ROAD, DUBLIN
Ireland 14 *T:* ATA Duggan 2, FPK Bresnihan
C: TJ Kiernan *PG:* TJ Kiernan
Scotland 6 *PG:* S Wilson 2
Referee: M Joseph (Wales)

09.03.1968 LANSDOWNE ROAD, DUBLIN
Ireland 9 *T:* MG Doyle *PG:* TJ Kiernan
DG: CMH Gibson
Wales 6 *PG:* D Rees *DG:* GO Edwards
Referee: MH Titcomb (England)

16.03.1968 MURRAYFIELD
Scotland 6 *PG:* S Wilson *DG:* GC Connell
England 8 *T:* MJ Coulman *C:* R Hiller *PG:* R Hiller
Referee: DP d'Arcy (Ireland)

23.03.1968 CARDIFF ARMS PARK
Wales 9 *T:* WK Jones *PG:* D Rees 2
France 14 *T:* L Camberabero, C Carrere
C: G Camberabero *PG:* G Camberabero
DG: G Camberabero
Referee: HB Laidlaw (Scotland)

	P	W	D	L	FOR	AGAINST	PTS
France	4	4	0	0	52	30	8
Ireland	4	2	1	1	38	37	5
England	4	1	2	1	37	40	4
Wales	4	1	1	2	31	34	3
Scotland	4	0	0	4	18	35	0

1968-69

11.01.1969 STADE COLOMBES, PARIS
France 3 *PG:* P Villepreux
Scotland 6 *T:* JW Telfer *PG:* CF Blaikie
Referee: GC Lamb (England)

25.01.1969 LANSDOWNE ROAD, DUBLIN
Ireland 17 *T:* JCM Moroney *C:* JCM Moroney
PG: JCM Moroney 3 *DG:* BJ McGann
France 9 *T:* J Trillo *PG:* P Villepreux 2
Referee: GC Lamb (England)

01.02.1969 MURRAYFIELD
Scotland 3 *PG:* CF Blaikie
Wales 17 *T:* B John, GO Edwards, MCR Richards
C: KS Jarrett *PG:* KS Jarrett 2
Referee: KD Kelleher (Ireland)

08.02.1969 LANSDOWNE ROAD, DUBLIN
Ireland 17 *T:* FPK Bresnihan, NAA Murphy
C: TJ Kiernan *PG:* TJ Kiernan 2 *DG:* BJ McGann
England 15 *T:* DJ Duckham *PG:* R Hiller 4
Referee: RP Burrell (Scotland)

22.02.1969 TWICKENHAM
England 22 *T:* KJ Fielding, DM Rollitt, RE Webb
C: R Hiller 2 *PG:* R Hiller 3
France 8 *T:* J-M Bonal *C:* C Lacaze *DG:* C Lacaze
Referee: DP d'Arcy (Ireland)

22.02.1969 MURRAYFIELD
Scotland 0
Ireland 16 *T:* ATA Duggan, BJ McGann, CMH Gibson,
FPK Bresnihan *C:* JCM Moroney 2
Referee: M Joseph (Wales)

08.03.1969 CARDIFF ARMS PARK
Wales 24 *T:* SJ Watkins, D Williams, WD Morris,
J Taylor *C:* KS Jarrett 3 *PG:* KS Jarrett *DG:* B John
Ireland 11 *T:* CMH Gibson *C:* TJ Kiernan
PG: TJ Kiernan 2
Referee: DCJ McMahon (Scotland)

15.03.1969 TWICKENHAM
England 8 *T:* DJ Duckham 2 *C:* R Hiller
Scotland 3 *PG:* PC Brown
Referee: C Durand (France)

22.03.1969 STADE COLOMBES, PARIS
France 8 *T:* A Campaes *C:* P Villepreux
PG: P Villepreux
Wales 8 *T:* GO Edwards, MCR Richards *C:* KS Jarrett
Referee: RP Burrell (Scotland)

12.04.1969 CARDIFF ARMS PARK
Wales 30 *T:* MCR Richards 4, B John *C:* KS Jarrett 3
PG: KS Jarrett 2 *DG:* B John
England 9 *PG:* R Hiller 3
Referee: DP d'Arcy (Ireland)

	P	W	D	L	FOR	AGAINST	PTS
Wales	4	3	1	0	79	31	7
Ireland	4	3	0	1	61	48	6
England	4	2	0	2	54	58	4
Scotland	4	1	0	3	12	44	2
France	4	0	1	3	28	53	1

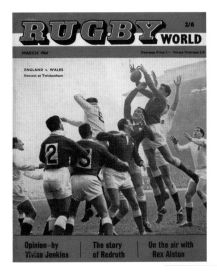

*LEFT AND BELOW **Two** national identities to the fore in the West Car Park before the game in 1973.*

" Was there ever a finer decade? Mean and magnificent were those guys, men who played with a swagger but also with a steely intent. **"**

1970s

How appropriate that it was an Englishman who penned the words 'It was the best of times, it was the worst of times'. If you were a Welshman, then you'd have drunk deep of the first part of that Dickens aphorism. Sadly, if you were a countryman of Dickens, you'd have taken the latter part on board. Only if you took the broad view of rugby life, would you as an England fan have felt uplifted by events in the 1970s. Was there ever a finer decade? Will we see the like again of Gareth and Barry and Benny and Gerald? What of the French trio of musketeers, Skréla, Rives and Bastiat? Mean and magnificent were those guys, men who played with a swagger but also with a steely intent.

And what of the Pontypool front row, Charlie Faulkner, Bobby Windsor and Graham Price, the 'Viet Gwent', a combination who terrorised the opposition and delighted in so doing? But they were no mere sluggers. They could play a bit, too, as illustrated so thrillingly in Price's lung-bursting 70-metre upfield burst at the Parc des Princes in 1975 to score Wales's fifth try on an invigorating afternoon. No, those lads could play.

There were Irish heroes to savour – Tom Kiernan, Mike Gibson and Willie John McBride. All the names are familiar to those who treasure their rugby memories, for it was the lure of the Lions that made the decade so special. They all came together in common cause, not once but twice within three years. For the one and only time in the entire history of the sport, it was the northern hemisphere that ruled the roost. John Dawes's tourists to New Zealand suffered only one defeat; Willie John's 1974 band of brothers in South Africa not even that. The Home Unions were in their element. The championship featured all the stars.

It was Wales, of course, who dominated the decade, with five outright championships, including three Grand Slams, plus a share in 1970 to their name. Nice work, eh? They also played

RIGHT The formidable Pontypool front row: (left to right) Graham Price, Bobby Windsor and Charlie Faulkner.

LEFT AND BELOW 10 February 1973: the match programme for the day that John Pullin (far left) and his England team 'turned up' to play Ireland in Dublin. BOTTOM The distinctive hippy look of Andy Ripley.

		IRELAND						ENGLAND	
				KICK OFF 3 PM					
FULL BACK	15	**T J KIERNAN** CORK CONSTITUTION	CAPTAIN			15	**A M JORDEN** BLACKHEATH	FULL BACK
THREEQUARTERS	14	**T O GRACE** ST MARY'S COLLEGE	Right Wing	Left Wing		11	**D J DUCKHAM** COVENTRY	THREEQUARTERS
	13	*****R A MILLIKEN** BANGOR	Right Centre	Left Centre		12	**P S PREECE** COVENTRY	
	12	**C M H GIBSON** N I F C	Left Centre	Right Centre		13	**P J WARFIELD** ROSSLYN PARK	
	11	**A W McMASTER** BALLYMENA	Left Wing	Right Wing		14	**A J MORLEY** BRISTOL	
HALF BACKS	10	**B J McGANN** CORK CONSTITUTION	Stand-Off	Stand-Off		10	**A R COWMAN** COVENTRY	HALF BACKS
	9	**J J MOLONEY** ST MARY'S COLLEGE	Scrum	Scrum		9	*****S J SMITH** SALE	
FORWARDS	8	**T A P MOORE** HIGHFIELD				8	**A G RIPLEY** ROSSLYN PARK	FORWARDS
	7	*****J H BUCKLEY** SUNDAY'S WELL				7	**A NEARY** BROUGHTON PARK	
	6	**J F SLATTERY** BLACKROCK COLLEGE				6	**P J DIXON** GOSFORTH	
	5	**W J McBRIDE** BALLYMENA				5	**C W RALSTON** RICHMOND	
	4	**K M A MAYS** UNIVERSITY COLLEGE DUBLIN				4	*****R UTTLEY** GOSFORTH	
	3	**J F LYNCH** ST MARY'S COLLEGE				3	**F E COTTON** LOUGHBOROUGH COLLEGES	
	2	**K W KENNEDY** LONDON-IRISH		*New Cap		2	**J V PULLIN** BRISTOL	CAPTAIN
	1	**R J McLOUGHLIN** BLACKROCK COLLEGE				1	**C B STEVENS** PENZANCE-NEWLYN	

Replacements	16	R J Clegg (Bangor)	17	P C Whelan (Garryowen)	Replacements	16	M J Cooper (Moseley)	17	G W Evans (Coventry)
	18	S A McKinney (Dungannon)	19	D M Canniffe (Cork Constitution)		18	J J Page (Northampton)	19	J D Gray (Coventry)
	20	J P Dennison (Garryowen)	21	A H Ensor (Wanderers)		20	R M Wilkinson (Cambridge University)	21	J A Watkins (Gloucester)

OFFICIALS

G A JAMISON (Irish Rugby Football Union) *Touch Judge* A M HOSIE (Scottish Rugby Union) *Referee* P E HUGHES (Rugby Football Union) *Touch Judge*

a part, naturally enough, in the tournament's only five-way tie, recorded in 1973. And the year before that, 1972, they were top of the table in an uncompleted championship. Neither Wales nor Scotland travelled to Ireland, such were the security fears over the Troubles in the North.

Famously, England did fulfil the fixture the following year, John Pullin leading out the side to great ovation at Lansdowne Road. That was as far as the welcome was extended as England went down to an 18-9 defeat, triggering the oft-quoted line by Pullin at the post-match banquet: 'We may not be very good, but at least we turn up.'

It was an era of enforced stoicism for England supporters. That loss at Lansdowne Road was England's seventh championship defeat in succession, a record low point, and their eighth match in a row without a win. Needless to say, it was the first time that had happened, too. From 1970 to 1976 inclusive, England finished last no fewer than five times, if you include ending up joint bottom with Scotland in 1970 and fifth in the truncated 1972 tournament in which England played and lost all their games. It was not a record that stood much scrutiny.

Of course, there were fine players in the white of England throughout the era, guys such as Bob Hiller, of the booming boot, or flaxen-locked David Duckham, all swaying hips and mesmerising feints. What, too, of the likes of Tony Neary, a stylish but hard-edged operator on the open side, and big, long-striding Andy Ripley, with his hippy,

Andy Ripley

'let's play man' outlook but brutally effective with it? Roger Uttley, Peter Dixon, Chris Ralston – these were not men of straw, yet even their heroics could not really drag England out of the mire for too long.

By the mid-point of the decade there were other behemoths beginning to show: Mike Burton, who knew a thing or two about getting the drop on his opposite number, so too Peter Wheeler and Fran Cotton alongside. As the wheel began to turn at the end of the 1970s, so a formidable England pack of forwards did begin to take shape, Bill Beaumont finally managing to rally everyone round and into productive action. But that was a far-off point as the 1960s closed. England, like so many others, were obliged to clutch at shadows as a golden age was launched west of the Severn.

It is strange to relate that England actually began the decade in decent heart. They had adopted a squad system for the first time, the benefits of which were to be seen in an impressive 11-8 victory over the Springboks just before Christmas 1969. The following championship opened with an encouraging 9-3 win over Ireland at Twickenham, a match notable for the re-emergence on the international scene of Tony O'Reilly, the burgeoning global businessman, recalled after a seven-year absence. Tales abound of O'Reilly turning up to training in his Rolls-Royce, about knocking on opposition dressing rooms and making merry. Part truth, part myth, the O'Reilly story is for real on one front: he knew the way to the try line. He had been top scorer on the 1959 Lions tour of Australia, New Zealand and Canada with an astonishing 22 tries in 23 games.

At Twickenham that Saturday in February 1970, though, it was Hiller's boot that made the difference. The Quins full back and England captain walloped over two monstrous dropped goals to break Irish hearts. Hiller, who was a rugby and cricket Blue at Oxford, never did let his head drop through all the struggles. In his time he was England's most capped full back with 19 caps and record points scorer with 138. He captained England on seven occasions, and was also a tourist with the 1968 and 1971 Lions, scoring 100 points on each tour yet never making the Test side. He was a fine ambassador for English rugby and has since served his time in the Harlequins committee room.

Early English promise, though, yielded nothing but disappointment and eventual despair. Wales dragged themselves off the floor to win at Twickenham 17-13, having trailed 13-3. A

Tony O'Reilly

TOP RIGHT Bob Hiller demonstrates the art of place-kicking to an audience of schoolboys. ABOVE Prolific try scorer and generally colourful character Tony O'Reilly of Ireland.

Barry John try had started to close the gap, but then Gareth Edwards departed the field through injury. If England fans were given something of a boost when they saw this, then they were rudely disabused of the notion by the performance of the replacement, Ray 'Chico' Hopkins of Maesteg. Hopkins, in his only Test for Wales, made a try for J.P.R. Williams, scored one himself, and a famous victory was rounded off by a dropped goal from Barry John.

England then went down 14-5 to Scotland at Murrayfield before travelling to France in mid-April for the final game of the championship. Several changes were made for the visit to the

ABOVE Demolition (35-13) followed against the French at Stade Colombes in 1970, but at least the England team enjoyed an evening at the Folies Bergère during the week before the game. BELOW J.P.R. Williams and Mervyn Davies, just two of the instantly recognisable figures in the Welsh teams of the 1970s.

Stade Colombes, the selectors reaching for the panic button after the pack were outplayed in Edinburgh. Any joy those guys had at winning an England cap had probably dissipated by the end of a dreadful day in Paris. France scored more points (35) against England than had any team in nearly 100 years of international matches up to that point. Ouch! France had gone from Wooden Spoon to a share of the championship; England from hope to desolation. It was a feeling that they were not to shake off too often over the coming years. Yet there was real tragedy to take on board, too, during the 1970s. In March 1974 a Turkish airliner taking England fans home after the 12-12 draw at the Parc des Princes crashed shortly after take-off from Orly Airport. All told, 346 people lost their lives. Heads were bowed for a long time thereafter.

In terms of rugby, the decade bore a finely etched thumbprint. The Welsh gallery of stars are still spoken of in reverential tones, and there was a grace and fluidity to their play that stirred the soul. Mind you, according to the actor Richard Burton, Welsh rugby was 'opera, ballet and sheer bloody murder' – and there was plenty of edge in the Welsh play, from the thunderous charges of J.P.R. Williams to the clattering tackles of Steve Fenwick. It was Wales's ability, though, to get the entire orchestra on song that was most impressive, from the big, bass beat to the flickering strings.

The first of this team's Grand Slams came in 1971,

Mervyn Davies

J.P.R. Williams

a campaign in which Wales used just 16 players. The side was built around those Welsh exiles at London Welsh – J.P.R., Gerald Davies, John Dawes, John Taylor, Mike Roberts and Mervyn Davies – all of whom would go to New Zealand that summer with the Lions, together with a seventh London Welshman, Geoff Evans, who did not feature for Wales in 1971 because of a back operation but joined the Lions tour as a replacement.

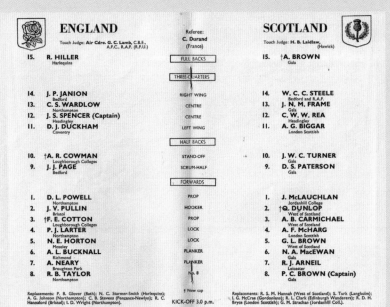

ENGLAND v SCOTLAND IN 1971.

LEFT, ABOVE AND BELOW Memories of the day that Scotland won at Twickenham for the first time since 1938 and (top) the team that achieved that narrow victory. Back row (left to right): C. Durand (referee), A.R. Brown, N.A.MacEwan, W.C.C. Steele, J.N.M. Frame, A.F. McHarg, A.G. Biggar, J.W.C. Turner, Q. Dunlop, C.W.W. Rea, H.B. Laidlaw (touch judge). Front row: J. McLauchlan, D.S. Paterson, A.B. Carmichael, P.C. Brown (capt), G.L. Brown, R.J. Arneil.

It all began at the rebuilt Cardiff Arms Park, Dawes's side easily despatching an inexperienced England parading eight new caps. Gerald Davies scored two tries in the 22-6 win. Wales's dominance was only really put to the test in a dramatic game at Murrayfield, bushy-haired flanker John 'Baz' Taylor caressing over a conversion from the touch line to nick a 19-18 victory at the death. Taylor was a round-the-corner kicker, his left foot deemed more suitable to the conversion of Gerald Davies' try in the right-hand corner. So it proved. That kick has gone down in the annals.

It was Wales's first Grand Slam in 19 years and they finished the tournament with 13 tries and 73 points, an indicator of their prowess. Yet it was a bizarre final table in 1971, in that Wooden Spoonists Scotland scored more points, 47, than any of the sides above them except Wales. Clearly Scotland's defence wasn't quite as efficient as their attack, with 12 tries conceded in four games. Easy pickings. Even so, in the RFU's centenary season, Scotland brought the curtain down on the championship for England with their first win (16-15) at Twickenham since 1938. Victory came with the last kick of the match, the incomparable Peter Brown converting Chris Rea's try. It was to be the last time that admirable pairing of John Spencer and David Duckham were to play together for England.

But all hail Wales! With Edwards and John in tandem, their control was all-encompassing, their potency marked and their enthusiasm for the task in hand unquenchable. Fittingly, a try each from these nonpareil half backs plus a penalty from John clinched the Grand Slam as Wales bested France 9-5 in Paris in a top-class game to round off the tournament. A legend had been created. The citizens of the Principality could sleep easy in their beds for many a year to come.

The following year, 1972, was to be one of those asterisk seasons, one in which Scotland and Wales failed to make the journey to Dublin because of concerns over the situation in Northern Ireland. Suggestions that the games might be played at a neutral venue did nothing to ease the ill-feeling caused by the refusal to travel. The sport suffered a loss of face, Ireland a loss of revenue and possibly an even greater reward given that they won both their away games against England and France. Might that elusive Grand Slam have materialised all those years ago? Or might it have gone again to John, Edwards, Williams & co, who were in their pomp and widely and rightly regarded as the finest side ever to wear the red of Wales?

Meanwhile, in an attempt to encourage attacking rugby, the administrators had upped the reward for a try from three points to four. Given that it was incomplete, the 1972 championship was not to prove the case for change conclusively, but there was certainly evidence of intent in attack. Wales, for example, recorded five tries in running up 35 points against Scotland. If there was one image that captured the irrepressible nature of the great Welsh adventure of the period, it came from that match. It was the smile of Gareth Edwards beaming through a mud-splattered face, his joy reflecting the brazen nature of the try he had just scored with a wonderful upfield run, kick and chase at a sodden Arms Park. This was Wales's fifth win in a row against Scotland and the highest championship score then conceded by the Scots, who didn't take it lying down. They promptly smashed hapless England 23-9, the fourth time in succession they had beaten the Auld Enemy if you include

FOLLOWING PAGES Chris Ralston touches down at Twickenham for England's first four-point try in the 1972 game against Ireland.

129

ABOVE *Plenty of talent in the team but bottom of the truncated 1972 championship: the England team that played Ireland that year. Back row (left to right): D.J. Duckham, C.W. Ralston, A. Brinn, M.A. Burton, P.J. Dixon, A.G. Ripley, M.C. Beese, A.G.B. Old, R.E. Webb. Front row: J.G. Webster, A.Neary, J.V. Pullin, R. Hiller (capt), K.J. Fielding, C.B. Stevens.*
BELOW *More points for Barry John as he moves past Jack Bancroft's record tally for Wales.*

the 1971 centenary match at Twickenham, which was not part of the Five Nations.

Poor, poor England. (Try to imagine saying that with a Scottish accent – it's good for the soul.) They lost all four matches in the championship for the first time ever and conceded a record 88 points in the process. After the opening losses to Wales and Ireland, the selectors dispensed with Bob Hiller. Good shout that one by the panel. England travelled to Paris for the final international match staged at the Stade Colombes and played the part of sacrificial lamb to perfection, losing by a catastrophic 37 points to 12. That was the highest score registered by any country against England and the margin of defeat – 25 points – was the widest since the 25-0 drubbing by Wales at Cardiff Arms Park in 1905.

Wales rounded off their truncated season with a 20-6 win over France. As he kicked his fourth penalty of the match, Barry John passed Jack Bancroft's Welsh record of 88 points in internationals, which had stood since 1914, and simultaneously created a new Welsh season record for the championship of 35 points. And then he walked away from it all at the age of 27.

Why? The question has been asked many times. John himself tells the tale of how he was spooked by a young girl kneeling down in front of him as if he were some sort of godlike figure. He was certainly that for many fans. The fame, the acclaim, the pressure, the scrutiny did not sit easily on his shoulders. He was Welsh rugby's George Best in many ways, lauded and feted wherever he went. How great might he have been if he'd played still more? Who knows? What he gave us was quite enough for one lifetime.

Other great, formative figures began to vacate the stage early on in the decade. Wales skipper John Dawes, leader of the 1971 Lions in New Zealand, was an understated man on the rugby field, something of a Mike Brearley almost. Others had more evident skills, but none his influence; 1971 was his final year of international rugby. Halfway through the 1973 campaign Tom Kiernan also departed, after a prodigious career. Kiernan first played for Ireland in 1960 and was a stalwart presence through 14 seasons of championship rugby. He scored his second

international try in his farewell outing against Scotland in 1973, his first having come 12 years previously. He finished up with 158 points from his 54 Tests for his country; 44 of those appearances had been in the championship. Then at the end of 1973 a fond adieu was wished to Walter Spanghero, elder brother of Claude and one of the greats of French rugby. He could fill any of the back-five roles and proved a charismatic captain.

Spanghero retired at the end of the season that saw the new Parc des Princes, built at a cost of £7.5 million, open its doors to rugby internationals for

INTERNATIONAL FAREWELLS.

ABOVE *Tom Kiernan on his last appearance for Ireland at Twickenham in 1972, the year before he retired from international rugby. It was Kiernan's fiftieth international appearance for Ireland.* LEFT *John Dawes makes his exit from Five Nations rugby at Stade Colombes in 1971, with the match ball and a Welsh Grand Slam.* BELOW *The Spanghero brothers, Walter (left) and Claude. Walter, who retired in 1973, had been an inspirational figure in what had been a successful period for French rugby.*

ABOVE AND ABOVE RIGHT
Seen from two angles: David Duckham scores England's only try against France at Parc des Princes in 1974.
RIGHT The legendary Willie John McBride leads the way as Ireland beat England 26-21 at Twickenham in 1974 and then go on to take the championship.

the first time. It still retains the affections of many rugby followers years later, despite, or perhaps because of, the fact that its capacity is 30,000 less than that of the space-age but rather soulless Stade de France. There was a novel – indeed unique – turn of events on the field that year, too. No one has ever come up with any convincing scientific reason why home advantage should count for so much. Pity. They'd have had a field day flogging their thesis that year, when every team won its home games only to lose every one on the road, producing a quintuple tie.

The following season's championship kicked off with an altered format. Until now, Five Nations fixtures had been arranged more or less according to tradition – the Calcutta Cup, for example, took place on the third Saturday in March. But from 1974 the structure was for two games to be played every other weekend, the fixtures to follow in strict rotation for periods of five years. The move was not universally popular at first but it endured.

Despite the change in the value of the try having been in place for less than three years, the 1974 campaign generated just 22 touchdowns. As with any initiative, there is a honeymoon period before the cynics get to grips with things and work out how to counter the

original intention. Ireland sneaked home to claim the title, scoring only 50 points in the process. More than half of those points came in one game, a 26-21 victory over England at Twickenham that came courtesy of four tries, two scored by Mike Gibson. England kept in touch mainly through the boot of Alan Old, who kicked five penalties as well as converting Peter Squires's try.

England had faltered once again after what had been a promising autumn. Hooker John Pullin, a seminal figure for England across these years with his uncompromising attitude, had led the team to a terrific 16-10 victory over the All Blacks in Auckland in September and then to a 20-3 win over Australia at Twickenham a couple of months later. So much promise, so little return in the championship.

England, though, were beginning to put together the pieces of a large-scale pack of forwards. Andy Ripley was in sumptuous form throughout the tournament, scoring a try early in the second half of the long-awaited victory over Wales. The 16-12 Twickenham win, with David Duckham also touching down, was England's first over Wales since 1963. Ripley, who won 24 caps at No. 8, a then England record for the position, formed an all-consuming back-row partnership with Peter Dixon and Tony Neary. That triumvirate played together on 12 occasions, an England record at the time for a breakaway trio, and was probably England's most complete back-row unit until the emergence of Hill, Back and Dallaglio.

LEFT The long-awaited win against Wales at Twickenham in 1974 featured many of the England squad that had finished at the foot of the table two years earlier. Back row (left to right): M.H. Titcomb (touch judge), J.R. West (referee), P.J. Dixon, C.W Ralston, R.M. Uttley, A.G.Ripley, K. Smith, M.A. Burton, A.G.B.Old. Middle row: A. Neary, G.W. Evans, D.J. Duckham, J.V Pullin (capt), C.B. Stevens, P.J. Squires. Front: W.H. Hare, J.G. Webster. BELOW During the same game: referee John West strides out impressively in pursuit of Alan Old as he breaks through the Welsh defence.

England were stirring but not delivering. They had a new captain in 1975 in the formidable Fran Cotton, a new coach in John Burgess and a couple of significant new faces in Bill Beaumont and Peter Wheeler, whose international careers got under way that year. But it was a case of the same old, same old. England were not the sum of their parts. They succumbed to Ireland 12-9 in Dublin, a defeat which prompted the usual knee-jerk reaction from the selectors, who made a raft of changes for the game against France. No prizes for guessing the outcome, a shattering 27-20 defeat, a new record number of points for France at Twickenham. How England kept the historians busy during this decade! Their blushes were only spared in 1975 by a nuggety 7-6 Calcutta Cup victory at Twickenham.

Ireland, meanwhile, had eyes on the title in their centenary season, but it was not to be, though they were in the mix until the final game. The scoreline, 32-4, told you all you needed to know as to who were the worthy winners. Wales, with the splendidly athletic Mervyn Davies at the helm, were back on top. They scored an impressive 14 tries in the campaign, with Ireland next in the rankings with eight. Wales's only defeat was the 12-10 reverse at Murrayfield, which was attended by a staggering 104,000 spectators, there as much to see the magic of the Welsh as the feats of their own. Indeed, every match of that championship was a sell-out. It was boom time for rugby.

ABOVE Andy Irvine (on the ground) and Jim Renwick watch helplessly as Tony Neary wins the loose ball during England's one-point (7-6) win in the 1975 Calcutta Cup match at Twickenham. RIGHT (Left to right) David Duckham (11), Mervyn Davies, Mike Burton, Terry Cobner and Phil Bennett watch as the two scrum halves, Mike Lampkowski and Gareth Edwards, sort things out between themselves in 1976. Edwards got the touchdown and Wales went on to win this encounter at Twickenham by the comfortable margin of 21-9.

A clutch of significant Irishmen blew the final whistle on their careers at no-side at Cardiff in 1975: Willie John McBride, Ray McLoughlin and Ken Kennedy. Willie John was without equal, notching up 17 Tests for the Lions on five tours. His captaincy on the 1974 tour to South Africa is the stuff of legend, as well as after-dinner speeches. McLoughlin and Kennedy, both also Lions Test players, were first-rate operators in the front row.

If England fans thought things couldn't get much worse, then they were in for a rude shock. The 1976 championship was a disaster. England finished bottom of the pile for the third year in a row, and suffered the indignity of being whitewashed for only the second time. Fifteen tries conceded – not so much a defence as a cop on point duty waving them through – and that after beating Australia 23-6 at Twickenham in early January. Oh, woe. Tony Neary led the side. It was not an enviable task.

At the other end of the table, there was a real tussle for the Grand Slam between Wales and France. The 'points for' column had to be stretched a notch to accommodate the former, who amassed a record 102 points, the largest total the championship had ever known. The fly-half conveyor belt was at full throttle, with Phil Bennett carrying on from where Barry John had left off. Bennett's 38-point haul was a new championship season best for a Welsh player.

France matched Wales stride for stride. They scored fewer points (82) but had a higher try count (13 to 11). Thrilling stuff. The decisive game was at Cardiff. Wales came through 19-13 despite being outscored two tries to one. Wings Jean-François Gourdon and Jean-Luc Averous touched down for France, J.J. Williams for Wales. Yet it was the trio of Bennett, Steve Fenwick and mighty lock forward Alan Martin who won the day for Wales with their penalty kicking.

Ray McLoughlin

ABOVE Ray McLoughlin, one of the Irish stalwarts who bowed out of international rugby at the end of the 1975 championship.

No one could have known at the time that the match against France would be the last international for Wales's Grand Slam captain, Mervyn Davies, who was obliged to retire after suffering a brain haemorrhage in a Welsh Cup tie between Swansea and Pontypool just a week later. Davies recovered but his career of 31 successive championship matches plus two Lions tours was at an end. He and Ripley, who also left international rugby that year, were two fine exponents of the art of No. 8 play.

Another to bid farewell to the Test arena in 1976 was one Englishman who might well have interested the Welsh selectors – David Duckham. Originally a centre, the Coventry man switched to the wing to great effect. His international career, which spanned lean years for England, ended in the 22-12 defeat at Murrayfield. Duckham scored ten tries in 36 international appearances for England; he also played in three Tests on the 1971 Lions tour of New Zealand.

England had had enough of being on their uppers, and in 1977, captain Roger Uttley paved the way for a more ferocious approach, leading his forwards in behind the crash ball of centre Charles Kent to exploit the second-phase possession created. The strategy brought immediate results with wins over Scotland (26-6) at Twickenham and Ireland (4-0) at Lansdowne Road.

There was an ominous note, though: full back Alastair Hignell missed three fairly routine kicks against the Scots. These blemishes didn't matter too much that day, but waywardness was

ONE WIN AND ONE LOSS AT TWICKENHAM IN 1977.

ABOVE *Evidence of the more robust approach introduced by Roger Uttley in 1977. England battle their way to a comprehensive 26-6 win against Scotland at Twickenham.* BELOW *But it was France who won the Grand Slam that year. Here captain Jacques Fouroux leads the way in their win at Twickenham, pursued by Bill Beaumont (left) and Fran Cotton.* LEFT *The French team that day. Back row (left to right): P.E. Hughes (touch judge), J. Desclaux (coach), A. Paco, R. Paparemborde, J-P. Rives, J-C. Skréla, G. Cholley, J-F. Imbernon, M. Palmié, J. Piqué (coach), J-P. Bastiat. Front row: D. Harize, R. Bertranne, J-M. Aguirre, J-P. Romeu, J. Fouroux (capt), F. Sangalli and J-L. Averous.*

to cost England dear later in the championship. Against France at Twickenham, Hignell missed five penalties as England succumbed 4-3. The great escape enabled France to go on to win the Grand Slam. Small wonder that Higgy still enjoys carte blanche at the bar wherever he goes in France. Hignell was nevertheless a colossus in defence, an indefatigable warrior.

The Grand Slam gone, England then narrowly lost the Triple Crown in Cardiff, Gareth Edwards dictating the tempo and eventual course of the match, the scrum half's name and that of J.P.R. Williams making their regular appearance on the scoresheet in a 14-9 victory. J.P.R. had a thing about the English. This was his fifth try against them. The torment was to continue for a few more years.

Meanwhile, France smashed their way to the Grand Slam, with 'Le Petit Caporal' Jacques Fouroux lashing his giant pack of forwards into productive action. Fouroux's marshalling of the troops was complemented by the tactical kicking of fly half Jean-Pierre Romeu. The French clinched the Slam in Dublin, winning 15-6 against Ireland, who lost all four matches for only the third time in their history and also had a share in the season's principal moment of controversy – the sending-off of Willie Duggan and Wales's Geoff Wheel at the Arms Park for scrapping.

Bill Beaumont took up the England captaincy in 1978, a notable moment in the country's rugby history. Beaumont went on to become one of the most admired and popular figures in the game. His quiet encouragement and unstinting commitment brought the best out of others. He was to lead England 21 times, claiming 11 victories, before he was forced into premature retirement from the game in 1982 after suffering a serious head injury playing for Lancashire against North Midlands in the County Championship final.

England's 1978 win at Murrayfield (15-0) was their first in Edinburgh in ten years, and all the more commendable given that they had opened their campaign with narrow defeats to France (15-6) in Paris and Wales (9-6) at Twickenham. Beaumont ensured that morale did not suffer, England rounding off with a 15-9 home win over Ireland.

Beaumont's side finished third, but again the championship contenders were Wales and France, with the key game this year taking place in Cardiff. Wales took the spoils and with it the championship and Grand Slam. Bennett scored two tries, and for all the mythology attached to the position, this was the first time since Raymond Ralph in 1931 that a Welsh fly half had crossed more than once in a championship

BELOW The teams as they appeared in the programme for the decisive encounter at Cardiff Arms Park in 1978.

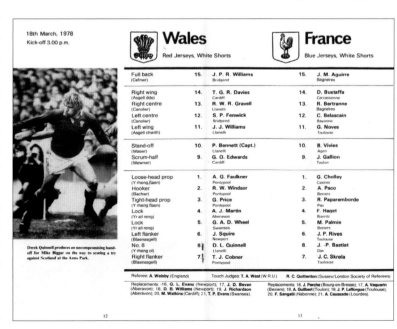

Derek Quinnell produces an uncompromising hand-off for Mike Biggar on the way to scoring a try against Scotland at the Arms Park.

18th March, 1978
Kick-off 3.00 p.m.

Wales
Red Jerseys, White Shorts

France
Blue Jerseys, White Shorts

		Wales		France
Full back (Cefnwr)	15.	J. P. R. Williams Bridgend	15.	J. M. Aguirre Bagnères
Right wing (Asgell dde)	14.	T. G. R. Davies Cardiff	14.	D. Bustaffa Carcassonne
Right centre (Canolwr)	13.	R. W. R. Gravell Llanelli	13.	R. Bertranne Bagnères
Left centre (Canolwr)	12.	S. P. Fenwick Bridgend	12.	C. Belascain Bayonne
Left wing (Asgell chwith)	11.	J. J. Williams Llanelli	11.	G. Noves Toulouse
Stand-off (Maswr)	10.	P. Bennett (Capt.) Llanelli	10.	B. Vivies Agen
Scrum-half (Mewnwr)	9.	G. O. Edwards Cardiff	9.	J. Gallion Toulon
Loose-head prop (Y rheng flaen)	1.	A. G. Faulkner Pontypool	1.	G. Cholley Castres
Hooker (Bachwr)	2.	R. W. Windsor Pontypool	2.	A. Paco Beziers
Tight-head prop (Y rheng flaen)	3.	G. Price Pontypool	3.	R. Paparemborde Pau
Lock (Yr ail reng)	4.	A. J. Martin Aberavon	4.	F. Haget Biarritz
Lock (Yr ail reng)	5.	A. G. D. Wheel Swansea	5.	M. Palmie Beziers
Left flanker (Blaenasgell)	6.	J. Squire Newport	6.	J. P. Rives Toulouse
No. 8 (Y rheng ol)	8.	D. L. Quinnell Llanelli	8.	J. -P. Bastiat Dax
Right flanker (Blaenasgell)	7.	T. J. Cobner Pontypool	7.	J. C. Skrela Toulouse

Referee: A. Welsby (England)   Touch Judges: T. A. West (W.R.U.)   R. C. Quittenton (Sussex/London Society of Referees)

Replacements: 16. G. L. Evans (Newport); 17. J. D. Bevan (Aberavon); 18. D. B. Williams (Newport); 19. J. Richardson (Aberavon); 20. M. Watkins (Cardiff); 21. T. P. Evans (Swansea).

Replacements: 16. J. Porche (Bourg-en-Bresse); 17. A. Vaquerin (Beziers); 18. A. Guilbert (Toulon); 19. J. P. Lafforgue (Toulouse); 20. F. Sangalli (Nabonne); 21. A. Caussade (Lourdes).

12   13

Phil Bennett

Gerald Davies

match. The result was 16-7, but joy was mixed with a certain mellow sorrow that this was to be the last time Edwards and Bennett were to be seen in the championship. No more sightings either of Terry Cobner or France back-row forwards Jean-Claude Skréla and Jean-Pierre Bastiat. It was Gerald Davies' last championship, too, while the following year Ireland's Mike Gibson brought the curtain down on his magnificent career after a record 56 championship games to his name across more than 15 years. Remarkable, quite remarkable. Some cast list, some era. Will we ever see their like again?

A frustrating and at times hugely demoralising decade for England ended in typical fashion. In 1979 they had a competitive pack of forwards, one that could take on the roughest and toughest in town, as evidenced in their heartening 7-6 win over France at Twickenham. But England still could not make the link work between forwards and backs. One step forwards, one step backwards. It was becoming an irritating pattern. England were maddeningly inconsistent.

Victory over France was followed by collapse at the Arms Park, England losing 27-3, only fly half Neil Bennett troubling the scorers with a solitary penalty goal. Not since 1905 had the Welsh margin of victory

been greater. And this overwhelming win was without those Welsh legends now in retirement. Steve Fenwick contrived to miss five penalties in the match yet still managed to equal Bennett's championship record of 38 points in a season, and thousands of Welsh fans were left rubbing their eyes in disbelief at the sight of J.P.R. being forced off the field with injury. Nevertheless, the win gave Wales the championship and their sixteenth Triple Crown to cap off their glorious decade.

LEFT J.P.R. Williams says farewell to the Welsh fans after the game against England at Cardiff Arms Park in 1979. It was to be a short retirement, since he returned for three more Tests in 1980-81 before finally calling it a day.
FACING PAGE TOP Two other Welsh legends, Phil Bennett and Gerald Davies, were seen no more in the championship after 1978.
CENTRE After England's hard-fought win over the French in 1979 the RFU entertained their guests at the London Hilton in Park Lane. BOTTOM Following the action: (left to right) English forwards Mike Rafter and Roger Uttley, referee Clive Norling and Scottish three-quarters Ian McGeechan and Jim Renwick watch as Malcolm Young gets his line moving during the 1979 Calcutta Cup match at Twickenham.

1969-70

10.01.1970 MURRAYFIELD
Scotland 9 *T:* ISG Smith *PG:* W Lauder 2
France 11 *T:* B Dauga, J-P Lux *C:* L Paries *DG:* L Paries
Referee: GC Lamb (England)

24.01.1970 STADE COLOMBES, PARIS
France 8 *T:* J Sillieres *C:* L Paries *DG:* L Paries
Ireland 0
Referee: RF Johnson (England)

07.02.1970 CARDIFF ARMS PARK
Wales 18 *T:* LTD Daniel, DB Llewellyn, SJ Dawes, WD Morris *C:* GO Edwards 2, LTD Daniel
Scotland 9 *T:* I Robertson *PG:* W Lauder
DG: I Robertson
Referee: DP d'Arcy (Ireland)

14.02.1970 TWICKENHAM
England 9 *T:* IR Shackleton *DG:* R Hiller 2
Ireland 3 *PG:* TJ Kiernan
Referee: AR Lewis (Wales)

28.02.1970 TWICKENHAM
England 13 *T:* DJ Duckham, MJ Novak *C:* R Hiller 2
PG: R Hiller
Wales 17 *T:* TM Davies, B John, JPR Williams, R Hopkins *C:* JPR Williams *DG:* B John
Referee: R Calmet (France), replaced by RF Johnson (England)

28.02.1970 LANSDOWNE ROAD, DUBLIN
Ireland 16 *T:* MG Molloy, KG Goodall, CMH Gibson, WJ Brown *C:* TJ Kiernan 2
Scotland 11 *T:* W Lauder, MA Smith *C:* ISG Smith
DG: I Robertson
Referee: C Durand (France)

14.03.1970 LANSDOWNE ROAD, DUBLIN
Ireland 14 *T:* ATA Duggan, KG Goodall *C:* TJ Kiernan
PG: TJ Kiernan *DG:* BJ McGann
Wales 0
Referee: GC Lamb (England)

21.03.1970 MURRAYFIELD
Scotland 14 *T:* AG Biggar, JWC Turner *C:* PC Brown
PG: PC Brown 2
England 5 *T:* JS Spencer *C:* R Hiller
Referee: M Joseph (Wales)

04.04.1970 CARDIFF ARMS PARK
Wales 11 *T:* WD Morris *C:* JPR Williams
PG: JPR Williams 2
France 6 *T:* J Cantoni, J-M Bonal
Referee: KD Kelleher (Ireland)

18.04.1970 STADE COLOMBES, PARIS
France 35 *T:* J-L Berot, J-M Bonal, R Bourgarel, B Dauga, J-P Lux, J Trillo *C:* P Villepreux 4
PG: P Villepreux *DG:* P Villepreux, J-L Berot
England 13 *T:* JS Spencer, RB Taylor *C:* AM Jorden 2
PG: AM Jorden
Referee: WKM Jones (Wales)

	P	W	D	L	FOR	AGAINST	PTS
France	4	3	0	1	60	33	6
Wales	4	3	0	1	46	42	6
Ireland	4	2	0	2	33	28	4
Scotland	4	1	0	3	43	50	2
England	4	1	0	3	40	69	2

1970-71

16.01.1971 STADE COLOMBES, PARIS
France 13 *T:* J Sillieres, P Villepreux *C:* P Villepreux 2
PG: P Villepreux
Scotland 8 *T:* WCC Steele *C:* PC Brown *PG:* ISG Smith
Referee: KD Kelleher (Ireland)

16.01.1971 CARDIFF ARMS PARK
Wales 22 *T:* TGR Davies 2, JC Bevan *C:* J Taylor 2
PG: JPR Williams *DG:* B John 2
England 6 *T:* RC Hannaford *PG:* PA Rossborough
Referee: DP d'Arcy (Ireland)

30.01.1971 LANSDOWNE ROAD, DUBLIN
Ireland 9 *T:* EL Grant *PG:* BJ O'Driscoll 2
France 9 *PG:* P Villepreux 2 *DG:* J-L Berot
Referee: GC Lamb (England)

06.02.1971 MURRAYFIELD
Scotland 18 *T:* AB Carmichael, CWW Rea
PG: PC Brown 4
Wales 19 *T:* J Taylor, GO Edwards, B John, TGR Davies *C:* B John, J Taylor *PG:* B John
Referee: MH Titcomb (England)

13.02.1971 LANSDOWNE ROAD, DUBLIN
Ireland 6 *T:* ATA Duggan, EL Grant
England 9 *PG:* R Hiller 3
Referee: M Joseph (Wales)

27.02.1971 TWICKENHAM
England 14 *T:* R Hiller *C:* R Hiller *PG:* R Hiller 3
France 14 *T:* R Bertranne, J Cantoni *C:* P Villepreux
PG: P Villepreux *DG:* J-L Berot
Referee: AR Lewis (Wales)

27.02.1971 MURRAYFIELD
Scotland 5 *T:* JNM Frame *C:* PC Brown
Ireland 17 *T:* ATA Duggan 2, EL Grant *C:* CMH Gibson
PG: CMH Gibson 2
Referee: WKM Jones (Wales)

13.03.1971 CARDIFF ARMS PARK
Wales 23 *T:* TGR Davies 2, GO Edwards 2 *C:* B John
PG: B John 2 *DG:* B John
Ireland 9 *PG:* CMH Gibson 3
Referee: RF Johnson (England)

20.03.1971 TWICKENHAM
England 15 *T:* R Hiller, A Neary *PG:* R Hiller 3
Scotland 16 *T:* PC Brown, DS Paterson, CWW Rea
C: PC Brown 2 *DG:* DS Paterson
Referee: C Durand (France)

27.03.1971 STADE COLOMBES, PARIS
France 5 *T:* B Dauga *C:* P Villepreux
Wales 9 *T:* GO Edwards, B John *PG:* B John
Referee: J Young (Scotland)

	P	W	D	L	FOR	AGAINST	PTS
Wales	4	4	0	0	73	38	8
France	4	1	2	1	41	40	4
England	4	1	1	2	44	58	3
Ireland	4	1	1	2	41	46	3
Scotland	4	1	0	3	47	64	2

1971-72

15.01.1972 TWICKENHAM
England 3 *PG:* R Hiller
Wales 12 *T:* JPR Williams *C:* B John *PG:* B John 2
Referee: J Young (Scotland)

15.01.1972 MURRAYFIELD
Scotland 20 *T:* CM Telfer, JM Renwick, JNM Frame
C: AR Brown *PG:* PC Brown *DG:* CM Telfer
France 9 *T:* B Dauga *C:* P Villepreux *PG:* P Villepreux
Referee: M Joseph (Wales)

29.01.1972 STADE COLOMBES, PARIS
France 9 *T:* J-P Lux *C:* P Villepreux *PG:* P Villepreux
Ireland 14 *T:* JJ Moloney, RJ McLoughlin
PG: TJ Kiernan 2
Referee: AR Lewis (Wales)

05.02.1972 CARDIFF ARMS PARK
Wales 35 *T:* GO Edwards 2, RTE Bergiers, TGR Davies, J Taylor 2 *C:* B John 3 *PG:* B John 3
Scotland 12 *T:* RL Clark *C:* PC Brown *PG:* JM Renwick, PC Brown
Referee: GA Jamison (Ireland)

12.02.1972 TWICKENHAM
England 12 *T:* CW Ralston *C:* R Hiller *PG:* R Hiller 2
Ireland 16 *T:* MK Flynn, TO Grace *C:* TJ Kiernan
PG: TJ Kiernan *DG:* BJ McGann
Referee: R Austry (France)

26.02.1972 STADE COLOMBES, PARIS
France 37 *T:* B Duprat 2, J-P Biemouret, J-P Lux, J Sillieres, W Spanghero *C:* P Villepreux 5
PG: P Villepreux
England 12 *T:* MC Beese *C:* AGB Old *PG:* AGB Old 2
Referee: TFE Grierson (Scotland)

18.03.1972 MURRAYFIELD
Scotland 23 *T:* PC Brown, NA MacEwan
PG: PC Brown 3, AR Brown *DG:* CM Telfer
England 9 *PG:* AGB Old 3
Referee: M Joseph (Wales)

25.03.1972 CARDIFF ARMS PARK
Wales 20 *T:* TGR Davies, JC Bevan *C:* B John 4
France 6 *PG:* P Villepreux 2
Referee: MH Titcomb (England)

	P	W	D	L	FOR	AGAINST	PTS
Wales	3	3	0	0	67	21	6
Scotland	3	2	0	1	55	53	4
Ireland	2	2	0	0	30	21	4
France	4	1	0	3	61	66	2
England	4	0	0	4	36	88	0

Ireland did not meet Wales or Scotland

1972-73

13.01.1973 PARC DES PRINCES, PARIS
France 16 *T:* C Dourthe *PG:* J-P Romeu 3
DG: J-P Romeu
Scotland 13 *T:* AJM Lawson *PG:* PC Brown 2
DG: IR McGeechan
Referee: KA Pattinson (England), replaced by F Palmade (France)

20.01.1973 CARDIFF ARMS PARK
Wales 25 *T:* JC Bevan 2, TGR Davies, GO Edwards, AJ Lewis *C:* P Bennett *PG:* J Taylor
England 9 *PG:* SA Doble 2 *DG:* AR Cowman
Referee: G Domercq (France)

03.02.1973 MURRAYFIELD
Scotland 10 *T:* CM Telfer, WCC Steele *C:* DW Morgan
Wales 9 *PG:* P Bennett 2, J Taylor
Referee: F Palmade (France)

10.02.1973 LANSDOWNE ROAD, DUBLIN
Ireland 18 *T:* TO Grace, RA Milliken *C:* BJ McGann 2
PG: BJ McGann *DG:* BJ McGann
England 9 *T:* A Neary *C:* AM Jorden *PG:* AM Jorden
Referee: AM Hosie (Scotland)

24.02.1973 TWICKENHAM
England 14 *T:* DJ Duckham 2 *PG:* AM Jorden 2
France 6 *T:* R Bertranne *C:* J-P Romeu
Referee: KH Clark (Ireland)

24.02.1973 MURRAYFIELD
Scotland 19 *T:* IW Forsyth *PG:* DW Morgan 2
DG: DW Morgan 2, IR McGeechan
Ireland 14 *T:* AW McMaster, TJ Kiernan
PG: BJ McGann 2
Referee: AR Lewis (Wales)

10.03.1973 CARDIFF ARMS PARK
Wales 16 *T:* JL Shanklin, GO Edwards *C:* P Bennett
PG: P Bennett 2
Ireland 12 *T:* CMH Gibson *C:* BJ McGann
PG: BJ McGann 2
Referee: TFE Grierson (Scotland)

17.03.1973 TWICKENHAM
England 20 *T:* PJ Dixon 2, GW Evans, PJ Squires
C: AM Jorden 2
Scotland 13 *T:* WCC Steele 2 *C:* AR Irvine
PG: DW Morgan
Referee: JC Kelleher (Wales)

24.03.1973 PARC DES PRINCES, PARIS
France 12 *PG:* J-P Romeu 3 *DG:* J-P Romeu
Wales 3 *PG:* P Bennett
Referee: DP d'Arcy (Ireland)

14.04.1973 LANSDOWNE ROAD, DUBLIN
Ireland 6 *PG:* CMH Gibson, AH Ensor
France 4 *T:* J-F Philipponneau
Referee: RF Johnson (England)

	P	W	D	L	FOR	AGAINST	PTS
Wales	4	2	0	2	53	43	4
Ireland	4	2	0	2	50	48	4
France	4	2	0	2	38	36	4
Scotland	4	2	0	2	55	59	4
England	4	2	0	2	52	62	4

1973-74

19.01.1974 PARC DES PRINCES, PARIS
France 9 *T:* V Boffelli *C:* J-M Aguirre *PG:* J-L Berot
Ireland 6 *PG:* AH Ensor 2
Referee: AM Hosie (Scotland)

19.01.1974 CARDIFF ARMS PARK
Wales 6 *T:* TJ Cobner *C:* P Bennett
Scotland 0
Referee: RF Johnson (England)

02.02.1974 LANSDOWNE ROAD, DUBLIN
Ireland 9 *PG:* AH Ensor 3
Wales 9 *T:* JJ Williams *C:* P Bennett *PG:* P Bennett
Referee: KA Pattinson (England)

02.02.1974 MURRAYFIELD
Scotland 16 *T:* AR Irvine, W Lauder *C:* AR Irvine
PG: AR Irvine 2
England 14 *T:* FE Cotton, A Neary *PG:* AGB Old
DG: PA Rossborough
Referee: J St Guilhem (France)

16.02.1974 TWICKENHAM
England 21 *T:* PJ Squires *C:* AGB Old *PG:* AGB Old 5
Ireland 26 *T:* CMH Gibson 2, JJ Moloney, TAP Moore
C: CMH Gibson 2 *PG:* AH Ensor *DG:* MAM Quinn
Referee: M Joseph (Wales)

16.02.1974 CARDIFF ARMS PARK
Wales 16 *T:* JJ Williams *PG:* P Bennett 3
DG: GO Edwards
France 16 *T:* J-P Lux *PG:* J-P Romeu 3 *DG:* J-P Romeu
Referee: NR Sanson (Scotland)

02.03.1974 LANSDOWNE ROAD, DUBLIN
Ireland 9 *T:* RA Milliken *C:* CMH Gibson
PG: SA McKinney
Scotland 6 *PG:* AR Irvine 2
Referee: F Palmade (France)

02.03.1974 PARC DES PRINCES, PARIS
France 12 *T:* J-P Romeu *C:* J-P Romeu *PG:* J-P Romeu
DG: J-P Romeu
England 12 *T:* DJ Duckham *C:* AGB Old *PG:* AGB Old
DG: GW Evans
Referee: JC Kelleher (Wales)

16.03.1974 TWICKENHAM
England 16 *T:* DJ Duckham, AG Ripley *C:* AGB Old
PG: AGB Old 2
Wales 12 *T:* TM Davies *C:* P Bennett *PG:* P Bennett 2
Referee: JR West (Ireland)

16.03.1974 MURRAYFIELD
Scotland 19 *T:* AF McHarg, LG Dick *C:* AR Irvine
PG: AR Irvine 2, DW Morgan
France 6 *PG:* J-P Romeu *DG:* J-P Romeu
Referee: KH Clark (Ireland)

	P	W	D	L	FOR	AGAINST	PTS
Ireland	4	2	1	1	50	45	5
Wales	4	1	2	1	43	41	4
France	4	1	2	1	43	53	4
Scotland	4	2	0	2	41	35	4
England	4	1	1	2	63	66	3

1974-75

18.01.1975 PARC DES PRINCES, PARIS
France 10 *T:* J-F Gourdon *PG:* M Taffray 2
Wales 25 *T:* SP Fenwick, TJ Cobner, TGR Davies,
GO Edwards, G Price *C:* SP Fenwick *PG:* SP Fenwick
Referee: KA Pattinson (England)

18.01.1975 LANSDOWNE ROAD, DUBLIN
Ireland 12 *T:* CMH Gibson, WMcM McCombe
C: WMcM McCombe 2
England 9 *T:* CB Stevens *C:* AGB Old *DG:* AGB Old
Referee: F Palmade (France)

01.02.1975 TWICKENHAM
England 20 *T:* DJ Duckham, PA Rossborough
PG: PA Rossborough 4
France 27 *T:* J-M Etchenique, J-F Gourdon, A Guilbert,
C Spanghero *C:* L Paries 4 *PG:* L Paries
Referee: TFE Grierson (Scotland)

01.02.1975 MURRAYFIELD
Scotland 20 *T:* JM Renwick, WCC Steele
PG: AR Irvine 2 *DG:* DW Morgan, IR McGeechan
Ireland 13 *T:* JP Dennison, TO Grace
C: WMcM McCombe *PG:* WMcM McCombe
Referee: RF Johnson (England)

15.02.1975 PARC DES PRINCES, PARIS
France 10 *T:* C Dourthe *PG:* L Paries *DG:* R Astre
Scotland 9 *PG:* AR Irvine 3
Referee: MS Lewis (Wales)

15.02.1975 CARDIFF ARMS PARK
Wales 20 *T:* TGR Davies, SP Fenwick, JJ Williams
C: AJ Martin *PG:* AJ Martin 2
England 4 *T:* NE Horton
Referee: AM Hosie (Scotland)

01.03.1975 LANSDOWNE ROAD, DUBLIN
Ireland 25 *T:* AH Ensor, TO Grace, WJ McBride
C: WMcM McCombe 2 *PG:* WMcM McCombe
DG: WMcM McCombe 2
France 6 *PG:* L Paries *DG:* L Paries
Referee: DM Lloyd (Wales)

01.03.1975 MURRAYFIELD
Scotland 12 *PG:* DW Morgan 3 *DG:* IR McGeechan
Wales 10 *T:* TP Evans *PG:* SP Fenwick 2
Referee: JR West (Ireland)

15.03.1975 CARDIFF ARMS PARK
Wales 32 *T:* GO Edwards, TGR Davies, AG Faulkner,
JJ Williams, RTE Bergiers *C:* P Bennett 3 *PG:* P Bennett 2
Ireland 4 *T:* WP Duggan
Referee: J St Guilhem (France)

15.03.1975 TWICKENHAM
England 7 *T:* AJ Morley *PG:* WN Bennett
Scotland 6 *PG:* DW Morgan 2
Referee: DP d'Arcy (Ireland)

	P	W	D	L	FOR	AGAINST	PTS
Wales	4	3	0	1	87	30	6
Ireland	4	2	0	2	54	67	4
France	4	2	0	2	53	79	4
Scotland	4	2	0	2	47	40	4
England	4	1	0	3	40	65	2

1975-76

10.01.1976 MURRAYFIELD
Scotland 6 *PG:* JM Renwick *DG:* DW Morgan
France 13 *T:* A Dubertrand *PG:* J-P Romeu 3
Referee: KA Pattinson (England)

17.01.1976 TWICKENHAM
England 9 *PG:* AJ Hignell 3
Wales 21 *T:* JPR Williams 2, GO Edwards
C: SP Fenwick 3 *PG:* AJ Martin
Referee: G Domercq (France)

07.02.1976 PARC DES PRINCES, PARIS
France 26 *T:* J Pecune, G Cholley, J Fouroux, J-P Rives
C: J-P Romeu, J-P Bastiat *PG:* J-P Romeu 2
Ireland 3 *PG:* JC Robbie
Referee: A Welsby (England)

07.02.1976 CARDIFF ARMS PARK
Wales 28 *T:* JJ Williams, TP Evans, GO Edwards
C: P Bennett 2 *PG:* P Bennett 3 *DG:* SP Fenwick
Scotland 6 *T:* AR Irvine *C:* DW Morgan
Referee: Dr A Cuny (France)

21.02.1976 LANSDOWNE ROAD, DUBLIN
Ireland 9 *PG:* BJ McGann 3
Wales 34 *T:* TGR Davies 2, GO Edwards, P Bennett
C: P Bennett 3 *PG:* P Bennett 3, AJ Martin
Referee: NR Sanson (Scotland)

21.02.1976 MURRAYFIELD
Scotland 22 *T:* AJM Lawson 2, DG Leslie
C: AR Irvine 2 *PG:* AR Irvine 2
England 12 *T:* AW Maxwell *C:* AGB Old
PG: AGB Old 2
Referee: DM Lloyd (Wales)

06.03.1976 TWICKENHAM
England 12 *PG:* AGB Old 4
Ireland 13 *T:* TO Grace *PG:* BJ McGann 2
DG: BJ McGann
Referee: AM Hosie (Scotland)

06.03.1976 CARDIFF ARMS PARK
Wales 19 *T:* JJ Williams *PG:* P Bennett 2, SP Fenwick 2,
AJ Martin
France 13 *T:* J-F Gourdon, J-L Averous *C:* J-P Romeu
PG: J-P Romeu
Referee: JR West (Ireland)

20.03.1976 LANSDOWNE ROAD, DUBLIN
Ireland 6 *PG:* BJ McGann 2
Scotland 15 *PG:* AR Irvine 4 *DG:* R Wilson
Referee: MS Lewis (Wales)

20.03.1976 PARC DES PRINCES, PARIS
France 30 *T:* R Paparemborde 2, J-P Bastiat, J Fouroux,
J-F Gourdon, J-P Romeu *C:* J-P Romeu 3
England 9 *T:* PJ Dixon *C:* PE Butler *PG:* PE Butler
Referee: KH Clark (Ireland)

	P	W	D	L	FOR	AGAINST	PTS
Wales	4	4	0	0	102	37	8
France	4	3	0	1	82	37	6
Scotland	4	2	0	2	49	59	4
Ireland	4	1	0	3	31	87	2
England	4	0	0	4	42	86	0

1976-77

15.01.1977 TWICKENHAM
England 26 *T:* CP Kent, MAC Slemen, RM Uttley, M Young *C:* AJ Hignell 2 *PG:* AJ Hignell 2
Scotland 6 *PG:* AR Irvine 2
Referee: M Joseph (Wales)

15.01.1977 CARDIFF ARMS PARK
Wales 25 *T:* TGR Davies, JPR Williams, RC Burgess *C:* P Bennett 2 *PG:* P Bennett 2 *DG:* SP Fenwick
Ireland 9 *PG:* CMH Gibson 3
Referee: NR Sanson (Scotland)

05.02.1977 PARC DES PRINCES, PARIS
France 16 *T:* J-C Skrela, D Harize *C:* J-P Romeu *PG:* J-P Romeu 2
Wales 9 *PG:* SP Fenwick 3
Referee: AM Hosie (Scotland)

05.02.1977 LANSDOWNE ROAD, DUBLIN
Ireland 0
England 4 *T:* MJ Cooper
Referee: F Palmade (France)

19.02.1977 TWICKENHAM
England 3 *PG:* AJ Hignell
France 4 *T:* F Sangalli
Referee: JC Kelleher (Wales)

19.02.1977 MURRAYFIELD
Scotland 21 *T:* WBB Gammell 2, DF Madsen *PG:* AR Irvine 2 *DG:* DW Morgan
Ireland 18 *T:* CMH Gibson *C:* CMH Gibson *PG:* CMH Gibson 2, MAM Quinn *DG:* MAM Quinn
Referee: M Joseph (Wales)

05.03.1977 PARC DES PRINCES, PARIS
France 23 *T:* A Paco, D Harize, R Bertranne, R Paparemborde *C:* J-P Romeu 2 *PG:* J-P Romeu
Scotland 3 *PG:* AR Irvine
Referee: M Joseph (Wales)

05.03.1977 CARDIFF ARMS PARK
Wales 14 *T:* GO Edwards, JPR Williams *PG:* SP Fenwick 2
England 9 *PG:* AJ Hignell 3
Referee: DIH Burnett (Ireland)

19.03.1977 LANSDOWNE ROAD, DUBLIN
Ireland 6 *PG:* CMH Gibson, MAM Quinn
France 15 *T:* J-P Bastiat *C:* J-M Aguirre *PG:* J-M Aguirre 2, J-P Romeu
Referee: AM Hosie (Scotland)

19.03.1977 MURRAYFIELD
Scotland 9 *T:* AR Irvine *C:* AR Irvine *DG:* IR McGeechan
Wales 18 *T:* JJ Williams, P Bennett *C:* P Bennett 2 *PG:* P Bennett 2
Referee: G Domercq (France)

	P	W	D	L	FOR	AGAINST	PTS
France	4	4	0	0	58	21	8
Wales	4	3	0	1	66	43	6
England	4	2	0	2	42	24	4
Scotland	4	1	0	3	39	85	2
Ireland	4	0	0	4	33	65	0

1977-78

21.01.1978 LANSDOWNE ROAD, DUBLIN
Ireland 12 *T:* SA McKinney *C:* AJP Ward *PG:* AJP Ward 2
Scotland 9 *PG:* DW Morgan 3
Referee: PE Hughes (England)

21.01.1978 PARC DES PRINCES, PARIS
France 15 *T:* J-L Averous, J Gallion *C:* J-M Aguirre 2 *PG:* J-M Aguirre
England 6 *DG:* AGB Old 2
Referee: NR Sanson (Scotland)

04.02.1978 TWICKENHAM
England 6 *PG:* AJ Hignell 2
Wales 9 *PG:* P Bennett 3
Referee: NR Sanson (Scotland)

04.02.1978 MURRAYFIELD
Scotland 16 *T:* D Shedden, AR Irvine *C:* DW Morgan *PG:* DW Morgan 2 *DG:* DW Morgan
France 19 *T:* J Gallion, F Haget *C:* J-M Aguirre *PG:* J-M Aguirre 3
Referee: CGP Thomas (Wales)

18.02.1978 PARC DES PRINCES, PARIS
France 10 *T:* J Gallion *PG:* J-M Aguirre 2
Ireland 9 *PG:* AJP Ward 3
Referee: CGP Thomas (Wales)

18.02.1978 CARDIFF ARMS PARK
Wales 22 *T:* GO Edwards, RWR Gravell, SP Fenwick, DL Quinnell *PG:* P Bennett *DG:* P Bennett
Scotland 14 *T:* JM Renwick, AJ Tomes *PG:* DW Morgan 2
Referee: JR West (Ireland)

04.03.1978 LANSDOWNE ROAD, DUBLIN
Ireland 16 *T:* JJ Moloney *PG:* AJP Ward 3 *DG:* AJP Ward
Wales 20 *T:* SP Fenwick, JJ Williams *PG:* SP Fenwick 4
Referee: G Domercq (France)

04.03.1978 MURRAYFIELD
Scotland 0
England 15 *T:* BG Nelmes, PJ Squires *C:* M Young 2 *PG:* PW Dodge
Referee: JR West (Ireland)

18.03.1978 TWICKENHAM
England 15 *T:* PJ Dixon, MAC Slemen *C:* M Young 2 *PG:* M Young
Ireland 9 *PG:* AJP Ward 2 *DG:* AJP Ward
Referee: F Palmade (France)

18.03.1978 CARDIFF ARMS PARK
Wales 16 *T:* P Bennett 2 *C:* P Bennett *DG:* GO Edwards, SP Fenwick
France 7 *T:* J-C Skrela *DG:* B Vivies
Referee: A Welsby (England)

	P	W	D	L	FOR	AGAINST	PTS
Wales	4	4	0	0	67	43	8
France	4	3	0	1	51	47	6
England	4	2	0	2	42	33	4
Ireland	4	1	0	3	46	54	2
Scotland	4	0	0	4	39	68	0

1978-79

20.01.1979 LANSDOWNE ROAD, DUBLIN
Ireland 9 *PG:* AJP Ward 3
France 9 *T:* A Caussade *C:* J-M Aguirre *PG:* J-M Aguirre
Referee: RC Quittenton (England)

20.01.1979 MURRAYFIELD
Scotland 13 *T:* AR Irvine *PG:* AR Irvine 3
Wales 19 *T:* HE Rees, TD Holmes *C:* SP Fenwick *PG:* SP Fenwick 3
Referee: F Palmade (France)

03.02.1979 TWICKENHAM
England 7 *T:* MAC Slemen *PG:* WN Bennett
Scotland 7 *T:* JY Rutherford *PG:* AR Irvine
Referee: C Norling (Wales)

03.02.1979 CARDIFF ARMS PARK
Wales 24 *T:* AJ Martin, P Ringer *C:* SP Fenwick 2 *PG:* SP Fenwick 4
Ireland 21 *T:* AC McLennan, CS Patterson *C:* AJP Ward 2 *PG:* AJP Ward 3
Referee: AM Hosie (Scotland)

17.02.1979 PARC DES PRINCES, PARIS
France 14 *T:* J-F Gourdon 2 *PG:* J-M Aguirre 2
Wales 13 *T:* TD Holmes *PG:* SP Fenwick 3
Referee: DIH Burnett (Ireland)

17.02.1979 LANSDOWNE ROAD, DUBLIN
Ireland 12 *T:* AC McLennan *C:* AJP Ward *PG:* AJP Ward *DG:* AJP Ward
England 7 *T:* WN Bennett *PG:* WN Bennett
Referee: AM Hosie (Scotland)

03.03.1979 TWICKENHAM
England 7 *T:* WN Bennett *PG:* WN Bennett
France 6 *T:* F Costes *C:* J-M Aguirre
Referee: JR West (Ireland)

03.03.1979 MURRAYFIELD
Scotland 11 *T:* KW Robertson, AR Irvine *PG:* AR Irvine
Ireland 11 *T:* CS Patterson 2 *PG:* AJP Ward
Referee: CGP Thomas (Wales)

17.03.1979 PARC DES PRINCES, PARIS
France 21 *T:* Y Malquier 2, C Belascain *PG:* R Aguerre, J-M Aguirre *DG:* R Aguerre
Scotland 17 *T:* KW Robertson, G Dickson, AR Irvine *C:* AR Irvine *PG:* AR Irvine
Referee: RC Quittenton (England)

17.03.1979 CARDIFF ARMS PARK
Wales 27 *T:* HE Rees, DS Richards, P Ringer, MG Roberts, JJ Williams *C:* AJ Martin, SP Fenwick *DG:* WG Davies
England 3 *PG:* WN Bennett
Referee: J-P Bonnet (France)

	P	W	D	L	FOR	AGAINST	PTS
Wales	4	3	0	1	83	51	6
France	4	2	1	1	50	46	5
Ireland	4	1	2	1	53	51	4
England	4	1	1	2	24	52	3
Scotland	4	0	2	2	48	58	2

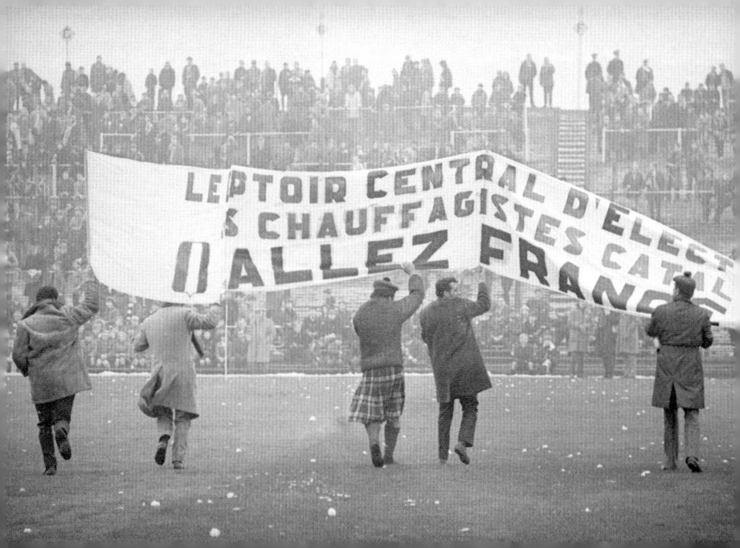
LEPTOIR CENTRAL D'ELECT
S CHAUFFAGISTES CATAL
ALLEZ FRANC

> "
> Why should England's
> Grand Slam of 1980 have
> been such a notable
> landmark? Primarily
> because of its rarity value
> in those days.
> "

1980s

Billy Beaumont: the sweat-drenched headband, the tache, the unruly mop of hair, the furrowed brow, the big backside, the unstinting effort, the wholehearted commitment, the sense of loyalty, the conscience of an England side that had endured so much hardship, so many years of underachievement and heartache, bearing the brunt of criticism, all taken with good-natured stoicism. Yes, Beaumont deserved to be the toast of Murrayfield, borne aloft by England after they had claimed their first Grand Slam in 23 years and closed it out with such a flourish.

Beaumont was, and is still, one of the most popular figures in the game. What he was on the field, he has remained since leaving it – a character of immense decency and trustworthiness. He would not make for an identikit picture of a ratings-winning TV personality, but that is exactly what he became as a long-running captain on the BBC's *A Question of Sport*, testimony to the regard in which he was held by the man in the street. That appeal had its roots in the manner and significance of England's Grand Slam in 1980, a long-awaited moment for followers of the red rose. As Beaumont toiled, supported by his chums in the impressive England pack, durable men such as the forbidding Gloucester prop Phil Blakeway, the implacable Angoulême lock Maurice Colclough, and the stylish breakaway Tony Neary, a man of immense skill and tenacity, so did England inch their way forward towards that elusive goal.

Beaumont was at the heart of that struggle. For England's Grand Slam did not come without a measure of pain and anxiety. England did not roll over their opponents without as much as a by your leave. True, they did send the champagne corks popping in style with that emphatic Slam-winning victory over Scotland – hat-trick hero John Carleton step forward and take your bow – but there were bruises along the way.

Why should England's Grand Slam of 1980 have been such a notable landmark, bearing in mind the years of success under Will Carling in the next decade? Primarily because of its rarity value in those days. While France managed a couple of Grand Slams later in the decade (1981 and 1987) and Scotland had an annus mirabilis in 1984, the feeling was that England ought to do better. That was always the complaint levelled at them during their years of desolation. They had many clubs, more players, more this, more that and still they came up short. That was why there was such an outpouring of relief when the goods were finally delivered on a jubilant March afternoon in 1980.

Beaumont had been an ever-present starter in the England engine room since the second Test against Australia in May 1975, his debut having come a few months earlier against Ireland at Lansdowne Road, when he had deputised for the injured Roger Uttley. His career began slowly, building towards that seminal 1980 season. He took over the captaincy in 1978, an honest, grafting lock who led by example, and England's Grand Slam success two years later propelled him into the Lions captaincy for the summer's tour of South Africa. When injury brought premature retirement, Beaumont was England's most capped lock (34 caps), had served most matches as captain (21 Tests) and had pulled on the white jersey a record 33 times in a row, a sequence that had begun with his second Test appearance, as a replacement, in the first Test against Australia way back in 1975; his last outing in an England shirt, although no one realised it at the time, was the 9-9 draw

BELOW England's Grand Slam skipper Bill Beaumont seen through the eyes of caricaturist John Ireland. FACING PAGE TOP Victorious at Murrayfield: Beaumont is chaired from the field by euphoric fans after England beat Scotland 30-18 to record their 1980 clean sweep. BOTTOM England wing John Carleton rounds the Scottish defence and touches down as part of his hat-trick in Edinburgh.

Bill Beaumont

ABOVE Beaumont and some of his trusty lieutenants against Ireland at Headquarters in 1980: (left to right) Steve Smith, Roger Uttley, Fran Cotton and the captain himself.
FACING PAGE BOTTOM The long-serving Tony Neary takes the ball into contact at Murrayfield. On the far left is Maurice Colclough, while Roger Uttley provides close support and Steve Smith arrives to link with the backs. TOP The reliable boot of Leicester's Dusty Hare served Beaumont and England well in Grand Slam year.

against Scotland at Murrayfield in January 1982. A couple of weeks later he took that blow to the head and a famous career was brought to an unfortunate close.

Bill had fine lieutenants around him. To paraphrase what Martin Johnson was later to say in a vain attempt to debunk the myths that swirled around his 2003 World Cup-winning captaincy, you are only as good as the blokes fighting in the trenches alongside you. Johnson had the likes of Lawrence Dallaglio, Jason Leonard and Matt Dawson, not to mention dropped-goal king Jonny Wilkinson, while Beaumont could call upon men such as Fran Cotton, Peter Wheeler, Roger Uttley, Tony Neary and Steve Smith, plus the big boot of Dusty Hare. In fact, when you run through that list of right-hand men you wonder that Beaumont managed to get a word in edgeways.

In fact, on one celebrated occasion in 1982 he didn't manage even that. As Bill was exhorting his troops to greater effort at half-time during a tight game against Australia at Twickenham, he was interrupted by scrum half Steve Smith, who was desperate to make an important observation. ''Ere, Bill,' said Smith. 'There's some bird just run past with your backside on her chest.' It was the well-endowed Erica Roe making her infamous topless dash across the Twickenham turf. God bless Erica. God bless Bill's backside. England went on to win that game 15-11, and Roe went on to a celebrity afterlife, still the proud perpetrator of one of the most uplifting runs ever seen at Twickenham.

The England of that period were a mature side, a hard-nosed outfit with a bit of glitter and dash in there as well. Neary was a stalwart figure on the flank, full of spiky intent but with a touch of class, too, in all that he did. He and Fergus Slattery had a wonderful duel for the coveted No. 7 shirt on the 1974 Lions tour to South Africa, the Irishman just getting the nod. But Neary was an unstinting servant of English rugby through the dark days of the 1970s, always tackling, always fetching and carrying, always unbowed, until ending in style at Murrayfield in 1980. At the time, Neary was England's most capped player, with 43 Tests under his belt, the ratio of wins to losses (15 to 25, plus three draws) reflecting England's struggles in the era in which he played.

Another legend of the English game to bow out in 1980 was Roger Uttley. Like Neary, Uttley spent time as England captain and he was then as he is now, a character of unflagging good spirit and integrity. He was selfless as well as relentless in his pursuit of whatever goal, happy to play wherever the selectors wanted him to play and took the fight to the opposition with customary zeal. Uttley, a schoolmaster at Harrow, went on to become a highly regarded and successful England coach. A Lion, too, a rugged individual, a faithful ally in arduous circumstances, Uttley deserves his place in the English pantheon.

If there was a defining feature of the 1980s, it was perhaps the rise of the goal-kicker. England's principal exponent of the goal-kicking art in the early years of the decade was Leicester's Dusty Hare. The Newark farmer had a personable character and a deadly boot. The easily recognisable bald pate and the swinging right peg, these were the hallmarks of Hare, unflustered and unflappable. Dusty had made his debut as far back as 1974, against Wales at Twickenham, but it was across these first few years of the 1980s that he came to the fore. He swung, and kept swinging. By the time he went off into international retirement in 1984, he was England's record points scorer with 240 from 25 Tests.

At no time was Hare's accuracy more valuable to England than in the 1980 game against Wales at Twickenham. Beaumont might never have gone on to acclaim and fame if Dusty's boot had not done the job that afternoon. Wales scored two tries, Hare three penalties. Result? England 9 Wales 8. It was a narrow victory, yet the scoreboard does not tell anything of that game – not the drama, nor the rancour, nor the controversy. It was a nasty old match, laced with spite and violence. Wales flanker Paul Ringer achieved lasting notoriety by being sent off by referee David Burnett for a late tackle on Bath fly half John Horton. The game had barely started, less than 14 minutes on the clock, and Wales were down to 14 men.

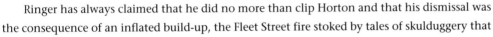

Dusty Hare

Ringer has always claimed that he did no more than clip Horton and that his dismissal was the consequence of an inflated build-up, the Fleet Street fire stoked by tales of skulduggery that

1980: ENGLAND'S GRAND SLAM YEAR.
ABOVE *The England team to play Scotland at Murrayfield. Back row (left to right): S.G.F. Mills (replacement), J-P. Bonnet (referee), W.H. Hare, P.W. Dodge, R.M. Uttley, M.J. Colclough, J.P. Scott, F.E. Cotton, A. Neary, M. Keyworth (replacement), G.A.F. Sargent (replacement), F. Palmade (touch judge). Middle row: G. Chevrier (touch judge), P.J. Wheeler, C.R. Woodward, M.A.C. Slemen, W.B. Beaumont (capt), S.J. Smith, J. Carleton, P.J. Blakeway. Front: A.G.B. Old (replacement), J.A. Palmer (replacement), I.G. Peck (replacement), J.P. Horton.*
RIGHT *Wales flanker Paul Ringer is on his way for an early bath after being dismissed at Twickenham.* BELOW *Clive Woodward takes on opposing centre David Richards during the same game.*
FACING PAGE *Andy Irvine – ace goal-kicker and running full back for Scotland.*

had followed Wales from their fractious opening game against France. Jean-Pierre Rives had denounced the over-robust attitude of Wales at the post-match banquet. Ringer was in the frame long before he scooted off the side of a scrum to put the heat on Horton. And so he became the first man to head for a disconsolate early bath at Twickenham since New Zealander Cyril Brownlie was dismissed in 1925.

But there was a game still to play as the black-haired figure of Ringer, still brooding, protesting his innocence (as thousands have done ever since, humming along to a Max Boyce ditty), trudged off down the Twickenham tunnel. If the thought was that his team-mates would be shocked and subdued by his premature exit, it proved to be anything but the case. The Welsh pack, with Alan Martin and Geoff Wheel grunting and straining to best effect in the engine room, made light of their handicap. England had to fight tooth and nail for every inch of turf. Wales were unstinting and unyielding that day, getting their touchdowns through captain Jeff Squire and wing Elgan Rees and looking for all the world as if they would snatch a dramatic, unexpected victory. In injury time Dusty's boot ensured that another tale was told, one of English escape and relief, a boost to England's championship hopes, and the third leg duly completed en route to the Grand Slam. It was a late, late show by England, but the result is there in the history books with its eventual contribution to an historic season.

Andy Irvine

England had begun their championship campaign with a comfortable 24-9 win over Ireland at Twickenham. Well, it wasn't too comfortable if you were Tony Bond. The hard-tackling Sale centre broke a leg. One person's misfortune was, as ever, another's opportunity. On came Clive Woodward, who was to become an integral part of England's Grand Slam side, his mazy, mesmeric run at Murrayfield having been recalled on many an occasion since. Woodward was also a tourist with the Lions to South Africa that summer under Beaumont's leadership. Years later, in 1997, Woodward was to get the backing of Beaumont, as well as that of Fran Cotton, another Lion and a fixture in the 1980 Grand Slam side, to become England's first professional coach.

England scored three tries against Ireland through John Scott, Mike Slemen and Steve Smith, Hare weighing in with three conversions and two penalty goals. The man kicking the goals for the opposition was the rather pasty figure of Old Belvedere's Ollie Campbell. His looks belied a hard inner self. Campbell's debut contribution that day was just three penalty goals, but there were to be many more points gleaned from that source. He finished the 1980 championship with a season record 46 points for Ireland. Elsewhere, Andy Irvine was clocking up a national best 35 championship points for Scotland. The era of the kicker had dawned. Mind you, Irvine in particular was no slouch when it came to stretching his legs as well.

That encouraging Twickenham opening was followed by an even more impressive win at the Parc des Princes, England scoring tries through John Carleton and Nick Preston in a 17-13 victory, their first in Paris since 1964. Once the discord from the Wales match had died down, it was onwards and upwards, north to Edinburgh and a date with – what? Destiny or more disenchantment? If there were any fears that England would fall at the final hurdle, flop when the scrutiny was at its fiercest, then they were quickly dispelled. No wobbles from Beaumont's

THIS PAGE Scenes from 1981.
TOP Scotland's Jim Calder
escapes the clutches of Mike
Slemen to score at
Twickenham. Slemen,
though, caused problems of
his own at the other end
(above right). Here he evades
Andy Irvine to touch down
but he also created a try for
Huw Davies in England's
23-17 win. ABOVE Marcus
Rose, assisted by Peter
Wheeler, in place-kicking
action against France.

side. Orrell's finest, John Carleton, nailed the first hat-trick for England in 56 years, further tries coming from Mike Slemen and Steve Smith. The final scoreline was 30-18, the 48-point aggregate the highest the fixture had ever produced. A grand Grand Slam, indeed.

That was as good as it got for England through the decade. It was an end, not a beginning, a fitting reward for those who had laboured for the cause through the unproductive 1970s. England did not throw in the towel the following year, far from it; they managed rousing wins over Scotland (23-17) at Twickenham and Ireland (10-6) away and came close to victory in their other two fixtures. England lost to Wales (21-19) at the Arms Park but might have pulled off a win but for a late penalty awarded against them in front of the posts, Steve Fenwick doing the business. Hare, for once, could not do likewise when offered a last-gasp chance to respond. England then lost their final game of the 1981 championship, against France at Twickenham, courtesy of a try by Bayonne's Laurent Pardo that ought not to have been given. The touchdown stemmed from France taking a quick throw, which is fine, but not if the ball has been returned by a bystander, as was the case here. France deserved their win, in truth, Cambridge University's Marcus Rose keeping England in the hunt with four penalty goals.

England were underpowered that season, with the loss to retirement of Uttley and Neary and an injury to Fran Cotton in the opening match against Wales; Cotton was never to play for England again. Another giant of the English game, Cotton appeared in 25 matches for England in the championship, 31 in all, and in seven Tests for the Lions. There was a shift in emphasis under way in the English game, with backs of the calibre and enterprise of Woodward, Paul Dodge, Slemen and Carleton coming

to the fore; fly half Huw Davies was more than happy to supply his men with the ball. England's points total of 64 reflected that audacity.

France, though, had chosen the way of the steamroller, new coach Jacques Fouroux carrying on where he had left off as a player, picking big and playing big. France, captained by Jean-Pierre Rives, the flamboyant flanker with the hard edge, won their third Grand Slam. There was a glimpse, too, of more adventurous times to come, with entrances on to the championship stage of the likes of Serge Blanco and Pierre Berbizier, both future captains.

There was to be one last sighting of the redoubtable J.P.R. Williams, the scourge of England, against whom he never lost, who came out of retirement to play in three games, against New Zealand, England and Ireland, before finally bringing the curtain down on a splendid career; he won a then Wales record 55 caps, plus eight for the Lions on their tours of 1971 and 1974. There was adieu to be bid, too, to a great servant of French rugby – Roland Bertranne, whose career had begun with a try on debut against England in 1971 and ended a further 16 Test tries and 68 international caps later against England in 1981.

LEFT France's captain for the 1981 campaign was classy flanker Jean-Pierre Rives, while the French line-up at Twickenham that year (above) included Serge Blanco, taking part in his first Five Nations Championship.

Ireland were on a roller-coaster ride – chumps in the 1981 campaign, losing the lot, champs in the next. France were on a similar trajectory but in the opposite direction – from Grand Slam to Wooden Spoon, albeit a share. No wonder coaches go grey so quickly. Trying to make sense of these matters is to invite madness to be your constant companion.

Ireland's pleasure was spoilt only by a hefty 22-9 defeat in their last game – against France in Paris. Perhaps celebrations had been a bit premature. There was no doubt that fly half Ollie Campbell was the star of Ireland's season. His three penalty goals at the Parc des Princes enabled him to equal his 1980 record mark of 46 championship points; his six penalties – matching the world record for a single player in an international match – plus a dropped goal had helped Ireland to a 21-12 victory over Scotland at Lansdowne Road and a first Triple Crown since 1949.

'I have turned wine into water,' was to be the wry, self-deprecating line of England coach Mike Davis, as he departed the scene at the end of the 1983 campaign. His side had just ended up with the Wooden Spoon, an ironic adjunct to the Grand Slam of three years earlier. England missed the drive and power of Beaumont, who had retired the previous season, as well as the injured Colclough, who went off in the opener against France and did not reappear that season. Tellingly, England registered only one try in the entire championship, scored by Carleton in the 13-13 draw with Wales in Cardiff.

Campbell was to be a particular scourge of England, the Old Belvedere man equalling his Irish individual points record of 21 in the 25-15 victory in Dublin, in which he broke his individual season record of 46 points, finishing up with an astonishing 52. Campbell underpinned another fine season for Ireland – a share of the championship spoils with France, who nevertheless managed to outscore Ireland in terms of tries and on points difference.

France, though, had a whirlwind on the wing – Patrick Estève – who set a new French try-scoring mark with five tries in the four games, including one in each game, which at the time

BELOW Forty-six points in 1982 for Ireland's kicking phenomenon Ollie Campbell, who set the standard for Five Nations individual points tallies in the early part of the decade. BELOW RIGHT Hugo MacNeill bursts through to score for Ireland in their 16-15 victory against England in 1982.

CALCUTTA CUP 1983.
ABOVE *Scotland lock Tom Smith heads groundwards to score on debut.*
LEFT *Jim Renwick passes to midfield partner Keith Robertson, who dropped a goal in Scotland's 22-12 victory.*

ENGLAND		SCOTLAND
Touch Judge: **J.-C. Yché** (F.F.R.)	Referee: **T. Doocey** (New Zealand)	Touch Judge: **M. Hourquet** (F.F.R.)
White Jerseys, White Shorts		**Blue Jerseys, White Shorts**

	ENGLAND			SCOTLAND
15.	**W. H. HARE** Leicester and Notts., Lincs and Derbyshire	FULL-BACK	15.	**P. W. DODS** Gala
		THREE-QUARTERS		
14.	**J. CARLETON** Orrell and Lancashire	RIGHT WING	14.	**J. A. POLLOCK** Gosforth
13.	**G. H. DAVIES** Coventry	CENTRE	13.	**J. M. RENWICK** Hawick
12.	**P. W. DODGE** Leicester	CENTRE	12.	**K. W. ROBERTSON** Melrose
11.	**A. H. SWIFT** Swansea	LEFT WING	11.	**G. R. T. BAIRD** Kelso
		HALF-BACKS		
10.	**J. P. HORTON** Bath and Somerset	STAND-OFF	10.	**J. Y. RUTHERFORD** Selkirk
9.	**S. J. SMITH** Sale and Lancashire	SCRUM-HALF	9.	**R. J. LAIDLAW** Jedforest
		FORWARDS		
1.	**C. E. SMART** Newport	PROP	1.	**J. AITKEN (captain)** Gala
2.	**P. J. WHEELER** Leicester	HOOKER	2.	**C. T. DEANS** Hawick
3.	**G. PEARCE** Northampton and Buckinghamshire	PROP	3.	**I. G. MILNE** Heriot's F.P.
4.	**S. B. BOYLE** Gloucester and Gloucestershire	LOCK	4. †	**T. J. SMITH** Gala
5.	**S. BAINBRIDGE** Gosforth and Northumberland	LOCK	5.	**I. A. M. PAXTON** Selkirk
6.	**N. C. JEAVONS** Moseley	FLANKER	6.	**J. H. CALDER** Stewart's Melville F.P.
7.	**P. J. WINTERBOTTOM** Headingley and Yorkshire	FLANKER	7.	**D. G. LESLIE** Gala
8.	**J. P. SCOTT (captain)** Cardiff	No. 8	8.	**J. R. BEATTIE** Glasgow Academicals

† New cap

Replacements: 16. N. C. Stringer (Wasps); 17. A. M. Bond (Sale); 18. N. C. Youngs (Bedford); 19. P. A. G. Rendall (Wasps); 20. S. G. F. Mills (Gloucester); 21. R. Hesford (Bristol).

KICK-OFF 3.00 p.m.

Replacements: 16. G. M. McGuinness (West of Scotland); 17. R. Cunningham (Bath); 18. A. J. Campbell (Hawick); 19. I. G. Hunter (Selkirk); 20. B. M. Gossman (West of Scotland); 21. D. I. Johnston (Watsonians).

RUGBY POST IS THE OFFICIAL MONTHLY MAGAZINE OF THE RUGBY FOOTBALL UNION:— ORDER NOW FROM YOUR NEWSAGENT

RUGBY FOOTBALL UNION

THE

Calcutta Cup

ENGLAND
V
SCOTLAND

TWICKENHAM
SATURDAY 5th MARCH
1983
Official Programme
Fifty Pence

Secretary R.F.U.

put him in a very select club of three with Carston Catcheside and Johnny Wallace. With nicknames including 'Le TGV' and the 'Narbonne Express', Estève was quick; indeed he had reached the 100m final in the French national athletics championships before turning to rugby. In the French pack, meanwhile, it was au revoir to prop Robert Paparemborde, a giant of a man, but one with a poacher's instinct, the Pau colossus scoring eight tries in his 55 Tests against all-comers.

Great expectations for England in 1984, on the back of a heartening 15-9 win over the All Blacks at Twickenham, quickly evaporated. With Derek Morgan and Dick Greenwood installed as the new management, and with Peter Wheeler at the helm in his last season, there was an air of freshness and possibility about the red rose team. It didn't come to pass, England losing 18-6 to Scotland at Murrayfield in their first match of the campaign, a reverse that caused them to look inward and become ever more narrow in their approach. A close win over Ireland (12-9) was followed by losses to France (32-18) and Wales (24-15), although the France match was notable for the first of 50 international tries (49 for England; one for the Lions) for Rory Underwood, scored in his second Test.

For Scotland, who had already won 15-9 in Cardiff on the opening day of the championship, the Calcutta Cup win provided the belief that they could win the championship. They duly did, and more, the Grand Slam being claimed for the first time since 1925. Once David Johnston had used his Hearts football skills to great effect to dribble over for

ABOVE The Narbonne Express arrives in style. Patrick Estève hurls himself into the corner to score at Parc des Princes in 1984, evading the pursuing Rory Underwood and Bryan Barley. The previous season the French flying machine had scored in each round of the championship. RIGHT Peter Wheeler, England's hooker and captain in 1984.

ABOVE *Robert Paparemborde, who bowed out at the end of the 1983 championship.* RIGHT *Rory Underwood in action against Wales in 1984, his debut season in international rugby.* BELOW *Scotland captain Jim Aitken celebrates with jubilant fans after the Grand Slam is clinched against France at Murrayfield in 1984.*

a try and his lanky centre partner, Alex Kennedy, had added a second to sink England, Scotland were halfway there.

Having crushed Ireland 32-9 in Dublin, the Scots closed out the deal in a tense 21-12 win over France at Murrayfield. Down 9-3, Scotland recovered to level at 12-12. Jim Calder then scored the crucial try. With Peter Dods's relentless kicking contributing 17 points in the game out of his Scottish record 50 scored in that championship, the deed was done. Prop Jim Aitken proved an astute, battle-hardened captain, but when he was not selected for the 1985 campaign, Scotland's sense of impregnability vanished, so much so that they proceeded to be whitewashed.

Indeed, 1985 was a case of the 'first shall be last; and the last shall be first'. For as Scotland descended, the previous year's whitewashed Wooden Spoonists, Ireland, shot to the top. A somewhat non-vintage season saw Ireland collect the Triple Crown and championship under the tutelage of new coach Mick Doyle. Meanwhile, the remaining sides stayed where they were. France let this one get away, drawing against Ireland at Lansdowne Road and against England at Twickenham, when scrum half Richard Harding dislodged the ball from the grasp of Patrick

Estève behind the English line to save a certain try. England themselves were all of a dither in the mid-1980s, not knowing which way to turn, who to pick, who to ditch, who to back and who to nurture. During a ten-month period to the end of the 1985 season, they used 20 new caps, an astonishing turnover of personnel. The inevitable upshot

159

BELOW Nigel Melville whips the ball away against Wales at Twickenham in 1985. Having skippered on international debut against Australia in November 1984, the injured Melville was replaced at scrum half by Richard Harding (right, closing down Serge Blanco) for the first part of the 1985 campaign, before returning against Ireland. ABOVE Melville regained the captaincy in 1986 and is here congratulating Dean Richards, who had just scored the first of his two tries on debut against Ireland.

was that England were inconsistent: a 10-7 win over Scotland, that 9-9 draw against France and defeat against Ireland and Wales (13-10 and 24-15 respectively) was the predictable narrative.

The 1986 season saw Nigel Melville installed as captain for the championship. Melville had made his debut (alongside fellow debutant Stuart Barnes) against Andrew Slack's all-conquering Wallabies at Twickenham in November 1984, skippering the side in the 19-3 defeat before succumbing to injury, Paul Dodge taking over as captain for the match against Romania and the 1985 championship. Yet there was to be no upturn in fortunes for England. A mixed bag was as good as it got, with victories over Wales (21-18) and Ireland (25-20) at Twickenham offset by defeats on the road to Scotland (33-6) and France (29-10). The Calcutta Cup defeat was particularly painful, all the more so after a last-minute Rob Andrew dropped goal to defeat Wales had given England a heartening start to the championship. Dean Richards announced himself on the international scene with a brace of tries against Ireland on debut.

Ireland and Scotland continued to trade places, passing each other on the up/down escalators. Ireland went back to the bottom, whitewashed once more, while the Scots finished top of the pile alongside France. A new name made a mark right at the start of this campaign, debutant Gavin Hastings landing six penalty goals to steer Scotland to an opening weekend 18-17 win over France. Hastings went on to rewrite the record books time and again that season, his Scottish best tally of 21 points in the subsequent Calcutta Cup triumph a hefty contribution to Scotland's biggest win in the fixture to date. Gavin's brother Scott also made his debut in the match against France, the pair becoming the first brothers to make their debuts together for Scotland in almost 100 years. Elsewhere, too, kickers were having an increasing influence on the scoreboard and outcome of matches. Wales's Paul Thorburn was among the best of the practitioners, demonstrating his prodigious power when landing a monstrous penalty goal from some 65 metres against Scotland. Thorburn kicked an all-championship record 16 penalty goals in the season.

France dominated the honours board in the last three years of the decade, winning a Grand Slam in 1987, finishing level on points with Wales in 1988 and taking a further outright title in 1989; they also reached the final of the inaugural Rugby World Cup in 1987 – their success testimony to the authoritative leadership of hooker Daniel Dubroca and the splendour of men such as Serge Blanco and Philippe Sella.

If the decade had begun with acrimony surrounding the England v Wales meeting, then the mood had certainly not got any better by 1987. Indeed, the fixture had been simmering in the intervening period and erupted once again that year. Four England players were disciplined by the RFU after a volatile match in Cardiff in which there were numerous acts of skulduggery. Captain and scrum half

Gavin Hastings

ABOVE Gavin Hastings, who broke records galore for Scotland. BELOW Paul Thorburn, who kicked frequent, and sometimes very long, goals for Wales. FOLLOWING PAGES After bubbling menacingly since 1980, the Wales against England fixture exploded at Cardiff in 1987, with fallout for a clutch of England players.

Richard Hill was sanctioned, as were hooker Graham Dawe, lock Wade Dooley and prop Gareth Chilcott – all of whom lost their places for England's final match of the championship. At Cardiff, England first lost the plot and then the match, going down to a 19-12 defeat. England's new captain for the Calcutta Cup match at Twickenham was wing Mike Harrison, nicknamed 'Burglar Bill' for his knack of grabbing breakaway tries. His side roused themselves to finish with a 21-12 victory, Harrison inducing a penalty try and Marcus Rose adding a second score plus the conversions and three penalties.

A tight championship in 1988 saw Wales going for a Grand Slam in Cardiff only to allow France to edge home 10-9 and grab a share of the title. Fly half Jean-Patrick Lescarboura touched down for a 10-3 lead, but Wales came back through a Ieuan Evans try and Paul Thorburn conversion to get to within one point in a game marred by torrential rain. Wales had got their championship off to a bright start with an 11-3 win at Twickenham, Adrian Hadley making best use of Robert Norster's dominant display in the line out to score two tries. As the Wales fans filed jubilantly from the stadium, few would have thought that it would be 20 years before they were to win again at HQ. The 1988 season was also the last campaign in which Robert Jones and Jonathan Davies operated together for Wales. The half-back partnership of this pair, both the equal of any of those who had worn the fabled Wales No. 9 and No. 10 jerseys, was broken up by Davies' move north to rugby league at Widnes.

Serge Blanco

England, by now under the management of Geoff Cooke and with Will Carling installed as captain in November 1988, aged 22, were beginning to get their act together as the decade drew to a close. They finished joint runners-up with Scotland behind France in 1989, losing as usual in Cardiff (12-9) and sharing the Calcutta Cup (12-12) – the trophy reshaped after celebrations by Dean Richards and John Jeffrey the previous year had threatened to transform the priceless item into the 'Calcutta Shield'. A good win in Dublin (16-3) and an 11-0 triumph over France at Twickenham hinted at bright prospects on the horizon. Appearances were not to be deceptive.

ENGLAND v WALES IN 1988.
LEFT *Wales lock and line-out master Robert Norster lines up opposite Mickey Skinner at Twickenham.* BELOW *Mark Ring (arm aloft) helps left wing Adrian Hadley celebrate the first of his two tries that day.* BOTTOM *The partnership of Jones and Davies at half back for Wales would not be seen again in the Five Nations after the 1988 season.*

RUGBY FOOTBALL UNION

ENGLAND
v
WALES

The British Gas Challenge

Secretary R.F.U.

TWICKENHAM
SATURDAY 6th FEBRUARY
1988

Official Programme
Sixty Pence

ENGLAND		Referee: S. R. Hilditch (Ireland) Touch Judges: O. E. Doyle (Ireland) B. Stirling (Ireland)	WALES	
White Jerseys, White Shorts			Red Jerseys, White Shorts	
15.	J. M. WEBB	FULLBACK	15.	A. CLEMENT
	Bristol			Swansea
		THREE QUARTERS		
14.	M. E. HARRISON (captain)	RIGHT WING	14.	I. C. EVANS
	Wakefield			Llanelli
13.	W. D. C. CARLING	CENTRE	13.	M. G. RING
	Durham Un. & Harlequins			Pontypool
12.	K. G. SIMMS	CENTRE	12.	B. BOWEN (captain)
	Wasps			South Wales Police
11.	R. UNDERWOOD	LEFT WING	11.	A. M. HADLEY
	Leicester & R.A.F.			Cardiff
		HALF BACKS		
10.	L. CUSWORTH	STAND-OFF	10.	J. DAVIES
	Leicester			Llanelli
9.	N. D. MELVILLE	SCRUM-HALF	9.	R. N. JONES
	Wasps			Swansea
		FORWARDS		
1.	P. A. G. RENDALL	PROP	1.	S. T. JONES
	Wasps			Pontypool
2.	B. C. MOORE	HOOKER	2.	K. H. PHILLIPS
	Nottingham			Neath
3.	J. A. PROBYN	PROP	3.	D. YOUNG
	Wasps			Swansea
4.	J. ORWIN	LOCK	4. †	P. MAY
	Bedford			Llanelli
5.	W. A. DOOLEY	LOCK	5.	R. L. NORSTER
	Fylde			Cardiff
6.	M. G. SKINNER	FLANKER	6.	R. PHILLIPS
	Harlequins			Neath
7.	P. J. WINTERBOTTOM	FLANKER	7.	R. G. COLLINS
	Headingley			South Wales Police
8.	D. RICHARDS	No. 8	8.	W. P. MORIARTY
	Leicester			Swansea

Replacements:
16. R. A. Adamson (Wakefield)
17. C. R. Andrew (Wasps)
18. R. M. Harding (Bristol)
19. G. J. Chilcott (Bath)
20. R. G. R. Dawe (Bath)
21. G. W. Rees (Nottingham)

† New cap

KICK-OFF 2.30 p.m.

Replacements:
16. G. M. C. Webbe (Bridgend)
17. M. R. Hall (Bridgend)
18. J. Griffiths (Llanelli)
19. J. Pugh (Neath)
20. I. Watkins (Ebbw Vale)
21. M. Jones (Neath)

The British Gas Challenge

The Rugby Football Union and the Welsh Rugby Union gratefully acknowledge the support of British Gas.

165

Five Nations Results 1980-89

1979-80

19.01.1980 CARDIFF ARMS PARK
Wales 18 *T:* HE Rees, TD Holmes, DS Richards, G Price
C: WG Davies
France 9 *T:* J-F Marchal *C:* A Caussade *DG:* A Caussade
Referee: AM Hosie (Scotland)

19.01.1980 TWICKENHAM
England 24 *T:* JP Scott, MAC Slemen, SJ Smith
C: WH Hare 3 *PG:* WH Hare 2
Ireland 9 *PG:* SO Campbell 3
Referee: C Thomas (Wales)

02.02.1980 PARC DES PRINCES, PARIS
France 13 *T:* J-L Averous, J-P Rives *C:* A Caussade
PG: A Caussade
England 17 *T:* J Carleton, NJ Preston *PG:* WH Hare
DG: JP Horton 2
Referee: C Norling (Wales)

02.02.1980 LANSDOWNE ROAD, DUBLIN
Ireland 22 *T:* MI Keane, TJ Kennedy *C:* SO Campbell
PG: SO Campbell 3 *DG:* SO Campbell
Scotland 15 *T:* DI Johnston 2 *C:* AR Irvine 2
PG: AR Irvine
Referee: G Chevrier (France)

16.02.1980 TWICKENHAM
England 9 *PG:* WH Hare 3
Wales 8 *T:* HE Rees, J Squire
Referee: DIH Burnett (Ireland)

16.02.1980 MURRAYFIELD
Scotland 22 *T:* AR Irvine 2, JY Rutherford *C:* AR Irvine,
JM Renwick *PG:* AR Irvine 2
France 14 *T:* J Gallion, S Gabernet *PG:* S Gabernet
DG: A Caussade
Referee: JR West (Ireland)

01.03.1980 PARC DES PRINCES, PARIS
France 19 *T:* J-F Gourdon 2 *C:* J-M Aguirre
PG: J-M Aguirre 2 *DG:* P Pedeutour
Ireland 18 *T:* AC McLennan *C:* SO Campbell
PG: SO Campbell 3 *DG:* SO Campbell
Referee: AM Hosie (Scotland)

01.03.1980 CARDIFF ARMS PARK
Wales 17 *T:* TD Holmes, L Keen, DS Richards
C: WR Blyth *PG:* SP Fenwick
Scotland 6 *T:* JM Renwick *C:* AR Irvine
Referee: LM Prideaux (England)

15.03.1980 LANSDOWNE ROAD, DUBLIN
Ireland 21 *T:* DG Irwin, JB O'Driscoll, CF Fitzgerald
C: SO Campbell 3 *PG:* SO Campbell
Wales 7 *T:* WR Blyth *PG:* SP Fenwick
Referee: LM Prideaux (England)

15.03.1980 MURRAYFIELD
Scotland 18 *T:* AJ Tomes, JY Rutherford *C:* AR Irvine 2
PG: AR Irvine 2
England 30 *T:* J Carleton 3, MAC Slemen, SJ Smith
C: WH Hare 2 *PG:* WH Hare 2
Referee: J-P Bonnet (France)

	P	W	D	L	FOR	AGAINST	PTS
England	4	4	0	0	80	48	8
Ireland	4	2	0	2	70	65	4
Wales	4	2	0	2	50	45	4
Scotland	4	1	0	3	61	83	2
France	4	1	0	3	55	75	2

1980-81

17.01.1981 PARC DES PRINCES, PARIS
France 16 *T:* S Blanco, R Bertranne *C:* A Caussade
PG: B Vivies, S Gabernet
Scotland 9 *T:* JY Rutherford *C:* JM Renwick
PG: AR Irvine
Referee: K Rowlands (Wales)

17.01.1981 CARDIFF ARMS PARK
Wales 21 *T:* CE Davis *C:* SP Fenwick
PG: SP Fenwick 4 *DG:* WG Davies
England 19 *T:* WH Hare *PG:* WH Hare 5
Referee: JB Anderson (Scotland)

07.02.1981 LANSDOWNE ROAD, DUBLIN
Ireland 13 *T:* HP MacNeill *PG:* SO Campbell 3
France 19 *T:* L Pardo *PG:* G Laporte 2, S Gabernet
DG: G Laporte 2
Referee: C Norling (Wales)

07.02.1981 MURRAYFIELD
Scotland 15 *T:* AJ Tomes, penalty try *C:* JM Renwick 2
PG: JM Renwick
Wales 6 *PG:* SP Fenwick 2
Referee: DIH Burnett (Ireland)

21.02.1981 TWICKENHAM
England 23 *T:* GH Davies, MAC Slemen,
CR Woodward *C:* WH Hare *PG:* WH Hare 3
Scotland 17 *T:* S Munro 2, JH Calder *C:* AR Irvine
PG: AR Irvine
Referee: DIH Burnett (Ireland)

21.02.1981 CARDIFF ARMS PARK
Wales 9 *PG:* G Evans 2 *DG:* GP Pearce
Ireland 8 *T:* JF Slattery, HP MacNeill
Referee: F Palmade (France)

07.03.1981 PARC DES PRINCES, PARIS
France 19 *T:* S Gabernet *PG:* G Laporte 3, S Gabernet 2
Wales 15 *T:* DS Richards *C:* G Evans *PG:* G Evans 3
Referee: A Welsby (England)

07.03.1981 LANSDOWNE ROAD, DUBLIN
Ireland 6 *DG:* SO Campbell, HP MacNeill
England 10 *T:* PW Dodge, WMH Rose *C:* WMH Rose
Referee: J-P Bonnet (France)

21.03.1981 TWICKENHAM
England 12 *PG:* WMH Rose 4
France 16 *T:* P Lacans, L Pardo *C:* G Laporte
DG: G Laporte 2
Referee: AM Hosie (Scotland)

21.03.1981 MURRAYFIELD
Scotland 10 *T:* BH Hay *PG:* AR Irvine
DG: JY Rutherford
Ireland 9 *T:* DG Irwin *C:* SO Campbell
PG: SO Campbell
Referee: LM Prideaux (England)

	P	W	D	L	FOR	AGAINST	PTS
France	4	4	0	0	70	49	8
England	4	2	0	2	64	60	4
Scotland	4	2	0	2	51	54	4
Wales	4	2	0	2	51	61	4
Ireland	4	0	0	4	36	48	0

1981-82

16.01.1982 MURRAYFIELD
Scotland 9 *PG:* AR Irvine 2 *DG:* JY Rutherford
England 9 *PG:* PW Dodge 2, WMH Rose
Referee: K Rowlands (Wales)

23.01.1982 LANSDOWNE ROAD, DUBLIN
Ireland 20 *T:* MC Finn 2, TM Ringland
C: SO Campbell *PG:* SO Campbell 2
Wales 12 *T:* TD Holmes *C:* G Evans *PG:* G Evans
DG: GP Pearce
Referee: JA Short (Scotland)

06.02.1982 TWICKENHAM
England 15 *T:* MAC Slemen *C:* WMH Rose
PG: WMH Rose 3
Ireland 16 *T:* HP MacNeill, GAJ McLoughlin
C: SO Campbell *PG:* SO Campbell 2
Referee: AM Hosie (Scotland)

06.02.1982 CARDIFF ARMS PARK
Wales 22 *T:* TD Holmes *PG:* G Evans 6
France 12 *T:* S Blanco *C:* M Sallefranque
PG: M Sallefranque, G Martinez
Referee: DIH Burnett (Ireland)

20.02.1982 PARC DES PRINCES, PARIS
France 15 *T:* L Pardo *C:* M Sallefranque
PG: M Sallefranque 2 *DG:* J-P Lescarboura
England 27 *T:* CR Woodward, J Carleton
C: WH Hare 2 *PG:* WH Hare 5
Referee: MDM Rea (Ireland)

20.02.1982 LANSDOWNE ROAD, DUBLIN
Ireland 21 *PG:* SO Campbell 6 *DG:* SO Campbell
Scotland 12 *T:* JY Rutherford *C:* AR Irvine
PG: JM Renwick 2
Referee: C Norling (Wales)

06.03.1982 TWICKENHAM
England 17 *T:* J Carleton, MAC Slemen *PG:* WH Hare 3
Wales 7 *T:* JR Lewis *DG:* WG Davies
Referee: F Palmade (France)

06.03.1982 MURRAYFIELD
Scotland 16 *T:* JY Rutherford *PG:* AR Irvine 3
DG: JM Renwick
France 7 *T:* J-P Rives *PG:* M Sallefranque
Referee: JAF Trigg (England)

20.03.1982 PARC DES PRINCES, PARIS
France 22 *T:* S Blanco, P Mesny *C:* S Gabernet
PG: S Gabernet 2, S Blanco 2
Ireland 9 *PG:* SO Campbell 3
Referee: A Welsby (England)

20.03.1982 CARDIFF ARMS PARK
Wales 18 *T:* ET Butler *C:* G Evans *PG:* G Evans 4
Scotland 34 *T:* JH Calder, JM Renwick, JA Pollock,
DB White, DI Johnston *C:* AR Irvine 4 *DG:* JM Renwick,
JY Rutherford
Referee: J-P Bonnet (France)

	P	W	D	L	FOR	AGAINST	PTS
Ireland	4	3	0	1	66	61	6
Scotland	4	2	1	1	71	55	5
England	4	2	1	1	68	47	5
Wales	4	1	0	3	59	83	2
France	4	1	0	3	56	74	2

1982-83

15.01.1983 TWICKENHAM
England 15 *PG:* WH Hare 4 *DG:* L Cusworth
France 19 *T:* P Esteve, P Sella, R Paparemborde
C: S Blanco 2 *PG:* D Camberabero
Referee: DIH Burnett (Ireland)

15.01.1983 MURRAYFIELD
Scotland 13 *T:* RJ Laidlaw *PG:* PW Dods 2
DG: JM Renwick
Ireland 15 *T:* MJ Kiernan *C:* SO Campbell
PG: SO Campbell 3
Referee: JC Yche (France)

05.02.1983 PARC DES PRINCES, PARIS
France 19 *T:* P Esteve 2 *C:* S Blanco *PG:* S Blanco 3
Scotland 15 *T:* KW Robertson *C:* PW Dods
PG: PW Dods *DG:* BM Gossman 2
Referee: A Richards (Wales)

05.02.1983 CARDIFF ARMS PARK
Wales 13 *T:* J Squire *PG:* MA Wyatt 2 *DG:* M Dacey
England 13 *T:* J Carleton *PG:* WH Hare 2
DG: L Cusworth
Referee: JR West (Ireland)

19.02.1983 LANSDOWNE ROAD, DUBLIN
Ireland 22 *T:* MC Finn 2 *C:* SO Campbell
PG: SO Campbell 4
France 16 *T:* S Blanco, P Esteve *C:* S Blanco
PG: S Blanco 2
Referee: AM Hosie (Scotland)

19.02.1983 MURRAYFIELD
Scotland 15 *T:* JM Renwick *C:* PW Dods
PG: PW Dods 3
Wales 19 *T:* ST Jones, HE Rees *C:* MA Wyatt
PG: MA Wyatt 3
Referee: RC Quittenton (England)

05.03.1983 TWICKENHAM
England 12 *PG:* WH Hare 3 *DG:* JP Horton
Scotland 22 *T:* RJ Laidlaw, TJ Smith *C:* PW Dods
PG: PW Dods 3 *DG:* KW Robertson
Referee: T Doocey (New Zealand)

05.03.1983 CARDIFF ARMS PARK
Wales 23 *T:* MA Wyatt, TD Holmes, HE Rees
C: MA Wyatt *PG:* MA Wyatt 3
Ireland 9 *PG:* SO Campbell 2, HP MacNeill
Referee: JAF Trigg (England)

19.03.1983 PARC DES PRINCES, PARIS
France 16 *T:* P Esteve *PG:* S Blanco 3
DG: D Camberabero
Wales 9 *T:* J Squire *C:* MA Wyatt *PG:* G Evans
Referee: T Doocey (New Zealand)

19.03.1983 LANSDOWNE ROAD, DUBLIN
Ireland 25 *T:* JF Slattery, SO Campbell *C:* SO Campbell
PG: SO Campbell 5
England 15 *PG:* WH Hare 5
Referee: JB Anderson (Scotland)

	P	W	D	L	FOR	AGAINST	PTS
France	4	3	0	1	70	61	6
Ireland	4	3	0	1	71	67	6
Wales	4	2	1	1	64	53	5
Scotland	4	1	0	3	65	65	2
England	4	0	1	3	55	79	1

1983-84

21.01.1984 PARC DES PRINCES, PARIS
France 25 *T:* J Gallion, P Sella *C:* J-P Lescaboura
PG: J-P Lescaboura 4 *DG:* J-P Lescaboura
Ireland 12 *PG:* SO Campbell 4
Referee: C Norling (Wales)

21.01.1984 CARDIFF ARMS PARK
Wales 9 *T:* MH Titley *C:* H Davies *PG:* H Davies
Scotland 15 *T:* IAM Paxton, J Aitken *C:* PW Dods 2
PG: PW Dods
Referee: OE Doyle (Ireland)

04.02.1984 MURRAYFIELD
Scotland 18 *T:* DI Johnston, AE Kennedy
C: PW Dods 2 *PG:* PW Dods 2
England 6 *PG:* WH Hare 2
Referee: DIH Burnett (Ireland)

04.02.1984 LANSDOWNE ROAD, DUBLIN
Ireland 9 *PG:* SO Campbell 3
Wales 18 *T:* RA Ackerman *C:* H Davies *PG:* H Davies 2,
B Bowen 2
Referee: RG Byres (Australia)

18.02.1984 TWICKENHAM
England 12 *PG:* WH Hare 3 *DG:* L Cusworth
Ireland 9 *PG:* AJP Ward 3
Referee: R Hourquet (France)

18.02.1984 CARDIFF ARMS PARK
Wales 16 *T:* H Davies, ET Butler *C:* H Davies
PG: H Davies 2
France 21 *T:* P Sella *C:* J-P Lescaboura
PG: J-P Lescaboura 4 *DG:* J-P Lescaboura
Referee: RG Byres (Australia)

03.03.1984 PARC DES PRINCES, PARIS
France 32 *T:* D Codorniou, P Sella, P Esteve, J Begu,
J Gallion *C:* J-P Lescaboura 3 *PG:* J-P Lescaboura
DG: J-P Lescaboura
England 18 *T:* R Underwood, WH Hare *C:* WH Hare 2
PG: WH Hare 2
Referee: AM Hosie (Scotland)

03.03.1984 LANSDOWNE ROAD, DUBLIN
Ireland 9 *T:* MJ Kiernan *C:* J Murphy *PG:* J Murphy
Scotland 32 *T:* RJ Laidlaw 2, penalty try,
KW Robertson, PW Dods *C:* PW Dods 3 *PG:* PW Dods 2
Referee: FA Howard (England)

17.03.1984 MURRAYFIELD
Scotland 21 *T:* JH Calder *C:* PW Dods *PG:* PW Dods 5
France 12 *T:* J Gallion *C:* J-P Lescaboura
PG: J-P Lescaboura *DG:* J-P Lescaboura
Referee: W Jones (Wales)

17.03.1984 TWICKENHAM
England 15 *PG:* WH Hare 5
Wales 24 *T:* AM Hadley *C:* H Davies *PG:* H Davies 4
DG: M Dacey 2
Referee: JB Anderson (Scotland)

	P	W	D	L	FOR	AGAINST	PTS
Scotland	4	4	0	0	86	36	8
France	4	3	0	1	90	67	6
Wales	4	2	0	2	67	60	4
England	4	1	0	3	51	83	2
Ireland	4	0	0	4	39	87	0

1984-85

02.02.1985 TWICKENHAM
England 9 *PG:* CR Andrew 2 *DG:* CR Andrew
France 9 *DG:* J-P Lescaboura 3
Referee: DIH Burnett (Ireland)

02.02.1985 MURRAYFIELD
Scotland 15 *PG:* PW Dods 4 *DG:* KW Robertson
Ireland 18 *T:* TM Ringland 2 *C:* MJ Kiernan 2
PG: MJ Kiernan *DG:* MJ Kiernan
Referee: S Strydom (South Africa)

16.02.1984 PARC DES PRINCES, PARIS
France 11 *T:* S Blanco 2 *PG:* J-P Lescaboura
Scotland 3 *PG:* PW Dods
Referee: LM Prideaux (England)

02.03.1985 LANSDOWNE ROAD, DUBLIN
Ireland 15 *PG:* MJ Kiernan 5
France 15 *T:* P Esteve, D Codorniou
C: J-P Lescaboura 2 *PG:* J-P Lescaboura
Referee: KVJ Fitzgerald (Australia)

02.03.1985 MURRAYFIELD
Scotland 21 *T:* IAM Paxton 2 *C:* PW Dods 2
PG: PW Dods *DG:* JY Rutherford 2
Wales 25 *T:* DF Pickering 2 *C:* MA Wyatt
PG: MA Wyatt 4 *DG:* WG Davies
Referee: R Hourquet (France)

16.03.1985 TWICKENHAM
England 10 *T:* ST Smith *PG:* CR Andrew 2
Scotland 7 *T:* KW Robertson *PG:* PW Dods
Referee: C Norling (Wales)

16.03.1985 CARDIFF ARMS PARK
Wales 9 *T:* PI Lewis *C:* MA Wyatt *DG:* WG Davies
Ireland 21 *T:* KD Crossan, TM Ringland
C: MJ Kiernan 2 *PG:* MJ Kiernan 3
Referee: KVJ Fitzgerald (Australia)

30.03.1985 LANSDOWNE ROAD, DUBLIN
Ireland 13 *T:* BJ Mullin *PG:* MJ Kiernan 2
DG: MJ Kiernan
England 10 *T:* R Underwood *PG:* CR Andrew 2
Referee: JM Fleming (Scotland)

30.03.1985 PARC DES PRINCES, PARIS
France 14 *T:* P Esteve, J Gallion *PG:* J-P Lescaboura 2
Wales 3 *PG:* PH Thorburn
Referee: S Strydom (South Africa)

20.04.1985 CARDIFF ARMS PARK
Wales 24 *T:* J Davies, G Roberts *C:* PH Thorburn 2
PG: PH Thorburn 3 *DG:* J Davies
England 15 *T:* ST Smith *C:* CR Andrew
PG: CR Andrew 2 *DG:* CR Andrew
Referee: F Palmade (France)

	P	W	D	L	FOR	AGAINST	PTS
Ireland	4	3	1	0	67	49	7
France	4	2	2	0	49	30	6
Wales	4	2	0	2	61	71	4
England	4	1	1	2	44	53	3
Scotland	4	0	0	4	46	64	0

1985-86

17.01.1986 TWICKENHAM
England 21 *PG:* CR Andrew 6 *DG:* CR Andrew
Wales 18 *T:* B Bowen *C:* PH Thorburn
PG: PH Thorburn 3 *DG:* J Davies
Referee: RJ Fordham (Australia)

17.01.1986 MURRAYFIELD
Scotland 18 *PG:* AG Hastings 6
France 17 *T:* P Berbizier, P Sella *PG:* G Laporte 2
DG: G Laporte
Referee: DIH Burnett (Ireland)

01.02.1986 CARDIFF ARMS PARK
Wales 22 *T:* AM Hadley *PG:* PH Thorburn 5
DG: J Davies
Scotland 15 *T:* MDF Duncan, J Jeffrey, AG Hastings
PG: AG Hastings
Referee: RC Francis (New Zealand)

01.02.1986 PARC DES PRINCES, PARIS
France 29 *T:* P Berbizier, P Marocco, P Sella
C: G Laporte *PG:* G Laporte 3, S Blanco *DG:* J-B Lafond
Ireland 9 *PG:* MJ Kiernan 3
Referee: RJ Fordham (Australia)

15.02.1986 MURRAYFIELD
Scotland 33 *T:* MDF Duncan, JY Rutherford,
S Hastings *C:* AG Hastings 3 *PG:* AG Hastings 5
England 6 *PG:* CR Andrew 2
Referee: RC Francis (New Zealand)

15.02.1986 LANSDOWNE ROAD, DUBLIN
Ireland 12 *T:* TM Ringland *C:* MJ Kiernan
PG: MJ Kiernan 2
Wales 19 *T:* PI Lewis, PT Davies *C:* PH Thorburn
PG: PH Thorburn 3
Referee: FA Howard (England)

01.03.1986 TWICKENHAM
England 25 *T:* D Richards 2, penalty try, GH Davies
C: CR Andrew 3 *PG:* CR Andrew
Ireland 20 *T:* TM Ringland, BJ Mullin, BW McCall
C: MJ Kiernan *PG:* MJ Kiernan 2
Referee: C Norling (Wales)

01.03.1986 CARDIFF ARMS PARK
Wales 15 *PG:* PH Thorburn 5
France 23 *T:* J-B Lafond, P Sella, S Blanco
C: G Laporte 2 *DG:* G Laporte
Referee: JB Anderson (Scotland)

15.03.1986 LANSDOWNE ROAD, DUBLIN
Ireland 9 *T:* TM Ringland *C:* MJ Kiernan
PG: MJ Kiernan
Scotland 10 *T:* RJ Laidlaw *PG:* AG Hastings 2
Referee: F Palmade (France)

15.03.1986 PARC DES PRINCES, PARIS
France 29 *T:* P Sella, G Laporte, penalty try, S Blanco
C: G Laporte 2 *PG:* G Laporte 3
England 10 *T:* WA Dooley *PG:* S Barnes 2
Referee: WD Bevan (Wales)

Five Nations Results 1980-89

	P	W	D	L	FOR	AGAINST	PTS
France	4	3	0	1	98	52	6
Scotland	4	3	0	1	76	54	6
Wales	4	2	0	2	74	71	4
England	4	2	0	2	62	100	4
Ireland	4	0	0	4	50	83	0

1986-87

07.02.1987 LANSDOWNE ROAD, DUBLIN
Ireland 17 *T:* MJ Kiernan, PM Matthews, KD Crossan
C: MJ Kiernan *PG:* MJ Kiernan
England 0
Referee: R Hourquet (France)

07.02.1987 PARC DES PRINCES, PARIS
France 16 *T:* E Bonneval, F Mesnel *C:* P Berot
PG: P Berot 2
Wales 9 *PG:* PH Thorburn 3
Referee: CJ High (England)

21.02.1987 MURRAYFIELD
Scotland 16 *T:* RJ Laidlaw, I Tukalo *C:* AG Hastings
DG: JY Rutherford 2
Ireland 12 *T:* DG Lenihan *C:* MJ Kiernan
PG: MJ Kiernan *DG:* MJ Kiernan
Referee: RC Quittenton (England)

21.02.1987 TWICKENHAM
England 15 *PG:* WMH Rose 4 *DG:* CR Andrew
France 19 *T:* E Bonneval, P Sella *C:* P Berot *PG:* P Berot
DG: F Mesnel, S Blanco
Referee: JM Fleming (Scotland)

07.03.1987 PARC DES PRINCES, PARIS
France 28 *T:* E Bonneval 3, P Berot *PG:* P Berot 3
DG: F Mesnel
Scotland 22 *T:* S Hastings, JR Beattie *C:* AG Hastings
PG: AG Hastings 4
Referee: KH Lawrence (New Zealand)

07.03.1987 CARDIFF ARMS PARK
Wales 19 *T:* S Evans *PG:* MA Wyatt 5
England 12 *PG:* WMH Rose 4
Referee: RJ Megson (Scotland)

21.03.1987 MURRAYFIELD
Scotland 21 *T:* JR Beattie, J Jeffrey *C:* AG Hastings 2
PG: AG Hastings 2 *DG:* JY Rutherford
Wales 15 *T:* M Jones *C:* MA Wyatt *PG:* MA Wyatt 2
DG: J Davies
Referee: KH Lawrence (New Zealand)

21.03.1987 LANSDOWNE ROAD, DUBLIN
Ireland 13 *T:* TM Ringland, MT Bradley *C:* MJ Kiernan
PG: MJ Kiernan
France 19 *T:* E Champ 2 *C:* P Berot *PG:* P Berot 3
Referee: C Norling (Wales)

04.04.1987 CARDIFF ARMS PARK
Wales 11 *T:* RL Norster, IC Evans *PG:* MA Wyatt
Ireland 15 *T:* PM Dean, BJ Mullin *C:* MJ Kiernan 2
PG: MJ Kiernan
Referee: G Maurette (France)

04.04.1987 TWICKENHAM
England 21 *T:* Penalty try, WMH Rose *C:* WMH Rose 2
PG: WMH Rose 3
Scotland 12 *T:* KW Robertson *C:* AG Hastings
PG: AG Hastings 2
Referee: OE Doyle (Ireland)

	P	W	D	L	FOR	AGAINST	PTS
France	4	4	0	0	82	59	8
Ireland	4	2	0	2	57	46	4
Scotland	4	2	0	2	71	76	4
Wales	4	1	0	3	54	64	2
England	4	1	0	3	48	67	2

1987-88

16.01.1988 PARC DES PRINCES, PARIS
France 10 *T:* L Rodriguez *PG:* P Berot 2
England 9 *PG:* JM Webb 2 *DG:* L Cusworth
Referee: OE Doyle (Ireland)

16.01.1988 LANSDOWNE ROAD, DUBLIN
Ireland 22 *T:* BJ Mullin, HP MacNeill, MT Bradley
C: MJ Kiernan 2 *PG:* MJ Kiernan *DG:* MJ Kiernan
Scotland 18 *T:* RJ Laidlaw, S Hastings *C:* AG Hastings 2
PG: AG Hastings 2
Referee: RC Quittenton (England)

06.02.1988 TWICKENHAM
England 3 *PG:* JM Webb
Wales 11 *T:* AM Hadley 2 *DG:* J Davies
Referee: SR Hilditch (Ireland)

06.02.1988 MURRAYFIELD
Scotland 23 *T:* AG Hastings, I Tukalo
PG: AG Hastings 4 *DG:* RI Cramb
France 12 *T:* P Lagisquet *C:* P Berot *PG:* P Berot
DG: J-P Lescarboura
Referee: F Muller (South Africa)

20.02.1988 PARC DES PRINCES, PARIS
France 25 *T:* S Blanco, P Lagisquet, D Camberabero,
A Carminati, P Sella *C:* P Berot *PG:* D Camberabero
Ireland 6 *PG:* MJ Kiernan 2
Referee: F Muller (South Africa)

20.02.1988 CARDIFF ARMS PARK
Wales 25 *T:* IC Evans, IJ Watkins, J Davies
C: PH Thorburn 2 *PG:* PH Thorburn *DG:* J Davies 2
Scotland 20 *T:* F Calder, MDF Duncan
PG: AG Hastings 4
Referee: Y Bressy (France)

05.03.1988 LANSDOWNE ROAD, DUBLIN
Ireland 9 *T:* TJ Kingston *C:* MJ Kiernan *PG:* MJ Kiernan
Wales 12 *T:* WP Moriarty *C:* PH Thorburn
PG: PH Thorburn *DG:* J Davies
Referee: RJ Megson (Scotland)

05.03.1988 MURRAYFIELD
Scotland 6 *PG:* AG Hastings 2
England 9 *PG:* JM Webb 2 *DG:* CR Andrew
Referee: W Jones (Wales)

19.03.1988 CARDIFF ARMS PARK
Wales 9 *T:* IC Evans *C:* PH Thorburn *PG:* PH Thorburn
France 10 *T:* J-P Lescarboura *PG:* J-B Lafond 2
Referee: FA Howard (England)

19.03.1988 TWICKENHAM
England 35 *T:* C Oti 3, R Underwood 2, GW Rees
C: CR Andrew 3, JM Webb 2 *PG:* JM Webb
Ireland 3 *DG:* MJ Kiernan
Referee: C Norling (Wales)

	P	W	D	L	FOR	AGAINST	PTS
Wales	4	3	0	1	57	42	6
France	4	3	0	1	57	47	6
England	4	2	0	2	56	30	4
Scotland	4	1	0	3	67	68	2
Ireland	4	1	0	3	40	90	2

1988-89

21.01.1989 MURRAYFIELD
Scotland 23 *T:* G Armstrong, DB White, CM Chalmers
C: PW Dods *PG:* PW Dods 2 *DG:* CM Chalmers
Wales 7 *T:* MR Hall *PG:* B Bowen
Referee: J-C Doulcet (France)

21.01.1989 LANSDOWNE ROAD, DUBLIN
Ireland 21 *T:* BJ Mullin *C:* MJ Kiernan
PG: MJ Kiernan 5
France 26 *T:* P Lagisquet 2, S Blanco, J-B Lafond
C: J-B Lafond 2 *PG:* J-B Lafond 2
Referee: JB Anderson (Scotland)

04.02.1989 CARDIFF ARMS PARK
Wales 13 *T:* MA Jones *PG:* PH Thorburn 3
Ireland 19 *T:* NP Mannion, PM Dean *C:* MJ Kiernan
PG: MJ Kiernan 3
Referee: RC Quittenton (England)

04.02.1989 TWICKENHAM
England 12 *PG:* CR Andrew 2, JM Webb 2
Scotland 12 *T:* J Jeffrey *C:* PW Dods *PG:* PW Dods 2
Referee: G Maurette (France)

18.02.1989 PARC DES PRINCES, PARIS
France 31 *T:* S Blanco 2, P Berbizier, P Dintrans
C: J-B Lafond 3 *PG:* J-B Lafond 2 *DG:* F Mesnel
Wales 12 *PG:* PH Thorburn 4
Referee: JM Fleming (Scotland)

18.02.1989 LANSDOWNE ROAD, DUBLIN
Ireland 3 *PG:* MJ Kiernan
England 16 *T:* BC Moore, D Richards *C:* CR Andrew
PG: CR Andrew 2
Referee: LJ Peard (Wales)

04.03.1989 TWICKENHAM
England 11 *T:* WDC Carling, RA Robinson
PG: CR Andrew
France 0
Referee: SR Hilditch (Ireland)

04.03.1989 MURRAYFIELD
Scotland 37 *T:* I Tukalo 3, J Jeffrey, DF Cronin
C: PW Dods 4 *PG:* PW Dods 3
Ireland 21 *T:* BJ Mullin 2, FJ Dunlea *C:* MJ Kiernan 3
PG: MJ Kiernan
Referee: KVJ Fitzgerald (Australia)

18.03.1989 PARC DES PRINCES, PARIS
France 19 *T:* P Berbizier, S Blanco, P Lagisquet
C: P Berot 2 *PG:* P Berot
Scotland 3 *PG:* PW Dods
Referee: OE Doyle (Ireland)

18.03.1989 CARDIFF ARMS PARK
Wales 12 *T:* MR Hall *C:* PH Thorburn
PG: PH Thorburn 2
England 9 *PG:* CR Andrew 2 *DG:* CR Andrew
Referee: KVJ Fitzgerald (Australia)

	P	W	D	L	FOR	AGAINST	PTS
France	4	3	0	1	76	47	6
England	4	2	1	1	48	27	5
Scotland	4	2	1	1	75	59	5
Ireland	4	1	0	3	64	92	2
Wales	4	1	0	3	44	82	2

"

At long last, woken from a slumber that had threatened to last forever, with only intermittent signs of life to offset huge slabs of torpor, England finally came good.

"

1990s

Cry 'God for Harry! England and St George!' At long last, woken from a slumber that had threatened to last forever, with only intermittent signs of life to offset huge slabs of torpor, England finally came good. The rest of the rugby world had always expressed concern that if England ever did get their act together, apply logic and method to their approach, come up with a system and stick with it, then the others might be in a bit of trouble. England had vast resources, and with the game going professional in the mid-1990s, increasing pots of money were to be ploughed into the professional game to maximise any advantages that they might have – they had riches at their disposal.

None of that would have been of any use, though, if the infrastructure creaked and groaned, or worse was non-existent. As the sport moved towards the moment when it had to turn professional, so all the structures underpinning the elite game became more and more streamlined. There was greater scrutiny, greater accountability, a greater need to get it right – even if the poor blokes at the sharp end, players and coaches, were still amateur.

The arrival of Geoff Cooke on the scene brought huge dividends to English rugby. Cooke's role in the whole drive towards World Cup success in 2003 has often been downplayed or even overlooked completely. It shouldn't be. Cooke was the first to recognise that greater rationality had to be applied to the selection process. There had to be criteria for selection, not mere gut instinct. There had to be more science, less whim. The players had to take greater responsibility for their actions, pay greater attention to their bodies, put a whole new emphasis on conditioning.

ABOVE England manager Geoff Cooke, here with coach Roger Uttley in 1991, brought a more scientific approach to running the national side.

Pints were still sunk, red meat was still gobbled up and late nights were still allowed. But the move towards a more professional set-up began long before professionalism itself arrived in 1995. Cooke came from a broad-based coaching background and knew the dedication that rowers and track-and-field athletes brought to their sport. He wanted English rugby to take that on board. Out with the old ways, in with the white-meat ways. Cooke put a lot of faith in the individual, which did not always sit that well with those in the committee rooms. His decision to make Will Carling captain in 1988 at such a young age was a bold move.

Carling was to become a seminal figure in England's renaissance through the 1990s, their most successful ever decade. Over a period of seven seasons, 1990-96, England won three Grand Slams (1991, 1992 and 1995), missed out on another by a whisker (not to mention a fierce Scottish uprising) in 1990, were champions in 1996 and lost out to Wales in 1994 only on the points difference system, which had been introduced, but not required, the previous year. That was some transformation from their years of underachievement.

The England captain became the figurehead, more and more of a magnet for television cameras not to mention the paparazzi once his friendship with Princess Diana got into the public domain. Carling was Cooke's man, a modern-day star, at ease with his profile and commercial possibilities. He was, of course, first and foremost a player. He still had to cut it as a centre-threequarter, which, to his credit, he did. Tough, durable, reliable, the perfect foil to the ghosting Jeremy Guscott, Carling was rarely spectacular, but nor was John Dawes and he led the Lions to one of their greatest ever triumphs in 1971. The beauty of rugby is that it is a game of many parts. Carling was one of those essential parts.

He was the first player to make playing for England a priority. Such a stance didn't always make Carling popular with those at Harlequins, and as the decade progressed, and the game become ever more popular, the tensions between club and country became more tense and fraught with friction. Carling spotted that long before it ever became an issue in the political battle between clubs and union. Eventually, a form of central contract was agreed, whereby clubs were compensated for the release of players to the national squad. England was Carling's prime focus, and he set just the sort of tunnel-vision tone that Cooke wanted to establish.

Carling was just 22 when he was appointed, the youngest England captain for 57 years. Cooke never presumed to tell the world that Carling was to be a fixture in the side come what may, for such is to tie a weight round a selector's neck. But Carling knew that as long as he performed on the field, then his was the first name on the team sheet. That sense of unity and collective purpose spread through the side.

National sides are often thrown together or brought together in unfavourable circumstances. The trick is to rise above the adversity, brought about by injury or a lack of

ABOVE Carling the leader talks to his troops at Twickenham in 1995. By this point he had been England captain for some seven years. BELOW LEFT Carling beats Neil Jenkins of Wales in 1992. Never a flashy player, Carling was nevertheless no slouch with ball in hand.

preparation, and foster a sense of togetherness. By the time the 1990 championship hove into view, there was a sense of Club England about the national side. It showed in their play. England were in their pomp, laying waste to the opposition. They rattled their way through games, playing with verve, vision, touch, hardness and potency. It's some task to get forwards and backs playing in perfect union. Too often one or the other holds sway. In 1990, England cracked it. They had a dominant line out through Wade Dooley and Paul Ackford, a strong, productive scrum, too, and a back-row mix that ticked all the boxes. The long-serving Peter Winterbottom, who had made his debut against Australia at Twickenham in 1982, could forage as well as tackle, while Mike Teague and Mickey Skinner were, well, just hard.

Outside, Richard Hill had learned his lesson from the hot-headed days of 1987 and was proving to be a reliable operator at the base. Hill had no need to resort to those head-banging, so-called motivational antics of earlier years: he had Brian 'the Pitbull' Moore for that, the Harlequins hooker ably supported by wily props Paul 'the Judge' Rendall and Jeff Probyn. Simon Hodgkinson was a reliable man at the rear, a formidable kicker, while Rory Underwood

knew how to finish off a move to deadly effect. Carling and Guscott were always a threat, while Simon Halliday outside was always shrewd, always dangerous.

The cast didn't change much throughout the 1990 campaign. Wasps wing Mark Bailey had an appearance, as did Bath No. 8 Dave Egerton, but it was a tightknit group that accounted so impressively for Ireland (23-0) at Twickenham and France (26-7) at a wind-lashed Parc des Princes, with

SCOTLAND v ENGLAND IN 1990.

England seemed destined to carry off the Grand Slam in 1990 but came up against a Scotland side with other ideas. LEFT *Tony Stanger and Chris Gray celebrate the former's try at Murrayfield.* ABOVE AND INSET *Grand Slam skipper David Sole is congratulated by the Scottish support after the 13-7 victory and enjoys a drink with coach Ian McGeechan.* BELOW *John Ireland's rendition of Scotland flanker John Jeffrey, aka 'the Great White Shark'.*

John Jeffrey

175

Underwood, Guscott and Carling all touching down on a day of delirium in the French capital for England followers. Wales were put to the sword back at Twickenham a fortnight later, Hill and once again Carling and Underwood scoring the tries in a 34-6 victory – an England record in terms of points and margin of victory. There was pace and efficiency in England's game and they headed to Murrayfield in good heart.

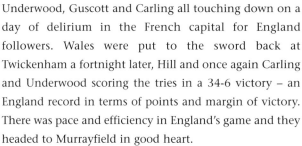

And then it all went horribly wrong. Why? Were England complacent? Probably. Were they arrogant imperialists of Thatcher's England, the banner-bearers of the Poll Tax brigade, hated and despised? Well, of course not. But the mood in Edinburgh that day was heavily charged. There was something unseemly about the atmosphere. Bannockburn was in the air, and Scotland played their hand magnificently, right from the moment that David Sole began his slow march out into the middle of the Murrayfield pitch, ratcheting up the tension and playing to the crowd.

Scotland, of course, still had to win the game. And to judge by the way that they had scuffed their way through the championship, they had it all to do. Scotland had sneaked past Ireland (13-10) and Wales (13-9), only really suggesting what they had to offer in dismantling a lacklustre French side 21-0 at Murrayfield. But do it they did. For all the recent input of science into the sport, rugby can still be reduced to elemental truths. If you smash the living daylights out of the opposition, harry and hound them at every turn (and was there ever a finer tartan trio to accomplish that than Finlay Calder, John Jeffrey and Derek White?) then you're in the ball game. Scotland did just that, took their opportunities – wing Tony Stanger capitalising on a fortunate bounce and dithering defence – and that was it. A legendary day was enshrined for Scotland and a complex was created for England.

Rory Underwood

England had scored 30 more points across the championship, but the Grand Slam was Scotland's. Small wonder that England were to retreat into themselves the following season: the 1990 campaign had repercussions way beyond mid-March of that year. England felt cheated by their defeat at Murrayfield, deserved as the Scottish victory had been on the day. This group felt that they had betrayed their potential, not made the most of their early championship excellence. England had played the best rugby they had played in at least a decade, and all they got for it was ridicule and gloating abuse.

In truth, England were right. They were far and away the best side. Scotland had scooped the pot, though, and the rest were nowhere. The overall quality was low. England were in a league of their own. For the next two seasons, they were to ensure that the rest of Europe had no reason but to acknowledge that. England won back-to-back Grand Slams, reached the final of the 1991 Rugby World Cup, too, and were the dominant force in the Home Unions. But instead of reaching out and trusting their talent as they had done for the early part of the 1990 championship, they became narrow and cautious, pragmatically inclined with the title their only goal. The end was to justify everything.

Pity, for there was a lot in that England side. England even managed to spoil their first victory in Cardiff for 28 years by throwing a strop against the media afterwards. Poor show. It was inevitable that there would be strain during these years, when players felt hard done by as the game attracted more and more money while they were still expected to doff the cap and be grateful for being granted the privilege of playing for England. The apogee of this tension was to come a few years later with Will Carling's famous quip about the '57 old farts' at the RFU. Pity he didn't patent the phrase for he would have made a fortune. It's been oft repeated since.

England didn't have an untroubled ride to their 1991 Grand Slam in that they had to really fight to beat France in a tumultuous final game at Twickenham. They got there, just, 21-19, but

LEFT The boot behind England's 1991 success: full back Simon Hodgkinson, seen here in the decider against France at Twickenham, in which he scored 14 of England's 21 points.
FOLLOWING PAGES England lock Paul Ackford leaps to snaffle line-out ball in the same game. And all his own efforts – no lifting here!

ENGLAND v FRANCE IN 1991.

ABOVE *Although England eventually pulled through 21-19, their first Grand Slam for 11 years was placed in jeopardy by one of the finest tries ever witnessed at Twickenham. Philippe Saint-André (11) finishes off under England's posts a move begun by the great Serge Blanco behind his own.* BOTTOM RIGHT *Former England captain and Lion Roger Uttley, coach to the 1991 Grand Slam winners.*

ENGLAND

White Jerseys, White Shorts

Referee:
L. J. Peard (Wales)
Touch Judges:
C. Norling (Wales)
D. Bevan (Wales)

FRANCE

Blue Jerseys, White Shorts

England	Position	France
15. S. D. HODGKINSON *Nottingham*	FULL BACK	15. S. BLANCO (captain) *Biarritz*
	THREE QUARTERS	
14. N. J. HESLOP *Orrell*	RIGHT WING	14. J.-B. LAFOND *Racing Club*
13. W. D. C. CARLING (captain) *Harlequins*	CENTRE	13. P. SELLA *Agen*
12. J. C. GUSCOTT *Bath*	CENTRE	12. F. MESNEL *Racing Club*
11. R. UNDERWOOD *RAF & Leicester*	LEFT WING	11. P. SAINT-ANDRÉ *Montferrand*
	HALF BACKS	
10. C. R. ANDREW *Wasps*	STAND-OFF	10. D. CAMBERABERO *Béziers*
9. R. J. HILL *Bath*	SCRUM-HALF	9. P. BERBIZIER *Agen*
	FORWARDS	
1. J. LEONARD *Harlequins*	PROP	1. G. LASCUBÉ *Agen*
2. B. C. MOORE *Harlequins*	HOOKER	2. P. MAROCCO *Montferrand*
3. J. A. PROBYN *Wasps*	PROP	3. P. ONDARTS *Biarritz*
4. P. J. ACKFORD *Harlequins*	LOCK	4. M. TACHDJIAN *Racing Club*
5. W. A. DOOLEY *Preston Grasshoppers*	LOCK	5. O. ROUMAT *Dax*
6. M. C. TEAGUE *Gloucester*	FLANKER	6. X. BLOND *Racing Club*
7. P. J. WINTERBOTTOM *Harlequins*	FLANKER	7. L. CABANNES *Racing Club*
8. D. RICHARDS *Leicester*	No. 8	8. A. BENAZZI *Agen*

Replacements: 16. J. M. Webb (Bath)
17. S. J. Halliday (Harlequins) 18. C. D. Morris (Orrell)
19. P. A. G. Rendall (Wasps) 20. C. J. Olver (Northampton)
21. M. G. Skinner (Harlequins)

KICK-OFF 2.45 p.m.

Replacements: 16. T. Lacroix (Dax)
17. E. Bonneval (Toulouse) 18. H. Sanz (Narbonne)
19. C. Deslandes (Racing Club) 20. M. Cécillon (Bourgoin)
21. P. Gimbert (Bègles)

Roger Uttley

it was France who stole away with the glory. They scored one of the best tries ever seen at Twickenham, started by Serge Blanco behind his own posts and finished several passes and a cross-field kick later by Philippe Saint-André. Brilliant, quite brilliant. Mind you, the try by Franck Mesnel wasn't bad either. France scored three tries to England's one, but as Carling's men had learnt painfully the year before, the only thing that matters is the final scoreboard. Simon Hodgkinson contributed a colossal 60 points to England's campaign, an all-Five Nations record.

Coach Roger Uttley gave way to Dick Best after the 1991 World Cup, but in the championship it was a case of *Plus ça change, plus c'est la même chose*, as our friends across the Channel are wont to say. England were clear victors, with the rest nowhere. An explosive match in Paris, which saw French forwards Grégoire Lascube and Vincent Moscato sent off, typified this hard-nosed England outfit. They put pressure on their opponents at every turn, forcing them into either error or indiscretion.

England had their own armoury, too, of course, as was reflected in their hugely impressive points total of 118 points. That's class. England's medic at the rear, Bath full back Jon Webb, who like J.P.R. became an orthopaedic surgeon, weighed in with a mighty, record-breaking 67 points, passing Simon Hodgkinson's Five Nations high-water mark of the previous season and overtaking Dusty Hare's all-time England record of 240 points into the bargain. Webb was outstanding in the 1992 season, and not just for his kicking. He scored two tries in the 38-9 win over Ireland at Twickenham and another in Paris.

Of the England set-up of the early 1990s, Paul Ackford hung up his boots after the 1991 World Cup to earn his living as a journalist, Martin Bayfield coming in to partner Wade 'the

THIS PAGE It was Slam number two for Will Carling's team in 1992. BOTTOM LEFT Jon Webb provided points aplenty with boot and ball in hand from full back. ABOVE 'Blackpool Tower' Wade Dooley crashes to earth to score in the 24-0 win over Wales on Grand Slam day. BELOW 'Swing Low, Sweet Chariot' (with some of the actions) rings out around Twickenham led by the players after the Wales match.

LEFT *The 22-year-old Martin Johnson takes his place in the line out on his international debut, against France at Twickenham in 1993. His name did not appear on the programme (below), since he was a last-minute replacement for the injured Wade Dooley.*

REFEREE	ENGLAND			FRANCE	
J. M. FLEMING (Scotland)		JERSEYS White SHORTS White			JERSEYS Blue SHORTS White
KICK-OFF 2.30pm					
FULL BACK	J. M. WEBB (Bath)		15	J-B LAFOND (Begles)	
RIGHT WING	I. HUNTER (Northampton)		14	P. SAINT-ANDRE (Montferrand)	
CENTRE	W. D. C. CARLING (Harlequins)(Captain)		13	P. SELLA (Agen)	
CENTRE	J. C. GUSCOTT (Bath)		12	T. LACROIX (Dax)	
LEFT WING	R. UNDERWOOD (R.A.F. and Leicester)		11	P. HONTAS (Biarritz)	
STAND OFF	C. R. ANDREW (Wasps)		10	D. CAMBERABERO (Beziers)	
SCRUM-HALF	C. D. MORRIS (Orrell)		9	A. HUEBER (Toulon)	
PROP	J. LEONARD (Harlequins)		1	L. ARMARY (Lourdes)	
HOOKER	B. C. MOORE (Harlequins)		2	J-F TORDO (Nice)(Captain)	
PROP	J. A. PROBYN (Wasps)		3	L. SEIGNE (Merignac)	
LOCK	M. C. BAYFIELD (Northampton)		4	A. BENAZZI (Agen)	
LOCK	W. A. DOOLEY (Preston Grasshoppers)		5	O. ROUMAT (Dax)	
FLANKER	M. C. TEAGUE (Moseley)		6	P. BENETTON (Agen)	
FLANKER	P. J. WINTERBOTTOM (Harlequins)		7	L. CABANNES (Racing Club)	
No. 8	B. B. CLARKE (Bath)		8	M. CECILLON (Bourgoin)	

TOUCH JUDGES	REPLACEMENTS	
R. J. MEGSON (Scotland)	16. P. R. DE GLANVILLE (Bath)	16. S. OUGIER (Toulouse)
D. LESLIE (Scotland)	17. S. BARNES (Bath)	17. F. MESNEL (Racing Club)
	18. S. M. BATES (Wasps)	18. J. CAZALBOU (Toulouse)
	19. V. E. UBOGU (Bath)	19. E. MELVILLE (Toulon)
	20. C. J. OLVER (Northampton)	20. S. GRAOU (Auch)
	21. T. A. K. RODBER (Army/Northampton)	21. F. LANDREAU (Grenoble)

The Rugby Football Union gratefully acknowledges the support of Save & Prosper.

ROB ANDREW, who spent last season with Toulouse, will have the opportunity of brushing up his French today.

RUGBY FOOTBALL UNION

ENGLAND
v
FRANCE

SAVE & PROSPER
THE INVESTMENT HOUSE

Official Programme
TWICKENHAM, 16th JANUARY 1993

Blackpool Tower' Dooley in the second row for 1992. Elsewhere, too, the early 1990s saw a changing of the guard. RWC 1991 was the swansong for Blanco of France; likewise Finlay Calder and John Jeffrey of Scotland. By the end of the 1992 championship, there was no more Donal Lenihan for Ireland and Scotland's Derek White had gone as well.

The 1993 season saw the five-point try arrive in the championship, having been brought in by the IRB in 1992 and first implemented in the southern hemisphere winter of that year. It was another supposed incentive to encourage attacking play; the flip side was that there was now a huge premium on making sure that tries were not given away, leading to more of an emphasis on stopping the opposition from scoring – by foul means if fair wouldn't get the job done. Oh, well.

Although England were powerful contenders for much of the decade, inevitably, and thankfully, they were not to have their own way in all things, and the 1993 season was to prove

LEFT England came unstuck against Ireland at Lansdowne Road in 1993, lock Mick Galwey going over for a try to add to Eric Elwood's two penalties and brace of dropped goals.

the point. In the year that also saw an official championship trophy for the first time, they still might have headed into Grand Slam territory had it not been for Rory Underwood being caught napping and allowing Ieuan Evans to dance in at the Arms Park to nick a 10-9 victory. True, it was Webb's boot that got them home 16-15 against France at Twickenham, Saint-André bagging a couple of tries to England's solitary effort from Ian Hunter, but even so England went into the last round of matches as 6/1-on favourites to beat Ireland at Lansdowne Road and finish top of the championship pile once again.

England were shaping up reasonably well on all fronts. And then they went to Dublin and got mugged. Ireland had done little to suggest that they had such a performance in them, losing 21-6 at home to France and 15-3 in their opening game against Scotland at Murrayfield. But they did have it in them, on one of those memorable Lansdowne Road days when the roar is mighty, the effort unstinting and the rage of the underdog is at its fiercest. Apparently, a drop of drink can be taken afterwards in this city for those of such persuasion.

England could manage only a solitary penalty goal through Webb, Munster's warrior figure Mick Galwey touching down for a try that sent Lansdowne Road potty. England's 17-3 defeat was to prove costly for several players nurturing hopes of going on the Lions tour to New Zealand. France, meanwhile, were seeing off championship strugglers Wales 26-10, and so became the first of the five to pick up the championship trophy.

Indeed, Wales had barely troubled the statisticians in those early years of the decade, historians being able to note only that the game in Wales seemed in turmoil. There was strife in the corridors of power and uncertainty out on the field. At the end of the 1993-94 season, however, Wales, who had lost to Canada 26-24 at Cardiff in the autumn, found themselves travelling to London for a crucial final game of the championship at Twickenham, the title within reach.

Rob Andrew

Opponents England had had a championship of tight scorelines, sneaking home 15-14 at Murrayfield thanks to a late, late 40-metre penalty from Jon Callard, only to undo the good of that fortunate escape two weeks later at Twickenham when Simon Geoghegan, a blond ball of energy on the Irish wing, helped bring off a famous 13-12 victory. In Paris England prevailed 18-14, Rob Andrew scoring all the visitors' points. Unbeaten Wales, on the other hand, had beaten Scotland 29-6, Ireland 17-15 and had sealed their first win over the French since 1982 (24-15) in their previous match, with fine tries from the barnstorming Scott Quinnell and classy Cardiff wing Nigel Walker, a former Olympic hurdler. Clearly Wales had superior points difference and needed only to avoid defeat by a 16-point margin and the title was theirs under the new system that brought an end to shared championships. Well, the title was theirs, but there were more than a few Welsh nerves shredded that afternoon. The 15-8 scoreline in England's favour prompted the bizarre scene of captain Ieuan Evans heading up the Twickenham steps to collect the Five Nations trophy while gloom filled Welsh hearts in the wake of defeat.

The following year was World Cup year, and England decided to bring in the much-garlanded Bath coach, Jack Rowell, to replace Best in the summer of 1994. There would be few who would argue against Rowell's involvement. He had proved himself time and time again on the club scene, keeping Bath ahead of their rivals season after season. No, there was nothing wrong with Rowell's credentials.

But nor was there with Best's either. Shortly before he was summarily moved aside, and that delicate matter was handled in a cack-handed manner, Best coached the side to a 32-15 victory over South Africa in Pretoria. His overall record was first-rate, and included a Grand Slam, but it was not enough to save him.

Rowell was the boss and it was to be his show. It wasn't a bad production, to be fair. England were back on Grand Slam form in 1995, sweeping the board and brooking little argument as far as that status was concerned. Andrew was kicking goals, Ben Clarke was proving a force in the middle of the back row and Tony Underwood was proving to be every bit as dangerous and accomplished as brother Rory. Underwood Minor scored against Ireland, then picked up a further two tries against France in an emphatic 31-10 victory at Twickenham,

ABOVE Rob Andrew of Wasps (later Newcastle) and England, fly half during the successful years of the 1990s and a major points contributor in the 1995 Grand Slam campaign. BELOW England coach Dick Best and manager Jack Rowell on the summer tour of South Africa in 1994. Despite Best's record of success in his post – he was coach to the 1992 Grand Slam side after all – he was soon to lose his job as Rowell was given the coaching duties in addition to his management role.

England's biggest over the French since 1914. England seemingly had a hex on France: that thumping win was also their eighth in a row over them. How France seethed at such indignity; England revelled in it. Brian Moore delighted in winding up his Gallic opponents, and they fell for it every time. The England hooker once likened them to '15 Eric Cantonas – brilliant but brutal'.

On 18 March England and Scotland squared up in the Grand Slam decider. If anyone was expecting a try-fest, they were to be disappointed. The kickers held sway: Rob Andrew bagged the lot for England in a 24-12 victory; Gavin Hastings and Craig Chalmers shared the spoils for Scotland. Grand Slam duly

1994: A DECISION ON POINTS.

LEFT *Simon Geoghegan is jubilant after scoring in Ireland's 13-12 defeat of England at Twickenham, which is in turn celebrated (below) by Denis McBride and a fan.*

BELOW LEFT *On the same day, Scott Quinnell powers away from the French defence to score in Cardiff as Wales keep their championship hopes alive. After England then won in Paris, the final match of the championship was an unusual shoot-out between England and Wales at Twickenham. Wales were on for a Grand Slam but England could still win the title if they beat Wales by enough points. England won but not heavily enough, and Ieuan Evans lifted the trophy (bottom).*

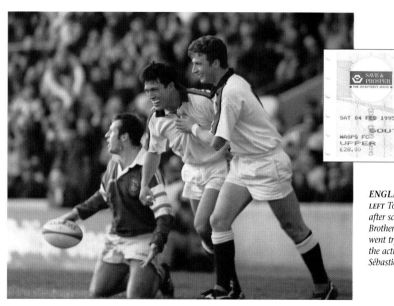

ENGLAND v FRANCE IN 1995.
LEFT Tony Underwood is congratulated by Mike Catt after scoring his second try in England's 31-10 win. Brother Rory was on the other wing that day but went tryless. FACING PAGE TOP Tony Underwood in the action again, this time beaten to a high ball by Sébastien Viars.

achieved. It was becoming almost a routine matter for England. Will Carling became the first player to captain his country to three Five Nations Grand Slams. Only two others had managed back-to-back Slams as captain.

It was the end of an era in many ways. By the time the players congregated for the 1996 championship the game had turned professional, sending many an old committee man spinning in his grave. What difference did it make? you might ask. Little in the short term, all the more so since the RFU insisted on a 12-month moratorium. In the long term, much did change. At long last, players were to be given a fair crack at getting the best out of themselves. No more juggling work and play, no more dashing from office, factory, hospital or school to put in a shift on the training field.

And no more excuses. Of course, you could argue that the rich got richer, that the gulf between the haves and have-nots in the four Home Unions was to grow wider still. Certainly France and England were to dominate the championship over the next decade to the point where it was decided to make that fixture the last in the schedule to provide an appropriate climax for television. That idea didn't last long. And thank goodness for that.

The amateur diehards had good reason to press their case in 1996, for it was a low-quality tournament, England coming through on points difference to take their twenty-second title and draw level with Wales at the top of the all-time honours board. England went with a young side – Lawrence Dallaglio, Mark Regan, Garath Archer, Matt Dawson, Paul Grayson and Jon Sleightholme were all new to the championship and Graham Rowntree had made his debut in the previous season's Grand Slam decider. One familiar,

shambling figure was not new, that of Dean Richards. Initially overlooked, Richards was drafted in for the Calcutta Cup as England got desperate. 'Deano' made it his own: England won 18-9 at Murrayfield, Grayson kicking all the points. 'He looks so strange,' said Scotland's Jim Telfer of Richards. 'But what a player.'

Money in the game brought its fair share of difficulties. There was a huge bust-up among the committees over the division of TV spoils. England, aware of their financial muscle, flexed it, signing an exclusive deal with satellite broadcaster BSkyB. There was no end of brinkmanship, no end of sabre-rattling, no end of name-calling. It all got rather messy, with the Celts turning on England for what they perceived to be their selfishness and lack of loyalty in brokering their own deal. The upshot was that England were turfed out of the championship. The news dominated the agenda during summer 1996. A Five Nations Championship without England? Unthinkable. Oh, no it wasn't.

Face had to be saved, of course, not to mention finances. The reality was that the Celts needed England as much, if not more, than England needed them. A truce was called, a peace treaty of sorts was cobbled together and the 1997 championship was saved. The news came in dramatic fashion, RFU treasurer Colin Herridge interrupting the official launch of the *Rothmans Rugby Yearbook* in August 1996, clutching confirmation that it was all back on again. It's

BELOW LEFT The England team for the Grand Slam decider against Scotland in 1995. Back row (left to right): C. Herridge (RFU), R.G.R. Dawe (replacement), L. Cusworth (assistant coach), C.G. Rowntree (replacement), M.J. Catt, V.E. Ubogu, D. Richards, B.B. Clarke, M.C. Bayfield, M.O. Johnson, T.A.K. Rodber, S.O. Ojomoh (replacement), J. Leonard, J. Rowell (coach), J. Elliott (selector), T. Moule (medic), K. Murphy (in front, physio). Front row: K.P.P. Bracken, G.R. Botterman (replacement), J.E.B. Callard (replacement), T. Underwood, J.C. Guscott, C.R. Andrew, W.D.C. Carling (capt), B.C. Moore, R. Underwood, P.R. de Glanville (replacement), C.D. Morris (replacement). Gregg Botterman was called up as a second replacement hooker after Graham Dawe, the incumbent reserve, was injured. FACING PAGE BOTTOM It's Grand Slam Carling for the third time, a first for a Five Nations captain, as England win 24-12 at Twickenham.

	SAVE & PROSPER THE INVESTMENT HOUSE		
ENGLAND			**WALES**
M. J. CATT (Bath)	FULL BACK	15	W. J. L. THOMAS (Llanelli)
J. M. SLEIGHTHOLME (Bath)	RIGHT WING	14	I. C. EVANS (Llanelli)
W. D. C. CARLING (Harlequins) *Capt.*	CENTRE	13	L. B. DAVIES (Neath)
J. C. GUSCOTT (Bath)	CENTRE	12	N. G. DAVIES (Llanelli)
R. UNDERWOOD (Leicester & RAF)	LEFT WING	11	W. T. PROCTOR (Llanelli)
P. J. GRAYSON (Northampton)	FLY HALF	10	A. C. THOMAS (Bristol)
M. J. S. DAWSON (Northampton)	SCRUM-HALF	9	R. HOWLEY* (Bridgend)
G. C. ROWNTREE (Leicester)	PROP	1	A. L. P. LEWIS (Cardiff)
M. P. REGAN (Bristol)	HOOKER	2	J. M. HUMPHREYS (Cardiff) *Capt.*
J. LEONARD (Harlequins)	PROP	3	J. D. DAVIES (Neath)
M. O. JOHNSON (Leicester)	LOCK	4	G. O. LLEWELLYN (Neath)
M. C. BAYFIELD (Northampton)	LOCK	5	D. JONES (Cardiff)
T. A. K. RODBER (Northampton & Army)	FLANKER	6	E. W. LEWIS (Cardiff)
L. B. N. DALLAGLIO (Wasps)	FLANKER	7	R. G. JONES (Llanelli)
B. B. CLARKE (Bath)	No. 8	8	H. T. TAYLOR (Cardiff)

Jerseys White
Shorts White

Jerseys Red
Shorts White

REPLACEMENTS

16 J. E. B. CALLARD (Bath)
17 P. R. DE GLANVILLE (Bath)
18 K. P. P. BRACKEN (Bristol)
19 V. E. UBOGU (Bath)
20 R. G. R. DAWE (Bath)
21 D. RICHARDS (Leicester)

REPLACEMENTS

16 G. THOMAS (Bridgend)
17 N. R. JENKINS (Pontypridd)
18 A. P. MOORE (Cardiff)
19 S. WILLIAMS (Neath)
20 L. MUSTOE (Cardiff)
21 G. R. JENKINS (Swansea)

REFEREE
K. W. McCARTNEY (Scotland)

TOUCH JUDGES
R. J. MEGSON (Scotland)
E. MURRAY (Scotland)

* = NEW CAP   The Rugby Football Union gratefully acknowledges the support of Save & Prosper.

1996: THE FIRST FIVE NATIONS OF THE PROFESSIONAL ERA.
TOP *Matt Dawson turns on the speed against Wales, while Jon Sleightholme (right) pins back his ears and heads for the try line against Ireland, both matches at Twickenham.* ABOVE *Souvenirs from the England v Wales game, including line-ups showing a good number of England names new to the championship, among them Lawrence Dallaglio and Paul Grayson as well as Dawson and Sleightholme themselves.*

ENGLAND v FRANCE IN 1997.
RIGHT Christophe Lamaison nabbed a full set for 18 points as France fought back at Twickenham to set themselves up for a Grand Slam of their own. ABOVE No-side and neither France nor England can believe the result – 23-20 to France, having been 20-6 down. BELOW The team line-ups in the match-day programme.

estimated that the RFU paid back some £20 million into the collective pot to assuage the ire of the Celtic nations. The RFU's £87.5-million deal with BSkyB stood.

On the field, England took their revenge on the Celts by dishing out savage beatings. In the final 1997 reckoning, England had scored an all-Five Nations record 141 points, 23 more than their previous best, achieved in 1992. But they lost the one that really mattered, against France at Twickenham, despite rattling up a 20-6 lead. In an amazing turnaround, France, kick-started by fly half Christophe Lamaison – who finished with a full set of try, conversions, penalties and dropped goal for a total of 18 points – stunned the Twickenham crowd as they ran out winners, 23-20. England had never lost a 14-point lead in their history, while for France it was their first win at Twickenham for ten years and their highest score at the ground in 22.

After beating England, France completed their fifth Grand Slam with a 47-20 win over Scotland at the Parc des Princes. France had roused themselves and went on to make it back-to-back Grand Slams in 1998. And they did it in true musketeer fashion, with plenty of panache and gung-ho, scoring 129 points and 14 tries – both French records for the championship. England had to settle for second place, but their celebrated pack of forwards, including Leonard, Johnson, Dallaglio and Richard Hill, was beginning to take shape.

At the end of the 1997 Five Nations, we bade adieu to the Parc des Princes, which is still much missed. To the north of Paris, the Stade de France was ready for action and began staging Five Nations matches from 1998. Wales, too, were in the business of bricks and mortar, steel and girders, and had to

FOLLOWING PAGES
Lawrence Dallaglio breaks from the scrum against France in 1999.

decamp to Wembley while the Millennium Stadium was rising magnificently from the ground. Wales had a funny championship in 1998, winning twice, against Scotland (19-13) and in Dublin (30-21), yet being humiliated by England (60-26) at Twickenham and by France (51-0) at Wembley. France, with Thomas Castaignède an impish presence, tormented Wales at the home of English football and delighted neutrals as they clinched back-to-back Slams for the first time. They scored seven tries on their way to the biggest ever winning margin recorded in a Five Nations match (it was not bettered until England's 80-23 win over Italy in 2001 in what was then the Six Nations). There was verve, effrontery, style and potency in all that they did.

England had their first professional coach, Clive Woodward, in charge by this time and were good value for their fourth Triple Crown in succession. But again they fluffed the test against France, losing the inaugural Five Nations match at the Stade de France by 24 points to 17, a scoreline that Woodward admitted flattered his side. One significant moment for England in the championship came with the introduction of Jonny Wilkinson as a substitute after 78 minutes of their win against Ireland. Wilkinson, aged 18 years 314 days, replaced Mike Catt on the wing, becoming the youngest player to be capped by England for 71 years.

Even those misguided administrators who were looking to gerrymander the fixture lists for the purposes of television could not

TOP David Rees, who scored two tries in England's 60-26 thumping of Wales in 1998, for which campaign England had a new boss in Clive Woodward (left). BELOW Nick Beal scores against Scotland in 1999. RIGHT Danny Grewcock stands tall in the line out in the same match.

have stage-managed the sort of finale that graced the 1999 championship. For the fourth season in succession, England lost only one match. But this was a crucial one, and how. On the Saturday of the final weekend of the championship, Scotland laid down the challenge with a brazen 36-22 victory in Paris; 36 points was, and remains, their highest score against France, Martin Leslie and Alan Tait scoring two tries apiece, with Gregor Townsend getting the other. All England had to do on Sunday was beat Wales at Wembley.

For long stretches of an impassioned game, it looked as though England would do exactly that, and with some margin to spare. They were in command 25-18 at the break, with tries by Dan Luger, Steve Hanley on debut and flanker Richard Hill. But England could not shake off Neil Jenkins. England kept infringing and Jenkins kept punishing. And then England got ahead of themselves. Rather than opting for a routine shot at the posts with five minutes remaining, captain Lawrence Dallaglio decided on a penalty kick to touch and a drive for a try. It didn't happen. Tim Rodber was yellow-carded for a high tackle, Wales came upfield, Scott Gibbs set off on a jinking run past five defenders, touched down, Jenkins converted and north London went absolutely bonkers. England had been beaten, 32-31, and Scotland were champions.

ABOVE Neil Jenkins played a central role in Wales's victory over England at Wembley in 1999, kicking six penalties plus two conversions, including that of Scott Gibbs's late try (below) to bring about a 32-31 scoreline.

Lloyds TSB
The Lloyds TSB Five Nations Championship
WALES v ENGLAND
SUNDAY 11TH APRIL 1999
KICK OFF 4.00PM TURNSTILES OPEN 2.00PM
PLEASE TAKE YOUR POSITIONS BY 3.15PM

TURNSTILE F
BLOCK 201 ROW 4 SEAT 7
00024991 £8.00
WEMBLEY

Five Nations Results 1990-99

1989-90

20.01.1990 TWICKENHAM
England 23 *T:* R Underwood, JA Probyn, DW Egerton, JC Guscott *C:* SD Hodgkinson 2 *PG:* SD Hodgkinson
Ireland 0
Referee: P Robin (France)

20.01.1990 CARDIFF ARMS PARK
Wales 19 *T:* MH Titley *PG:* PH Thorburn 4
DG: DW Evans
France 29 *T:* J-B Lafond, P Sella, D Camberabero, P Lagisquet, L Rodriguez *C:* D Camberabero 3
PG: D Camberabero
Referee: FA Howard (England)

03.02.1990 PARC DES PRINCES, PARIS
France 7 *T:* P Lagisquet *PG:* D Charvet
England 26 *T:* R Underwood, JC Guscott, WDC Carling *C:* SD Hodgkinson *PG:* SD Hodgkinson 4
Referee: OE Doyle (Ireland)

03.02.1990 LANSDOWNE ROAD, DUBLIN
Ireland 10 *T:* JJ Fitzgerald *PG:* MJ Kiernan 2
Scotland 13 *T:* DB White 2 *C:* CM Chalmers
PG: CM Chalmers
Referee: C Norling (Wales)

17.02.1990 TWICKENHAM
England 34 *T:* R Underwood 2, WDC Carling, RJ Hill *C:* SD Hodgkinson 3 *PG:* SD Hodgkinson 4
Wales 6 *T:* PT Davies *C:* PH Thorburn
Referee: D Leslie (Scotland)

17.02.1990 MURRAYFIELD
Scotland 21 *T:* F Calder, I Tukalo *C:* CM Chalmers 2 *PG:* CM Chalmers 2, AG Hastings
France 0
Referee: FA Howard (England)

03.03.1990 CARDIFF ARMS PARK
Wales 9 *T:* A Emyr *C:* PH Thorburn *PG:* PH Thorburn
Scotland 13 *T:* DF Cronin *PG:* CM Chalmers 3
Referee: R Hourquet (France)

03.03.1990 PARC DES PRINCES, PARIS
France 31 *T:* F Mesnel 2, P Lagisquet
C: D Camberabero 2 *PG:* D Camberabero 5
Ireland 12 *PG:* MJ Kiernan 4
Referee: K McCartney (Scotland)

17.03.1990 MURRAYFIELD
Scotland 13 *T:* AG Stanger *PG:* CM Chalmers 3
England 7 *T:* JC Guscott *PG:* SD Hodgkinson
Referee: DJ Bishop (New Zealand)

24.03.1990 LANSDOWNE ROAD, DUBLIN
Ireland 14 *T:* BA Smith, WD McBride, TJ Kingston
C: MJ Kiernan
Wales 8 *T:* SP Ford, GO Llewellyn
Referee: DJ Bishop (New Zealand)

	P	W	D	L	FOR	AGAINST	PTS
Scotland	4	4	0	0	60	26	8
England	4	3	0	1	90	26	6
France	4	2	0	2	61	78	4
Ireland	4	1	0	3	36	75	2
Wales	4	0	0	4	42	84	0

1990-91

19.01.1991 PARC DES PRINCES, PARIS
France 15 *PG:* D Camberabero 2
DG: D Camberabero 2, S Blanco
Scotland 9 *PG:* CM Chalmers 2 *DG:* CM Chalmers
Referee: EF Morrison (England)

19.01.1991 CARDIFF ARMS PARK
Wales 6 *PG:* PH Thorburn, NR Jenkins
England 25 *T:* MC Teague *PG:* SD Hodgkinson 7
Referee: RJ Megson (Scotland)

02.02.1991 MURRAYFIELD
Scotland 32 *T:* DB White 2, CM Chalmers, G Armstrong *C:* CM Chalmers, AG Hastings
PG: AG Hastings 2, CM Chalmers *DG:* CM Chalmers
Wales 12 *T:* SP Ford *C:* PH Thorburn
PG: PH Thorburn 2
Referee: DJ Bishop (New Zealand)

02.02.1991 LANSDOWNE ROAD, DUBLIN
Ireland 13 *T:* SJ Smith *PG:* MJ Kiernan 3
France 21 *T:* L Cabannes, P Lagisquet
C: D Camberabero 2 *PG:* D Camberabero 3
Referee: WD Bevan (Wales)

16.02.1991 TWICKENHAM
England 21 *T:* NJ Heslop *C:* SD Hodgkinson
PG: SD Hodgkinson 5
Scotland 12 *PG:* CM Chalmers 4
Referee: SR Hilditch (Ireland)

16.02.1991 CARDIFF ARMS PARK
Wales 21 *T:* P Arnold, NR Jenkins *C:* PH Thorburn 2
PG: PH Thorburn 2 *DG:* NR Jenkins
Ireland 21 *T:* DJ Clarke, BJ Mullin, SP Geoghegan, JE Staples *C:* BA Smith *DG:* BA Smith
Referee: DJ Bishop (New Zealand)

02.03.1991 LANSDOWNE ROAD, DUBLIN
Ireland 7 *T:* SP Geoghegan *PG:* BA Smith
England 16 *T:* R Underwood, MC Teague
C: SD Hodgkinson *PG:* SD Hodgkinson 2
Referee: A Ceccon (France)

02.03.1991 PARC DES PRINCES, PARIS
France 36 *T:* S Blanco, P Saint-Andre, F Mesnel, O Roumat, P Sella, J-B Lafond *C:* D Camberabero 2, S Blanco *PG:* D Camberabero 2
Wales 3 *PG:* PH Thorburn
Referee: KVJ Fitzgerald (Australia)

16.03.1991 MURRAYFIELD
Scotland 28 *T:* AG Hastings, AG Stanger, S Hastings *C:* CM Chalmers 2 *PG:* CM Chalmers 3, AG Hastings
Ireland 25 *T:* KD Crossan, BF Robinson, SP Geoghegan, BJ Mullin *C:* BA Smith 3 *DG:* BA Smith
Referee: KVJ Fitzgerald (Australia)

16.03.1991 TWICKENHAM
England 21 *T:* R Underwood *C:* SD Hodgkinson
PG: SD Hodgkinson 4 *DG:* CR Andrew
France 19 *T:* P Saint-Andre, D Camberabero, F Mesnel
C: D Camberabero 2 *PG:* D Camberabero
Referee: LJ Peard (Wales)

	P	W	D	L	FOR	AGAINST	PTS
England	4	4	0	0	83	44	8
France	4	3	0	1	91	46	6
Scotland	4	2	0	2	81	73	4
Ireland	4	0	1	3	66	86	1
Wales	4	0	1	3	42	114	1

1991-92

18.01.1992 LANSDOWNE ROAD, DUBLIN
Ireland 15 *T:* RM Wallace *C:* RP Keyes *PG:* RP Keyes 3
Wales 16 *T:* S Davies *PG:* NR Jenkins 3
DG: CJ Stephens
Referee: FA Howard (England)

18.01.1992 MURRAYFIELD
Scotland 7 *T:* DB White *PG:* AG Hastings
England 25 *T:* R Underwood, CD Morris *C:* JM Webb
PG: JM Webb 4 *DG:* JC Guscott
Referee: WD Bevan (Wales)

01.02.1992 TWICKENHAM
England 38 *T:* JM Webb 2, CD Morris, JC Guscott, R Underwood, SJ Halliday *C:* JM Webb 4 *PG:* JM Webb 2
Ireland 9 *T:* RP Keyes *C:* RP Keyes *PG:* RP Keyes
Referee: WD Bevan (Wales)

01.02.1992 CARDIFF ARMS PARK
Wales 9 *PG:* NR Jenkins 3
France 12 *T:* P Saint-Andre *C:* J-B Lafond
PG: S Viars *DG:* A Penaud
Referee: OE Doyle (Ireland)

15.02.1992 PARC DES PRINCES, PARIS
France 13 *T:* S Viars, A Penaud *C:* S Viars *PG:* S Viars
England 31 *T:* JM Webb, R Underwood, CD Morris, penalty try *C:* JM Webb 3 *PG:* JM Webb 3
Referee: SR Hilditch (Ireland)

15.02.1992 LANSDOWNE ROAD, DUBLIN
Ireland 10 *T:* RM Wallace *PG:* RP Keyes 2
Scotland 18 *T:* AG Stanger, AD Nicol *C:* AG Hastings 2
PG: AG Hastings 2
Referee: AJ Spreadbury (England)

07.03.1992 TWICKENHAM
England 24 *T:* WDC Carling, MG Skinner, WA Dooley
C: JM Webb 3 *PG:* JM Webb 2
Wales 0
Referee: RJ Megson (Scotland)

07.03.1992 MURRAYFIELD
Scotland 10 *T:* NGB Edwards *PG:* AG Hastings 2
France 6 *PG:* J-B Lafond 2
Referee: F Burger (South Africa)

21.03.1992 CARDIFF ARMS PARK
Wales 15 *T:* RE Webster *C:* NR Jenkins
PG: NR Jenkins 3
Scotland 12 *T:* CM Chalmers 2, AG Hastings
DG: CM Chalmers
Referee: M Desclaux (France)

21.03.1992 PARC DES PRINCES, PARIS
France 44 *T:* S Viars 2, A Penaud 2, M Cecillon, L Cabannes, J-L Sadourny *C:* S Viars 5 *PG:* S Viars 2
Ireland 12 *PG:* DR McAleese 4
Referee: F Burger (South Africa)

	P	W	D	L	FOR	AGAINST	PTS
England	4	4	0	0	118	29	8
France	4	2	0	2	75	62	4
Scotland	4	2	0	2	47	56	4
Wales	4	2	0	2	40	63	4
Ireland	4	0	0	4	46	116	0

1992-93

16.01.1993 MURRAYFIELD
Scotland 15 *T:* DA Stark, AG Stanger *C:* AG Hastings
PG: AG Hastings
Ireland 3 *PG:* NG Malone
Referee: EF Morrison (England)

16.01.1993 TWICKENHAM
England 16 *T:* I Hunter *C:* JM Webb *PG:* JM Webb 3
France 15 *T:* P Saint-Andre 2 *C:* D Camberabero
PG: D Camberabero
Referee: JM Fleming (Scotland)

06.02.1993 CARDIFF ARMS PARK
Wales 10 *T:* IC Evans *C:* NR Jenkins *PG:* NR Jenkins
England 9 *PG:* JM Webb 2 *DG:* JC Guscott
Referee: J Dume (France)

06.02.1993 PARC DES PRINCES, PARIS
France 11 *T:* T Lacroix *PG:* D Camberabero 2
Scotland 3 *PG:* AG Hastings
Referee: WD Bevan (Wales)

20.02.1993 LANSDOWNE ROAD, DUBLIN
Ireland 6 *PG:* NG Malone 2
France 21 *T:* P Saint-Andre, P Sella *C:* D Camberabero
PG: D Camberabero 2 *DG:* D Camberabero
Referee: D Leslie (Scotland)

20.02.1993 MURRAYFIELD
Scotland 20 *T:* DJ Turnbull *PG:* AG Hastings 5
Wales 0
Referee: J Dume (France)

06.03.1993 CARDIFF ARMS PARK
Wales 14 *T:* IC Evans *PG:* NR Jenkins 3
Ireland 19 *T:* BF Robinson *C:* EP Elwood
PG: EP Elwood 3 *DG:* CP Clarke
Referee: AR MacNeill (Australia)

06.03.1993 TWICKENHAM
England 26 *T:* JC Guscott, R Underwood,
T Underwood *C:* JM Webb *PG:* JM Webb 3
Scotland 12 *PG:* AG Hastings 3 *DG:* CM Chalmers
Referee: BW Stirling (Ireland)

20.03.1993 LANSDOWNE ROAD, DUBLIN
Ireland 17 *T:* MJ Galwey *PG:* EP Elwood 2
DG: EP Elwood 2
England 3 *PG:* JM Webb
Referee: AR MacNeill (Australia)

20.03.1993 PARC DES PRINCES, PARIS
France 26 *T:* P Benetton 2, J-B Lafond *C:* J-B Lafond
PG: T Lacroix 3
Wales 10 *T:* N Walker *C:* NR Jenkins *PG:* NR Jenkins
Referee: OE Doyle (Ireland)

	P	W	D	L	FOR	AGAINST	PTS
France	4	3	0	1	73	35	6
Scotland	4	2	0	2	50	40	4
England	4	2	0	2	54	54	4
Ireland	4	2	0	2	45	53	4
Wales	4	1	0	3	34	74	2

1993-94

15.01.1994 CARDIFF ARMS PARK
Wales 29 *T:* MA Rayer 2, IC Evans *C:* NR Jenkins
PG: NR Jenkins 4
Scotland 6 *PG:* AG Hastings 2
Referee: P Robin (France)

15.01.1994 PARC DES PRINCES, PARIS
France 35 *T:* P Benetton, P Saint-Andre, T Lacroix,
O Merle *C:* T Lacroix 3 *PG:* T Lacroix 3
Ireland 15 *PG:* EP Elwood 5
Referee: JM Fleming (Scotland)

05.02.1994 MURRAYFIELD
Scotland 14 *T:* RI Wainwright *PG:* AG Hastings 2
DG: GPJ Townsend
England 15 *PG:* JEB Callard 5
Referee: LL McLachlan (New Zealand)

05.02.1994 LANSDOWNE ROAD, DUBLIN
Ireland 15 *PG:* EP Elwood 5
Wales 17 *T:* NR Jenkins *PG:* NR Jenkins 4
Referee: AJ Spreadbury (England)

19.02.1994 TWICKENHAM
England 12 *PG:* JEB Callard 4
Ireland 13 *T:* SP Geoghegan *C:* EP Elwood
PG: EP Elwood 2
Referee: P Thomas (France)

19.02.1994 CARDIFF ARMS PARK
Wales 24 *T:* LS Quinnell, N Walker *C:* NR Jenkins
PG: NR Jenkins 4
France 15 *T:* O Roumat, P Sella *C:* T Lacroix
PG: T Lacroix
Referee: LL McLachlan (New Zealand)

05.03.1994 PARC DES PRINCES, PARIS
France 14 *T:* A Benazzi *PG:* T Lacroix 3
England 18 *PG:* CR Andrew 5 *DG:* CR Andrew
Referee: SR Hilditch (Ireland)

05.03.1994 LANSDOWNE ROAD, DUBLIN
Ireland 6 *PG:* EP Elwood 2
Scotland 6 *PG:* AG Hastings 2
Referee: EF Morrison (England)

19.03.1994 MURRAYFIELD
Scotland 12 *PG:* AG Hastings 4
France 20 *T:* J-L Sadourny, P Saint-Andre *C:* T Lacroix,
P Montlaur *PG:* T Lacroix 2
Referee: WD Bevan (Wales)

19.03.1994 TWICKENHAM
England 15 *T:* R Underwood, TAK Rodber
C: CR Andrew *PG:* CR Andrew
Wales 8 *T:* N Walker *PG:* NR Jenkins
Referee: JM Fleming (Scotland)

	P	W	D	L	FOR	AGAINST	PTS
Wales	4	3	0	1	78	51	6
England	4	3	0	1	60	49	6
France	4	2	0	2	84	69	4
Ireland	4	1	1	2	49	70	3
Scotland	4	0	1	3	38	70	1

1994-95

21.01.1995 LANSDOWNE ROAD, DUBLIN
Ireland 8 *T:* A Foley *PG:* PA Burke
England 20 *T:* WDC Carling, BB Clarke, T Underwood
C: CR Andrew *PG:* CR Andrew
Referee: P Thomas (France)

21.01.1995 PARC DES PRINCES, PARIS
France 21 *T:* E Ntamack, P Saint-Andre *C:* T Lacroix
PG: T Lacroix 3
Wales 9 *PG:* NR Jenkins 3
Referee: J Pearson (England)

04.02.1995 MURRAYFIELD
Scotland 26 *T:* CA Joiner, DF Cronin *C:* AG Hastings 2
PG: AG Hastings 4
Ireland 13 *T:* BJ Mullin, JC Bell *PG:* PA Burke
Referee: WD Bevan (Wales)

04.02.1995 TWICKENHAM
England 31 *T:* T Underwood 2, JC Guscott
C: CR Andrew 2 *PG:* CR Andrew 4
France 10 *T:* S Viars *C:* T Lacroix *PG:* T Lacroix
Referee: KW McCartney (Scotland)

18.02.1995 CARDIFF ARMS PARK
Wales 9 *PG:* NR Jenkins 3
England 23 *T:* R Underwood 2, VE Ubogu
C: CR Andrew 2 *PG:* CR Andrew 2
Referee: D Mene (France)

18.02.1995 PARC DES PRINCES, PARIS
France 21 *T:* P Saint-Andre 2, J-L Sadourny
PG: T Lacroix *DG:* C Deylaud
Scotland 23 *T:* GPJ Townsend, AG Hastings
C: AG Hastings 2 *PG:* AG Hastings 3
Referee: DTM McHugh (Ireland)

04.03.1995 MURRAYFIELD
Scotland 26 *T:* EW Peters, DIW Hilton
C: AG Hastings 2 *PG:* AG Hastings 4
Wales 13 *T:* RN Jones *C:* NR Jenkins *PG:* NR Jenkins 2
Referee: S Lander (England)

04.03.1995 LANSDOWNE ROAD, DUBLIN
Ireland 7 *T:* SP Geoghegan *C:* EP Elwood
France 25 *T:* Y Delaigue, M Cecillon, E Ntamack,
P Saint-Andre *C:* E Ntamack *PG:* E Ntamack
Referee: C Thomas (Wales)

18.03.1995 CARDIFF ARMS PARK
Wales 12 *PG:* NR Jenkins 4
Ireland 16 *T:* BJ Mullin *C:* PA Burke *PG:* PA Burke 2
DG: PA Burke
Referee: RJ Megson (Scotland)

18.03.1995 TWICKENHAM
England 24 *PG:* CR Andrew 7 *DG:* CR Andrew
Scotland 12 *PG:* AG Hastings 2 *DG:* CM Chalmers 2
Referee: BW Stirling (Ireland)

	P	W	D	L	FOR	AGAINST	PTS
England	4	4	0	0	98	39	8
Scotland	4	3	0	1	87	71	6
France	4	2	0	2	77	70	4
Ireland	4	1	0	3	44	83	2
Wales	4	0	0	4	43	86	0

1995-96

20.01.1996 LANSDOWNE ROAD, DUBLIN
Ireland 10 *T:* PM Clohessy *C:* EP Elwood
PG: EP Elwood
Scotland 16 *T:* KD McKenzie, M Dods *PG:* M Dods
DG: GPJ Townsend
Referee: B Campsall (England)

20.01.1996 PARC DES PRINCES, PARIS
France 15 *PG:* T Lacroix 3 *DG:* T Lacroix,
T Castaignede
England 12 *PG:* PJ Grayson 2 *DG:* PJ Grayson 2
Referee: DTM McHugh (Ireland)

03.02.1996 TWICKENHAM
England 21 *T:* R Underwood, JC Guscott
C: PJ Grayson *PG:* PJ Grayson 3
Wales 15 *T:* HT Taylor, R Howley *C:* AC Thomas
PG: AC Thomas
Referee: KW McCartney (Scotland)

03.02.1996 MURRAYFIELD
Scotland 19 *T:* M Dods 2 *PG:* M Dods 3
France 14 *T:* A Benazzi *PG:* T Lacroix 2, T Castaignede
Referee: C Thomas (Wales)

17.02.1996 PARC DES PRINCES, PARIS
France 45 *T:* E Ntamack 2, R Castel 2, P Saint-Andre,
O Campan, G Accoceberry *C:* T Castaignede 5
Ireland 10 *T:* Penalty try *C:* DG Humphreys
PG: DG Humphreys
Referee: EF Morrison (England)

17.02.1996 CARDIFF ARMS PARK
Wales 14 *T:* WT Proctor *PG:* AC Thomas 3
Scotland 16 *T:* GPJ Townsend *C:* M Dods
PG: M Dods 3
Referee: J Dume (France)

02.03.1996 LANSDOWNE ROAD, DUBLIN
Ireland 30 *T:* SP Geoghegan, NKPJ Woods,
GM Fulcher, DS Corkery *C:* SJP Mason 2
PG: SJP Mason 2
Wales 17 *T:* IC Evans 2 *C:* AC Thomas 2
PG: AC Thomas
Referee: D Mene (France)

02.03.1996 MURRAYFIELD
Scotland 9 *PG:* M Dods 3
England 18 *PG:* PJ Grayson 6
Referee: WD Bevan (Wales)

16.03.1996 CARDIFF ARMS PARK
Wales 16 *T:* R Howley *C:* NR Jenkins *PG:* NR Jenkins 3
France 15 *T:* T Castaignede, E Ntamack
C: T Castaignede *PG:* T Castaignede
Referee: BW Stirling (Ireland)

16.03.1996 TWICKENHAM
England 28 *T:* JM Sleightholme *C:* PJ Grayson
PG: PJ Grayson 6 *DG:* PJ Grayson
Ireland 15 *T:* SJP Mason 4 *DG:* DG Humphreys
Referee: E Murray (Scotland)

	P	W	D	L	FOR	AGAINST	PTS
England	4	3	0	1	79	54	6
Scotland	4	3	0	1	60	56	6
France	4	2	0	2	89	57	4
Wales	4	1	0	3	62	82	2
Ireland	4	1	0	3	65	106	2

Five Nations Results 1990-99

1996-97

18.01.1997 MURRAYFIELD
Scotland 19 *T*: S Hastings *C*: RJS Shepherd
PG: RJS Shepherd 3 *DG*: CM Chalmers
Wales 34 *T*: LS Quinnell, NR Jenkins, AC Thomas,
IC Evans *C*: NR Jenkins 4 *PG*: NR Jenkins 2
Referee: HA Smith (Ireland)

18.01.1997 LANSDOWNE ROAD, DUBLIN
Ireland 15 *PG*: EP Elwood 5
France 32 *T*: D Venditti 3, F Galthie
C: T Castaignede 3 *PG*: T Castaignede 2
Referee: A Watson (South Africa)

01.02.1997 CARDIFF ARMS PARK
Wales 25 *T*: IC Evans 2, LS Quinnell *C*: NR Jenkins 2
PG: NR Jenkins 2
Ireland 26 *T*: JA Bell, ERP Miller, DA Hickie
C: EP Elwood *PG*: EP Elwood 3
Referee: WJ Erickson (Australia)

01.02.1997 TWICKENHAM
England 41 *T*: Penalty try, WDC Carling,
ACT Gomarsall, PR de Glanville *C*: PJ Grayson 3
PG: PJ Grayson 5
Scotland 13 *T*: BRS Eriksson *C*: RJS Shepherd
PG: RJS Shepherd 2
Referee: PD O'Brien (New Zealand)

15.02.1997 LANSDOWNE ROAD, DUBLIN
Ireland 6 *PG*: EP Elwood 2
England 46 *T*: JM Sleightholme 2, T Underwood 2,
ACT Gomarsall, RA Hill *C*: PJ Grayson 2
PG: PJ Grayson 4
Referee: CJ Hawke (New Zealand)

15.02.1997 PARC DES PRINCES, PARIS
France 27 *T*: L Leflamand 2, O Merle, D Venditti
C: R Dourthe, D Aucagne *PG*: D Aucagne
Wales 22 *T*: G Thomas, AG Bateman, R Howley
C: NR Jenkins 2 *PG*: NR Jenkins
Referee: PL Marshall (Australia)

01.03.1997 MURRAYFIELD
Scotland 38 *T*: AV Tait, GPJ Townsend, GW Weir,
P Walton, AG Stanger *C*: RJS Shepherd 5
PG: RJS Shepherd
Ireland 10 *T*: DA Hickie *C*: DG Humphreys
PG: DG Humphreys
Referee: G Simmonds (Wales)

01.03.1997 TWICKENHAM
England 20 *T*: LBN Dallaglio *PG*: PJ Grayson 4
DG: PJ Grayson
France 23 *T*: L Leflamand, C Lamaison
C: C Lamaison 2 *PG*: C Lamaison 2 *DG*: C Lamaison
Referee: JM Fleming (Scotland)

15.03.1997 PARC DES PRINCES, PARIS
France 47 *T*: A Benazzi, L Leflamand, O Magne,
F Tournaire *C*: C Lamaison 3 *PG*: C Lamaison 6
DG: J-L Sadourny
Scotland 20 *T*: AV Tait 2 *C*: RJS Shepherd 2
PG: RJS Shepherd 2
Referee: EF Morrison (England)

15.03.1997 CARDIFF ARMS PARK
Wales 13 *T*: R Howley *C*: J Davies *PG*: J Davies 2
England 34 *T*: TRG Stimpson, T Underwood, RA Hill,
PR de Glanville *C*: MJ Catt 4 *PG*: MJ Catt 2
Referee: J Dume (France)

	P	W	D	L	FOR	AGAINST	PTS
France	4	4	0	0	129	77	8
England	4	3	0	1	141	55	6
Wales	4	1	0	3	94	106	2
Scotland	4	1	0	3	90	132	2
Ireland	4	1	0	3	57	141	2

1997-98

07.02.1998 LANSDOWNE ROAD, DUBLIN
Ireland 16 *T*: Penalty try *C*: DG Humphreys
PG: DG Humphreys 2 *DG*: DG Humphreys
Scotland 17 *T*: AV Tait *PG*: RJS Shepherd 2,
CM Chalmers 2
Referee: A Watson (South Africa)

07.02.1998 STADE DE FRANCE, PARIS
France 24 *T*: P Bernat-Salles, C Dominici
C: C Lamaison *PG*: C Lamaison 2 *DG*: T Castaignede,
J-L Sadourny
England 17 *T*: NA Back *PG*: PJ Grayson 4
Referee: DTM McHugh (Ireland)

21.02.1998 TWICKENHAM
England 60 *T*: DL Rees 2, NA Back, KPP Bracken,
LBN Dallaglio, AS Healey, WJH Greenwood,
MJS Dawson *C*: PJ Grayson 7 *PG*: PJ Grayson 2
Wales 26 *T*: AG Bateman 2, G Thomas, IS Gibbs
C: NR Jenkins 3
Referee: CJ Hawke (New Zealand)

21.02.1998 MURRAYFIELD
Scotland 16 *T*: AG Stanger *C*: CM Chalmers
PG: CM Chalmers 3
France 51 *T*: P Bernat-Salles 2, O Brouzet,
M Lievremont, C Califano, P Carbonneau,
T Castaignede *C*: C Lamaison 2, T Castaignede 3
PG: C Lamaison, T Castaignede
Referee: PD O'Brien (New Zealand)

07.03.1998 STADE DE FRANCE, PARIS
France 18 *T*: P Bernat-Salles, R Ibanez *C*: C Lamaison
PG: C Lamaison 2
Ireland 16 *T*: DA Hickie *C*: EP Elwood
PG: EP Elwood 3
Referee: JM Fleming (Scotland)

07.03.1998 WEMBLEY
Wales 19 *T*: WT Proctor *C*: AC Thomas *PG*: NR Jenkins,
AC Thomas 3
Scotland 13 *T*: GPJ Townsend, DF Cronin
PG: CM Chalmers
Referee: J Dume (France)

21.03.1998 LANSDOWNE ROAD, DUBLIN
Ireland 21 *T*: AJ Ward, VCP Costello *C*: EP Elwood
PG: EP Elwood 3
Wales 30 *T*: AG Bateman, KA Morgan, NR Jenkins
C: NR Jenkins 3 *PG*: NR Jenkins 3
Referee: EF Morrison (England)

22.03.1998 MURRAYFIELD
Scotland 20 *T*: AG Stanger, SL Longstaff *C*: DJ Lee 2
PG: CM Chalmers
England 34 *T*: Penalty try, MJS Dawson, AS Healey,
PJ Grayson *C*: PJ Grayson 4 *PG*: PJ Grayson
DG: PJ Grayson
Referee: C Thomas (Wales)

04.04.1998 TWICKENHAM
England 35 *T*: MB Perry, MJ Catt, R Cockerill,
PR de Glanville *C*: PJ Grayson 3 *PG*: PJ Grayson 3
Ireland 17 *T*: DA Hickie 2 *C*: EP Elwood 2
PG: EP Elwood
Referee: WD Bevan (Wales)

05.04.1998 WEMBLEY
Wales 0
France 51 *T*: J-L Sadourny 2, X Garbajosa 2,
T Lievremont, S Glas, F Galthie *C*: C Lamaison 5
PG: C Lamaison 2
Referee: PL Marshall (Australia)

	P	W	D	L	FOR	AGAINST	PTS
France	4	4	0	0	144	49	8
England	4	3	0	1	146	87	6
Wales	4	2	0	2	75	145	4
Scotland	4	1	0	3	66	120	2
Ireland	4	0	0	4	70	100	0

1998-99

06.02.1999 LANSDOWNE ROAD, DUBLIN
Ireland 9 *PG*: DG Humphreys 3
France 10 *T*: E Ntamack *C*: T Castaignede
PG: T Castaignede
Referee: PL Marshall (Australia)

06.02.1999 MURRAYFIELD
Scotland 33 *T*: GPJ Townsend, JA Leslie, S Murray,
AV Tait *C*: KM Logan 2 *PG*: KM Logan 2, DW Hodge
Wales 20 *T*: DR James, IS Gibbs *C*: NR Jenkins 2
PG: NR Jenkins 2
Referee: EF Morrison (England)

20.02.1999 TWICKENHAM
England 24 *T*: TAK Rodber, DD Luger, ND Beal
C: JP Wilkinson 3 *PG*: JP Wilkinson
Scotland 21 *T*: AV Tait 2, GPJ Townsend
C: KM Logan 3
Referee: DTM McHugh (Ireland)

20.02.1999 WEMBLEY
Wales 23 *T*: JC Quinnell, SP Howarth *C*: NR Jenkins 2
PG: NR Jenkins 3
Ireland 29 *T*: KM Maggs, KGM Wood
C: DG Humphreys 2 *PG*: DG Humphreys 3
DG: DG Humphreys 2
Referee: SJ Young (Australia)

06.03.1999 STADE DE FRANCE, PARIS
France 33 *T*: E Ntamack 3, T Castaignede
C: T Castaignede 2 *PG*: T Castaignede 3
Wales 34 *T*: CL Charvis, DR James, JC Quinnell
C: NR Jenkins 2 *PG*: NR Jenkins 5
Referee: JM Fleming (Scotland)

06.03.1999 LANSDOWNE ROAD, DUBLIN
Ireland 15 *PG*: DG Humphreys 5
England 27 *T*: TAK Rodber, MB Perry *C*: JP Wilkinson
PG: JP Wilkinson 4 *DG*: PJ Grayson
Referee: PD O'Brien (New Zealand)

20.03.1999 TWICKENHAM
England 21 *PG*: JP Wilkinson 7
France 10 *T*: F Comba *C*: T Castaignede
PG: T Castaignede
Referee: CJ Hawke (New Zealand), replaced by
JM Fleming (Scotland)

20.03.1999 MURRAYFIELD
Scotland 30 *T*: CA Murray 2, SB Grimes,
GPJ Townsend *C*: KM Logan 2 *PG*: KM Logan 2
Ireland 13 *T*: Penalty try *C*: DG Humphreys
PG: DG Humphreys 2
Referee: WD Bevan (Wales)

10.04.1999 STADE DE FRANCE, PARIS
France 22 *T*: E Ntamack, C Juillet, C Dominici
C: D Aucagne 2 *PG*: D Aucagne
Scotland 36 *T*: MD Leslie 2, AV Tait 2, GPJ Townsend
C: KM Logan 4 *PG*: KM Logan
Referee: C Thomas (Wales)

11.04.1999 WEMBLEY
Wales 32 *T*: SP Howarth, IS Gibbs *C*: NR Jenkins 2
PG: NR Jenkins 6
England 31 *T*: DD Luger, SM Hanley, RA Hill
C: JP Wilkinson 2 *PG*: JP Wilkinson 4
Referee: A Watson (South Africa)

	P	W	D	L	FOR	AGAINST	PTS
Scotland	4	3	0	1	120	79	6
England	4	3	0	1	103	78	6
Wales	4	2	0	2	109	126	4
Ireland	4	1	0	3	66	90	2
France	4	1	0	3	75	100	2

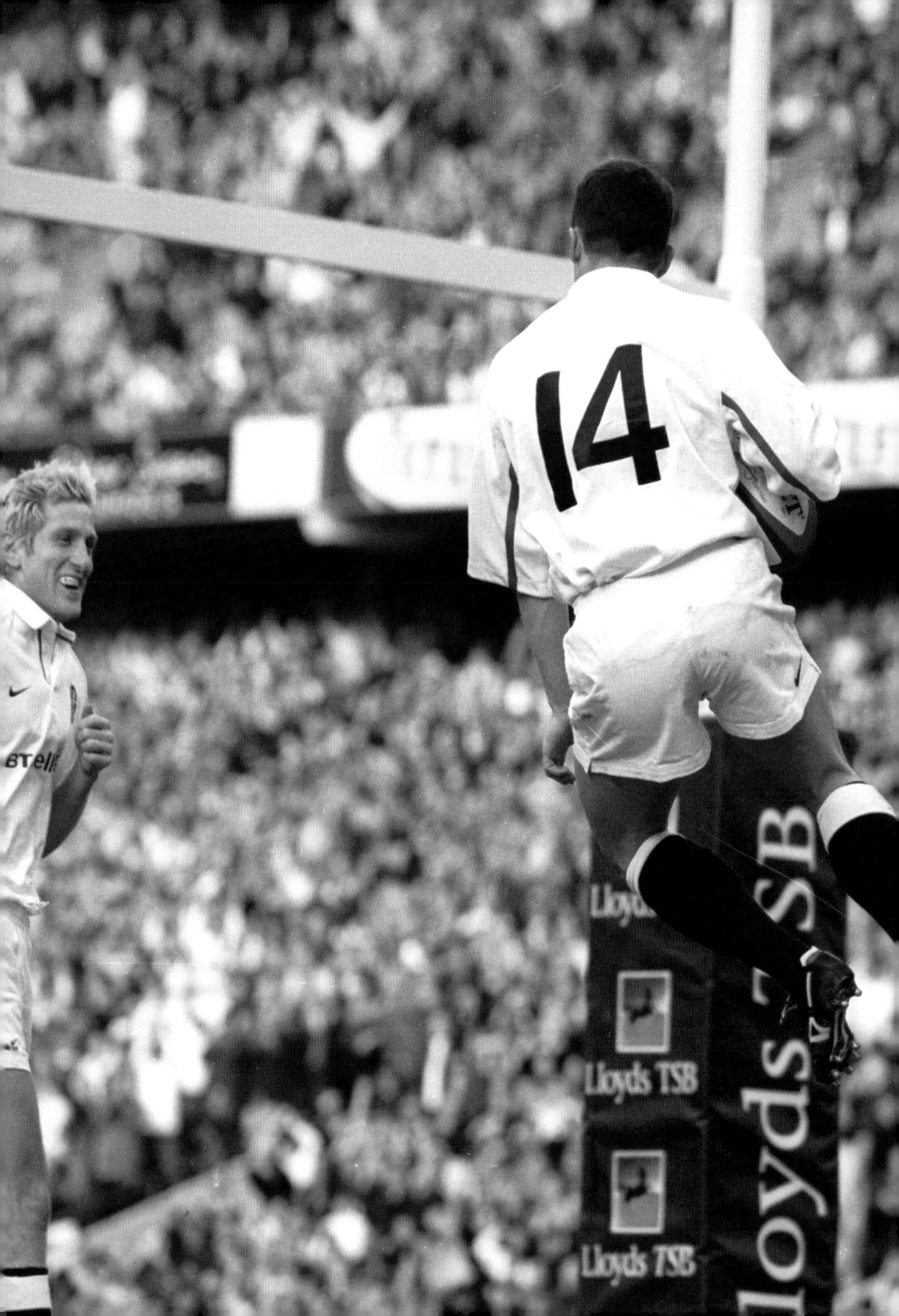
14
Lloyds TSB
Lloyds TSB
Lloyds TSB

"

Nevertheless Italy deserved their place at the top table. They had strived and seduced, waited and hoped, lobbied and cajoled, and most importantly, played with vigour and pride.

"

2000s

Lawrence Dallaglio

Jason Leonard

Five became six, the brotherhood was extended, even if the big boy, England, was still to boss the playground, winning three of the first four championships of the decade. These titles included the little matter of a Grand Slam, which was nailed down in 2003 after much mishap and soul-searching down the years as the landmark continued to elude England for all manner of reasons. Clive Woodward's England imposed their footprint on not just European rugby during this period but also world rugby. They were the dominant force, and ought to have had further Grand Slams but for being frustrated by fate and those pesky lot known as the opposition. But by the time they headed to Australia to contest the World Cup in October 2003, they were the number-one-rated side in the world, and deservedly so. They had come through adversity and a twinge of self-doubt; strife, too, the players creating uproar when they staged a 24-hour strike over a pay dispute (or, more properly, flexed their muscles at a sense of grievance about control) prior to the game against Argentina in November 2000. Emotions ran high, postures were struck, disagreements were aired and face was quickly saved. In his inimitable fashion, Woodward managed to turn a negative into a positive, stating that even though he was against the strike, he admired his players' fighting spirit.

Woodward was right in many ways. England brooked little argument in the championship in those early years of the decade. They were stern and unforgiving up front, with beetle-browed Martin Johnson setting the tone, ably supported by a cast of hard-nut lieutenants – Richard Hill, Jason Leonard, Lawrence Dallaglio and Neil Back to name but a few.

If you wanted a snapshot of differing fortunes and the gulf in standard, then a glance at England's replacements in Rome in 2002 told you all you needed to know. Woodward could afford the luxury of having four captains on the bench – Johnson (coming back from a 21-day suspension), Matt Dawson, Dallaglio and Leonard – this heavyweight army not making an appearance until near the hour mark. What resources, what riches. Italy did what they could, manful and hearty as ever, but they had neither the personnel nor the fitness to sustain the fight, losing 45-9 on that occasion.

Nevertheless Italy deserved their place at the top table. They had strived and seduced, waited and hoped, lobbied and cajoled, and most importantly, played with vigour and pride. Finally, they got their

ABOVE RIGHT England's power pack of the early 2000s included such uncompromising characters as Lawrence Dallaglio and the long-serving Jason Leonard, both of whom had experience of England captaincy, as did scrum half Matt Dawson (below).

reward when they made their entrance into what was now the Six Nations. The decision to grant the Italians championship status had been made in 1998, but the celebrated day did not dawn until 5 February 2000, when the Stadio Flaminio in Rome played host to Scotland. Not that it or its team were particularly generous hosts, Italy sending the locals – some diehard fans, many merely curious – into raptures by beating the Scots 34-20. It had never happened before, and it has rarely happened since, but for one day at least, rugby edged football from the front of the Italian sports pages.

Despite their stunning first-day success – and how wonderful it was to see the *Azzurri* cock an immediate snook at those who questioned their right to be admitted to the prestigious tournament – this generation of mighty Italian warriors was already coming down the other side of the summit. Fly half Diego Domínguez, Massimo Giovanelli in the back row and Carlo Checchinato in the second row held the line for as long as they could, picking up the occasional result through the sheer cussedness of their being as well as the unerring boot of Domínguez.

Some sceptics claimed, and continue to claim, that Italy bring little sparkle to the party, that they have limited horizons and a conservative game plan. Those narrow-minded people would do well to remember just how long it took France to establish themselves as any sort of force in the championship. It took them until 1959 to win their first title; until 1968 to win their first Grand Slam – yet by the start of the 2000s France had increased their Slam count to six. Italy brought, and continue to bring, colour, diversity, courage and conviction to the

ABOVE Giampiero de Carli forces his way over for Italy's try as the new boys stun Scotland at the Stadio Flaminio in their first Six Nations outing in 2000. LEFT Elation post-match after the 34-20 victory. Playmaker and goal-kicker Diego Domínguez (far left, in white) contributed 29 points – a conversion, six penalties and three dropped goals.

			Lloyds TSB			
	15	**Matt Perry** (Bath)	Full Back	**Conor O'Shea** (London Irish)	15	
	14	**Austin Healey** (Leicester Tigers)	Right Wing	**Justin Bishop** (London Irish)	14	
	13	**Mike Tindall *** (Bath)	Centre	**Brian O'Driscoll** (Blackrock College)	13	
	12	**Mike Catt** (Bath)	Centre	**Mike Mullins** (Young Munster)	12	
	11	**Ben Cohen *** (Northampton Saints)	Left Wing	**Kevin Maggs** (Bath)	11	
	10	**Jonny Wilkinson** (Newcastle Falcons)	Stand-Off	**David Humphreys** (Dungannon)	10	
	9	**Matt Dawson** (Northampton Saints) CAPTAIN	Scrum-Half	**Tom Tierney** (Garryowen)	9	
	1	**Jason Leonard** (NEC Harlequins)	Prop	**Peter Clohessy** (Young Munster)	1	
	2	**Phil Greening** (Sale Sharks)	Hooker	**Keith Wood** CAPTAIN (Garryowen)	2	
	3	**Phil Vickery** (Gloucester)	Prop	**Paul Wallace** (Saracens)	3	
	4	**Garath Archer** (Bristol)	Lock	**Robert Casey** (Blackrock College)	4	
	5	**Simon Shaw** (London Wasps)	Lock	**Malcolm O'Kelly** (St. Mary's College)	5	
	6	**Richard Hill** (Saracens)	Flanker	**Dion O'Cuinneagain** (Ballymena)	6	
	7	**Neil Back** (Leicester Tigers)	Flanker	**Kieron Dawson** (London Irish)	7	
	8	**Lawrence Dallaglio** (London Wasps)	No. 8	**Anthony Foley** (Shannon)	8	

ENGLAND
This team was accurate as at 03.02.2000

IRELAND
This team was accurate as at 03.02.2000

Replacements

16	**Iain Balshaw** (Bath)
17	**Alex King** (London Wasps)
18	**Andy Gomarsall** (Bedford)
19	**Martin Corry** (Leicester Tigers)
20	**Joe Worsley** (London Wasps)
21	**Trevor Woodman** (Gloucester)
22	**Neil McCarthy** (Gloucester)

Replacements

16	**Frank Sheahan** (Cork Constitution)
17	**Justin Fitzpatrick** (Dungannon)
18	**Mick Galwey** (Shannon)
19	**Trevor Brennan** (St. Mary's College)
20	**Peter Stringer** (Shannon)
21	**Eric Elwood** (Galwegians)
22	**Girvan Dempsey** (Terenure College)

* NEW CAP

Referee Steve Walsh (New Zealand)

Touch Judges Derek Bevan (Wales) & Rob Dickson (Scotland)

R.F.U. website: www.rfu.com

championship. Their victories have been no flukes, their compelling engagement a source of concern for every opponent. And Rome, of course, has been a wondrous addition to the whirling carnival that winds its way round Europe's great capital cities in the early part of every year, illuminating many a dark day.

There was untold drama in the 2000 championship, with England once again showing that their Achilles' heel was sore and vulnerable. The fact that they topped the championship table, having scored more than double the points managed by Scotland, was of little consolation to them on a dismal day (in all senses) at Murrayfield in early April. England had travelled north in similar spirit to a decade earlier, buoyed by their impressive performance up to that point. Ireland had been routinely dismantled at Twickenham, Ben Cohen and Austin Healey scoring a brace of tries apiece in a 50-18 victory; England then showed their strong spine and hard-headedness to win 15-9 in Paris, Jonny Wilkinson scoring all their points with the boot. Wales were rolled over with ease at Twickenham, 46-12, the visitors scoring not a single point in the second half, causing their conditioning coach, Steve Black, to bemoan the fitness levels of players at Welsh

ABOVE Ben Cohen, pictured going round Kevin Maggs, scored two tries on debut in an impressive England victory over Ireland in 2000 that also saw first caps given to Mike Tindall and, from the bench, Iain Balshaw. RIGHT Lawrence Dallaglio and Neil Back are all smiles after the former touches down for one of five tries scored by England against Wales in 2000.

clubs. England's first trip for a cap international to the Stadio Flaminio, that stylish, open-fronted 25,000-capacity stadium near central Rome, proved to be a straightforward matter once those burly Italian forwards had been quelled. Healey did the damage, his energetic, intelligent running bringing him a hat-trick, Cohen and Dawson also weighing in with two tries each. The final scoreline was 59-12 and England looked irresistible.

Scotland, meanwhile, were at the other end of the spectrum, hangdog and struggling to recover from that shock opening defeat. A thumping 44-22 loss at Lansdowne Road did little to improve the mood. They then went

down 28-16 to France at Murrayfield and 26-18 to Wales in Cardiff. So who, then, might have expected Scotland to deny England their coveted Grand Slam? Ten years earlier David Sole had led Scotland into the final game against England with three victories under his belt. Andy Nicol had no such succour. The well-regarded scrum half, who'd plied his trade among the English at Bath, had but the snarl of the underdog to offer as resistance, the pride of the jersey, too, of course, and the filthiest day imaginable to put England off their game.

It was enough. Nicol was an impassioned, pivotal figure, stirring his men to great deeds, hounding England to distraction. England did not cope with either the weight of expectation, the foul conditions or the heroic, demented play of the opposition. Crucially, England failed to adapt their game to what was happening around them. Johnson was missing and it fell to Dawson to lead the side through its difficulties. The failure, in the end, was a collective one.

Naturally enough there was bedlam when Duncan Hodge ploughed through for a muddy try; indeed the fly half scored all Scotland's points in the stunning 19-13 win. The championship was still England's, although there was a minor diplomatic incident when they failed to emerge from their dressing room to collect the trophy. Scotland, despite keeping Italy company at the bottom of the table, were more than happy with the Calcutta Cup. England were sent homeward 'tae think again'.

One other notable issue to arise during that year's championship was the scandal tagged 'Grannygate', which saw the International Rugby Board investigating the eligibility claims of Kiwi duo Shane Howarth and Brett Sinkinson, who were

ABOVE In 2000 Scotland destroyed England's Grand Slam ambitions once again, Duncan Hodge, here the try scorer, recording all Scotland's points in their 19-13 win at Murrayfield. BELOW Earlier that season, a 21-year-old by the name of Brian O'Driscoll, in his first championship season, had run in three tries as Ireland won in Paris for the first time in 28 years.

ENGLAND IN 2001.
ABOVE *Jonny Wilkinson set a new individual points record for the championship with 89 points in the season, including a match record 35 against Italy, while Will Greenwood (inset) ran in six tries in the tournament.* BELOW *Austin Healey crossed for two tries as England beat Italy 80-23, to add to the three he had scored against them the previous season.* BELOW LEFT *The incomparable Martin Johnson, England skipper in the 2001 Six Nations and captain of the Lions to Australia that summer.*

Martin Johnson

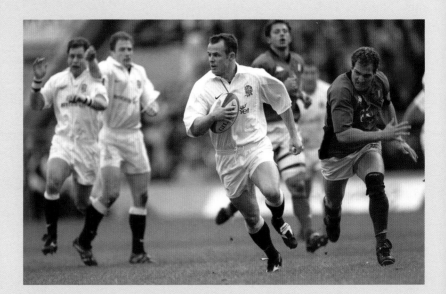

supposedly qualified for Wales on the strength of their grandparentage. It transpired that they weren't. Scotland prop Dave Hilton also came forward to state that his grandfather hadn't been born in Edinburgh as thought, but in Bristol. Oops!

If that incident was a distraction, then foot-and-mouth disease proved to be a major disruption to the 2001 championship. Felled by the tartan fervour one year, derailed by swine the next. It would have been small wonder had England thought that someone up above did not like them. True, the championship was eventually completed in September/October with the three outstanding games taking place involving Ireland, whose government had earlier imposed travel restrictions to prevent the spread of the outbreak. By that time, though, England's momentum had stalled. Once again, the red rose had blazed a trail of glory, reaching a fabulous record mark of 229 points in their five games, an average of almost 46 points per match. Quite remarkable. They shredded their opponents with a deft brand of rugby: tough and imposing up front, crafty and varied at half back, deadly in their finishing. Jonny Wilkinson set a new individual points record for a championship with 89, while Will Greenwood scored six tries, two short of the all-time season record.

England had one aim when they arrived at the Millennium Stadium for the first time for their championship curtain-raiser: to silence the crowd. Martin Johnson said as much as they stood in the tunnel and listened to the spine-tingling wall of sound sweeping round the stands. The din didn't last long. Greenwood had his hat-trick all sorted by the 41st minute and an impressive 44-15 win was in the bag. In their following match, England even managed to improve on that uplifting opening, with an utter rout of Italy, who were perhaps bemused by how it all went so horribly wrong given that they scored tries through Denis Dallan and Carlo Checchinato to be only 33-23 down at half-time. Yet England rattled up 47 unanswered points after the interval, finishing with ten tries in all from eight different players. Wilkinson kept the historians busy with a personal haul of 35 points for a new individual match record for the championship in a final score of 80-23.

And so it continued. 'Rugby is the best it's ever been' was the opinion of Scotland coach Ian McGeechan, dwelling on a 43-3 beating at Twickenham. What about mighty France, surely

BELOW In 2001 French wing Philippe Bernat-Salles, 'the Pau Rocket', became the first player to score a try in each round of a Six Nations Championship, completing the set against England at Twickenham.

they could cause England problems? Nope. The scoreline of 48-19 at Twickenham was in England's favour, with six tries for the men in white from six different players. France wing Philippe Bernat-Salles touched down to become the first player to score a try in each match of a Six Nations Championship, scant consolation as England breezed past their championship season record of 183 points, set in 2000, during the game.

Fast-forward to 20 October at Lansdowne Road and what had changed? Well, there was the draining effect of a Lions tour, which featured many Englishmen, to factor in. More significantly, England were deprived of

DEFEAT IN DUBLIN.
Scotland coach Ian McGeechan (right) was highly impressed with England's rugby when they beat Scotland 43-3 in March 2001, but when they played Ireland, in October because of foot-and-mouth, England came off second-best. Keith Wood (left, tackling Danny Grewcock) scored in Ireland's 20-14 win. England (below) were still champions, but losing the Slam was painful.

Ian McGeechan

Martin Johnson, Lawrence Dallaglio and Phil Vickery through injury. Stand-in captain Matt Dawson was then crocked before half-time. On the run of play, this was no upset. Ireland were in the driving seat from the first whistle. England's scrum was poor, the line out wobbly and the rest just appendages. The ubiquitous Keith Wood scored Ireland's try, and what a one-man show that was, Wood hurling himself towards the try line from a peeled line out with the fury of the possessed. England had no chance. A third Grand Slam was blown. A complex was taking deep root. Once again, England were champions, but it didn't feel like it.

France had fared poorly in 2001, struggling to put away Scotland at home and being defeated by England, Wales and Ireland. It was a great day for Wales fans in the French capital, a four-try romp seeing the side to an extravagant 43-35 victory. In typical French fashion, the side went from chumps to champs. England again were strong in 2002 but lost out in the decisive game in Paris, 20-15. France coach Bernard Laporte was cracking the whip, paying

LEFT *Imanol Harinordoquy touches down for France in their 2002 victory over England in Paris, which opened the way to a Grand Slam. That year once again England saw off four out of five opponents, rattling up 183 points, including 45 against Ireland. Joe Worsley (below) was one of the five English try scorers that day.*

Clive Woodward's side the great compliment of playing *à la manière anglaise*. Self-control and discipline were to be Laporte's watchwords. He was turning France into England. Frills were frowned upon. The fact that France gave away only six penalties in two of the championship matches suggested that Laporte's message was getting through. Their reward was a seventh Grand Slam.

France were rigorous in seeing off England, leading 14-0 after just 18 minutes through tries from Gérald Merceron and Imanol Harinordoquy. A trademark Jason Robinson try on the stroke of half-time got England on the scoreboard, but France were not to be denied, Ben Cohen's 85th-minute try for England coming too late to affect the result. France completed the Slam in style, demolishing Ireland 44-5 at the Stade de France in early April. France made it look easy. Now why couldn't England do that?

Finally, in 2003, they did. They had learnt their lessons, eaten their humble pie, banished the demons and got on with the job. Lawrence Dallaglio stated at the start of the championship that England would deserve shooting if they failed again. No rifles were needed. As France had aped England, so in one regard did England copy our friends

ENGLAND v FRANCE IN 2003.
Jason Leonard emerges from the Twickenham tunnel ahead of the team in recognition of his 100th England cap. It was nevertheless an occasion marred by tragedy: the previous day, England scrum half Nick Duncombe, Leonard's Harlequins clubmate, had died, aged just 21. The players wore black armbands, and Twickenham observed a minute's silence (top right) before the start of the match.

from across the Channel in that they too finished it all with a rousing win over Ireland. This victory, though, was in Dublin, when the Grand Slam was up for grabs for both sides. It was a terrific finale, the 42-6 scoreline not reflecting what a close, competitive game it had been for the first 60 minutes. But then England hit overdrive and showed their class. It was not that Ireland fell away, giving in to fatigue and failing to sustain the pace. No, England delivered.

Woodward had challenged his men to get their act together. In such circumstances, and with all those past failures hanging in the air, many coaches would play down the significance of the occasion, forbidding any mention of a possible Grand Slam. Woodward did the opposite. He figured that if England flopped again, then they might as well give up any notion of going to Australia later in the year with any credible hopes of winning the World Cup. The ploy worked. The inner man did not wilt in the face of such pressure.

Lawrence Dallaglio opened England's try-scoring account early in the match, but it was nip and tuck. Then as the clock ticked to the hour mark it all changed. Mike Tindall cut a fine line off Will Greenwood to power past Brian O'Driscoll on his way to the try line. Suddenly Ireland were on the back foot. The game was up. Will Greenwood scored two tries, the second of them a cheeky interception as Ireland threw caution to the wind. Dan Luger added a fifth and final score and Englishmen could sleep easy. It was all over.

A MONKEY OFF THEIR BACK.
Clive Woodward's England finally nailed down a Grand Slam at Lansdowne Road in 2003.
TOP *Mike Tindall breaks through Geordan Murphy's tackle to score.*
ABOVE *Clive Woodward and the England staff are brought to their feet by a passage of play.* RIGHT *Martin Johnson lifts the Six Nations trophy – eight months later it would be the World Cup.* LEFT *The team relax having delivered the goods.*

This was England's first Grand Slam since 1995, their twelfth in all. Once again they were the highest points scorers in the championship with 173, and in Jonny Wilkinson with 77 points, a dozen short of his 2001 record, they once more boasted the highest individual scorer. England could head to Australia in good heart.

Italy had had another championship opener to treasure under their new coach, former All Black wing John Kirwan, beating Wales 30-22 at the Stadio Flaminio. In the course of recording 15 points, Diego Domínguez passed 1000 points in international rugby, including 27 scored in two matches for Argentina in 1989. Wales's season did not get any better. They were whitewashed for the first time since 1995.

With England in rebuilding mode post their World Cup triumph of November 2003, it was left to France and Wales to rule the roost in the Six Nations, the two sides winning respective Grand Slams in 2004 and 2005. It was inevitable that England would take time to find themselves after the tumult of Sydney. Martin Johnson led the charge into retirement, and while there was a sense of things coming back together and new targets being set, it was all

ABOVE Italy's experienced half-back combination Diego Domínguez and Alessandro Troncon fly the flag after the defeat of Wales in Rome in 2003. BELOW Jason Robinson embarks on a trademark run during England's 2004 win over Wales at Twickenham. RIGHT 2004 was France's year, though. Sir Clive Woodward, who was to depart as England coach in September, congratulates French opposite number Bernard Laporte on the Grand Slam, while France scrum half Dimitri Yachvili (bottom right) shows off the trophy.

thrown into disorder again by Sir Clive Woodward's surprise resignation in September 2004. Lawrence Dallaglio had announced his retirement from international rugby at around the same time. That he was back in an England shirt within 18 months, difficulties in his personal life having been sorted, was a boon to those fans who saw him as the embodiment of the values that had characterised English rugby during the decade.

Andy Robinson was promoted from within to take over Woodward's role of head coach. It was a tough first championship in 2005 for Robinson, one that was to bring glory for Mike Ruddock down in Wales as his side won an unexpected Grand Slam, getting the campaign off to a heartening start with an 11-9 win over England at the Millennium Stadium. After this defeat in Cardiff, Robinson's England slipped to a frustrating 18-17 loss against France at Twickenham despite scoring the only tries of the game through Olly Barkley and Josh Lewsey. It was the boot of Dimitri Yachvili that held sway, however, the former Gloucester scrum half landing six penalty goals. Robinson was to encounter the blues again a fortnight

ABOVE LEFT Gavin Henson watches as his long, late touch-line penalty finds its mark to give Wales victory over England in Cardiff in 2005. ABOVE England coach Andy Robinson, who had taken over from Sir Clive Woodward in autumn 2004, had a difficult time of it in his first championship in charge. LEFT Kevin Morgan puts Wales 29-6 up against Ireland on the final day of the 2005 Six Nations, and despite an Irish comeback, the match and the Grand Slam were secured by Mike Ruddock's side.

211

later in Dublin as Ireland won 19-13, England suffering from some marginal calls by South African referee Jonathan Kaplan. Heated post-match comment on the referee by the England head coach drew a rebuke from the Rugby Football Union. Three defeats from three matches was not the stuff of world champions. England were labouring, struggling for form, vitality and consistency, albeit they did round off the 2005 championship with wins over Italy (39-7) and Scotland (43-22), Newcastle centre Jamie Noon scoring a hat-trick in the latter.

Life in the doldrums didn't seem to be coming to an end any time soon. The 2006 campaign followed the same dispiriting and baffling pattern. True, England smashed Grand Slam champions Wales 47-13 with a six-try salvo in the opening match of the championship at Twickenham; Mark Cueto, Lewis Moody, Mike Tindall, Lawrence Dallaglio, Matt Dawson and Tom Voyce touched down. But that was to prove the falsest of dawns. England, and Robinson in particular, were criticised for being too conservative. They had to clutch at straws, earning their first away victory since the opening match of the 2004 Six Nations when winning 31-16 in Rome.

After going down 18-12 at Murrayfield, England, weakened by a stomach virus prior to the match, then lost 31-6 in Paris, their heaviest defeat in the championship in 20 years. It equalled their worst ever margin of defeat against France and was their seventh loss in 14 championship matches since the 2003 World Cup. Eight of the last nine Test matches away from home had ended in defeat. For the second match in succession, England failed to score a try. The depressing litany of statistics told its own sorry tale.

England fared little better next time out, despite Robinson making eight changes for the match against Ireland at Twickenham. Six World Cup winners were dropped, five of them to the bench. England had not made as many changes since the mid-1980s. It didn't make much difference: Ireland secured their eighth Triple Crown with a 28-24 victory, Shane Horgan getting the benefit of a dodgy-looking call by the video referee to score his and his side's first try. Ireland took full advantage.

Meanwhile, Frank Hadden got his coaching tenure off to a bright start, Scotland playing attractive, purposeful rugby to finish mid-table with three wins, over France, England and Italy. Wales, though, imploded, with Grand

ABOVE LEFT AND ABOVE England v Ireland 2006. Shane Horgan's second try of the match, scored in the dying seconds, puts paid to England and brings Ireland the Triple Crown. BELOW Frank Hadden, in his first season in charge of Scotland, oversaw three wins, including the 2006 Calcutta Cup match at Murrayfield. FACING PAGE England's 2006 season had started promisingly with a 47-13 victory over Wales at Twickenham. TOP England rise unchallenged in the line out at the start of the match. BOTTOM Steve Borthwick takes an unorthodox route down with the ball later on in the game.

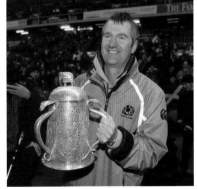

213

Slam-winning coach Mike Ruddock departing in mid-tournament, the victim of dressing-room backbiting, and the side going from the Slam to a fifth-place finish. Italy, the one team below them, had an encouraging campaign under Pierre Berbizier, despite their lowly position, causing all five opponents problems along the way. Their 18-18 draw at the Millennium Stadium was heartening for all their loyal followers. But for the third time in five seasons the championship went to France, although Laporte's ageing side were far from convincing. In fact, that was the hallmark of a tournament in which defences ruled.

By the time England congregated for the 2007 Six Nations Championship, Andy Robinson had gone. A careworn autumn campaign ended with defeat by South Africa, 25-14, England's eighth loss in nine games. Robinson, who had lost 13 of his 22 matches in charge, was removed from office and replaced by Brian Ashton.

England played with the mark of Ashton in his opening game in charge, registering their second highest ever Calcutta Cup score in winning 42-20 at Twickenham, Wilkinson posting a Calcutta Cup record 27 points. Jason Robinson had been coaxed out of retirement by Ashton and repaid the faith invested in him by scoring two tries. Whatever your affiliation, it was good to see Wilkinson out in the middle doing what he enjoyed so much. He had had so much injury, so many setbacks, since that Sydney night of glory that you could not but wish him well – all the more so in that the respite from the ravages was not to last long.

Jason Robinson

ABOVE Jason Robinson, as captured by John Ireland. Having retired from international rugby in September 2005, 'Billy Whizz' returned to the colours in 2007 under Brian Ashton, scoring four tries in the championship. RIGHT Jonny Wilkinson, kept out of an England shirt by injury since the 2003 World Cup final, was another to make a comeback in the 2007 Six Nations. In his first match back, he scored a Calcutta Cup record 27 points, his full set of scores including this try in the corner.

England's uplift was not to last long, either. 'We were stuffed,' said Ashton honestly and bluntly after their emotive, ground-breaking first appearance at Croke Park. The England coach was not wrong. England were blown away, losing 43-13, the only glimmer being the try-scoring debut performance of David Strettle. It was a record defeat for England against Ireland.

Yet England entered the final weekend of the championship with a long-shot chance of claiming the title. True, it was an unlikely scenario in that they needed to win by 57 points to do so and results elsewhere to go their way. In the end, Wales managed to avoid their second whitewash in five years with a 27-18 victory. England's difficulties on the road continued. Encompassing all Tests, the ledger now stood at 12 defeats in their last 13 away games.

That final weekend of the 2007 tournament contained great drama. Last-minute tries in Rome and Paris settled the outcome in the most theatrical of circumstances. Ireland's goose was cooked, though they did not know it yet, when they conceded a try to Roland de Marigny, which was

MEMORIES OF 2007.
TOP *England's debutant fly half Shane Geraghty, off the bench for Toby Flood, makes the searing break against France at Twickenham that led to Mike Tindall's crucial try.* ABOVE *Alessandro Zanni escapes from Ryan Jones as Italy beat Wales 23-20 at the Stadio Flaminio.* RIGHT *Yannick Jauzion jumps with delight as referee Craig Joubert signals Elvis Vermeulen's last-play try, which brought France the title in dramatic style.*

converted to close their winning margin to 51-24. Even so, France only just breasted the tape in first place with their late, late score at the Stade de France, Elvis Vermeulen's touchdown sealing a 46-19 win and a points difference that was superior by four. The trophy went to France for the third time in four years.

This was the championship in which Italy won two games for the first time – Wales (23-20) in Rome and Scotland at Murrayfield. This was a first away win for the *Azzurri* and Scotland's generosity and carelessness lent proceedings a pantomime feel at times. Nonetheless Italy's 37-17 victory was deserved.

The 2007 Rugby World Cup ought to have been a formative influence on the 2008 Six Nations Championship. But how then to explain Wales's Grand Slam, their second in four years? In the autumn they'd beaten a baleful retreat from Nantes after losing their final pool game of RWC 2007 38-34 against Fiji. It was the most magnificent of matches unless you happened to be sporting the colours of Wales, who were thus knocked out at the group stage.

Coach Gareth Jenkins was summarily dismissed, to be replaced eventually by Warren Gatland, who winged in from Waikato. Was it all down to him? Perhaps. The coach's magic touch.

What then to make of England? Against all odds, odds that went stratospheric after they were humiliated 36-0 by South Africa at the pool stage, England reached the World Cup final,

ENGLAND v WALES IN 2008.
RIGHT Wales boss Warren Gatland and his defence coach Shaun Edwards in conversation on the Twickenham pitch before kick-off on the opening day of the championship. BELOW Toby Flood heads for the line as England build up a 19-6 lead. BELOW RIGHT Full back Lee Byrne signals his score as Wales fight back to win 26-19 and take the first step on the road to the Grand Slam.

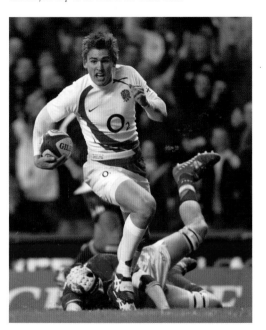

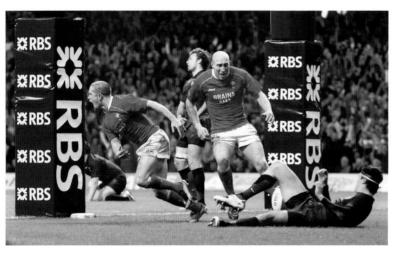

losing to the Boks in a tight game. Brian Ashton was still in charge and finishing runners-up in a Rugby World Cup is no mean achievement. Nor is finishing in the same position in the championship, which England did in 2008, though admittedly a long way behind Wales.

ABOVE Shane Williams turns away after scoring against France at the Millennium Stadium and bringing the Grand Slam that little bit closer. It was Williams' sixth try of the 2008 tournament and the forty-first of his international career, putting him top of the Wales all-time try scorers list. BELOW With tries against Italy, France and Ireland in 2008, Paul Sackey showed himself to be a dangerous international finisher.

Yet Ashton, too, was to be shown the door in the aftermath of what was perceived to be another frustrating Six Nations. In fact, the World Cup was playing its part, for tales of discord and confusion in the ranks had emerged from that tournament, Ashton coming in for caustic criticism from Lawrence Dallaglio and Mike Catt in ghosted post-World Cup books. Little better at one stage than 'a pub team' was the most damning of the verdicts.

There was little sign of what was to come when England led Wales 19-6 as the hour approached in their opening game of the championship at Twickenham. England, showing six changes from the World Cup final, were brisk and purposeful, good value for their lead. And then it began to go horribly wrong. Wales, riding their luck, scored 20 unanswered points in 13 minutes, tries rattling in from Lee Byrne and Mike Phillips to complement James Hook's penalties. England were shell-shocked and on the slide, Wales were euphoric and on their way.

England alternated between Jekyll and Hyde for the rest of the tournament. They escaped with their modesty barely intact in Rome, coming through by just four points, 23-19, their narrowest margin of victory ever over Italy, now coached by South African Nick Mallett.

Paul Sackey

England, wracked by injury, began well enough with early tries from Paul Sackey and Toby Flood, but then they stuttered. An incident involving Danny Cipriani captured the malaise. Arriving in place of Jonny Wilkinson in the 67th minute, the young Wasps fly half, in only his second Test, was charged down almost immediately for a try by Simon Picone.

Close, very close, and many feared the worst as England travelled to Paris to take on France, who also had a new coach in Marc Lièvremont. That day, though, it was Hyde (or was it Jekyll who was the accomplished rugby player?) who emerged as England won 24-13, Jonny Wilkinson scoring 14 to draw level with Neil Jenkins' world record mark of 1090 international points. That was England's first win in the Six Nations at the Stade de France since 2000.

Cipriani was due to start England's next game, against Scotland, only to be dropped hours after being named in the side when photographs appeared in the press of him coming out of a London nightclub in midweek shortly after midnight. Cipriani's explanation that he had been there for just a few minutes to drop off tickets cut no ice with Ashton. As it happened, the Calcutta Cup match was a good one to miss. England were lamentable in losing 15-9. If one match shaped the RFU's decision to part company with Ashton, that was it, the really fine win over Ireland (33-10) in the last match notwithstanding.

Wilkinson was dropped for that final game for only the second time in his career and Cipriani, making his first start, was outstanding. That at least was one positive for England from the tournament, along with the emergence of the Wasps back-row forward James Haskell.

That last-day thumping by England capped off a poor showing by Ireland in the tournament, coming on top of an underachieving World Cup: Ireland coach Eddie O'Sullivan stood down and Munster's Declan Kidney took over the reins. It was the change that was finally to galvanise Ireland into achieving that which they had striven after so long and so hard – the Grand Slam. To the joy and wonder of many, on a delirious day in Cardiff in 2009 Ireland finally claimed their prize, but, boy, was it close.

Had things turned out differently, Ireland substitute Paddy Wallace might well have had to leave the ground in disguise after giving away the last-minute penalty that could have snatched glory away from Ireland. How his heart must have been racing, his stomach

ABOVE Brian Ashton's days as England coach were numbered despite the optimistic way in which his side finished the 2008 season – beating Ireland 33-10 at Twickenham, with Danny Cipriani (left) starring at fly half. Coach Ashton is pictured in conversation with Rob Andrew, the RFU's director of elite rugby.
FOLLOWING PAGES Italy look set to win ball on their throw at Twickenham, February 2009.

churning. Wales fly half Stephen Jones lined up that kick from around halfway and off it went, straight and true. It was on target … on target … but a few feet short. Ireland had won 17-15, the cherished Grand Slam was theirs for the first time since 1948. Those heroes of long ago – and venerated fly half Jackie Kyle was at the Millennium Stadium – were happy to cede their place in history.

It was a dramatic finale to a middling championship, one with a decent narrative thread but not too much glittering rugby. Ireland were good value for their Grand Slam, even if they only nipped past England by one point, 14-13, at Croke Park. It was England's yellow-card fever that cost them, the giant fist of new manager Martin Johnson caught on camera smashing down in rage after scrum half Danny Care was sent to the sin-bin. That made it ten yellow cards in four matches for England, beginning with the autumn international against New Zealand.

Johnson was no angel on the rugby field. But, in a strange way, he was not ill-disciplined. He knew the consequences of his actions and he knew when it was time to back away. It's hard to imagine that the players were not listening to Johnson, for who wouldn't? But that was the impression. Johnson was having a bumpy ride in his first season in charge. He'd been the populist choice to take over. Yet the hard fact of the matter was that he had no experience. He was in it for the long haul, and after thumping, record defeats in the autumn against South Africa (42-6 – biggest defeat ever at Twickenham) and New Zealand (32-6 – biggest All Black winning margin at Twickenham), that road must have stretched far ahead of him.

At least, though, by the end of the 2009 championship there was a sense of his team taking shape. The influence of new attack coach Brian Smith was also being felt. One of his former charges at London Irish, Delon Armitage, had been a great success, Riki Flutey was becoming more authoritative at inside centre, Ugo Monye was shaping up on the wing, Leicester's Tom Croft likewise in the back row. England finished well, beating France 34-10 and Scotland 26-12. Significantly, those two matches saw England field the same XV in consecutive games for the first time since the quarters and semis of RWC 2007. England were rewarded with second place in the championship, but the real celebrations were elsewhere.

THIS PAGE 2009: Ireland deliver. ABOVE The Wales defence cannot get to Ronan O'Gara in time to stop him kicking a 78th-minute dropped goal at the Millennium Stadium to put Ireland 17-15 ahead. ABOVE RIGHT Just moments later, Wales kicking coach Neil Jenkins looks on in disbelief and Stephen Jones clasps his hands to his head as his last-gasp penalty shot to snatch victory falls short. BELOW Brian O'Driscoll hoists high the trophy as the celebrations begin in honour of Ireland's first Grand Slam since 1948.

SCENES FROM TWICKENHAM IN 2009.
TOP *Ugo Monye and Joe Worsley celebrate the latter's try for England as they defeat France 34-10.* ABOVE LEFT *England's new supremo Martin Johnson watches his charges during his first championship in the job.* ABOVE RIGHT *Quick-footed centre Riki Flutey dives over to score as Scotland go down 26-12 to the Auld Enemy.*
LEFT *'Billy Williams' Cabbage Patch' today: Twickenham full to the rafters for the 2009 Calcutta Cup match.*
FOLLOWING PAGES *The view from the south that greets spectators in autumn 2009.*

1999-2000

05.02.2000 STADIO FLAMINIO, ROME
Italy 34 *T:* G-P de Carli *C:* D Dominguez
PG: D Dominguez 6 *DG:* D Dominguez 3
Scotland 20 *T:* GC Bulloch, MD Leslie *C:* KM Logan
GPJ Townsend *PG:* GPJ Townsend *DG:* GPJ Townsend
Referee: JI Kaplan (South Africa)

05.02.2000 MILLENNIUM STADIUM, CARDIFF
Wales 3 *PG:* NR Jenkins
France 36 *T:* T Castaignede, O Magne, E Ntamack
C: C Lamaison 3 *PG:* C Lamaison 4 *DG:* C Lamaison
Referee: C White (England)

05.02.2000 TWICKENHAM
England 50 *T:* BC Cohen 2, AS Healey 2, MJ Tindall,
NA Back *C:* JP Wilkinson 4 *PG:* JP Wilkinson 4
Ireland 18 *T:* KM Maggs, MJ Galwey
C: DG Humphreys *PG:* DG Humphreys 2
Referee: SR Walsh (New Zealand)

19.02.2000 STADE DE FRANCE, PARIS
France 9 *PG:* R Dourthe 3
England 15 *PG:* JP Wilkinson 5
Referee: SJ Dickinson (Australia)

19.02.2000 MILLENNIUM STADIUM, CARDIFF
Wales 47 *T:* SP Howarth, AG Bateman, SM Williams,
LS Quinnell *C:* NR Jenkins 3 *PG:* NR Jenkins 7
Italy 16 *T:* W Visser *C:* D Dominguez
PG: D Dominguez 2 *DG:* D Dominguez
Referee: I Ramage (Scotland)

19.02.2000 LANSDOWNE ROAD, DUBLIN
Ireland 44 *T:* BG O'Driscoll, DG Humphreys,
KGM Wood, SP Horgan, ME O'Kelly *C:* RJR O'Gara 2,
DG Humphreys 3 *PG:* RJR O'Gara 2, DG Humphreys
Scotland 22 *T:* KM Logan, GH Metcalfe, G Graham
C: KM Logan 2 *PG:* KM Logan
Referee: J Dume (France)

04.03.2000 MURRAYFIELD
Scotland 16 *T:* AD Nicol *C:* CD Paterson
PG: KM Logan, CD Paterson 2
France 28 *T:* O Magne 2, T Castaignede
C: G Merceron 2 *PG:* G Merceron 3
Referee: SJ Lander (England)

04.03.2000 TWICKENHAM
England 46 *T:* BC Cohen, PBT Greening, RA Hill,
NA Back, LBN Dallaglio *C:* JP Wilkinson 3
PG: JP Wilkinson 5
Wales 12 *PG:* NR Jenkins 3 *DG:* NR Jenkins
Referee: JM Fleming (Scotland)

04.03.2000 LANSDOWNE ROAD, DUBLIN
Ireland 60 *T:* SP Horgan 2, KGM Wood, K Dawson,
GT Dempsey, BG O'Driscoll *C:* RJR O'Gara 6
PG: RJR O'Gara 6
Italy 13 *T:* A de Rossi *C:* D Dominguez
PG: D Dominguez 2
Referee: WD Bevan (Wales)

18.03.2000 STADIO FLAMINIO, ROME
Italy 12 *T:* L Martin, CA Stoica *C:* D Dominguez
England 59 *T:* AS Healey 3, BC Cohen 2,
MJS Dawson 2, penalty try *C:* JP Wilkinson 4, AD King
PG: JP Wilkinson 2 *DG:* NA Back
Referee: A Lewis (Ireland)

18.03.2000 MILLENNIUM STADIUM, CARDIFF
Wales 26 *T:* SM Williams 2 *C:* SM Jones 2
PG: SM Jones 4
Scotland 18 *T:* GPJ Townsend, MD Leslie
C: DW Hodge *PG:* DW Hodge 2
Referee: DTM McHugh (Ireland)

19.03.2000 STADE DE FRANCE, PARIS
France 25 *T:* C Laussucq *C:* G Merceron
PG: G Merceron 6
Ireland 27 *T:* BG O'Driscoll 3 *C:* RJR O'Gara 2,
DG Humphreys *PG:* DG Humphreys 2
Referee: PG Honiss (New Zealand)

01.04.2000 STADE DE FRANCE, PARIS
France 42 *T:* A Penaud 2, T Castaignede, F Pelous,
A Benazzi *C:* R Dourthe 4 *PG:* R Dourthe 3
Italy 31 *T:* A Troncon 2, L Martin, N Mazzucato
C: D Dominguez 4 *DG:* D Dominguez 2
Referee: P Deluca (Argentina)

01.04.2000 LANSDOWNE ROAD, DUBLIN
Ireland 19 *T:* SP Horgan *C:* RJR O'Gara
PG: RJR O'Gara 4
Wales 23 *T:* SM Jones, NJ Budgett *C:* SM Jones 2
PG: SM Jones, NR Jenkins 3
Referee: A Cole (Australia)

02.04.2000 MURRAYFIELD
Scotland 19 *T:* DW Hodge *C:* DW Hodge
PG: DW Hodge 4
England 13 *T:* LBN Dallaglio *C:* JP Wilkinson
PG: JP Wilkinson 2
Referee: C Thomas (Wales)

	P	W	D	L	FOR	AGAINST	PTS
England	5	4	0	1	183	70	8
France	5	3	0	2	140	92	6
Ireland	5	3	0	2	168	133	6
Wales	5	3	0	2	111	135	6
Scotland	5	1	0	4	95	145	2
Italy	5	1	0	4	106	228	2

2000-01

03.02.2001 STADIO FLAMINIO, ROME
Italy 22 *T:* Ma Bergamasco, C Checchinato, C Pilat
C: R Pez 2 *PG:* C Pilat
Ireland 41 *T:* RAJ Henderson 3, SP Horgan, RJR O'Gara
C: RJR O'Gara 2 *PG:* RJR O'Gara 4
Referee: JI Kaplan (South Africa)

03.02.2001 MILLENNIUM STADIUM, CARDIFF
Wales 15 *T:* R Howley, LS Quinnell *C:* NR Jenkins
PG: NR Jenkins
England 44 *T:* WJH Greenwood 3, MJS Dawson 2,
BC Cohen *C:* JP Wilkinson 4 *PG:* JP Wilkinson 2
Referee: J Dume (France)

04.02.2001 STADE DE FRANCE, PARIS
France 16 *T:* P Bernat-Salles *C:* C Lamaison
PG: C Lamaison 3
Scotland 6 *PG:* KM Logan 2
Referee: SJ Dickinson (Australia)

17.02.2001 LANSDOWNE ROAD, DUBLIN
Ireland 22 *T:* BG O'Driscoll *C:* RJR O'Gara
PG: RJR O'Gara 5
France 15 *T:* P Bernat-Salles, F Pelous *C:* C Lamaison
PG: C Lamaison
Referee: SJ Young (Australia)

17.02.2001 TWICKENHAM
England 80 *T:* IR Balshaw 2, AS Healey 2, BC Cohen,
LBN Dallaglio, WJH Greenwood, MP Regan,
JP Wilkinson, JPR Worsley *C:* JP Wilkinson 9
PG: JP Wilkinson
Italy 23 *T:* C Checchinato, D Dallan *C:* A Scanavacca 2
PG: A Scanavacca 3
Referee: SJ Dickinson (Australia)

17.02.2001 MURRAYFIELD
Scotland 28 *T:* JG McLaren, TJ Smith, CD Paterson
C: KM Logan, DW Hodge *PG:* KM Logan 3
Wales 28 *T:* M Taylor *C:* NR Jenkins *PG:* NR Jenkins 4
DG: NR Jenkins 3
Referee: SJ Lander (England)

03.03.2001 STADIO FLAMINIO, ROME
Italy 19 *T:* M Perziano *C:* D Dominguez
PG: D Dominguez 4
France 30 *T:* P Bernat-Salles, S Bonetti, J-L Sadourny
C: C Lamaison 3 *PG:* C Lamaison 3

03.03.2001 TWICKENHAM
England 43 *T:* IR Balshaw 2, LBN Dallaglio 2,
WJH Greenwood, RA Hill *C:* JP Wilkinson 5
PG: JP Wilkinson
Scotland 3 *PG:* DW Hodge
Referee: R Davies (Wales)

17.03.2001 STADE DE FRANCE, PARIS
France 35 *T:* P Bernat-Salles, S Bonetti *C:* C Lamaison,
G Merceron *PG:* G Merceron 4, C Lamaison 3
Wales 43 *T:* R Howley, NR Jenkins, DR James,
LS Quinnell *C:* NR Jenkins 4 *PG:* NR Jenkins 3
DG: NR Jenkins 2
Referee: A Lewis (Ireland)

17.03.2001 MURRAYFIELD
Scotland 23 *T:* TJ Smith *PG:* DW Hodge 5
DG: DW Hodge
Italy 19 *T:* Ma Bergamasco *C:* D Dominguez
PG: D Dominguez 4
Referee: J Dume (France)

07.04.2001 TWICKENHAM
England 48 *T:* IR Balshaw, MJ Catt, PBT Greening,
WJH Greenwood, RA Hill, MB Perry *C:* JP Wilkinson 6
PG: JP Wilkinson 2
France 19 *T:* P Bernat-Salles *C:* G Merceron
PG: G Merceron 3 *DG:* G Merceron
Referee: WTS Henning (South Africa), replaced by
DTM McHugh (Ireland)

08.04.2001 STADIO FLAMINIO, ROME
Italy 23 *T:* C Checchinato *PG:* D Dominguez 5
DG: D Dominguez
Wales 33 *T:* IS Gibbs 2, GJ Cooper *C:* NR Jenkins 3
PG: NR Jenkins 4
Referee: PG Honiss (New Zealand)

Delayed matches

22.09.2001 MURRAYFIELD
Scotland 32 *T:* A Henderson, JA Leslie, AC Pountney,
TJ Smith *C:* CD Paterson 2, GPJ Townsend
PG: CD Paterson 2
Ireland 10 *T:* GT Dempsey *C:* DG Humphreys
PG: RJR O'Gara
Referee: C White (England)

13.10.2001 MILLENNIUM STADIUM, CARDIFF
Wales 6 *PG:* SM Jones 2
Ireland 36 *T:* DA Hickie, SP Horgan, BG O'Driscoll
C: DG Humphreys 2, RJR O'Gara *PG:* DG Humphreys 5
Referee: JI Kaplan (South Africa)

20.10.2001 LANSDOWNE ROAD, DUBLIN
Ireland 20 *T:* KGM Wood *PG:* DG Humphreys 3,
RJR O'Gara 2
England 14 *T:* AS Healey *PG:* JP Wilkinson 3
Referee: PG Honiss (New Zealand)

	P	W	D	L	FOR	AGAINST	PTS
England	5	4	0	1	229	80	8
Ireland	5	4	0	1	129	89	8
Scotland	5	2	1	2	92	116	5
Wales	5	2	1	2	125	166	5
France	5	2	0	3	115	138	4
Italy	5	0	0	5	106	207	0

2001-02

02.02.2002 MURRAYFIELD
Scotland 3 *PG:* DW Hodge
England 29 *T:* J Robinson 2, MJ Tindall, BC Cohen
C: JP Wilkinson 2, CC Hodgson *PG:* JP Wilkinson
Referee: S Walsh (New Zealand)

02.02.2002 STADE DE FRANCE, PARIS
France 33 *T:* D Traille, S Betsen *C:* G Merceron
PG: G Merceron 7
Italy 12 *PG:* D Dominguez 4
Referee: A Lewis (Ireland)

03.02.2002 LANSDOWNE ROAD, DUBLIN
Ireland 54 *T:* GEA Murphy 2, PJ O'Connell,
DA Hickie, KD Gleeson, RJR O'Gara
C: DG Humphreys 2, RJR O'Gara *PG:* DG Humphreys 6
Wales 10 *T:* SM Jones *C:* SM Jones *PG:* SM Jones
Referee: P Deluca (Argentina)

16.02.2002 MILLENNIUM STADIUM, CARDIFF
Wales 33 *T:* JC Quinnell, KA Morgan, NJ Budgett
C: SM Jones 3 *PG:* SM Jones 4
France 37 *T:* T Marsh 2, A Rougerie *C:* G Merceron 2
PG: G Merceron 4, D Traille *DG:* G Merceron
Referee: DTM McHugh (Ireland)

16.02.2002 TWICKENHAM
England 45 *T:* WJH Greenwood 2, JP Wilkinson,
BC Cohen, JPR Worsley, BJ Kay *C:* JP Wilkinson 6
PG: JP Wilkinson
Ireland 11 *T:* RJR O'Gara *PG:* PG Humphreys 2
Referee: PR Marshall (Australia)

16.02.2002 STADIO FLAMINIO, ROME
Italy 12 *PG:* D Dominguez 4
Scotland 29 *T:* GPJ Townsend, BJ Laney *C:* BJ Laney 2
PG: BJ Laney 5
Referee: KM Deaker (New Zealand)

02.03.2002 LANSDOWNE ROAD, DUBLIN
Ireland 43 *T:* BG O'Driscoll 3, SP Horgan, SH Easterby
C: DG Humphreys 2, RJR O'Gara *PG:* DG Humphreys 4
Scotland 22 *T:* MD Leslie *C:* BJ Laney *PG:* BJ Laney 5
Referee: N Whitehouse (Wales)

02.03.2002 MILLENNIUM STADIUM, CARDIFF
Wales 44 *T:* CS Morgan, DR James, GR Williams,
LS Quinnell, AWN Marinos *C:* SM Jones 5
PG: SM Jones 3
Italy 20 *T:* C Checchinato, N Mazzariol *C:* R Pez,
G Peens *PG:* R Pez, G Peens
Referee: C White (England)

02.03.2002 STADE DE FRANCE, PARIS
France 20 *T:* G Merceron, I Harinordoquy
C: G Merceron 2 *PG:* G Merceron 2
England 15 *T:* J Robinson, BC Cohen *C:* JP Wilkinson
PG: JP Wilkinson
Referee: A Watson (South Africa)

23.03.2002 TWICKENHAM
England 50 *T:* DD Luger 2, WJH Greenwood,
JP Wilkinson, TRG Stimpson *C:* JP Wilkinson 5
PG: JP Wilkinson 4 *DG:* JP Wilkinson
Wales 10 *T:* IR Harris *C:* IR Harris *PG:* IR Harris
Referee: AJ Cole (Australia)

23.03.2002 MURRAYFIELD
Scotland 10 *T:* BW Redpath *C:* BJ Laney *PG:* BJ Laney
France 22 *T:* T Marsh 2, F Galthie *C:* G Merceron 2
PG: G Merceron
Referee: AC Rolland (Ireland)

23.03.2002 LANSDOWNE ROAD, DUBLIN
Ireland 32 *T:* JP Kelly 2, DA Hickie *C:* RJR O'Gara
PG: DG Humphreys 4, RJR O'Gara
Italy 17 *T:* Ma Bergamasco, GP de Carli
C: D Dominguez 2 *DG:* G Peens
Referee: R Dickson (Scotland)

06.04.2002 STADE DE FRANCE, PARIS
France 44 *T:* S Betsen 2, N Brusque 2, A Rougerie
C: G Merceron 2 *PG:* G Merceron 4, F Gelez
Ireland 5 *T:* KGM Wood
Referee: PD O'Brien (New Zealand)

06.04.2002 MILLENNIUM STADIUM, CARDIFF
Wales 22 *T:* GR Williams, C Charvis *PG:* SM Jones 5
Scotland 27 *T:* GC Bulloch 2 *C:* BJ Laney
PG: BJ Laney 4, DW Hodge
Referee: J Jutge (France)

07.04.2002 STADIO FLAMINIO, ROME
Italy 9 *PG:* D Dominguez 3
England 45 *T:* WJH Greenwood 2, J Robinson,
BC Cohen, LBN Dallaglio, AS Healey *C:* JP Wilkinson 5,
MJS Dawson *PG:* JP Wilkinson
Referee: M Lawrence (South Africa)

	P	W	D	L	FOR	AGAINST	PTS
France	5	5	0	0	156	75	10
England	5	4	0	1	184	53	8
Ireland	5	3	0	2	145	138	6
Scotland	5	2	0	3	91	128	4
Wales	5	1	0	4	119	188	2
Italy	5	0	0	5	70	183	0

2002-03

15.02.2003 STADIO FLAMINIO, ROME
Italy 30 *T:* GP de Carli, C Festuccia, M Phillips
C: D Dominguez 3 *PG:* D Dominguez
DG: D Dominguez 2
Wales 22 *T:* T Shanklin, SM Williams, D Peel
C: IR Harris 2 *PG:* IR Harris
Referee: J Jutge (France)

15.02.2003 TWICKENHAM
England 25 *T:* J Robinson *C:* JP Wilkinson
PG: JP Wilkinson 5 *DG:* JP Wilkinson
France 17 *T:* O Magne, C Poitrenaud, D Traille
C: G Merceron
Referee: PG Honiss (New Zealand)

16.02.2003 MURRAYFIELD
Scotland 6 *PG:* G Ross 2
Ireland 36 *T:* DA Hickie, GEA Murphy,
DG Humphreys *C:* DG Humphreys 3
PG: DG Humphreys 5
Referee: A Cole (Australia)

22.02.2003 STADIO FLAMINIO, ROME
Italy 13 *T:* D Dallan *C:* R Pez *PG:* D Dominguez, R Pez
Ireland 37 *T:* PA Stringer, BG O'Driscoll, JP Kelly,
DG Humphreys, GEA Murphy *C:* DG Humphreys 3
PG: DG Humphreys
Referee: AJ Spreadbury (England)

22.02.2003 MILLENNIUM STADIUM, CARDIFF
Wales 9 *PG:* C Sweeney 3
England 26 *T:* WJH Greenwood, JPR Worsley
C: JP Wilkinson 2 *PG:* JP Wilkinson 2
DG: JP Wilkinson
Referee: SR Walsh (New Zealand)

23.02.2003 STADE DE FRANCE, PARIS
France 38 *T:* F Pelous, C Poitrenaud, D Traille,
A Rougerie *C:* F Gelez 3 *PG:* F Gelez 4
Scotland 3 *PG:* CD Paterson
Referee: PR Marshall (Australia)

08.03.2003 LANSDOWNE ROAD, DUBLIN
Ireland 15 *PG:* DG Humphreys 4 *DG:* GEA Murphy
France 12 *PG:* F Gelez 4
Referee: A Watson (South Africa)

08.03.2003 MURRAYFIELD
Scotland 30 *T:* BAF Douglas, SM Taylor, CD Paterson
C: CD Paterson 3 *PG:* CD Paterson 3
Wales 22 *T:* GJ Cooper, M Taylor, GR Williams
C: SM Jones 2 *PG:* SM Jones
Referee: PC Deluca (Argentina), replaced by
AJ Spreadbury (England)

09.03.2003 TWICKENHAM
England 40 *T:* OJ Lewsey 2, S Thompson, J Simpson-
Daniel, MJ Tindall, DD Luger *C:* JP Wilkinson 4,
MJS Dawson
Italy 5 *T:* Mi Bergamasco
Referee: AC Rolland (Ireland)

22.03.2003 TWICKENHAM
England 40 *T:* J Robinson 2, BC Cohen, OJ Lewsey
C: JP Wilkinson 3, PJ Grayson *PG:* JP Wilkinson 4
Scotland 9 *PG:* CD Paterson 3
Referee: A Lewis (Ireland)

22.03.2003 MILLENNIUM STADIUM, CARDIFF
Wales 24 *T:* SM Jones, ME Williams, G Thomas
C: SM Jones 3 *DG:* SM Jones
Ireland 25 *T:* KD Gleeson 2 *PG:* DG Humphreys 4
DG: RJR O'Gara
Referee: SJ Lander (England)

23.03.2003 STADIO FLAMINIO, ROME
Italy 27 *T:* R Pez, Mi Bergamasco, A Persico, M Phillips
C: R Pez 2 *PG:* R Pez
France 53 *T:* D Traille 2, A Rougerie 2, S Betsen,
F Michalak, T Castaignede *C:* D Yachvili 6
PG: D Yachvili 2
Referee: N Williams (Wales)

29.03.2003 STADE DE FRANCE, PARIS
France 33 *T:* T Castaignede, V Clerc, F Michalak
C: D Yachvili 3 *PG:* D Yachvili 4
Wales 5 *T:* G Thomas
Referee: PD O'Brien (New Zealand)

29.03.2003 MURRAYFIELD
Scotland 33 *T:* JPR White, JG McLaren, KM Logan,
CD Paterson *C:* CD Paterson 2 *PG:* CD Paterson 3
Italy 25 *T:* Mi Bergamasco, R Pez, S Palmer *C:* R Pez 2
PG: R Pez 2
Referee: DTM McHugh (Ireland)

30.03.2003 LANSDOWNE ROAD, DUBLIN
Ireland 6 *PG:* DG Humphreys *DG:* DG Humphreys
England 42 *T:* WJH Greenwood 2, LBN Dallaglio,
MJ Tindall, DD Luger *C:* JP Wilkinson 3, PJ Grayson
PG: JP Wilkinson *DG:* JP Wilkinson 2
Referee: JI Kaplan (South Africa)

	P	W	D	L	FOR	AGAINST	PTS
England	5	5	0	0	173	46	10
Ireland	5	4	0	1	119	97	8
France	5	3	0	2	153	75	6
Scotland	5	2	0	3	81	161	4
Italy	5	1	0	4	100	185	2
Wales	5	0	0	5	82	144	0

2003-04

14.02.2004 STADE DE FRANCE, PARIS
France 35 *T:* V Clerc, P Pape, Y Jauzion, J-B Elissalde
C: F Michalak 3 *PG:* F Michalak 3
Ireland 17 *T:* AG Foley, TG Howe *C:* RJR O'Gara 2
PG: RJR O'Gara
Referee: C White (England)

14.02.2004 MILLENNIUM STADIUM, CARDIFF
Wales 23 *T:* GR Williams 2, AR Jones *C:* SM Jones
PG: SM Jones 2
Scotland 10 *T:* SM Taylor *C:* CD Paterson
DG: CD Paterson
Referee: D Courtney (Ireland)

15.02.2004 STADIO FLAMINIO, ROME
Italy 9 *PG:* RS Wakarua 2 *DG:* RS Wakarua
England 50 *T:* J Robinson 3, IR Balshaw, OJ Lewsey,
PJ Grayson, CM Jones *C:* PJ Grayson 3 *PG:* PJ Grayson 3
Referee: A Turner (South Africa)

21.02.2004 MURRAYFIELD
Scotland 13 *T:* SCJ Danielli *C:* CD Paterson
PG: CD Paterson 2
England 35 *T:* BC Cohen, OJ Lewsey, IR Balshaw,
DJ Grewcock *C:* PJ Grayson 3 *PG:* PJ Grayson 3
Referee: DTM McHugh (Ireland)

21.02.2004 STADE DE FRANCE, PARIS
France 25 *T:* I Harinordoquy 2, P Elhorga
C: J-B Elissalde 2 *PG:* J-B Elissalde, D Traille
Italy 0
Referee: A Lewis (Ireland)

22.02.2004 LANSDOWNE ROAD, DUBLIN
Ireland 36 *T:* JS Byrne 2, BG O'Driscoll 2, RJR O'Gara,
AG Foley *C:* RJR O'Gara 3
Wales 15 *T:* T Shanklin 2 *C:* SM Jones *PG:* SM Jones
Referee: J Jutge (France)

06.03.2004 STADIO FLAMINIO, ROME
Italy 20 *T:* F Ongaro *PG:* R de Marigny 5
Scotland 14 *T:* SL Webster *PG:* CD Paterson 3
Referee: N Whitehouse (Wales)

06.03.2004 TWICKENHAM
England 13 *T:* MJS Dawson *C:* PJ Grayson
PG: PJ Grayson 2
Ireland 19 *T:* GT Dempsey *C:* RJR O'Gara
PG: RJR O'Gara 4
Referee: PG Honiss (New Zealand)

07.03.2004 MILLENNIUM STADIUM, CARDIFF
Wales 22 *T:* ME Williams *C:* SM Jones *PG:* SM Jones 5
France 29 *T:* I Harinordoquy, J-B Elissalde
C: J-B Elissalde 2 *PG:* J-B Elissalde 5
Referee: SJ Dickinson (Australia)

20.03.2004 LANSDOWNE ROAD, DUBLIN
Ireland 19 *T:* ME O'Kelly, BG O'Driscoll, SP Horgan
C: RJR O'Gara 2
Italy 3 *PG:* R de Marigny
Referee: KM Deaker (New Zealand)

20.03.2004 TWICKENHAM
England 31 *T:* BC Cohen 2, JPR Worsley
C: OJ Barkley 2 *PG:* OJ Barkley 4
Wales 21 *T:* G Thomas, M Taylor *C:* SM Jones
PG: SM Jones 3
Referee: AJ Cole (Australia)

21.03.2004 MURRAYFIELD
Scotland 0
France 31 *T:* O Magne, Y Jauzion 2 *C:* D Yachvili 2
PG: D Yachvili 4
Referee: SJ Young (Australia)

27.03.2004 MILLENNIUM STADIUM, CARDIFF
Wales 44 *T:* SM Williams 2, GR Williams 2, G Thomas,
T Shanklin *C:* SM Jones 4 *PG:* SM Jones 2
Italy 10 *T:* A Masi *C:* RS Wakarua *PG:* R de Marigny
Referee: M Lawrence (South Africa)

27.03.2004 LANSDOWNE ROAD, DUBLIN
Ireland 37 *T:* GM D'Arcy 2, GEA Murphy, DP Wallace,
PA Stringer *C:* RJR O'Gara 3 *PG:* RJR O'Gara 2
Scotland 16 *T:* A Hogg *C:* CD Paterson
PG: CD Paterson 2 *DG:* DA Parks
Referee: N Williams (Wales)

27.03.2004 STADE DE FRANCE, PARIS
France 24 *T:* I Harinordoquy, D Yachvili *C:* D Yachvili
PG: D Yachvili 4
England 21 *T:* BC Cohen, OJ Lewsey *C:* OJ Barkley
PG: OJ Barkley 3
Referee: AC Rolland (Ireland)

	P	W	D	L	FOR	AGAINST	PTS
France	5	5	0	0	144	60	10
Ireland	5	4	0	1	128	82	8
England	5	3	0	2	150	86	6
Wales	5	2	0	3	125	116	4
Italy	5	1	0	4	42	152	2
Scotland	5	0	0	5	53	146	0

2004-05

05.02.2005 STADE DE FRANCE, PARIS
France 16 *T:* D Traille *C:* F Michalak *PG:* Y Delaigue 2
DG: Y Delaigue
Scotland 9 *PG:* CD Paterson 3
Referee: N Williams (Wales)

05.02.2005 MILLENNIUM STADIUM, CARDIFF
Wales 11 *T:* SM Williams *PG:* SM Jones, GL Henson
England 9 *PG:* CC Hodgson 3
Referee: SR Walsh (New Zealand)

06.02.2005 STADIO FLAMINIO, ROME
Italy 17 *T:* ML Castrogiovanni *PG:* L Orquera,
R de Marigny 3
Ireland 28 *T:* GEA Murphy, PA Stringer, DA Hickie
C: RJR O'Gara 2 *PG:* RJR O'Gara 3
Referee: PD O'Brien (New Zealand)

12.02.2005 STADIO FLAMINIO, ROME
Italy 8 *T:* L Orquera *PG:* R de Marigny
Wales 38 *T:* J Thomas, T Shanklin, ME Williams,
BJ Cockbain, SM Williams, RA Sidoli *C:* SM Jones 4
Referee: A Cole (Australia)

12.02.2005 MURRAYFIELD
Scotland 13 *T:* HFG Southwell, JM Petrie
PG: CD Paterson
Ireland 40 *T:* ME O'Kelly, PJ O'Connell, DA Hickie,
JJ Hayes, GW Duffy *C:* RJR O'Gara 2, DG Humphreys
PG: RJR O'Gara 3
Referee: J Jutge (France)

13.02.2005 TWICKENHAM
England 17 *T:* OJ Barkley, OJ Lewsey *C:* CC Hodgson 2
PG: CC Hodgson
France 18 *PG:* D Yachvili 6
Referee: PD O'Brien (New Zealand)

26.02.2005 MURRAYFIELD
Scotland 18 *PG:* CD Paterson 6
Italy 10 *T:* A Masi *C:* R de Marigny *PG:* R de Marigny
Referee: SJ Dickinson (Australia)

26.02.2005 STADE DE FRANCE, PARIS
France 18 *T:* D Yachvili, A Rougerie *C:* D Yachvili
PG: D Yachvili *DG:* F Michalak
Wales 24 *T:* ME Williams 2 *C:* SM Jones *PG:* SM Jones 3
DG: SM Jones
Referee: PG Honiss (New Zealand)

27.02.2005 LANSDOWNE ROAD, DUBLIN
Ireland 19 *T:* BG O'Driscoll *C:* RJR O'Gara
PG: RJR O'Gara 2 *DG:* RJR O'Gara 2
England 13 *T:* ME Corry *C:* CC Hodgson
PG: CC Hodgson *DG:* CC Hodgson
Referee: JI Kaplan (South Africa)

12.03.2005 LANSDOWNE ROAD, DUBLIN
Ireland 19 *T:* BG O'Driscoll *C:* RJR O'Gara
PG: RJR O'Gara 4
France 26 *T:* C Dominici 2, B Baby *C:* D Yachvili
PG: D Yachvili 2 *DG:* Y Delaigue
Referee: AJ Spreadbury (England)

12.03.2005 TWICKENHAM
England 39 *T:* MJ Cueto 3, S Thompson, IR Balshaw,
AR Hazell *C:* CC Hodgson 3, AJ Goode *PG:* CC Hodgson
Italy 7 *T:* A Troncon *C:* G Peens
Referee: M Lawrence (South Africa)

13.03.2005 MURRAYFIELD
Scotland 22 *T:* A Craig, RA Lamont, CD Paterson
C: CD Paterson 2 *PG:* CD Paterson
Wales 46 *T:* GR Williams 2, KA Morgan 2, RP Jones,
SM Williams *C:* SM Jones 5 *PG:* SM Jones 2
Referee: JI Kaplan (South Africa)

19.03.2005 STADIO FLAMINIO, ROME
Italy 13 *T:* K Robertson *C:* G Peens *PG:* G Peens 2
France 56 *T:* D Marty 2, Y Nyanga, Y Jauzion,
J Laharrague, G Lamboley, P Mignoni *C:* D Yachvili 4,
F Michalak 2 *PG:* D Yachvili 3
Referee: D Courtney (Ireland)

19.03.2005 MILLENNIUM STADIUM, CARDIFF
Wales 32 *T:* GD Jenkins, KA Morgan *C:* SM Jones 2
PG: SM Jones 4, GL Henson *DG:* GL Henson
Ireland 20 *T:* MJ Horan, GEA Murphy
C: DG Humphreys 2 *PG:* RJR O'Gara 2
Referee: C White (England)

19.03.2005 TWICKENHAM
England 43 *T:* JD Noon 3, JPR Worsley, OJ Lewsey,
HA Ellis, MJ Cueto *C:* CC Hodgson 4
Scotland 22 *T:* SF Lamont, A Craig, SM Taylor
C: CD Paterson 2 *PG:* CD Paterson
Referee: AC Rolland (Ireland)

	P	W	D	L	FOR	AGAINST	PTS
Wales	5	5	0	0	151	77	10
France	5	4	0	1	134	82	8
Ireland	5	3	0	2	126	101	6
England	5	2	0	3	121	77	4
Scotland	5	1	0	4	84	155	2
Italy	5	0	0	5	55	179	0

2005-06

04.02.2006 LANSDOWNE ROAD, DUBLIN
Ireland 26 *T:* JP Flannery, TJ Bowe *C:* RJR O'Gara 2
PG: RJR O'Gara 4
Italy 16 *T:* Mi Bergamasco *C:* R Pez *PG:* R Pez 2,
PR Griffen
Referee: D Pearson (England)

04.02.2006 TWICKENHAM
England 47 *T:* MJ Cueto, LW Moody, MJ Tindall,
LBN Dallaglio, MJS Dawson, TMD Voyce
C: CC Hodgson 2, AJ Goode 2 *PG:* CC Hodgson 3
Wales 13 *T:* ME Williams *C:* SM Jones *PG:* SM Jones 2
Referee: PG Honiss (New Zealand)

05.02.2006 MURRAYFIELD
Scotland 20 *T:* SF Lamont 2 *C:* CD Paterson 2
PG: CD Paterson 2
France 16 *T:* J Bonnaire, S Bruno *PG:* J-B Elissalde 2
Referee: JI Kaplan (South Africa)

11.02.2006 STADE DE FRANCE, PARIS
France 43 *T:* C Heymans 2, D Marty 2, A Rougerie,
O Magne *C:* J-B Elissalde 5 *PG:* J-B Elissalde
Ireland 31 *T:* RJR O'Gara, GM D'Arcy,
DP O'Callaghan, AD Trimble *C:* RJR O'Gara 4
PG: RJR O'Gara
Referee: PG Honiss (New Zealand)

11.02.2006 STADIO FLAMINIO, ROME
Italy 16 *T:* Mi Bergamasco *C:* R Pez *PG:* R Pez
DG: R Pez 2
England 31 *T:* MJ Tindall, CC Hodgson, MJ Cueto,
J Simpson-Daniel *C:* CC Hodgson 4 *PG:* CC Hodgson
Referee: KM Deaker (New Zealand)

12.02.2006 MILLENNIUM STADIUM, CARDIFF
Wales 28 *T:* Penalty try, G Thomas 2, RA Sidoli
C: SM Jones 4
Scotland 18 *T:* HFG Southwell, CD Paterson
C: CD Paterson *PG:* CD Paterson 2
Referee: S Walsh (New Zealand)

25.02.2006 STADE DE FRANCE, PARIS
France 37 *T:* T Lievremont, Y Nyanga, P de Villiers,
A Rougerie, F Michalak *C:* D Yachvili 3 *PG:* J-B Elissalde,
D Yachvili
Italy 12 *PG:* R Pez 3 *DG:* R Pez
Referee: AJ Spreadbury (England)

25.02.2006 MURRAYFIELD
Scotland 18 *PG:* CD Paterson 5 *DG:* DA Parks
England 12 *PG:* CC Hodgson 4
Referee: A Lewis (Ireland)

26.02.2006 LANSDOWNE ROAD, DUBLIN
Ireland 31 *T:* DP Wallace, SP Horgan, PA Stringer
C: RJR O'Gara 2 *PG:* RJR O'Gara 4
Wales 5 *T:* MA Jones
Referee: JI Kaplan (South Africa)

11.03.2006 MILLENNIUM STADIUM, CARDIFF
Wales 18 *T:* MA Jones, SM Jones *C:* SM Jones
PG: SM Jones 2
Italy 18 *T:* E Galon, P Canavosio *C:* R Pez *PG:* R Pez 2
Referee: J Jutge (France)

11.03.2006 LANSDOWNE ROAD, DUBLIN
Ireland 15 *PG:* RJR O'Gara 5
Scotland 9 *PG:* CD Paterson 3
Referee: SJ Dickinson (Australia)

12.03.2006 STADE DE FRANCE, PARIS
France 31 *T:* F Fritz, D Traille, C Dominici
C: D Yachvili 2 *PG:* D Yachvili 4
England 6 *PG:* CC Hodgson, AJ Goode
Referee: AC Rolland (Ireland)

18.03.2006 STADIO FLAMINIO, ROME
Italy 10 *T:* Mi Bergamasco *C:* R Pez *PG:* R Pez
Scotland 13 *T:* CD Paterson *C:* CD Paterson
PG: CD Paterson *DG:* G Ross
Referee: AC Rolland (Ireland)

18.03.2006 MILLENNIUM STADIUM, CARDIFF
Wales 16 *T:* HN Luscombe *C:* SM Jones
PG: SM Jones 2, GL Henson
France 21 *T:* D Szarzewski, F Fritz *C:* J-B Elissalde
PG: D Yachvili 2, J-B Elissalde
Referee: C White (England)

18.03.2006 TWICKENHAM
England 24 *T:* JD Noon, SW Borthwick
C: AJ Goode *PG:* AJ Goode 4
Ireland 28 *T:* SP Horgan 2, DP Leamy *C:* RJR O'Gara 2
PG: RJR O'Gara 3
Referee: N Whitehouse (Wales)

	P	W	D	L	FOR	AGAINST	PTS
France	5	4	0	1	148	85	8
Ireland	5	4	0	1	131	97	8
Scotland	5	3	0	2	78	81	6
England	5	2	0	3	120	106	4
Wales	5	1	1	3	80	135	3
Italy	5	0	1	4	72	125	1

2006-07

03.02.2007 STADIO FLAMINIO, ROME
Italy 3 *PG:* R Pez
France 39 *T:* S Chabal 2, C Dominici, C Heymans,
Y Jauzion *C:* D Skrela 4 *PG:* D Skrela, L Beauxis
Referee: W Barnes (England)

03.02.2007 TWICKENHAM
England 42 *T:* J Robinson 2, JP Wilkinson, MB Lund
C: JP Wilkinson 2 *PG:* JP Wilkinson 5 *DG:* JP Wilkinson
Scotland 20 *T:* SM Taylor, RE Dewey *C:* CD Paterson 2
PG: CD Paterson 2
Referee: M Jonker (South Africa)

04.02.2007 MILLENNIUM STADIUM, CARDIFF
Wales 9 *PG:* SM Jones 3
Ireland 19 *T:* R Best, BG O'Driscoll, RJR O'Gara
C: RJR O'Gara 2
Referee: KM Deaker (New Zealand)

10.02.2007 TWICKENHAM
England 20 *T:* J Robinson *PG:* JP Wilkinson 5
Italy 7 *T:* A Scanavacca *C:* A Scanavacca
Referee: N Owens (Wales)

10.02.2007 MURRAYFIELD
Scotland 21 *PG:* CD Paterson 7
Wales 9 *PG:* SM Jones 3
Referee: A Lewis (Ireland)

11.02.2007 CROKE PARK, DUBLIN
Ireland 17 *T:* RJR O'Gara *PG:* RJR O'Gara 4
France 20 *T:* R Ibanez, V Clerc *C:* D Skrela, L Beauxis
PG: D Skrela 2
Referee: S Walsh (New Zealand)

24.02.2007 MURRAYFIELD
Scotland 17 *T:* RE Dewey, CD Paterson
C: CD Paterson 2 *PG:* CD Paterson
Italy 37 *T:* Ma Bergamasco, A Scanavacca, K Robertson,
A Troncon *C:* A Scanavacca 4 *PG:* A Scanavacca 3
Referee: D Courtney (Ireland)

24.02.2007 CROKE PARK, DUBLIN
Ireland 43 *T:* GT Dempsey, DP Wallace, SP Horgan,
IJ Boss *C:* RJR O'Gara 3, PW Wallace *PG:* RJR O'Gara 5
England 13 *T:* D Strettle *C:* JP Wilkinson
PG: JP Wilkinson 2
Referee: J Jutge (France)

24.02.2007 STADE DE FRANCE, PARIS
France 32 *T:* C Dominici, L Nallet *C:* D Skrela 2
PG: D Skrela 5, L Beauxis
Wales 21 *T:* AJ Popham, T Shanklin, JP Robinson
C: SM Jones 3
Referee: AJ Spreadbury (England)

10.03.2007 MURRAYFIELD
Scotland 18 *PG:* CD Paterson 6
Ireland 19 *T:* RJR O'Gara *C:* RJR O'Gara
PG: RJR O'Gara 4
Referee: D Pearson (England)

10.03.2007 STADIO FLAMINIO, ROME
Italy 23 *T:* K Robertson, Ma Bergamasco *C:* R Pez 2
PG: R Pez 3
Wales 20 *T:* SM Williams, M Rees *C:* SM Jones,
JW Hook *PG:* JW Hook 2
Referee: C White (England)

11.03.2007 TWICKENHAM
England 26 *T:* TGAL Flood, MJ Tindall *C:* TGAL Flood,
S Geraghty *PG:* TGAL Flood 3, S Geraghty
France 18 *PG:* D Skrela 3, D Yachvili 3
Referee: JI Kaplan (South Africa)

17.03.2007 STADIO FLAMINIO, ROME
Italy 24 *T:* M Bortolami, R de Marigny *C:* A Scanavacca
PG: R Pez 2 *DG:* R Pez 2
Ireland 51 *T:* GT Dempsey 2, DA Hickie 2,
SH Easterby, GM D'Arcy, SP Horgan, RJR O'Gara
C: RJR O'Gara 4 *PG:* RJR O'Gara
Referee: JI Kaplan (South Africa)

17.03.2007 STADE DE FRANCE, PARIS
France 46 *T:* I Harinordoquy, Y Jauzion, D Marty,
C Heymans, O Milloud, E Vermeulen *C:* L Beauxis 5
PG: L Beauxis 2
Scotland 19 *T:* N Walker, SF Lamont, EA Murray
C: CD Paterson 2
Referee: C Joubert (South Africa)

17.03.2007 MILLENNIUM STADIUM, CARDIFF
Wales 27 *T:* JW Hook, CL Horsman *C:* JW Hook
PG: JW Hook 4 *DG:* JW Hook
England 18 *T:* HA Ellis, J Robinson *C:* TGAL Flood
PG: TGAL Flood *DG:* TGAL Flood
Referee: AC Rolland (Ireland)

	P	W	D	L	FOR	AGAINST	PTS
France	5	4	0	1	155	86	8
Ireland	5	4	0	1	149	84	8
England	5	3	0	2	119	115	6
Italy	5	2	0	3	94	147	4
Wales	5	1	0	4	86	113	2
Scotland	5	1	0	4	95	153	2

2007-08

02.02.2008 CROKE PARK, DUBLIN
Ireland 16 *T:* GT Dempsey *C:* RJR O'Gara
PG: RJR O'Gara 3
Italy 11 *T:* ML Castrogiovanni *PG:* D Bortolussi 2
Referee: JI Kaplan (South Africa)

02.02.2008 TWICKENHAM
England 19 *T:* TGAL Flood *C:* JP Wilkinson
PG: JP Wilkinson 3 *DG:* JP Wilkinson
Wales 26 *T:* LM Byrne, WM Phillips *C:* JW Hook 2
PG: JW Hook 4
Referee: C Joubert (South Africa)

03.02.2008 MURRAYFIELD
Scotland 6 *PG:* DA Parks *DG:* DA Parks
France 27 *T:* V Clerc 2, J Malzieu *C:* J-B Elissalde 2,
D Skrela *PG:* D Traille 2
Referee: AC Rolland (Ireland)

09.02.2008 MILLENNIUM STADIUM, CARDIFF
Wales 30 *T:* SM Williams 2, JW Hook *C:* JW Hook 2,
SM Jones *PG:* JW Hook, SM Jones 2
Scotland 15 *PG:* CD Paterson 5
Referee: B Lawrence (New Zealand)

09.02.2008 STADE DE FRANCE, PARIS
France 26 *T:* V Clerc 3, C Heymans *C:* J-B Elissalde 3
Ireland 21 *T:* Penalty try, DP Wallace *C:* RJR O'Gara
PG: RJR O'Gara 3
Referee: N Owens (Wales)

10.02.2008 STADIO FLAMINIO, ROME
Italy 19 *T:* S Picone *C:* D Bortolussi *PG:* D Bortolussi 4
England 23 *T:* PH Sackey, TGAL Flood
C: JP Wilkinson 2 *PG:* JP Wilkinson 3
Referee: AC Rolland (Ireland)

23.02.2008 MILLENNIUM STADIUM, CARDIFF
Wales 47 *T:* LM Byrne 2, SM Williams 2, T Shanklin
C: SM Jones 3, JW Hook 2 *PG:* SM Jones 4
Italy 8 *T:* ML Castrogiovanni *PG:* A Marcato
Referee: D Pearson (England)

Six Nations Results 2000-09

23.02.2008 CROKE PARK, DUBLIN
Ireland 34 *T:* DP Wallace, RDJ Kearney, MJ Horan,
TJ Bowe 2 *C:* RJR O'Gara 3 *PG:* RJR O'Gara
Scotland 13 *T:* SL Webster *C:* CD Paterson
PG: CD Paterson 2
Referee: C Berdos (France)

23.02.2008 STADE DE FRANCE, PARIS
France 13 *T:* L Nallet *C:* D Traille *PG:* M Parra,
D Yachvili
England 24 *T:* PH Sackey, REP Wigglesworth
C: JP Wilkinson *PG:* JP Wilkinson 3 *DG:* JP Wilkinson
Referee: SR Walsh (New Zealand)

08.03.2008 CROKE PARK, DUBLIN
Ireland 12 *PG:* RJR O'Gara 4
Wales 16 *T:* SM Williams *C:* SM Jones *PG:* SM Jones 2,
JW Hook
Referee: W Barnes (England)

08.03.2008 MURRAYFIELD
Scotland 15 *PG:* CD Paterson 4, DA Parks
England 9 *PG:* JP Wilkinson 3
Referee: JI Kaplan (South Africa)

09.03.2008 STADE DE FRANCE, PARIS
France 25 *T:* A Floch, Y Jauzion, A Rougerie
C: D Yachvili 2 *PG:* D Yachvili 2
Italy 13 *T:* ML Castrogiovanni *C:* A Marcato
PG: A Marcato 2
Referee: A Lewis (Ireland)

15.03.2008 STADIO FLAMINIO, ROME
Italy 23 *T:* Penalty try, G-J Canale *C:* A Marcato 2
PG: A Marcato 2 *DG:* A Marcato
Scotland 20 *T:* A Hogg, MRL Blair *C:* CD Paterson 2
PG: CD Paterson, DA Parks
Referee: N Owens (Wales)

15.03.2008 TWICKENHAM
England 33 *T:* PH Sackey, MJ Tait, JD Noon
C: DJ Cipriani 3 *PG:* DJ Cipriani 4
Ireland 10 *T:* RDJ Kearney *C:* RJR O'Gara
PG: RJR O'Gara
Referee: SJ Dickinson (Australia)

15.03.2008 MILLENNIUM STADIUM, CARDIFF
Wales 29 *T:* SM Williams, ME Williams *C:* SM Jones 2
PG: JW Hook 3, SM Jones 2
France 12 *PG:* J-B Elissalde 3, D Yachvili
Referee: M Jonker (South Africa)

	P	W	D	L	FOR	AGAINST	PTS
Wales	5	5	0	0	148	66	10
England	5	3	0	2	108	83	6
France	5	3	0	2	103	93	6
Ireland	5	2	0	3	93	99	4
Scotland	5	1	0	4	69	123	2
Italy	5	1	0	4	74	131	2

2008-09

07.02.2009 TWICKENHAM
England 36 *T:* AJ Goode, HA Ellis 2, R Flutey,
MJ Cueto *C:* AJ Goode 4 *PG:* AJ Goode
Italy 11 *T:* Mi Bergamasco *PG:* L McLean 2
Referee: M Lawrence (South Africa)

07.02.2009 CROKE PARK, DUBLIN
Ireland 30 *T:* JPR Heaslip, BG O'Driscoll, GM D'Arcy
C: RJR O'Gara 3 *PG:* RJR O'Gara 3
France 21 *T:* I Harinordoquy, M Medard *C:* L Beauxis
PG: L Beauxis *DG:* L Beauxis 2
Referee: N Owens (Wales)

08.02.2009 MURRAYFIELD
Scotland 13 *T:* MB Evans *C:* CD Paterson
PG: CD Paterson 2
Wales 26 *T:* T Shanklin, A-W Jones, SL Halfpenny,
SM Williams *PG:* SM Jones 2
Referee: AC Rolland (Ireland)

14.02.2009 STADE DE FRANCE, PARIS
France 22 *T:* F Ouedraogo *C:* L Beauxis *PG:* L Beauxis 5
Scotland 13 *T:* T Evans *C:* CD Paterson
PG: PJ Godman 2
Referee: G Clancy (Ireland)

14.02.2009 MILLENNIUM STADIUM, CARDIFF
Wales 23 *T:* SL Halfpenny *PG:* SM Jones 5,
SL Halfpenny
England 15 *T:* PH Sackey, D Armitage *C:* TGAL Flood
DG: AJ Goode
Referee: JI Kaplan (South Africa)

15.02.2009 STADIO FLAMINIO, ROME
Italy 9 *PG:* L McLean 3
Ireland 38 *T:* TJ Bowe, L Fitzgerald 2, DP Wallace,
BG O'Driscoll *C:* RJR O'Gara 4, RDJ Kearney
PG: RJR O'Gara
Referee: C White (England)

27.02.2009 STADE DE FRANCE, PARIS
France 21 *T:* T Dusautoir, C Heymans *C:* M Parra
PG: M Parra 3
Wales 16 *T:* LM Byrne *C:* SM Jones *PG:* SM Jones 2,
JW Hook
Referee: M Lawrence (South Africa)

28.02.2009 MURRAYFIELD
Scotland 26 *T:* SCJ Danielli, S Gray *C:* PJ Godman,
CD Paterson *PG:* CD Paterson 3, PJ Godman
Italy 6 *PG:* L McLean *DG:* S Parisse
Referee: N Owens (Wales)

28.02.2009 CROKE PARK, DUBLIN
Ireland 14 *T:* BG O'Driscoll *PG:* RJR O'Gara 2
DG: BG O'Driscoll
England 13 *T:* D Armitage *C:* AJ Goode
PG: TGAL Flood, D Armitage
Referee: C Joubert (South Africa)

14.03.2009 STADIO FLAMINIO, ROME
Italy 15 *PG:* A Marcato 5
Wales 20 *T:* SM Williams, T Shanklin *C:* JW Hook 2
PG: JW Hook 2
Referee: A Lewis (Ireland)

14.03.2009 MURRAYFIELD
Scotland 15 *PG:* CD Paterson 5
Ireland 22 *T:* JPR Heaslip *C:* RJR O'Gara
PG: RJR O'Gara 4 *DG:* RJR O'Gara
Referee: JI Kaplan (South Africa)

15.03.2009 TWICKENHAM
England 34 *T:* MJ Cueto, R Flutey 2, D Armitage,
JPR Worsley *C:* TGAL Flood 3 *PG:* TGAL Flood
France 10 *T:* D Szarzewski, J Malzieu
Referee: SJ Dickinson (Australia)

21.03.2009 STADIO FLAMINIO, ROME
Italy 8 *T:* S Parisse *PG:* A Marcato
France 50 *T:* S Chabal, F Trinh-Duc, M Medard 2,
C Heymans, T Domingo, J Malzieu *C:* M Parra 3
PG: M Parra 3
Referee: AC Rolland (Ireland)

21.03.2009 TWICKENHAM
England 26 *T:* U Monye, R Flutey, MJ Tait
C: TGAL Flood *PG:* TGAL Flood 2 *DG:* DS Care
Scotland 12 *PG:* CD Paterson 3, PJ Godman
Referee: M Jonker (South Africa)

21.03.2009 MILLENNIUM STADIUM, CARDIFF
Wales 15 *PG:* SM Jones 4 *DG:* SM Jones
Ireland 17 *T:* BG O'Driscoll, TJ Bowe *C:* RJR O'Gara 2
DG: RJR O'Gara
Referee: W Barnes (England)

	P	W	D	L	FOR	AGAINST	PTS
Ireland	5	5	0	0	121	73	10
England	5	3	0	2	124	70	6
France	5	3	0	2	124	101	6
Wales	5	3	0	2	100	81	6
Scotland	5	1	0	4	79	102	2
Italy	5	0	0	5	49	170	0

Sebastien Chabal

appendix

EXPERIENCE TWICKENHAM

A VISIT TO TWICKENHAM STADIUM IS A MUST FOR ALL RUGBY FANS

GET BEHIND THE SCENES AT THE HOME OF ENGLAND RUGBY

WHICHEVER RUGBY TEAM YOU SUPPORT, THE HOME OF ENGLAND RUGBY IS THE PERFECT PLACE FOR A DAY TRIP.

Tour the world's most famous rugby stadium, visit the World Rugby Museum, enjoy lunch at the Marriott Hotel and take home some souvenirs from the Rugby Store.

MILESTONES

1905 & 1906
England's home games against New Zealand (1905) and South Africa (1906) at the Crystal Palace are sell-outs, so the RFU set about acquiring their own ground.

1907
RFU committee man Billy Williams sets up the purchase of a 101/4-acre market garden where cabbages had been grown, hence the nickname of the stadium as 'the Cabbage Patch'; the cost is £5572 12s 6d.

1908
First stands constructed – East and West – with mounds of earth as viewpoints behind the goalposts.

1909
First match played on 2 October – Harlequins v Richmond.

1910
First international played on 15 January between England and Wales before a capacity crowd of 20,000.

1914-19
Twickenham used for sheep and cattle grazing during World War I.

1921
Stand built above North Terrace.

1926
First Middlesex Sevens.

1927
First University match.
Extension of East Stand to a two-tiered structure with a capacity of 12,000; South Terrace enlarged to a capacity of 20,000.

1932
New West Stand completed – also two-tiered – with offices for the RFU.

1981
South Terrace rebuilt as two-tiered South Stand.

1988
First rendition of 'Swing Low, Sweet Chariot', by boys of Douai School to celebrate Chris Oti's hat-trick of tries in England's 35-3 win over Ireland.
Start of two-year building programme to extend North Stand as a three-tiered structure.

1991
IRB Rugby World Cup in England and France: England play group games at the stadium and lose the final there, 12-6 to Australia.

1992
Start of rebuilding of East Stand, then West Stand; stadium capacity increased to 75,000.

1999
England play IRB Rugby World Cup group and second-round games at Twickenham; stadium also stages both semi-finals.

2000
Whilst Wembley is rebuilt, Twickenham stages 2000 Rugby League World Cup and hosts two Challenge Cup finals.

2005
Start of complete redevelopment of South Stand – including hotel, leisure centre, offices and shops – to bring stadium capacity to 82,000; seating completed in November 2006 and roof in 2008, making ground now completely enclosed.

2009-10
Twickenham Stadium's Centenary Season.

NATURAL BORN COMPETITORS
wanted for the PokerStars
ENGLAND RUGBY CHALLENGE

To succeed at tournament poker you need a razor-sharp competitive streak – something the England rugby boys know all about. That's why we've teamed up with the RFU for the PokerStars England Rugby Challenge, a free-to-enter tournament series with match tickets to be won throughout the year.

If you think you have what it takes to win, register at PokerStars.com and put yourself to the test.

POKERSTARS
ENGLAND
RUGBY
CHALLENGE

ENGLAND
RUGBY
OFFICIAL
PARTNER

PokerStars.com
Find the Poker Star in you

FIVE/SIX NATIONS CHAMPIONSHIP RECORDS 1910-2009

PREVIOUS WINNERS (* Grand Slam)

1910s – 1910 England; 1911 Wales*; 1912 England & Ireland; 1913 England*; 1914 England*.

1920s – 1920 England & Scotland & Wales; 1921 England*; 1922 Wales; 1923 England*; 1924 England*; 1925 Scotland*; 1926 Scotland & Ireland; 1927 Scotland & Ireland; 1928 England*; 1929 Scotland.

1930s – 1930 England; 1931 Wales; 1932 England & Ireland & Wales; 1933 Scotland; 1934 England; 1935 Ireland; 1936 Wales; 1937 England; 1938 Scotland; 1939 England & Ireland & Wales.

1940s – 1947 England & Wales; 1948 Ireland*; 1949 Ireland.

1950s – 1950 Wales*; 1951 Ireland; 1952 Wales*; 1953 England; 1954 England & Wales & France; 1955 Wales & France; 1956 Wales; 1957 England*; 1958 England; 1959 France.

1960s – 1960 England & France; 1961 France; 1962 France; 1963 England; 1964 Scotland & Wales; 1965 Wales; 1966 Wales; 1967 France; 1968 France*; 1969 Wales.

1970s – 1970 Wales & France; 1971 Wales*; 1972 Not completed; 1973 Five Nations tie; 1974 Ireland; 1975 Wales; 1976 Wales*; 1977 France*; 1978 Wales*; 1979 Wales.

1980s – 1980 England*; 1981 France*; 1982 Ireland; 1983 Ireland & France; 1984 Scotland*; 1985 Ireland; 1986 Scotland & France; 1987 France*; 1988 Wales & France; 1989 France.

1990s – 1990 Scotland*; 1991 England*; 1992 England*; 1993 France; 1994 Wales; 1995 England*; 1996 England; 1997 France*; 1998 France*; 1999 Scotland.

2000s – 2000 England; 2001 England; 2002 France*; 2003 England*; 2004 France*; 2005 Wales*; 2006 France; 2007 France; 2008 Wales*; 2009 Ireland*.

HIGHEST TEAM MATCH SCORES IN THE FIVE/SIX NATIONS CHAMPIONSHIP (1910-2009)

80-23	England v Italy	Twickenham	2001
60-26	England v Wales	Twickenham	1998
60-13	Ireland v Italy	Dublin	2000
59-12	England v Italy	Rome	2000
56-13	France v Italy	Rome	2005
54-10	Ireland v Wales	Dublin	2002
53-27	France v Italy	Rome	2003
51-16	France v Scotland	Murrayfield	1998
51-0	France v Wales	Wembley	1998
51-24	Ireland v Italy	Rome	2007

LEADING POINTS SCORERS IN THE FIVE/SIX NATIONS CHAMPIONSHIP (1910-2009)

RJR O'Gara	Ireland	(2000-09)	499
JP Wilkinson	England	(1998-2008)	479
NR Jenkins	Wales	(1991-2001)	406
SM Jones	Wales	(2000-09)	382
CD Paterson	Scotland	(2000-09)	361
AG Hastings	Scotland	(1986-95)	288
DG Humphreys	Ireland	(1996-2005)	275*
PJ Grayson	England	(1996-2004)	232
MJ Kiernan	Ireland	(1982-91)	207
AR Irvine	Scotland	(1973-82)	201*

* indicates that player's total includes one penalty try.

HIGHEST INDIVIDUAL MATCH SCORES IN THE FIVE/SIX NATIONS CHAMPIONSHIP (1910-2009)

35	JP Wilkinson	England v Italy	Twickenham	2001
30	RJR O'Gara	Ireland v Italy	Dublin	2000
30	JP Wilkinson	England v Wales	Twickenham	2002
29	D Dominguez	Italy v Scotland	Rome	2000
28	NR Jenkins	Wales v France	Paris	2001
27	NR Jenkins	Wales v Italy	Cardiff	2000
27	JP Wilkinson	England v Scotland	Twickenham	2007
26	DG Humphreys	Ireland v Scotland	Murrayfield	2003
24	by five other players in matches in the tournament			

LEADING TRY SCORERS IN THE FIVE/SIX NATIONS CHAMPIONSHIP (1910-2009)

IS Smith	Scotland	(1924-33)	24
BG O'Driscoll	Ireland	(2000-09)	21
CN Lowe	England	(1913-23)	18
GO Edwards	Wales	(1967-78)	18
R Underwood	England	(1984-96)	18
SM Williams	Wales	(2000-09)	17
KJ Jones	Wales	(1947-57)	16
TGR Davies	Wales	(1967-78)	16
BC Cohen	England	(2000-06)	16
WJH Greenwood	England	(1998-2004)	15

RUGBY SCORING SYSTEM 1910 TO DATE

January 1910 – When the Five Nations began in 1909-10, the following points system was in force: try (T) 3 points; conversion (C) 2 points; penalty goal (PG) 3 points; dropped goal (DG) 4 points; goal from mark (GM) 3 points.

March 1948 – The value of the dropped goal (DG) is reduced from 4 to 3 points.

September 1971 – The value of the try (T) is increased from 3 to 4 points, initially as a trial measure.

September 1977 – The goal from mark (GM) ceases to exist as a mode of scoring: a mark is now followed by a free kick, from which a player may not score direct.

April 1992 – The value of the try (T) is increased from 4 to 5 points.

RFUDIRECT.COM
DELIVERING THE RUGBY STORE DIRECT TO YOU

ENGLAND
RUGBY

NEW ENGLAND 2009/10 HOME RUGBY KIT

ORDER ONLINE AT
RFUDIRECT.COM OR
CALL 0871 222 2003

NEW ENGLAND 2009/10 TRAINING RANGE

VIEW THE ENTIRE
RANGE ONLINE
TODAY A
RFUDIRECT.CO

LEADING APPEARANCES IN THE FIVE/SIX NATIONS CHAMPIONSHIP (1910-2009)

CMH Gibson	Ireland	(1964-79)	56
J Leonard	England	(1991-2004)	54
WJ McBride	Ireland	(1962-75)	53
P Sella	France	(1983-95)	50
R Underwood	England	(1984-96)	50
JF Slattery	Ireland	(1970-84)	49
F Pelous	France	(1996-2006)	49
JJ Hayes	Ireland	(2000-09)	49
CD Paterson	Scotland	(2000-09)	48
ME Williams	Wales	(1998-2009)	47

Ireland's CMH Gibson (1964-79) and AJF O'Reilly (1955-70) share the record for the longest championship careers. Each had 15 years and 23 days between their first and last appearances in the tournament.

ENGLAND'S FIVE/SIX NATIONS RECORDS (1910-2009)

Record	Detail	Set	
Most points in season	229	in five matches	2001
Most tries in season	29	in five matches	2001
Highest score	80	80-23 v Italy	2001
Biggest win	57	80-23 v Italy	2001
Highest score conceded	43	13-43 v Ireland	2007
Biggest defeat	30	13-43 v Ireland	2007
Most appearances	54	J Leonard	1991-2004
Most points in matches	479	JP Wilkinson	1998-2008
Most points in season	89	JP Wilkinson	2001
Most points in match	35	JP Wilkinson	v Italy, 2001
Most tries in matches	18	CN Lowe	1913-23
	18	R Underwood	1984-96
Most tries in season	8	CN Lowe	1914
Most tries in match	4	RW Poulton-Palmer	v France, 1914
Most cons in matches	81	JP Wilkinson	1998-2008
Most cons in season	24	JP Wilkinson	2001
Most cons in match	9	JP Wilkinson	v Italy, 2001
Most pens in matches	90	JP Wilkinson	1998-2008
Most pens in season	18	SD Hodgkinson	1991
	18	JP Wilkinson	2000
Most pens in match	7	SD Hodgkinson	v Wales, 1991
	7	CR Andrew	v Scotland, 1995
	7	JP Wilkinson	v France, 1999
Most drops in matches	9	CR Andrew	1985-97
	9	JP Wilkinson	1998-2008
Most drops in season	5	JP Wilkinson	2003
Most drops in match	2	R Hiller	v Ireland, 1970
	2	AGB Old	v France, 1978
	2	JP Horton	v France, 1980
	2	PJ Grayson	v France, 1996
	2	JP Wilkinson	v Wales, 2003
	2	JP Wilkinson	v Ireland, 2003

OVERALL FIVE/SIX NATIONS RECORDS (1910-2009)

Record	Detail	Set	
Most team points in season	229 by England	in five matches	2001
Most team tries in season	29 by England	in five matches	2001
Highest team score	80 by England	80-23 v Italy	2001
Biggest team win	57 by England	80-23 v Italy	2001
Most appearances	56 for Ireland	CMH Gibson	1964-79
Most points in matches	499 for Ireland	RJR O'Gara	2000-09
Most points in season	89 for England	JP Wilkinson	2001
Most points in match	35 for England	JP Wilkinson	v Italy, 2001
Most tries in matches	24 for Scotland	IS Smith	1924-33
Most tries in season	8 for England	CN Lowe	1914
	8 for Scotland	IS Smith	1925
Most cons in matches	81 for England	JP Wilkinson	1998-2008
Most cons in season	24 for England	JP Wilkinson	2001
Most cons in match	9 for England	JP Wilkinson	v Italy, 2001
Most pens in matches	99 for Ireland	RJR O'Gara	2000-09
Most pens in season	18 for England	SD Hodgkinson	1991
	18 for England	JP Wilkinson	2000
	18 for France	G Merceron	2002
Most pens in match	7 for England	SD Hodgkinson	v Wales, 1991
	7 for England	CR Andrew	v Scotland, 1995
	7 for England	JP Wilkinson	v France, 1999
	7 for Wales	NR Jenkins	v Italy, 2000
	7 for France	G Merceron	v Italy, 2002
	7 for Scotland	CD Paterson	v Wales, 2007
Most drops in matches	9 for France	J-P Lescarboura	1982-88
	9 for England	CR Andrew	1985-97
	9 for England	JP Wilkinson	1998-2008
Most drops in season	5 for France	G Camberabero	1967
	5 for Italy	D Dominguez	2000
	5 for Wales	NR Jenkins	2001
	5 for England	JP Wilkinson	2003
Most drops in match	3 for France	P Albaladejo	v Ireland, 1960
	3 for France	J-P Lescarboura	v England, 1985
	3 for Italy	D Dominguez	v Scotland, 2000
	3 for Wales	NR Jenkins	v Scotland, 2001

appendix

PICTURE ACKNOWLEDGEMENTS

Where there is more than one image on a page the pictures are numbered in sequence from left to right and top to bottom. Where a match programme is reproduced with a front cover and internal spread this is treated for numbering purposes as one picture, as are those occasions where two or more cigarette cards are grouped together on the page.

Associated Press 127 (i)
Colorsport 134 (iii), 126 (i), 141, 146, 149 (ii), 150, 152 (all), 154 (all), 155 (ii), 156 (i & ii), 157 (i & ii), 158 (i), 159 (i & iii), 160 (i), 161 (ii), 164 (i), 165 (i & ii), 172, 173 (ii), 175 (i), 180 (i), 181 (i & ii), 183, 184 (ii), 185 (iv), 187 (ii), 192 (i & ii), 193 (i & iii)
Colorsport/Andrew Cowie 160 (ii), 177, 181 (iii), 185 (i). 189 (ii), 223 (ii)
Colorsport/Colin Elsey 149 (i), 151 (ii), 159 (ii), 162-163, 174 (ii), 175 (ii), 182 (i), 197, 208 (i)
Colorsport/Kieran Galvin 213 (i & ii), 219 (i)
Colorsport/Matthew Impey 209 (iii)
Colorsport/Stuart McFarlane 173 (i), 186 (i), 187 (i)
Fotosport/Matt Browne 222 (iii)
Fotosport/David Gibson 203 (i), 216 (ii), 217 (i)
Getty Images 170
Getty Images/AFP/Odd Andersen 212 (i)
Getty Images/AFP/Nicolas Asfouri 207 (ii)
Getty Images/AFP/Adrian Dennis 212 (ii), 217 (ii)
Getty Images/Allsport/Shaun Botterill 202 (ii), 211 (iii), 214 (iii), 223 (i)
Getty Images/Allsport/David Cannon 186 (ii), 210 (iii), 169
Getty Images/Allsport /Russell Cheyne 171, 174 (i), 176 (i), 178-179
Getty Images/Allsport/Mike Hewitt 206 (iii), 216 (iii)
Getty Images/Allsport/Ross Kinnaird 192 (iii)
Getty Images/Allsport/Alex Livesey 190-191
Getty Images/Allsport/Clive Mason 198, 200 (iii), 204 (ii), 205
Getty Images/Allsport/Jamie McDonald 204 (i)
Getty Images/Allsport/Adrian Murrell 158 (ii)
Getty Images/Allsport/Mike Powell 160 (iii)
Getty Images/Allsport/Gary M Prior 8
Getty Images/Allsport/Dave Rogers 185 (i & iii), 188 (i & iv), 189 (i), 199, 201 (i & ii), 203 (ii), 206 (ii), 209 (iv), 210 (ii & iv), 211 (i & ii), 215 (i), 216 (i), 219 (ii), 222 (i & ii), 231
Getty Images/Central Press 75, 83 (i), 136 (ii), 138 (i), 145
Getty Images/Phil Cole 209 (i), 210 (i)
Getty Images/Tony Duffy 124
Getty Images/Evening Standard 15 (i), 138 (iii)
Getty Images/Express 133 (i)
Getty Images/Stu Forster 217 (iii)
Getty Images/Fox Photos 68 (i), 71 (i)

Getty Images/Paul Gilham 223 (iii)
Getty Images/Laurence Griffiths 218 (i)
Getty Images/Richard Heathcote 15 (iv), 214 (i)
Getty Images/Hulton Archive 12 (i), 110 (i)
Getty Images/Keystone 15 (iii), 74 (i), 126 (i), 133 (ii & iii)
Getty Images/Chris Lee 209 (ii)
Getty Images/Warren Little 220-221
Getty Images/Dean Mouhtaropoulos 17
Getty Images/Picture Post 76
Getty Images/Popperfoto 12 (ii), 24 (ii), 27 (ii), 51, 58 (i), 78, 79, 192 (iv), 202 (iii), 204 (iv), 207 (i)
Getty Images/RBS 223 (iv)
Getty Images/DR Stuart 74 (iii), 83 (iii & iv)
Getty Images/Bob Thomas 147
Getty Images/Mark Thompson 208 (ii)
Getty Images/Topical Press 13 (i & ii), 20, 22 (ii), 61 (i)
John Ireland 16 (i), 103 (i), 104 (ii), 112 (ii), 125 (iii), 126 (ii), 127 (ii), 137, 140 (i), 200 (i & ii), 148, 151 (i), 153, 161 (i), 164 (ii), 175 (iii), 176 (iii), 180 (iii), 184 (i), 204 (iii), 206 (ii), 214 (ii), 218 (ii), 230
Lennard Associates 16 (ii & iii), 29, 33, 35 (i), 40, 41 (i), 44 (i), 55 (i), 56 (i), 60 (iii), 62, 71 (ii), 85, 104 (i), 106 (i), 112 (i), 116, 120, 125 (ii), 128 (ii), 139, 155 (i), 157 (iii), 165 (iii), 168, 176 (ii), 180 (ii), 182 (ii), 186 (iii), 188 (ii & iii), 189 (iii), 202 (i), 208 (iii), 213 (i), 215 (ii)
Mary Evans Library/Illustrated Sporting and Dramatic News 39 (ii)
Mary Evans Library/Illustrated London News 60 (i)
Offside/Gerry Cranham 101, 105, 122, 123
Offside/L'Equipe 134 (i & ii), 193 (ii)
Press Association 140 (iii)
Rugby Relics 74 (ii)
S&G and Barratts/Empics Sport 30, 31, 36, 38 (i & iii), 41 (ii), 42-43, 45, 50, 52 (i & ii), 60 (ii & iv), 61 (iii), 63 (i & ii), 66, 67, 69 (ii), 70 (i), 72 (iii), 73 (ii), 77, 80 (i & ii), 81, 82, 83 (ii & v), 84 (ii & iii), 86-87, 88 (ii & iii), 89 (ii), 90, 91 (i), 92, 94 (i & ii), 95 (ii), 99, 100, 102, 106 (ii & iii), 107, 108, 109 (i & ii), 110 (ii & iii), 111, 113 (i), 114-115, 116 (i & iii), 117, 121, 125 (i), 128 (i), 130-131, 132 (i & ii), 135 (i & ii), 138 (ii), 232
JA Thorpe 22 (i)
Twickenham Experience Endpaper (back)
Leo Wilkinson Photography 224-225
World of Rugby Museum, Twickenham Endpaper (front), 9, 11 (all), 14 (all), 15 (ii), 18, 19, 21 (all), 22 (iii), 23 (i & ii), 24 (i & iii), 25, 26 (all), 27 (i & iii), 34, 35 (ii), 37 (i & ii), 38 (ii), 39 (i), 44 (ii), 48, 49, 52 (iii), 54, 55 (ii), 56 (ii), 57, 58 (ii), 59, 61 (ii), 63 (iii & iv), 68 (ii), 69 (i), 70 (ii), 72 (i & ii), 73 (i & iii), 84 (i), 88 (i), 89 (i), 91 (ii & iii), 93 (all), 95 (i, iii & iv), 103 (ii), 113 (ii), 128 (iii), 140 (ii)

BIBLIOGRAPHY

The authors would like to acknowledge the following valuable sources:

La Fabuleuse Histoire du Rugby – Henri Garcia
The International Rugby Championship 1883-1983 – Terry Godwin
Guinness Book of Rugby Facts and Feats – Terry Godwin and Chris Rhys
The History of Scottish Rugby – Sandy Thorburn
Welsh International Matches 1881-2000 – Howard Evans
100 Years of Irish Rugby – Edmund van Esbeck
Playfair Rugby Football Annuals 1955-72

Rothmans Rugby Yearbooks 1972-2000
IRB International Rugby Yearbooks 2001-04
IRB World Rugby Yearbooks 2007-09
Book of English International Rugby: 1871 to 1982 – John Griffiths
The Phoenix Book of International Rugby Records – John Griffiths

And thanks also to Scrum.com